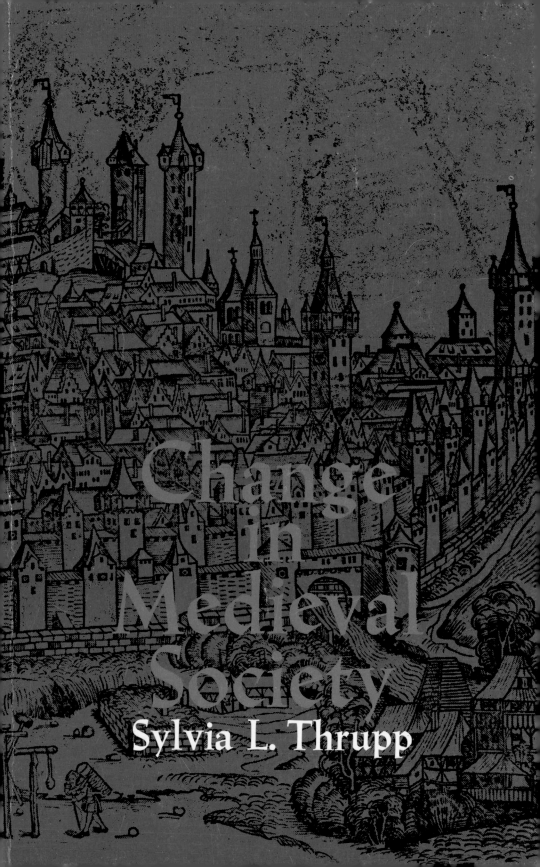

Change
in
Medieval
Society

Sylvia L. Thrupp

CHANGE
IN
MEDIEVAL SOCIETY

CHANGE

IN

MEDIEVAL SOCIETY

Europe North of the Alps, 1050-1500

1344

Edited by

SYLVIA L. THRUPP
The University of Michigan

New York: APPLETON-CENTURY-CROFTS
Division of Meredith Publishing Company

Preface

THE CIVILIZATION of Western Europe in the latter half of the middle ages, from the late eleventh to the late fifteenth century, is the earliest for which we have written records relating to almost all aspects of life. Our picture of civilizations older than this is drawn from the work of their more successful political and religious leaders and lawmakers, and from the ideas of their philosophers, men of letters, and artists. Skilled archaeologists, and economic and legal historians can round out the picture, in some cases very considerably. Yet the patterns of loyalty and organization among the people who built and ran the cities of the ancient and classical civilizations, who made the tools and worked the land, whose sons willingly or unwillingly manned the armies, remain very much of a blank. We interpret, in the main, the rise and fate of these civilizations through their forms of political power. We have to assume that the ideas and ideals in the writing and art that has survived were influential.

But the last four centuries of the Medieval West have left enough administrative, legal, economic, and personal records to bring the middling and lower ranks of people before us objectively. When people of this kind appear in the literary sources, they are likely to be caricatured or shown only as a moralist thought they ought to behave. The nonliterary sources provide a check. These sources are vast, but they are accessible to any scholar, and they are not, like the records of the recent past, so bulky as to be unmanageable. Research in them has opened up many new perspectives that are not yet fully explored and raised new questions to be asked of the literary sources and the chronicles.

The new research makes older attempts to simplify medieval history by reducing it to a single theme, suggestive and dramatic though these may be, unsatisfactory. The interpretations of this kind that have been most influential have been based either on politics or on philosophy. To many writers, the key theme of medieval history has been the rise of the nation-state, or of middle-class liberties and the principles that these invoked. The other most popular type of interpretation rested on the overriding medieval faith in God, and on the curious survival of the idea of one Empire. The leading characteristic of the age then becomes the quest for unity. A variant of this view makes the idea of law the driving force of the age. This is more subtle, since the idea made for debate over the sources of authority.

Brilliant use has been made of such interpretations. Without them, medieval history would hardly exist for us. It would be no more than the chaos of wars, intrigue, and local disaster which is all that the chronicles, at first sight, seem to contain. The historians' ideas may often have been one-sided. They may have represented medieval men as owing everything to ancient Rome, or to idealized ancient Germans. They may have shown them too much in the light of religion, or of nineteenth-century liberalism or romanticism. But they made the age interesting, they aroused curiosity, and they opened up the documents to research. Stress on the middle class, for example, led to research into the development of urban life and the economy. Nor is it really fair to complain of their one-sidedness, for none of these interpretations ever professed to do more than describe certain aspects of medieval life or to show more than a few links of causation. Their causal analysis may sometimes have leaned too heavily on the influence of heroes. But it led also to study of the development of institutions, and of the bearing of abstract principles on political action.

If medievalists have been turning away from older interpretations, it is from curiosity about matters that these passed over. There had been at least a tacit implication that apart from the movement of politics, law, philosophy, and art, the medieval world was simple and more or less static. Now that we know more about its scientific effort, its technology, medicine, music, diplomacy, finance, population problems, and opportunities for social mobility, this impression is seen to be illusory. On all sides there is evidence of change. This came either through slight but cumulative adaptations to new circumstances, or through the influence and spread of imaginative innovations.

Change of course occurred within a framework of order which, if we contrast it with our own, had certain fixed characteristics. But a medieval man, if he could have read a general history of the future, would similarly have found certain fixed characteristics in the modern world. The contours of change in a remote time are always foreshortened, just as in a remote landscape, even in rolling country, the contours around the more striking landmarks blur into an impression of flatness. It is only through detailed research that historians discover how the conditions of life and thought in a past age were actually altering. This is not to say that the pace of change is always the same. In the medieval world communications were slow, population being small and for the most part scattered in small villages and tiny towns. England's population at the time of the Norman Conquest could be housed in Detroit, and the population of medieval France at its height was not very much greater than New York's. This in itself made for regional diversity. Innovations were more likely to arise in centers of discussion, that is, in the larger cities, in universities, among the upper echelons of government servants, or in reformist circles in the Church. Adaptive change, however, occurred everywhere. Custom and tradition were flexible. Handicraftmen had always to be ready to adapt their techniques to changes in the quality or nature of their materials and also to changes in demand, as their customers' standards of living rose. They were inventive in devising new uses of waterpower, wind power and animal-power. The peasantry, too, even in backward regions, used their small resources rationally and adapted as best they could to long-run economic trends. It is a libel to stereotype them as cabbages. In short, though change was in many directions slow, and was contained always within limits that are clear, there could have been few men in the last half of the middle ages who faced quite the same life situation as their fathers did.

Obviously it is becoming harder now to give any ordered picture of the medieval world that will do justice to its diversity and complexity. But this is a chronic problem in all fields of historical knowledge as specialist research advances. There are three ways of dealing with it. Some writers are temperamentally able only to take an artist's view, putting what interests them personally at the center, and leaving out or treating only vaguely what bores or confuses them. Others try to be scientific in the sense of applying broad theoretical generalizations, leaving out exceptional situations or regions. Certainly a few exceptions need not invalidate a generalization. These writers try to unify the picture by leaning on the type of cultural theory that insists on the interrelatedness of all aspects of a society. Marxism is one form of such theory. In any form this type of theory leads one to look for interconnections between the development of thought and institutions, and to take account of environmental influences. Yet social anthropology found long ago that even in very simple societies, though there may be some environmental influence, for example, on religion, it cannot explain the variety of religious customs one meets. People's response to a physical environment depends on the way in which they perceive it, and the same is true of their response to the traditions that have shaped their social environment. These perceptions alter in subtle ways and by no means necessarily all at the same time. One can discover important interconnections between the development of medieval philosophy, art, political leadership, and the economy, yet change in these different spheres went on very unevenly.

A third and more hopeful way of advance is along the lines mapped out by the French scholar, Marc Bloch. Only one of Bloch's major books

—*Feudal Society*—has been translated into English, and much of his most important work is scattered through the files of the magazine that he and Lucien Febvre founded, the *Annales d'histoire économique et sociale,* now entitled *Annales—Economies—Sociétés—Civilisations.* But he has exercised a profound influence on medievalists everywhere. Both he and Febvre seem to have felt that the heart of the historian's problem lies in understanding the social influences by which, in any age, people's perception of natural and social phenomena is shaped, and also their consciousness of a past, of values that maintain a sense of continuity. Only in this way can we grasp the quality of experience in another age, discover the starting points of any type of change, the reasons for readiness or unreadiness to accept change, the reasons for borrowing from other cultures, the reasons for the success or failure of innovations originating in creative minds.

This view calls for a still further extension of research interests. At the same time it holds out some promise of unifying them, not through straining to discover connections between the course of different types of change—connections that may or may not exist—but in relation to a common denominator, a common base. Interest in the influence of social experience on perception and readiness to change can never become a narrow specialty, for it is equally important to the understanding of all aspects of an age; all alert imaginative scholars share in it. Every medieval historian and biographer is aware that members of the upper classes and elites were steeped, at least in their childhood, in the popular culture of the localities where they grew up. Their horizon was extended by the discussion that went on in the universities, the courts, and the councils into which their careers led, yet their outlook usually retained much in common with that of humbler people.

This book is designed to illustrate the liveliness of research into medieval communities and the channels of communication through which new movements of thought and aspiration took form and spread. It illustrates conservatism, conflict, failures, and circumstances that resisted control—monetary inflation, decline of population, the misery and isolation of the very poor—as well as triumphs of innovation. It shows how medievalists work, how they pose problems for research, and the innumerable kinds of evidence, literary and nonliterary, on which they draw.

The book does not in any way profess to give a complete picture of the last half of the middle ages. The more familiar themes that are well treated in well-known books are deliberately omitted. The book is also deliberately confined for the most part to countries north of the Alps. The far-reaching influence of the Mediterranean world on the North needs a volume to itself.

It is only fair to add that the views expressed in this preface are my own, and that several of the authors whose work is represented here might disagree with them at some points or even entirely. All, however, have written in a spirit more or less akin to that of Marc Bloch.

S. L. T.

ACKNOWLEDGMENTS

THIS BOOK has been made possible by the kind permission to reproduce or translate the essays it contains, granted by the following: The Casa Editrice Dott. A. Giuffrè (Milan), the Secretary of the UNESCO Commission on the Cultural and Scientific History of Mankind (Paris), the editors of *Annales—Economies—Sociétés—Civilisations* (Paris); Professor C. N. L. Brooke (Liverpool University) and the editor of *The Historical Journal* (Cambridge); the editor of *Mediaeval Studies* and the Director of the University of Notre Dame Press; Mr. H. G. Richardson; Professor J. R. Strayer (Princeton) and the Mediaeval Academy of America; Dr. Edward Miller (Cambridge); Professor F. L. Carsten (London) and the Council of The Royal Historical Society (London); the editor of *The American Historical Review;* Professor Sir Hamilton Gibb and the Librarian of the John Rylands Library (Manchester); Dr. Otto G. von Simson and the Society of Architectural Historians; Dr. A. C. Crombie (Oxford), Heinemann Educational Books Ltd. (London), and the University of Chicago Press; the editor of the *Revue des Etudes Juives* (Paris); Professor E. Perroy (Paris) and the Council of the Economic History Society; the editor of *Church History*.

My thanks go also to Professor Carlo Cipolla (Turin) for making a few changes in the original version of his essay, to Professor John A. Yunck (Michigan State University) for permission to omit some Latin verses from his article, to Professor Howard Kaminsky (University of Washington) for permission to omit lengthy quotations in three footnotes and for furnishing a new bibliographical note, and to Professor L. Génicot (Louvain) for taking the trouble to correct my translation of his article. For typing and assistance in assembling the book I am indebted to Miss Ann Alexander.

Contents

2 15 8 6

The essays in this book first appeared in the following publications:

Marc Bloch	*Studi di Storia e Diritto in Onore di Enrico Besta,* Vol. II (1939)
Léopold Génicot	*Cahiers d'histoire mondiale,* Vol. I (1953)
Richard Koebner	*Annales d'histoire économique et sociale,* Vol. IX (1937)
C. N. L. Brooke	*The Cambridge Historical Journal,* Vol. XII (1956)
John A. Yunck	*Mediaeval Studies,* Vol. XXIII (1961) and incorporated in *The Lineage of Lady Meed,* University of Notre Dame Press, Notre Dame, Indiana, 1963
H. G. Richardson	*History,* Vol. 46 (1961)
J. R. Strayer	*Speculum,* Vol. XV (1940)
Edward Miller	*Transactions of the Royal Historical Society,* 5th Series, Vol. II (1952)
Laurence M. Larson	*The American Historical Review,* Vol. 13 (1908)
Sir Hamilton Gibb	*The Bulletin of the John Rylands Library* (1955)
Otto G. von Simson	*The Journal of the Society of Architectural Historians,* Vol. XI (1952)
A. C. Crombie	*Isis* (1961) and in Harry Woolf, ed., *Quantification: A History of Measurement in the Natural & Social Sciences.* New York, Bobbs-Merrill, 1961
Séraphine Guerchberg	*Revue des Etudes Juives,* Vol. 108 (1948)
Carlo Cipolla	*The Economic History Review* (1963)
E. Perroy	*The Economic History Review* (1955)
Howard Kaminsky	*Church History* (1957)
Louise R. Loomis	*The American Historical Review,* Vol. 44 (1939)
F. L. Carsten	*Transactions of the Royal Historical Society,* 4th Series, Vol. XXV (1943)
F. Graus	*Annales—Economies—Sociétés—Civilisations,* Vol. XVI (1961)

Communities

From the Royal Court to the Court of Rome

The Suit of the Serfs of Rosny-Sous-Bois[1]

MARC BLOCH

I

THE VILLAGE OF Rosny-sous-Bois, to the east of Paris,[2] had for its lord, towards the end of the 12th century, one of the most famous religious foundations of Paris: the abbey of St. Genevieve on the *Mont*. An ancient royal possession, it had become part of the abbey's patrimony through the generosity of a king. We do not know exactly when. We know only that the gift goes back before 1163[3] but not into so ancient a past as to have been forgotten in the village; memory of it still lingered there in the early 13th century.[4] The gift, however, was not without thorns. By 1179, perhaps even earlier, a passionate dispute had broken out between the canons and the peasants. Were the latter serfs? They denied this as vigorously as their masters affirmed it, and a lengthy suit followed. The history of this is most illuminating. Before discussing its significance, it will be best to outline briefly the story of what happened.

II

Our evidence begins with a diploma of Louis VII, issued at some time between December 25, 1178 and the end of August, 1179.[5] It records a judgment of the royal court, on which our story turns. The decision is unambiguous: "We have ordained", says the king, "that henceforth the men of Rosny be subject to the church of St. Genevieve as serfs to their lords".[6] After Louis' death the canons prudently had the award confirmed by his successor, Philip Augustus.[7] They had already taken another precaution, a less usual one. On February 1, 1182, they had obtained a bull from Pope Lucius III which gave the late king's "constitution" the sanction of the supreme moral authority of Christendom.[8] This was the Roman Curia's first intervention in the affair. It was by no means to be the last. For although the king had expressly forbidden them "de jamais soulever à nouveau ce débat", the peasants did not accept defeat. Rebuffed at Paris, they too turned to Rome. Quietly ignoring the royal decision and its personal confirmation by the Pope, they very quickly managed to obtain letters from this same Lucius III appointing apostolic judges to settle their case, as though it were still pending.[9] The Holy See thus contradicted itself, within a few months, in the most flagrant fashion. Lucius later excused himself in terms too delightful not to be quoted: "Because of the multitude of affairs that are brought before the apostolic chair, we cannot possibly remember the tenor of our letters and our other decisions. For this reason we may be tricked unawares into contradicting what we have written earlier." [10] As we see, the pontiff had soon been enlightened, doubtless by the canons. Their abbot, who was then the celebrated Stephen of Tournai, kept in close touch with the Curia.[11] The passage justed cited is from a bull of September 25, 1184, which restored the status quo.[12] Having learnt his lesson, Lucius was not content merely to revoke the letters of commission that he had despatched, appointing judges in the case: he annulled in advance any further letters of the kind that the men of Rosny might be cunning enough to obtain.

In spite of this shift, or before word of it had arrived, action apparently had been taken along normal procedural lines. In all probability it was in his capacity as apostolic judge that Henry, Bishop of Senlis, at some time between February 1, 1182 and February 21, 1185, summoned the villagers to appear before him. Recorded in the form of a recognizance, or oath, taken by the peasants themselves, his decision, like that of the royal tribunal before, was in favor of the abbey.[13] Everything goes to show that the peasants had indeed for many years been subject to the obligations characteristic of serfdom. It therefore counted for little that their claims may have rested on memory of an earlier and different state of affairs. Custom, the source of law, had ceased to speak in their favor.

Although they took care to have the bishop's decision copied into their cartulary, the canons were not anxious to invoke it. On principle, they had been opposed to any reopening of the dispute, taking their stand on Louis VII's award. They had a confirmation of this inserted in each of the bulls by which, according to custom, each successive pope approved their privileges: first under Clement III, who gave them a special bull confirming it, and then under Celestine III.[14] In this way they made certain that it would not fall into oblivion.

The rustics of Rosny, however—to use a term that recurs quite often in monastic writing—were of "stiff-necked" stock. Toward the end of Innocent III's pontificate, they returned to the fray. Again they addressed themselves to the Curia. Again they obtained a hearing. A second set of apostolic judges was appointed to hear their case. At this point the canons outwitted them by a clever ruse. Pretending to be eager to reach an amicable agreement, they arranged that the bull be deposited, probably by the judges to whom it had been sent, with the treasurer of the Templars in Paris. They were no doubt assured of the latter's complicity beforehand, for he hastened to pass the document on to them. Since they refused to give it up, there was then no possibility of acting on it. But their adversaries were not to be caught napping. They let the new Pope, Honorius III, know what had happened. Properly indignant, on February 13, 1219 he wrote the abbot and convent a very sharp reminder of the duties of their position: "It is most unfitting for religious men to act in a manner so contrary to mercy, for the perfection at which they must aim obliges them to abstain from many things which may be permitted to others." [15] The peasants had really disturbed the spiritual head of Christendom. They had done more than simply inform him of the hocus-pocus of which their lords were guilty: they had gone on to explain how the state of serfdom to which they were reduced obliged them continually to violate, against their will, the laws of the Church. Because their neighbors refused to intermarry with them, they were obliged "de se mêler entre soi", marrying among themselves up to the fourth or even the third degree of consanguinity.[16] This grievance was not invented for the occasion. It is echoed in a great deal of other evidence: by reason both of the ban on *formariage* and of the taint to which the spouse of a serf was exposed, serfs found it difficult to marry. Hence they were often driven to take concubines or to marry within the forbidden degrees of consanguinity. Despite its neutrality as regards the principle of serfdom, the Church could not entirely ignore the fact that the juridical definition of the status had these effects. Honorius commanded the canons to give their people justice. Failing this, three judges, already designated, were to determine the case.

Then, once more, the canons won the next round. They sent the Pope the decision of Louis VII, with the bulls which had confirmed it. Like Lucius III before him, Honorius, on February 7, 1220, reversed his decision.[17] But not for long. For the peasants now tried an audacious manoeuvre that proved brilliantly successful. The bull ordering the apostolic judges to drop the case had, they asserted, merely deferred to the judgment of the royal court. Had it not missed the point—that they were appealing this judgment? They had regarded the heir of the apostles as supreme, as able to correct the judgments even of kings. The successor of Innocent III could not but be moved by so astounding a declaration of Papal supremacy. On the 28th of May, 1221, he appointed three new judges.[18] Better still, he conceded both parties the right to make a final appeal, if they wished, directly to the ruling pontiff. The earlier bulls had made no such provision.

The case was thus definitely reopened. Like any other case, it dragged along slowly, suffering procedural delays which are unfortunately not well documented. The best-known incident was that in which the new Abbot of St. Genevieve, Galon, was in 1232 held in contempt for not responding to a summons by the apostolic judges. Galon gave the apparently reasonable excuse that at the time of the summons he was in Rome, where he had gone for papal confirmation of his election, and to receive the papal blessing. On July 1 Honorius revoked Galon's sentence and decided to call the case before his own tribunal.[19] However, this order appears not to have been followed up, perhaps because Galon died the following month. There were no new developments until 1224.

The new turn of events seems to have begun with the canons obtaining royal support for a ruthless resort to force. Herbert, the new abbot, noted in his records that early in 1224 Louis VII granted the canons, at their request, permission to build a prison for Rosny, subject only to the condition that they imprison no one without the king's assent and only for so long as the king approved.[20] Whether or not it was the persuasive effect of the new jail, we know that on February 4, 1224, two men and one woman from the village appeared before the Official of the Archdeacon of Paris and promised under oath to withdraw from the suit against the abbey, which was still before the apostolic judges. By January 5, 1225, eleven similar declarations had come from groups that included in all 89 heads of families; probably the whole or almost the whole population of the village was involved.[21] We see that even under severe pressure, the peasants gave way only gradually. Nor did they give up the battle altogether. If we may believe the canons, several peasants, "oublieux de foi jurée",[22] had tried to reopen the case. The final result, however, was as one would expect. Well-disposed though he had always been toward the plaintiffs, Honorius was obliged to take formal note (on July 6, 1226) of the fact that they themselves were dropping the suit.[23] His action closed this extraordinary case, which had lasted for over 47 years and had set three kings and five popes at odds.

Yet the peasants were not to linger in the bonds which they had so tenaciously tried to shake off. In August, 1246 they won their enfranchisement, at the cost of an annual rent of 60 *livres parisis,* which was apportioned among the various properties of the estate.[24] At this time lords in all parts of the Ile-de-France were selling freedom to their *hommes de corps.* Interestingly enough, however, among the "general manumissions" involving whole villages in the Parisian region, that of Rosny is, to my knowledge, the earliest. St. Louis granted his charter to Villeneuve-le-Roi in the same year but not until October. The canons of Notre Dame of Paris apparently opened similar negotiations with the serfs of several of their estates around 1246 but did not complete them until much later.[25] The men of Rosny had always chafed so much under the stigma of serfdom that they gladly seized on the first opportunity to be rid of it, even at a money price. As we shall see, they did not lack money. The religious, for their part, were doubtless not sorry to receive good money for parting with rights which had been very expensive to defend. Yet, desirous to uphold the legitimacy of their claims to the end, they were at pains to add to the stereotyped form of the deeds of enfranchisement a significant little phrase: "the men of our vill of Rosny, who are *hommes de corps,* that is, serfs of our church, the which servitude they admit".[26]

III

The record of so long a dispute does much to illuminate, among other things, the history and the nature of the servile bond. In the judgment of the Bishop of Senlis, for example, we find one of the few precise definitions of servile status that survives from the Ile-de-France of the 13th century. A document of this kind can of course be interpreted only by comparing it with other analogous evidence. I have attempted such an analysis elsewhere.[27] The only point to be stressed here is the fact that juridical classification was often a matter of uncertainty. The history of the people of Rosny shows, once more, that it could be extremely difficult to determine the exact juridical status, not merely of an individual, but of a group of men, not merely of a few vagrants or fugitives, but of a collectivity firmly fixed to the soil. Was it true, as the peasants claimed, that their condition had worsened after they passed from the royal regime to that of the abbey? We do not know. Whether their enserfment was recent or not, there is one circumstance that explains the ambiguity of the situation. As the bishop informs us, "peu de personnes" at Rosny owed the chevage payment of four pennies. This payment was in many places already obsolete. Thanks to the fact that it was an annual payment, chevage had been both the one sure means by which a lord could keep the listing of his serfs up-to-date and the one inescapable reminder, for the serfs, of their condition. None of the other burdens or disabilities of serfdom—mainmorte in the form that prevailed in France except in the extreme north, the prohibition of *formariage,* exclusion from holy orders—were clear characteristics. After all, they applied only in exceptional circumstances. When the latter were lacking for any length of time, the door was open to the destroying action of prescription, that worm which in the Middle Ages ate away all manner of rights.[28]

The course of the proceedings in the royal court, where the contest began, is interesting. The abbot and canons took the first step, bringing before the king a plaint against their rebellious subjects. The first question is whether the king undertook to settle the dispute. The "custom" of the *royaume de France,* which was well established, gave him no power to do so. For in denying that they were serfs of St. Genevieve, the men of Rosny were in effect admitting that they were "hôtes et colons". These terms were synonymous, the first coming from the vernacular, the second from the pseudo-classical language to which the notaries who drew up charters were so long attached. In either case it was understood that the peasants lived in the seigneurie of the abbot and canons and held their lands of them. Since the religious possessed high as well as low justice at Rosny, the peasants were justiciable only to them; on these grounds, at least according to the principles of jurisprudence that held throughout the 12th century, the suit ought to have been returned to the abbot's court. Indeed, as late as the reign of St. Louis, Pierre de Fontaines was still declaring that between a lord and his villein (that is to say, his tenant) there is no judge but God.[29] Later on, it is true—actually from the reign of St. Louis—,[30] we find the *Parlement* judging disputes over servile status without any hesitation, even when the parties were a lord and his own tenant. But this remarkable extension of royal jurisdiction came about only gradually and, as it were, insidiously. Under Louis VII, it was still far in the future. The king was content to rule that the case be tried in the abbot's court, by combat. This was a perfectly normal custom. He also delegated several of his followers to observe the procedure. At first sight this is rather surprising, but it is readily explained by the circumstance that the abbey stood in a special relation to the royal power. After a period of independence, it had, in the reign of Henry I, been brought back under the "power and patronage of the kings" and, as a diploma of Louis VI shows, had thereafter been regarded as the perfect type of "royal church".[31] This is why its justice could be supervised.

On the day set for the suit, when the abbot's court was filled with "important men" (evidently the principal vassals of the Church), the peasants refused combat. Such a refusal was not at all uncommon. If we had statistical data on trials by combat, we would probably find that most cases ended like this. From our own rationalist point of view, fighting a duel seems one of the most absurd methods of justice ever invented. Yet in an age when people firmly believed that it was God who gave judgment, they might be frightened of being beaten if they knew they were not really in the right: it was not enough to have a strong champion. There are instances of refusal of combat through such fears. The curious thing is that after the peasants' refusal, the abbot and his advisers did not feel able to pronounce judgment; instead, they came to an agreement with their subjects to take the case back to the king. It was the king who had ordered procedure by combat, and since his orders had not been carried out, it was for him to rule on the default. Louis VII duly heard the sworn testimony of his observers, along with less formal corroborative statements of many other eye-witnesses—clerks, knights, sergeants, and bourgeois. Acting with the advice of his barons, the king then passed judgment on the peasants' default. As we have seen, he declared the peasants to be serfs. The proceedings had thus preserved formal respect for seigneurial judicial rights while at the same time reflecting the supremacy of the Capetian king over one of his principal churches.

But temporal princes were not, or were no longer, the sole sovereign judges in Christendom. Exalted by the Gregorian spirit, the Papacy had assumed an enormously extended role: it was trying to intervene in every dispute in the Catholic world that in any way concerned a church. There could hardly be a more striking example of this situation than its repeated intervention in a quarrel between a Parisian abbey and a little group of villagers in the Ile-de-France. The case had virtually no bearing on the general problems of Christendom, yet we find the papacy stepping in, first to lend a royal judgment superfluous support and later to summon to its own bar a case known to have been settled already by a king.

There is still more to the story: the Curia was obviously unable to realize its high ambitions. Lacking reliable local means of intelligence and control, the papacy was wildly presumptuous, as indeed were all the great powers of the time. Techniques of communication were still too rudimentary to permit effective supervision of such an affair, to ensure that orders would be obeyed or to keep the pope abreast of new developments. The Curia's own internal organization lacked system and was unreliable. We have Lucius III's own word that his registers were carelessly kept. We get the impression that any suitor with an iota of perseverance, who knew his way about, could ultimately obtain a bull in his favor, even though this might flagrantly contradict a previous decision. By the simple means of confiscating apostolic letters that were unfavorable to them, the canons of St. Genevieve successfully held up all action for a considerable time. And despite all Honorius III's good will, it was not his mandates as the vicar of Christ and supreme judge over men, it was not his scruples as a priest who felt that even rustics deserved mercy, it was the solid walls of the abbot's prison, built by leave of the king, that decided the peasants' case. It is abundantly clear that the last word lay with the authorities that were on the scene and in command of physical force.

The peasants' long resistance does credit to more than their obstinacy. It implies some rudiments of collective organization. How far had this developed? It is significant that a clause in the manumission of 1246 forbids the newly enfranchised to form a commune without the consent of the religious and of the king.[32] This provision is found in only one of the other acts of enfranchisement under the seal of St. Genevieve, that of Borest (February, 1245).[33] Being very near Senlis, whose commune is indeed mentioned in the act, Borest lay on the frontier of the classical zone of the communal movement in both its urban and its rural forms. In the Parisian region the only acts of enfranchisement, apart from Rosny's, which anticipate and place a ban on communal movements are all from St. Germain-des-Prés.[34] The clause was not therefore a matter of common form. Had Rosny, like the bourg of Schelles nearby, developed a communal conspiracy? [35] Possibly, though we have no evidence of it. Certainly the canons had reason enough to dread the potentialities of the collective spirit which had so interminably prolonged their suit. For these wretched clodhoppers, forced into submission only by the necessity of gaining their daily bread, had displayed an amazingly sophisticated knowledge of the wider world. In 1220 there is direct evidence of their sending procurators to the court of Rome—they had no doubt done so earlier—, and they must have been in touch with them. This is one of the most intriguing aspects of the enterprise of these incorrigible suitors.

Again, such suits were undoubtedly very expensive. The notion that a purely "natural" economy prevailed in the countryside is once again shown to be a myth, at least for the Ile-de-France in the 13th century. On this point the charter of enfranchisement reinforces the evidence of the dealings in the Curia. An annual charge of 60 *livres parisis*—in the money of the time, roughly 6.3 kilograms of silver—shared among a population of about 89 families, no more than 400 or 500 souls, was no inconsiderable sum.[36] Yet its availability is easily explained. Peasants could acquire this much only by selling what they produced. Now our men were fortunate in being very close to an important market—that of Paris. Hence they were relatively prosperous and could probably borrow easily. There must have been an active exchange economy in the wheat lands from which the already great city drew its supplies. This is the final conclusion to be drawn from the sinuous history of the bitter quarrel between the canons of St. Genevieve and their villeins of Rosny.

NOTES

1 The documents on which this paper is based are for the most part taken either from the 13th century cartulary of St. Genevieve (Paris, Bibliothèveue Saint-Geneviève, ms. 356), hereafter referred to as *Cartul.*, or from various sources in the National Archives which will be referred to by the lettering of their series followed by the number of the file. There is a rather inaccurate outline of the facts in Giard, *Etude sur l'histoire de l'abbaye de Sainte-Geneviève de Paris jusqu'à la fin du XIIIᵉ siècle*, in *Mémoires de la Société de l'Histoire de Paris*, t. XXX (1903).

2 Seine, cant. Vincennes.

3 Bull of Alexander III, 1163, April 24: *Gallia christiana*, t. VII, *instr.* col. 241. Giard to the contrary, it is nevertheless certain that the *Redomatum* mentioned in the *Miracula S. Genovefae* (AA. SS., jun. 1, p. 150) is to be identified with Rosny; in any case the text in no way indicates that this *Redomatum*, whatever it was, belonged then to the abbey.

4 Text cited above, n. 3.

5 *Cartul.*, p. 94. Fragments of the text have been printed several times: Du Cange, *Glossarium, vox Hospites*; *Gallia Christ.*, t. VII, col. 721; A. Luchaire, *Histoire des institutions monarchiques de la France sous les premiers Capétiens*, 2nd ed., vol. II, p. 343 (following an 18th-century copy; cf. correction in *Etude sur les actes*, cited later); J. Desilve, *Lettres d'Etienne de Tournai*, p. 421. It has also been catalogued in A. Luchaire, *Etude sur les actes de Louis VII*, no. 758 and A. Cartellieri, *Philipp II*

August, t. 1, *Beilagen*, p. 59, no. 41. The text gives no date but 1179 A.D. But the methods of dating used in Louis VII's chancellery are obscure and may have varied: cf. L. Halphen, in *Revue Historique*, CVIII, p. 55. The earliest date possible is December 25, 1178 and the latest possible date is fixed by mention of the chancellery being vacant. This doubtless refers to the disgrace of Hugues de Champfleuri (1172). The act must therefore antedate the giving of the seals to Hugues du Puiset, which could not have occurred before the end of August, 1179. Cartellieri favored April 1179, saying that the presence of a number of the witnesses at court is to be explained only by their having come for the recent election of the young Philip Augustus as associate king. But actually the only persons named in the diploma as barons participating in the judgment are the king's brother and the seneschal, Thibaud de Blois, along with six high dignitaries from the Parisian clergy representing the court of St. Genevieve, and the usual high officials. There was nothing exceptional about the presence of any of these at the *palais*. Cartellieri was in error in taking the *Symon de Sancto Dyonisio*, whose name follows that of the Archdeacon of Paris, for abbot of the celebrated monastery. Surely he was Prior of Saint-Denis de la-Châtre?

6 "Ut et deinceps homines de Rodoniaco ecclesie Sancte Genovefe subiecti sint, sicut servi dominis suis, precepimus, et ne aliquam in posterum inde questionem moveant modis omnibus prohibuimus."

7 Delaborde, *Recueil*, no. 65 (Nov. 1, 1182-April 16, 1183).

8 *Cartul.*, p. 86. Dated Feb. 1, at the Lateran, from the itinerary.

9 The letters mentioned in the bull have been lost.

10 "Cum autem pro negociorum multitudine que ad sedem apostolicam referuntur non possint scriptorum nostrorum tenor et alia que facimus memoriter retineri, quorumdam circumvenimur quandoque versutia et ad scribendum ignorantur inducimur contra ea que antea scripseramus."

11 Desilve, *Lettres d'Etienne de Tournai*, no. LXIII, LXXI, XCIX, *CLXVIII*. It is impossible to tell whether any of these letters relate to the Rosny affair.

12 *Cartul.*, p. 87: dated at Verona, 25 Sept. From the pope's itinerary this might be 1184 or 1185, but another bull approving the privileges of the abbey is expressly dated from Verona, 1184, Oct. 25 (*Cartul.*, pp. 3ff.). This removes all doubt about the year of the bull of Sept. 25.

13 *Cartul.*, p. 98, undated. The date must be prior to the bishop's death, which occurred before Feb. 21, 1185 (*Gallia*, no. X, col. 1404–1405) and if Henry was acting on the papal letters of commission, after Lucius III's bull of Feb. 1, 1182, which confirmed the royal judgment. As we know from the bull of Sept. 25, 1184, the peasants had only managed to get these letters by prudently avoiding any mention of the confirmation that the canons had obtained on Feb. 1, 1182.

14 *Cartul.*, p. 88: June 19, 1190 (specific confirmation); p. 9, July 6, 1190; p. 12, March 22, 1196 (new style).

15 *Cartul.*, p. 88, Lateran. Edited, with mistakes, by Giard, as his document no. X. Catalogued in Presutti, *Regesta Honorii*, p. 1, no. 1847, where the act is dated 28 January, "Cum religiosos omnino non deceat sic immisericorditer agere, sed a multis, que licerent forsitan aliis, cum arripuerint perfectionis (*ms.:* profectionis) propositum, abstinere." The letters of commission to the apostolic judges: Presutti, *loc. cit.* The treasurer of the Temple of Paris, Aimard, is a well-known figure: cf. L. Delisle, *Mém. Acad. Inscriptions*, XXXIII, 1889, p. 61ff.

16 "Homines de Rodiniaco suam ad nos querimoniam destinarunt quod vos, abutentes eorum dominio quo se vobis tenere cognoscunt, eos quodam servitutis (iure) quod manus mortua dicitur, opprimitis minus iuste, ita ut ipsi, qui olim sub dominio regum Francie prosperitate florebant, nunc a vobis, ad quos eorum dominium ex munificentia regali pervenit, adeo importabilis servitutis onere deprimuntur ut, vicinorum locorum hominibus eorum evitantibus copulam nuptialem, in tercio et in quarto gradu consanguinitatis matrimonialiter invicem misceantur".

17 *Cartul.*, p. 89: Viterbo.

18 *Ibid.*, p. 90: Lateran.

19 *Ibid.*, p. 92: Lateran.

20 J, 152, no. 5. Cf. Ch. Petit-Dutaillis, *Etude sur la vie et le règne de Louis VIII*,

p. 479, n. 222, 14 April, 1224 to 29 March, 1225. "Notum facimus universis quod cum karissimus dominus noster Ludovicus, rex Francorum illustris, ad requisitionem nostram nobis concessisset quod pro iusticiandis hominibus nostris de Rooni tantummodo prisoniam faceremus, nos presentibus litteris confitemur et concedimus quod nec ponere nec tenere possimus ipsos homines de Rooni vel alios qualescumque in dicta prisonia nostra nisi de voluntate et licentia eiusdem domini regis et quamdiu placuerit eidem".

21 The renunciations were entered in a *vidimus* under the seal of the apostolic judges and bearing the date July 1227. This record, probably a roll, is lost. But it was copied in two different places in the cartularies: the first part on pp. 125–127, the concluding part on pp. 55–58. Naturally we cannot tell if some parts have not been omitted. We have the original of one of the acts of renunciation, which is copied correctly on p. 55 of the cartulary, with the date Nov. 10, 1224: S 1572 no. 1.

22 Bull of Honorius III: Lateran, 13 May, 1224. *Cartul.*, p. 92.

23 By two bulls of the same date, one addressed to the abbot and the convent, the other to the Abbot of Saint-Denis and St. Germain-des-Prés and to the Prior of St. Martin-des-Champs: *Cartul.*, pp. 93–94. *Cf.* Presutti, II, no. 5975 (dated June 4). It was probably by virtue of the second bull that the Abbot of St. Germain, on April 3, 1222, "by apostolic authority" summoned a certain Pierre, son of Roger *deu Perer* before him and obtained his admission that he was *homme de corps* of St. Germain (*Cartul.*, p. 220).

24 Original: S 1574, no. 1. Royal confirmation in the same month: K 30, no. 13. Copies of this confirmation, of the 13th century, *Cartul.*, p. 84 and in the *Registre de comptes du celerier,* Bibl. St. Genev. ms. 351 fol. 83.

25 Marc Bloch, *Rois et serfs,* pp. 61 and 67–68.

26 "Homines ville nostre de Rodoniaco qui ecclesie nostre sunt homines de corpore sive servi ecclesie, quam etiam servitutem confitentur".

27 See my "Liberté et Servitude personelles au moyen âge, particulièrement en France", in *Anuario de Historia del derecho español* (1933). For a slightly different view of the development of French serfdom, see P. Petot, "L'évolution du servage dans la France coutumière du XIe au XIVe siècle" in *Le servage. Communications présentées à la Société Jean Bodin* (Brussels, 1937).

28 The term "prescription" refers to legitimation through unchallenged usage or practice over a period of time. If the disabilities of serfdom were not enforced, serfs would claim exemption from them by prescription. Alternately, one could say they were claiming freedom by prescriptive right.—Ed. note.

29 Ed. Marnier, XIX, 8, p. 225. On suits relating to serfdom, see Beaumanoir, no. 1431, ed. Salmon, p. 222.

30 See especially a trial of 1263: *Olim.* t. 1, no. XIII; p. 446, no. XXIV; LL 79 fol. 36.

31 Diploma of Henry I, 1035, r. 4: Tardif, *Cartons des rois,* no. 264. On the situation of St. Genevieve, see W. M. Newman, *Le domaine royal sous les premiers Capétiens,* pp. 76 and 207. In a rather forward-looking clause, Henry I had promised the canons that they would always remain under the authority of his successors, the kings or princes holding the city of Paris.

32 "Item additum est quod homines de Rodoniaco non poterunt facere communiam nisi de licentia nostra et domini regis super hoc obtenta".

33 Royal confirmation, Compiègne, 1–15 April, 1245: K 30, no. 13 bis, and copy in *Cartul.*, p. 79.

34 Enfranchisement of Antony, June, 1248 (in a royal confirmation of the same date: K 30, no. 16); of Villeneuve-Saint-Georges, February, 1250 (Guérard, *Polyptyque de l'abbé Irminon,* II, p. 383); of Thiais, November, 1250 (Guérard, p. 390).

35 Cf. Marc Bloch, in *Bulletin de la Soc. de l'Histoire de Paris,* XL (1913), p. 17.

36 The 60 livres were not, however, claimed for long. An act of Jan. 1277 (L 887 no. 43) indicates that the figure has been reduced to 54 livres, the remainder having been compounded for by a lump sum of 200 livres, an extraordinarily advantageous deal for the canons. The odd thing is that the 200 livres were not paid directly by the men of Rosny but were paid in their name by the men of the nearby village of Chenevières-sur-Marne (Seine-et-Oise, cant. Boissy-Saint-Léger). This place was divided between

the two abbeys of St. Genevieve and St. Maur des Fossés. Its inhabitants had been included in two acts of enfranchisement that had been granted, for a money payment, one by the first-mentioned monastery, in March, 1248, to the men of Créteil (*Cartul.*, p. 284: Bibl. St. Genev., ms. 351 fol. 96; and *littera obligationis*, of the previous January, ms. 351, fol. 99); the other was granted by the second monastery in March, 1251 to St. Maur itself and several other places (L 455 no. 4). Had the men of Rosny lent money to their neighbors at this time? And had the latter paid them back in 1277? We cannot tell. But these transactions by communities are clearly signs of a singularly well developed money economy.

2

On the Evidence of Growth of Population in the West From the Eleventh to the Thirteenth Century

LÉOPOLD GÉNICOT

ECONOMIC EXPANSION, religious ferment, renaissance of letters and development of science, creation of an original art, territorial gains at the expense of the infidel world, all these phenomena of which the life of Christian Europe was woven between the 11th century and the 13th are in some way related to a net growth of the population. Consequently, almost all historians hold that, during what Marc Bloch called the second feudal age, the West went through a strong demographic surge.

This virtual unanimity is, however, a little deceptive: no one ordinarily doubts the fact or its importance yet we really know little about it. Actually, no one has had the courage to study it very closely. The documentation is so poor as at first sight to seem unable to sustain more than vague general conclusions. It has not been interrogated methodically, for fear that the effort would be futile.[1] Perhaps this pessimism is justified, but how can we tell? We cannot be certain until at least one scholar has carried out systematic and exhaustive research in some definite region, and has then tried to draw together all the forms of evidence that reveal the shape of demographic trends from the post-Carolingian period up to the end of the Middle Ages.

This article tries to show what types of research would be feasible. It offers, not a finished history of the population of the different regions of the West between the years 1000 and 1300—indeed, the present state of knowledge would barely permit of an outline—but a list of the various indices of population growth that the monographs we need ought to collect and analyze. We shall illustrate the uses and the significance of each of these indices. Perhaps this will stimulate more careful research into "demographic prehistory". In any case I hope it will show that, although some historians may have exaggerated in speaking of the "demographic revolution of the 11th, 12th, and 13th centuries" and although our knowledge is still far from precise, the impression that population was growing is well founded.

To speak of demography means that we must seek quantitative measures, even though the figures may only partially reflect the reality and be no more than a basis for interpretation. Accordingly, we shall classify the numerous and varied indices of population growth in order of decreasing precision, that is to say, according as they may be expressed in more or less rigorous mathematical form, or better still—for history is concerned with evolution—, in statistical series. They might be ranged as follows: the evidence given in military or fiscal documents; information gained from inventories of seigneurial property and rights; birth rates to be deduced from genealogical study and from the descriptions of families to be found in many charters; long-term price trends, in particular of agricultural prices; the multiplication and expansion of towns; land clearance, technological advances, and the fragmentation of traditional land holdings; changes in ecclesiastical geography and construction or alteration of public buildings, especially of churches and chapels; and colonization of the vast regions seized from the Infidel.

Medievalists do not hope to find a complete census of any population. They are happy enough to find incomplete or indirect data, such as lists of men liable to military service, or accounts of hearth taxes or poll taxes. The former are rather rare and late; only in Italy do we have any that antedate the 14th century.[2] Again, they concern only the towns and we cannot be certain that urban population fluctuated in the same way as rural population. And their use depends on the calculation of a multiplier, usually on uncertain grounds, that will represent the ratio between the number of men capable of bearing arms and the total population.[3] The second type of data, as presented by the celebrated "Etat des paroisses et des feux" of 1328 and the Poll tax returns of 1377, is more valuable because it ordinarily covers a wide region, not just a single town. But it raises even more difficult problems. What was a hearth and what is the average number of individuals it indicates?[4] Or what was the ratio between the number of adults who paid a poll tax and the number of children? What percentage of the population did exempt groups form—clergy, often nobles and their households, and vagrants? Were the enumerators and collectors conscientious? Was it hard to evade payment? How are we to fill the frequent gaps in the records? To what extent and under what conditions is it legitimate to argue from the part to the whole? All these questions are extremely delicate.[5] On the other hand, again with exceptions in Italy (the *generales subventiones* of Frederick II and Charles of Anjou [6]), the fiscal records, like the military lists, are all later than 1300. Yet for our purpose they are still relevant and useful, even for the earlier period. They furnish figures which, when compared with earlier data from other sources, show very convincingly that the population of the West had grown before the 14th century, and they help us to form a rough idea of the amplitude and the rhythm of this growth. Without the poll tax referred to above, J. C. Russell would not have been able to establish so firmly the fact that the population of England more than tripled in some 250 years, between 1086 and 1346.[7]

Among the oldest of the other auxiliary sources are the surveys known as the polyptyques. Sometimes these give a fully detailed inventory of all the lands and dues belonging to a lay or ecclesiastical lord. In the 13th century many great and middling lords whose classical manorial regime had weathered a crisis drew up surveys of this kind in order, so to speak, to take their bearings.[8] Sometimes the survey is merely a concise description of a single manor, compiled on the occasion of a pious donation or of a dispute or of what was later called a *dénombrement* of a fief. But whatever their form or scope, the polyptyques all contain similar statistical data: the number of settlements on the estate, for at least from the 11th century this often comprised more than one; the number of holdings of each type; the total area, in the ancient and the current measures, of fields and meadows [9]; the number of tenants and the average extent of their holdings [10]; and finally, in so far as one can tell from figures based on dues levied on individuals or on hearths, the total population and its density.[11] If one has, then, for all or part of an estate, several polyptyques or related documents, such as accounts, it is possible to establish these facts at a series of dates and hence to deduce, more or less exactly, the demographic trend of the period and region in question. New settlements may appear,[12] or the older ones may come to be more densely populated. For example, the 81 people living on the lands of Weedon Beck in 1248 had by 1300 grown to 110.[13] Such a record is a valid measure of population growth if all other things remain equal at the two dates, namely, the area of land in question and the hearth or household unit. We must also be certain that an increase in one item is not offset by a decrease in another, for example, that an increase in the number of tenants does not simply reflect a decrease in the number of sub-tenants or of landless people.

Another way of measuring population change is through calculations of the average number of children per household. With luck, if our documentation is good enough, there will be two ways of doing this. One is through compiling genealogies. If genealogies compiled in the

middle ages are used they of course have to be checked, and may sometimes be amplified, by new research.[14] In this way it was discovered that
the eldest branches of two of the greatest families of the region of Namur
in each generation between the dates 1000 and 1250, had respectively a
minimum of 5.75 and 4.30 children who came of age.[15] The method is
however applicable only in the case of great families.[16] And the average
number of children surviving may have varied considerably between
one social level and another. There is however another procedure, one
that to my knowledge has never been tried,[17] namely, the gathering of
the descriptions of complete families to be found in charters.[18] These
quite often, when referring to pious donations of land, or in the case of
liberi who donated themselves or of serfs who were donated to a religious
foundation, name parents and their children.[19] This information should
be classified by date, by social class, by regions, etc. It would then show
how the average number of children altered between one period and
another. It might also resolve other problems, especially the question
whether, as many historians have maintained, the serfs died out through
having a particularly low birth rate. Having obtained the average by
one or the other of these methods, one then has to estimate the number
of children per couple, in the period and region in question, that would
have been requisite simply to maintain the population level. Ideally one
would deduce this from local documents of the period. In practice the
best plan is to take a coefficient calculated by modern specialists, say 2.7,
modifying it in the light of differences in the relevant variables. We are
unable to take account of infant mortality, because the documents mention only children who have lived for some years, indeed usually only
those who have grown up. But we have to take account of the nuptuality
rate. This was undoubtedly lower in the Middle Ages than today because of a more pronounced disequilibrium between the sexes and because of more frequent entry into religious orders.[20] Again, we have to
bear in mind that the average duration of life was also lower in that
age of all too frequent famine and epidemic.[21]

Price trends, especially in agricultural prices, also demand attention. They are or may be, to an extent which has to be determined for
every case, a function of demographic change.[22] A fall in the rent of fields
and meadows, accompanied by a rise in wages, especially of farm hands,
such as we see in 14th-century England [23], is an unequivocal sign of a
fall in population. Inversely, a rise in the value of arable land, above
all if it is accompanied by a fall in wages, is a clue to population increase. Although we may never be able to trace the course of wages with
any exactness before 1300, it is possible to form a general idea of their
movement in the regions that are better documented. As to land values,
at least in the 13th century, it is quite easy to show that they were rising:
one may do so either by comparing average figures in successive years [24]

or, more surely, by charting the course of the rents on specific pieces of land.[25]

Other indices lend themselves less easily to measurement, chief among these being the growth of towns. In some regions, such as the Low Countries, these probably originated in the 9th century; in others, such as Lombardy, they were revivified in the 10th century; everywhere they were in full expansion between the 11th century and the 13th.[26] Proof of this lies in the continual enlargement of their bounds that is revealed by the successive construction of new outworks and by the re-ordering of their ancient parish divisions.[27] The extension of their areas was not, however, exactly proportionate to increase in the number of inhabitants, for the density of urban population was not a constant. It varied from one town to another and within the same town, not only from one period to another but from one quarter to another, as, for example, between the market quarter and what modern architects would call the residential quarters, or from the ancient *civitas* to newly built suburbs. Besides, the walled area was seldom if ever completely built up; especially towards the close of the Middle Ages, it might include fields and meadows and other vacant sites. Yet in default of any more exact measure, the extension of the area enclosed is of some significance. To cite only two instances, the area enclosed by the fortifications of Ghent, one of the greatest towns of the age, had by the 14th century grown from 80 hectares to 644; the fortified area of Aix, a lesser town, grew from 50 hectares to 175.[28]

Parallel with this urban movement ran another which some historians overlook: the transformation of villages into little towns.[29] Places that had hitherto been simply agricultural acquire market rights and a market place, and sometimes a fair. They become petty commercial centers.

One should beware of exaggerating the demographic significance of these urban phenomena. Urban growth is not a precise index of total population growth. Even if the area of Ghent grew almost tenfold in 250 years or the population of some town in central Italy grew in the same period from 5,000 to 30,000 [30], it does not follow that the population of Flanders or of Tuscany or of Umbria had grown tenfold or sixfold. Towns have always [31] tended to absorb the people of their immediate environs; in some regions, as in Italy, they have attracted the artisans of whole regions [32], and even the peasants.[33] They have continually drained the open country. All the same, and this is the point to be emphasized here, they did not empty the countryside.[34] They drained off only its surplus human output.

They did not even take the whole of that surplus. Between the 11th and the 13th century, the rural population grew appreciably. The considerable extension of arable land during this period is sufficient evidence of this.[35] For this was the age of the great work of dyking and drainage in fenlands. In Flanders, nature and man combined in the 11th century to push back the sea.[36] In Lombardy, bishops, monasteries, and finally communes, endeavoured to tame the Po and make its valley fertile.[37] By 1250 the work was finished: Milan by then, for instance, had its great irrigation canal, the Muzza, while downstream, between the tributaries of the Oglio and the Molinella, the river was well under control.[38]

This is also, notably in such regions of France as the Parisian basin, the great age of the "villes neuves". The "villes neuves" were new settlements founded on open waste and in forest clearings by enlightened lords and their colonists (*hôtes*).[39] We have the foundation charters of some of these places. For others the place name attests their origin [40] by referring to new foundation (the French *Villeneuve*) or to the proprietor (Créon, Libourne), or by indicating their privileged status (the Italian *Villafranca*), or by copying the name of some great city far off (Bruges or Ghent in Béarn), or above all, by preserving the memory of the ancient forests and of the clearing process which eroded it, as in the German place names ending in *rade, raut, rode, roth, reut, riet, holz, wald, forst, hausen, hain, hagen, bruch, brand, scheid, schlag,* etc. Often the ground plan [41] is our evidence, a grid pattern or the angling of intersections proving that the whole place was laid out in one operation.

Even where there was no dyking, no drainage, and no planting of new settlements, there was still new activity, although it may be more difficult for us to trace it. Yet careful examination of the old landscapes and attentive reading of the documents relating to them will often reveal that arable and pasture areas were being enlarged. Sometimes the structure of villages is significant, as in the intercalary type of settlement. Here there is a nucleus around which lie hamlets, scattered houses, or, less frequently, isolated manors. Records and source data prove these to be relatively new. They may, for example, be mentioned as inhabited places only rather late; they may be served by a little chapel dependent on the church in the central settlement, or they may be located in the middle of a huge tract of land owned by a single tenant, while the surrounding lands lie in open fields cultivated in strips, etc.[42] Sometimes holdings are classified in such a way as to indicate that new clearing has taken place. A 13th century polyptyque, for instance, distinguishes the older tenements—manses, *més,* quarters, and *masale* land—from the assarts (newly broken land). Or study of the names of fields and holdings reveals the presence of *courts, vents, artigues, arsis,* and *mesnils,* dating from Roman or early Frankish times. Again, the documents may speak of the tithes known as *novales,* those levied on newly cultivated land, which may go back to a 9th century origin but more often only to the 11th century.[43] Finally, a charter or a saint's life may mention the new de-

velopment of forest or wasteland: for example, a property may be deeded
to an individual or to a religious foundation to be cleared (*ad extir-
pandum*), or someone struck by paralysis has to lease out land that he
had brought under cultivation.[44]

All of these indices of the advance of cultivation have been known
to us for a long time. The need now is to examine them in a more
methodical and rigorous way. Research should focus on clearly defined
areas and should exploit every existing source of information.[45] Local
study should deal simultaneously with water problems, with the appearance [46], the number and the importance of *villes neuves* [47], and with
clearing operations within older lands in order to identify and date
each assart.[48] By doing so, it would be possible to measure the advance
of cultivation in the region in question as accurately as possible.

The increase of the cultivated area would be a main clue to the
degree of population growth. Yet although the two phenomena certainly move together, there is nothing to show that they must vary
equally. Conceivably the breaking in of more land might be due less
to an increase in population than to a fall in the number of the landless,
or to a general rise in standards of living. The problem in each case
would be to decide how far the movement was the result of population
pressure. To know the motivation of the people or the communities
concerned would be helpful. The founding of a *ville neuve* by a king or
a territorial prince whose aims were political, strategic, or fiscal rather
than truly economic [49] and whose call for immigrants drew a response
mainly from more or less remote countries [50], or the creation of a grange
(outlying farm) by some Cistercian abbey would be less significant for
the region we were studying [51] than clearing planned by the cadets of
seigneurial families or by peasants. Work of this kind was often more
important than has been generally recognized.[52]

To attack forest and wasteland is one means of dealing with population pressure. Another way is to improve technique. Agricultural methods progressed through fallowing every third year instead of every second
and, on some plots, by sowing legumes in the fallow, through plowing
more frequently and more deeply and fertilizing the soil more, and by
specialization, for example, in vine culture or market gardening. All
this was going on in the valley of the Rhine in the 12th and 13th centuries.[53] What was achieved there may have been achieved elsewhere.
In studying the demographic history of a region, it is important to look
into all this.

But not everyone with too many children made an effort to get
more land or to farm better. When population began to grow families
at first continued to live on their patrimony. After a time, if juridical
and other customs permitted [54], they would simply divide it. Fragmentation of manorial units, both of a whole vill and of the peasant *mansus,*

was thus to some extent [55] a consequence [56] of population growth. It is one of our indices. It is true that the movement began well before 1100; in some places, for example in Lorraine [57], it was by then general. Of greater interest for us is the further fragmentation of the units, especially the quarter, into which the ancient manse had been split, but its occurrence is not easy to date.

Population growth bore not only on the secular "cell" of the social organism, the vill, but also on its religious "cell", the parish. Sometimes the parish disintegrated, though less often than has been supposed.[58] The proprietors and the incumbents of the old churches, both rural and urban, defended their privileges fiercely and often victoriously.[59] Thus the spiritual problems consequent on the growth of the flock had to be met by other means than subdivision of parishes. The old churches, and the bodies of clergy serving them, had to be enlarged [60] or else new *loci religiosi* had to be set up, that is, chapels served more or less regularly by a priest, so that the faithful could at least hear Sunday Mass.[61] Construction or alteration of churches and chapels is thus evidence of population growth [62]; here the historian should consult the archeologist.

Finally, along with chance references to the development of this or that rural industry, we have clear proof of a rise in the population curve—in the expansion of the West. *Reconquista*, the feudal operations of the Hautevilles and their rivals in Southern Italy and Sicily, Crusades, and the *Drang nach Osten*—these movements are too familiar and too far-reaching to be discussed here. Between the 11th century and the 13th, and even into the 14th century, they were drawing colonists from all parts of the Christian West.[63] In research in the population history of a region one must never forget to find out whether any of its people emigrated—either in large groups, like the Flemish peasants who went off to the Baltic fenlands, or singly, like the barons of Perche or of Béarn who straggled off to Spain.[64] One should also try to find out why they went. Land hunger need not have been the only motive.

These then are the kinds of evidence which tend to show that from 1000 or 1050 to 1300 or 1350 the Christian West was becoming more thickly settled. Taken by itself, each piece of evidence is debatable. For example, the clearing of new land is not in itself "decisive evidence of an unusual growth of population, of a demographic revolution [65]". It is the consistency of the evidence that brings conviction. Increase in the number of households or of individuals within a given area, birth rates higher than would have been necessary to mere maintenance of the population, a rise in land values coinciding with a probable fall in wages, growth in the size and number of towns, the promotion of more and more villages to the status of a little town and the rise of God knows how many new villages and hamlets, the pushing back of seas, marshes, wasteland, and forest by the advance of fields and pastures, improvements in the yield of land, fragmentation of old manorial units, subdivision of parishes or enlargement of churches and building of chapels, the expansion of the West to the South and to the East—how are we to explain all this going on at the same time, except by a net increase of population?

But though the nature of the process is clear enough, its working is in many respects still hazy. The evidence has not been systematically interrogated. We are still much in the dark about the starting points, the duration, the intensity and the phasing of the movement. When did it begin? We say, in the mid-11th century. But is this true of Italy? [66] Or of Germany? [67] Or of the Low Countries, Flanders or Normandy? [68] When did it die down? Most historians would say, in the 14th century; many towns were then stagnating or declining, while marginal lands and even whole villages [69] were being deserted. But there is still controversy as to whether these developments came in the early or middle years of the century. Those who believe that they came around 1300 point to the impossibility of bringing any more land under wheat, and to evidence of soil exhaustion on many of the assarts.[70] They argue that in these circumstances population must already have ceased to grow and may already have begun to fall. But the majority still holds to the contrary thesis that the Black Death was responsible for reversing the trend.[71] Again, some researchers take an entirely different view of the phasing of the movement. One writer claims that the Bavarian plain was already fully exploited by the end of the 12th century and the mountain zones not yet fully exploited at the end of the 13th.[72] Another claims, after comparing two fiscal records, that between 1312 and 1427 the population of the Tirol grew by 50%.[73]

The extent to which population grew is also a matter of debate. To speak of a revolution is perhaps to exaggerate. Even by the rather generous estimates of Levasseur or of Lamprecht, the average annual increase comes out far below that of England or Germany between 1800 and 1850—a percentage of 3.8 or 4.8 instead of 14 or 11.[74] As to the possible phases of the movement, we are still unable to distinguish and describe them.

Almost everything that we know or postulate on this subject therefore requires to be verified and restated in quantitative terms. This can be done only through meticulously careful regional study. We cannot even be certain of reaching precise quantative results. But the attempt has to be made, for although it has been long neglected [75], the problem is nonetheless important. Indeed, in all medieval history there are few questions so fundamental as this one.

P.S. On reading the manuscript of this article my esteemed colleague and friend Professor Philippe Wolff of the University of Toulouse suggested to me that the improvement in the status of peasants, especially the relaxation of the bonds attaching them to the soil, may equally be a consequence of population growth. This is certainly true, yet the interpretation of this index is a particularly delicate matter, one that does not lend itself well to statistical study.

NOTES

[1] This seems to be the conviction of C. Cipolla, J. Dhondt, M. Postan, and P. Wolff, authors of the remarkable "Rapport sur la démographie au moyen âge" presented at the Ninth International Congress of the Historical Sciences and published in Vol. I of the *Rapports* of that Congress (Paris, 1950), pp. 55ff.

[2] K. J. Beloch, *Bevölkerungsgeschichte Italiens* (Berlin and Leipzig, 1937), vol. I, pp. 1ff.

[3] Good examples of the use of these lists are offered for the Flemish towns, which in the 14th century rivalled the Italian cities, by Jos. De Smet, "L'effectif des milices brugeoises et la population de la ville en 1340", *Revue belge de philologie et d'histoire*, t. XII (1933), pp. 636ff. and H. van Werveke, "Het bevolkingscijfer van de stad Gent in de veertiende eeuw", *Miscellanea historica in honorem L. van der Essen*, t. I (Brussels and Paris, 1947), pp. 345ff.

 K. Bücher, *Die Bevölkerung von Frankfurt-am-Main* (Leipzig, 1886) is still useful for anyone interested in the history of the medieval urban population.

[4] There is no doubt that this average varied from one region to another with the strength or weakness of a communal spirit, with conceptions of the family, and with inheritance customs; it varied also from one period to another according as the population was tending to grow, to become stabilized, or to fall. The search for a multiplier valid for all countries and all periods, on which some authors are bent, is therefore futile and seriously mistaken.

[5] On the handling of these questions see especially J. Cuvelier, "Les dénombrements de foyers en Brabant (XIVe–XVIe siècle)", *Publications de la Commission royale d'histoire de Belgique* (Brussels, 1912) and F. Lot, "L'état des paroisses et des feux de 1328", *Bibliothèque de l'Ecole des Chartes*, t. XC (1929), p. 51.

[6] K. J. Beloch, *op. cit.*, pp. 91ff.

[7] J. C. Russell, *British Medieval Population* (Albuquerque, 1948). If the auxiliary calculations of this author, such as the average expectation of life, are debatable, the total figures that he suggests for the years 1086, 1346, and 1377 are more certain. On the basis of the Polyptyque of Saint-Germain-des-Prés, compiled at the end of the reign of Charlemagne or early in that of Louis the Pious, and on *L'Etat des paroisses et des feux* of 1328, E. Levasseur, in *La population française* (Paris, 1889), t. I, pp. 139 and 168, proposed the figures of 8 to 9 million inhabitants for France in the Carolingian period and of 20 to 22 million for the first third of the 14th century. But he almost immediately modified these figures by reason of the analysis of A. Longnon, *Polyptyques de l'abbaye de Saint-Germain-des-Prés* (Paris, 1895), t. I, p. 250. His inquiries were resumed with more rigor by F. Lot, "Conjectures démographiques sur la France au IXe siècle", in *Le Moyen Age*, t. XXXII (1921), pp. 1ff. For this scholar the density of rural population in France about 810–820 was between 34 and 39 per square kilometer. These new conclusions were confirmed with the help of the polyptyque of Saint-Bertin relating to French Flanders, by H. van Werveke, "De bevolkingsdichtheid in de IXe eeuw. Poging tot schatting", *XXXe Congrès de la Fédération archéologique et historique de Belgique* (Brussels, 1935), *Annales* (Brussels, 1936), pp. 107ff. On the other hand, in his edition of the Etat of 1328, F. Lot estimated the density of population at this date as between 35 and 38 per square kilometer, a figure sharply rejected by so learned a scholar as E. Perroy, "A l'origine d'une économie contractée. Les crises du XIVe siècle", *Annales. Economies. Sociétés. Civilisations* (4e Année, 1949), p. 168, n. 1. This would imply that between the age of Charlemagne and that of Philip VI, the population of the

French countryside did not grow or that if it increased after 1050 this merely compensated for probable losses between 850 and 1050, as M. Bloch believed, "Les invasions: occupation du sol et peuplement", *Annales d'histoire sociale,* II (1945), p. 26. These deductions are much more speculative than those of English researchers, especially because the basis of Lot's estimates for the Carolingian period is so much narrower than that of Domesday Book. To generalize about France as a whole from about twenty estates is indeed reckless. Surely the polyptyques of Saint-Germain and of Saint-Bertin refer to estates better furnished with manpower than neighboring estates, simply because they were monastic and also because they refer to regions that were drawing immigrants? Even supposing that their populations were as large in 800 as in 1300, would it follow that this was true throughout France? Besides, is it certain that the French population had not grown between these dates? The only way to be certain of this would be to study identical estates at different dates from the point of view of the extent of cultivated land, the number of tenants and of hearths, etc.

8 See, for England, J. C. Russell, *op. cit.,* pp. 76ff. and, for the continent, L. Verriest, *Institutions médiévales* (Mons et Frameries, 1946), p. 117.

9 Conversion into modern measures is always hazardous. It is usually done with the help of tables drawn up at the end of the Ancien Régime or at the beginning of the 19th century, on the assumption that no modification had occurred since the Middle Ages. It is best, therefore, not to use these unless it is necessary, that is to say, unless one needs to compare data from different estates.

10 From the post-Carolingian age, indeed in some cases earlier, there ceases to be any correlation between the number of tenures and the number of tenants. Calculation of the latter runs up against the difficulty of vague references to partners *(conparticipes)* or by the recurrence in the lists of the same names, which may or may not refer to the same people.

11 As A. E. Levett has noted, *Studies in Manorial History* (Oxford, 1938), p. 249, it is rash to deduce the number of inhabitants from the number of tenants. The former included, besides the tenants, the following categories whose importance varied from estate to estate: subtenants, farmhands lodging with their masters, artisans without a scrap of land—perhaps not even their own house and garden—, rear-vassals of whom polyptyques usually give no hints, and small independent freeholders.

12 It was by counting inhabited centers as they appeared in the documents that K. Lamprecht, *Deutsches Wirtschaftsleben im Mittelalter* (Leipzig, 1885), I, pp. 163ff. and II, pp. 17ff., thought he had discovered the phases of demographic history in the Moselle valley between the 10th century and the 15th. The method is defensible, since new settlements usually indicate new population. However, in striving to be statistical the German historian laid himself open to serious criticism. He proceeded as though he had full information on all the inhabited places in the years 1000, 1050, 1100, etc., or as though the percentage that he did not know was a constant; this is to suppose that one's documentation is either complete or bears a constant relation to the facts throughout the whole period. He gave the same weight to all inhabited centers, although in an age of intensive clearing the new settlements are usually mere hamlets or isolated farms, with many fewer inhabitants than the old settlements. He overlooked the abandonment of some villages between the 11th century and the 13th. From the fact that there appeared to have been no new settlements in this region after 1240, he arbitrarily concluded that population ceased to grow at that date.

13 M. Morgan, *The English Lands of the Abbey of Bec* (Oxford, 1946), p. 111.

14 For examples of the ancient genealogies, useful but to be checked with extreme care, see "Chronicon Hanoniense quod dicitur Balduini Avennensis", ed. J. Heller, in *Monumenta Germaniae Historica. Scriptores,* XXV, pp. 421ff.

15 L. Génicot, *L'économie rurale namuroise au bas moyen âge,* T. I, *La seigneurie foncière* (Louvain and Namur, 1943), p. 66. The same method has been applied by P. Feuchère, "Histoire sociale et généalogie. La noblesse du Nord de la France", *Annales. Economies. Sociétés. Civilisations,* VI (1951), pp. 315ff.

16 At least for the 11th, 12th, and 13th century. From the late Middle Ages and espe-

cially from 1400, it is possible to draw up most interesting genealogies of bourgeois families, like that of the Rohrbachs of Frankfurt-am-Main, analyzed by H. Boos, *Geschichte der rheinischen Städtekultur* (2nd ed., Berlin, 1899), III, p. 44, and set out in detail in H. Grotefend, ed., *Quellen zur Frankfürter Geschichte* (Frankfurt, 1884), table 19, pp. 434ff.

[17] The example in *Beilage V: Beispiele der Kinderfrequenz der abhängigen Bevölkerung* for the Carolingian age, established from the *libri traditionum* of Fulda and other German abbeys in K. Th. von Inama-Sternegg, *Deutsche Wirtschaftsgeschichte* (2nd ed., Leipzig, 1909), is only a rough sketch of what could be done.

[18] Obviously other types of documents may be used for this purpose, such as the polyptyques, like that of Irminon, and for the later Middle Ages tax rolls, like the Tyrolese rolls of 1427 used by K. Schadelbauer, "Die Kopfzahl der bäuerlichen Familien in Tirol im 15 Jahrhundert", in *Quellen zur Steuer-, Bevölkerungs- und Sippengeschichte des Landes Tirol im 13, 14, und 15 Jahrhundert. Festgabe zum 80 Lebensjahre O. Redlichs. Schlern-Schriften*, Heft 44 (Innsbrück, 1939).

[19] One must of course always make sure that the data are clearly representative. For example, one cannot exclude the possibility that figures drawn from pious donations are above the average, such transactions being sometimes the alternative to excessive fragmentation. In that case, however, a statistician would term the error a more or less strictly systematic one, which would not invalidate the evolutionary study of which we are speaking. On account of this bias one should not, however, mix data drawn from pious donations with those drawn from other sources.

[20] On this point see K. Kulischer, *Allgemeine Wirtschaftsgeschichte des Mittelalters und der Neuzeit* (Munich and Berlin, 1927), I, p. 173 or the well-known book of K. Buecher, *Die Frauenfrage im Mittelalter* (2nd ed., Leipzig, 1910), summarized in *Abhandlung XI* of the first volume of *Die Entstehung der Volkswirtschaft* (17th ed., Tübingen, 1926).

[21] With the exception of some historians of medicine who have dealt with this briefly and indirectly and whose chief works are listed in E. Keyser, *Bevölkerungsgeschichte Deutschlands* (2nd ed., Leipzig, 1941) (the only edition I was able to procure), the epidemics and plagues of our period have received little attention from 20th century researchers. We still have little to go on beyond F. Curschmann, *Hungersnöte im Mittelalter* (Leipzig, 1900) or even older works, such as A. Corradi, *Annali delle Epidemie occorse in Italia* (Bologna, 1865), or L. Torfs, *Fastes des calamités publiques survenues dans les Pays-Bas*, 2 vols. (Paris and Tournay, 1859), or chapter 21 in L. Delisle, *Etudes sur la condition de la classe agricole et l'état de l'agriculture en Normandie au moyen âge* (Evreux, 1851) and appendix 1 to vol. I of K. Lamprecht, *op. cit.*, pp. 1537ff.

[22] Agricultural prices seem to me to be more closely related to the demographic situation and more likely to show changes in this if they are expressed in wheat and not in money or when they move in a different direction from other prices or have a different amplitude in their fluctuations.

[23] M. Postan, "Some Economic Evidence of Declining Population in the later Middle Ages", *Economic History Review*, 2nd series, vol. II, no. 3 (1950), pp. 225ff. See also W. Abel, "Bevölkerungsgang und Landwirtschaft im ausgehenden Mittelalter im Lichte der Preis und Lohnbewegung", *Schmoller's Jahrbücher*, 58th year (1934), pp. 33ff.

[24] This is the method used in France by d'Avenel and in Germany by Lamprecht and used again by W. Abel, *Agrarkrisen und Agrarkonjunktur in Mitteleuropa vom 13 bis zum 19 Jahrhundert* (Berlin, 1935), pp. 24ff. It is also the one which J. R. Strayer, in *The Royal Domain in the Bailliage of Rouen* (Princeton, 1936) suggested applying to Normandy when he wrote (p. 24) that it is sometimes possible to make a comparison between the prices given in the document which he was publishing and those of 1180–1200, that is, 70 or 80 years before, given by L. Delisle in ch. XX of the work cited in n. 21.

[25] We have indicated this method in a table on p. 289 of the work cited above in n. 15.

[26] The best general exposition is still that of H. Pirenne, "Le mouvement économique

et social au moyen âge, du XIe au milieu du XVe siècle" in G. Glotz, ed., *Histoire générale*, 2nd part, *Histoire du moyen âge* (Paris, 1933), VIII (reprinted in *Histoire économique de l'Occident médiéval*, pp. 155ff.). However, it needs revision in the way indicated in R. Latouche, *Les origines de l'économie occidentale, IVe–XIe siècle* (Paris, 1956), pp. 271ff. and in my *Lignes de faîte du moyen âge* (2nd ed., Tournai and Paris, 1962), p. 334, n. 27.

27 The criteria of urban growth have been very carefully analyzed by F. L. Ganshof, *Over stadsontwikkeling tusschen Loire en Rijn gedurende de Middeleeuven* (2nd ed., Brussels, 1944) and in remarks reported in the *Acts* of the Ninth International Congress of the Historical Sciences (Paris), II, pp. 34–35.

28 Figures drawn from the work of Ganshof just cited. For other important examples see F. Lot, *Recherches sur la population et la superficie des cités remontant à la période gallo-romaine (Bibliothèque de l'Ecole des Hautes Etudes. Sciences historiques et philologiques)* (Paris, 1945 and 1950), vols. 287 and 296; L. Blondel, "Le développement urbain de Genève à travers les siècles", *Cahiers de préhistoire et d'archéologie* (Geneva and Nyon, 1946), III, and also I. von Strampf, *Die Entstehung und mittelalterliche Entwicklung der Stadt Nürnberg* (Erlangen, 1929).

29 A. E. Levett, *op. cit.*, p. 181, remarked on this.

30 G. Luzzatto, *Storia economica d'Italia* (Rome, 1949), vol. I, p. 241, writes that many Italian towns between 1100 and 1250 grew from 5 to 6,000 souls to 30 or 40,000; the bounds sometimes finally enclosed an area tenfold the size of the original area yet building still went on beyond them.

31 On this point see very precise data in E. Keyser, *op. cit.*, pp. 268ff.

32 Italian historians have paid particular attention to the process of urbanization. See the survey by G. Luzzatto, "L'inurbamento delle popolazioni rurali in Italia nei secoli XII e XIII", *Studi di storia e diritto in onore di E. Besta* (Milan, 1939), II, pp. 185ff.

33 E. Lipson, *The Economic History of England* (10th ed., London, 1949), I, p. 185, says that at the end of the 13th century half the inhabitants of Colchester lived by agriculture.

34 Except for a narrow radius of four or five kilometers around little towns; see M. C. Daviso, "I piu antichi catasti del commune di Chieri (1253)", *Bollettino storico-bibliografico subalpino*, vol. XXXIX (1937), p. 75.

35 See R. Koebner's excellent survey on this matter in *The Cambridge Economic History of Europe* (Cambridge, 1941), I, pp. 61ff., and G. Duby, *L'économie rurale et la vie des campagnes dans l'Occident médiéval* (Paris, 1962), pp. 133–169.

36 F. L. Ganshof, *La Flandre sous les premiers comtes*, 2nd ed., p. 54, in the collection *Notre Passé* (Brussels, 1944) and S. J. Fockerma-Andreae, "Embanking and Drainage Authorities in the Netherlands in the Middle Ages", *Speculum*, XXVII (1952), pp. 158ff.

37 G. Mickwitz in the *Cambridge Economic History*, I, pp. 323ff. and G. Luzzatto, *Storia economica d'Italia*, p. 212.

38 On work on the Po, see especially P. Torelli, *Un comune cittadino in territorio ad economia agricola*, in *Pubblicazioni della R. Accademia Virgiliana di Mantova. Serie miscellanee*, III (1930), vol. I, pp. 105ff.

39 M. Bloch, *Les caractères originaux de l'histoire rurale française* (Oslo, 1931 and Paris), pp. 5ff.

40 See A. Longnon, *Les noms de lieu de la France* (Paris, 1920–1929), pp. 515ff.

41 Typical plans will be found in P. Lavendan, *Histoire de l'urbanisme* (Paris, 1926), I, pp. 296ff.; M. Bloch, *op. cit.*, pl. I in the appendix; *Cambridge Economic History*, I, p. 45.

42 See a study of my own, "Le destin d'une famille noble. Les Noville aux XIIIe et XIVe siècles", *Annales de la Société archéologique de Namur*, t. XLVI (1952), p. 216.

43 A. Poeschl, "Der Neubruchzehent", *Archiv für katholisches Kirchenrecht*, t. XCVIII (1918), pp. 33ff.

44 "Miracles de la Sainte Croix de Brogne", 1. 3, c. 8, ed. by F. Baix in the *Annales de la Société archéologique de Namur*, vol. XLV (1950), p. 260. Needless to say, the indices listed here are only the most obvious ones. Others can be found, such as a

fall in the number of pigs that a village can fatten: see H. E. Darby, *An Historical Geography of England before 1800* (Cambridge, 1936), p. 181.

[45] It is better to take a compact district than to pick villages here and there, if only to rule out the effect of local migration.

[46] There has been a good deal of systematic study of the *villes neuves* of Southwest France, called *bastides*. One of the most recent contributions is by L. Higounet, "Cisterciens et Bastides", in *Le Moyen Age*, vol. LVI (1950), pp. 69ff.

[47] As names by themselves are deceptive—there was clearing before the 11th and even before the 10th century!—, it may be useful, in the interests of exactness, to follow the methods of A. Helbok, *Grundlagen der Volksgeschichte Deutschlands und Frankreichs* (Leipzig and Berlin, 1937), maps 53ff.: draw two series of maps, one showing the various types of place names, the other showing the first mention of each place in a document, and then construct colonization maps after comparing these two. In default of maps the data of place names and of documents may simply be tabulated as in A. Bach, "Die Siedlungsnamen des Taunusgebiets in ihrer Bedeutung für die Besiedlungsgeschichte", in *Veröffentlichungen des Instituts für geschichtliche Landeskunde der Rheinlande an der Universität Bonn. Herausgegeben von F. Steinbach* (Bonn, 1927), vol. I, pp. 207ff.

[48] On this see C. Higounet, "Les artigues dans les vallées luchonnaises", *Mélanges géographiques offerts en hommage à Monsieur le doyen D. Faucher* (Toulouse, 1948–1949), vol. II, pp. 555ff. and "Contribution à l'étude de la toponymie du défrichement: les artigues du Bordelais et du Bazadais", in *IIIe Congrès international de toponymie et anthroponymie. Vol. III: Actes et Mémoires* (Louvain, 1951), pp. 595ff.

[49] On all of the towns of central Flanders and some of the Norman towns, see J. Dhondt, "Développement urbain et initiative comtale au XIe siècle", *Revue du Nord*, vol. XXX (1948), pp. 133ff. and J. F. Lemarignier, *Revue du moyen âge latin*, vol. IV (1948), p. 191. The first-mentioned author seems to me to exaggerate the role of material factors in the birth of these towns.

[50] There were undoubtedly migrations even in the heart of the Christian West: see R. Boutruche, "Les courants de peuplement dans l'Entre-Deux-Mers", *Annales d'histoire économique et sociale,* vol. VII (1935), pp. 13ff. and 124ff.

[51] Their significance is chiefly for the regions from which settlers are drawn or for places victualled by the grange.

[52] Most authors follow F. L. Ganshof (*Cambridge Economic History*, I, pp. 279ff.) and Marc Bloch (*Les caractères originaux, loc. cit.*), in so emphasizing magnates and abbeys as founders of *villes neuves* as to give the reader the impression that assarting within old lands by petty lords or peasants was of only secondary importance. This is probably an error; in regard to peasant clearing see T. A. M. Bishop, "Assarting and the Growth of the Open Fields", *Economic History Review*, VI, no. 1 (1935), pp. 17ff. and R. Latouche, "Agrarzustände im westlichen Frankreich während des Hochmittelalters", *Vierteljahrschrift für Sozial- und Wirtschaftsgeschichte*, XXIX (1936), p. 111, and on the work of petty lords see my article cited in n. 42.

[53] W. Abel, *Agrarkrisen*, p. 22. An increasing yield is the best proof we can get of more rational exploitation. The data on this point have, however, to be handled with great care, even for England, where the statistical data are best. See M. K. Bennet, "British Wheat Yield per Acre for Seven Centuries", *Economic History. A supplement of The Economic Journal*, III, no. 10 (February, 1935), pp. 12–20, and B. A. Slicher van Bath, "De oogstophengsten van verschillende gewassen, voornamelijk granen, in verhouding tot het Zaaizaad ca. 810–1820", in *A. A. G. Bijdragen*, vol. 9 (1963), pp. 29–126.

[54] Several factors may have contributed to keep manorial units stable. For example, it was in the interests of royal power and lords to keep the manse intact as a fiscal unit, and local inheritance customs could have the same effect. The reciprocal of our proposition therefore does not hold, that is to say, the survival of the old units does not prove demographic stagnation. At Bobbio the manse was preserved throughout the Middle Ages solely for fiscal reasons; see C. M. Cipolla, "Per la storia della crisi del sistema curtense in Italia. Lo sfaldamento del manso nell'Appennino bob-

biese", *Bollettino dell'Istituto Storico Italiano per il Medio Evo ed Archivie Muratoriano*, n. 62 (1950), pp. 283ff.

55 The splitting up of estates could occur through pious donations or subinfeudation; see my *Economie rurale namuroise*, I, pp. 37ff.

56 It would usually follow after a lag; as a consequence of the practice of indivision, the splitting up of holdings frequently happened one or two generations after the growth of population.

57 C. E. Perrin, *Recherches sur la seigneurie rurale en Lorraine d'après les plus anciens censiers (IXe–XIIe siècles)* (Paris, 1935), pp. 634ff.

58 A. Hauck, *Kirchengeschichte Deutschlands*, vol. IV (3rd ed., Leipzig, 1913), pp. 24ff.

59 This also introduced a lag.

60 See R. Rey, *L'art roman et ses origines. Archéologie pré-romane et romane* (Toulouse and Paris, 1945), p. 147 and K. Lamprecht, *op. cit.*, I, p. 164.

61 The monasteries that multiplied from the 11th century on helped to meet this need.

62 Although they can constitute proof, they need not; a chapel might have been founded through piety and a church altered simply because architectural taste was changing.

63 M. Postan, *Cambridge Economic History* (Cambridge, 1952), II, p. 160.

64 For North Germany see R. Koebner and H. Aubin, *Cambridge Economic History*, I, pp. 80ff. and 364ff. and E. Keyser, *op. cit.*, pp. 212ff., and for Belgium, R. Doehaerd, *L'expansion économique belge au moyen âge*, in the collection *Notre Passé* (Brussels, 1946), pp. 38ff. For Spain see M. Defourneaux, *Les Français en Espagne aux XIe et XIIe siècles* (Paris, 1949), pp. 214ff. and the remarks of J. M. Lacarra in the *IXe Congrès international des Sciences historiques*, II, p. 43.

65 The phrase is taken from R. Koebner, *loc. cit.*, p. 69. He may not have intended to exaggerate. It may be admitted as true, if the emphasis is on the word revolution.

66 G. Luzzatto, *Storia economica*, p. 212, thinks that the Italian growth began in the 10th century. P. Torelli, *Un comune cittadino, op. cit.*, pp. 151ff., takes the same view.

67 R. Koetzschke, *Allgemeine Wirtschaftsgeschichte des Mittelalters*, in the *Handbuch der Wirtschaftsgeschichte*, ed. G. Brodnitz (Iena, 1924), II, pp. 361–362, in view of new settlements in Lower Saxony, in the Harz region, at the edges of the forest in Thuringia, and in Austria, described German population growth between the Carolingian and the Hohenstaufen period as "not negligible". II. Aubin, *op. cit.*, p. 365, also sees German colonization of Austria as occurring between 800 and 1100. P. Dollinger, *L'évolution des classes rurales en Bavière* (Paris, 1949), p. 79, holds that though new settlement in Bavaria was interrupted by the Hungarian invasion, it was vigorously resumed from the mid-10th century.

68 H. van der Linden, *De Cope* (Assen, 1955); C. E. Perrin, *Les classes rurales et le régime seigneurial au moyen âge* (mimeographed, Paris, 1949), p. 134; F. L. Ganshof, *op. cit.*, p. 278.

69 See in general W. Abel, "Wachstumsschwankungen mitteleuropäischer Völker seit dem Mittelalter", *Jahrbücher für Nationalökonomie und Statistik*, CXLII (1935), pp. 675ff.; and on Germany his "Die Wüstungen des ausgehenden Mittelalters. Ein Beitrag zur Siedlungs- und Agrargeschichte Deutschlands", *Quellen und Forschungen zur Agrargeschichte* (2nd ed., Iena, 1955), vol. I. Signs of the desertion of land multiply in the 15th century.

70 See M. Postan, *loc. cit.* above, n. 23. Similarly in France, according to G. d'Avenel, *Histoire économique de la propriété, des salaires, des denrées et de tous les prix en général depuis l'an 1200 jusqu'en l'an 1800* (2nd ed., Paris, 1914), II, p. 508. The price of land ceased to rise from the beginning of the 14th century.

71 See especially J. C. Russell, *op. cit.* and F. Luetge, "Das 14–15 Jahrhundert in der Sozial- und Wirtschaftsgeschichte", *Jahrbücher für Nationalökonomie und Statistik*, CLXII (1950), pp. 165ff.

72 P. Dollinger, *loc cit.*

73 O. Stolz, "Zur Statistik der Haushalte nach den Listen von 1312 und 1427", pp. 5 and 6 (in the Redlich Festschrift, cited above in n. 18). R. Koetzschke, "Grundzüge

der deutschen Wirtschaftsgeschichte bis zum 17 Jahrhundert" (2nd ed.), *Grundriss der Geschichtswissenschaft* (Leipzig and Berlin, 1923), 2nd series, fasc. I, p. 116, although he believes that the Black Death reduced German population, estimates that for the 13th and 14th century it had a density of 20 to 30 per square kilometer and that in "favorable situations" the density around 1450 may have been from 30 to 40.

[74] K. F. Helleiner, "Population Movement and Agrarian Depression in the Later Middle Ages", *Canadian Journal of Economics and Political Science*, XV (1949), p. 371.

[75] None of the classical textbooks of medieval and modern economic history devotes even a section of a chapter to this problem.

3

German Towns and
Slav Markets

RICHARD KOEBNER

I

BETWEEN APPROXIMATELY 1150 and 1250, a wave of urban and rural colonization transformed the economic and social structure of the eastern parts of Central Europe (the Western Slav world), from top to bottom. The two forms of colonization usually went on together in close connection. Yet the urban form had a momentum of its own. While there was nowhere any creation of new estates and villages without the founding also of new towns, urban colonization penetrated many districts of Bohemia, Poland, and Pomerania where there was as yet no rural colonization. Again, although it was the Germans who introduced new methods of organizing rural colonization, the Slavs everywhere followed their example. The newly established towns, on the contrary, were at first peopled only by Germans. Indeed, as long as the town-founding movement lasted—up to the beginning of the 14th century—, it continued to rely, directly or indirectly, on the flow of German immigration.

These circumstances are to be explained by the fact that before the wave of colonization arrived, the Western Slav world had no towns— no forms of settlement resembling the towns of Germany or of the rest of Western Europe. The foundation of towns was everywhere, whether or not it was accompanied by rural colonization, an entirely new movement. If the Western Slav world had already developed places with an economic character like that of German towns and a comparable way of life, despite juridical differences, the Slav princes could have favored the new urban colonists only at the cost of disrupting native groups and ruining some of their hereditary subjects. Nothing of this sort ever occurred.

What exactly were the innovations involved in the founding of towns of the German type? The market, which lay at the centre of every colonial town, was in itself certainly no novelty. Well-organized markets were by 1100 an important element of the territorial regimes of Bohemia, Poland, and Pomerania; legal rights over them were uniform in nature and precisely defined. The most important markets were those in the vicinity of the chief centers of political life—the great forts of the princes. All carried on a regular trade, some being held weekly, some annually. All had shops for the sale of wine, bread, meat, and shoes, and most of these shops had fixed owners. The merchants and artisans who regularly supplied and ran the market appear to have lived nearby. Is it an error, then, to say that these Slav countries had no towns? Was the difference between the Slav market and the German town merely one of size or of the degree of social differentiation? The answer has up to now been largely a matter of opinion. Some writers have preferred to view the old Slav markets as so backward that they were incapable of surviving alongside the German towns. Others have maintained that when the Germans arrived and took over the direction of economic life, the Slav markets were already on the verge of developing an urban culture. We propose to analyze the question here rather more fully.

II

In the first place, one cannot help noticing that the Slav princes took a long time to decide on the reorganization of their regime along the new lines that the foundation of German towns introduced.

German towns first entered the Western Slav world around 1150. Colonization was by then on the move on the German side of the whole eastern frontier strip of the Empire that lay along the Elbe, from Holstein to Meissen. Lübeck, Schwerin, Jüterborg, Leipzig, and other towns arose here at that time: the urban movement, the spontaneous development of town life, was spreading from the older regions of German culture west of the river. It was only recently, since about 1100, that the western citizen groups had been winning administrative and juridical autonomy. These privileges became the basis of colonial enterprise through the founding of new communities and towns. But there was a striking lag in the further spread of the movement across the German-Slav frontiers into the Slav principalities of Mecklenburg, Pomerania, Poland, Silesia, and Bohemia.

It was not until 1210 that Henry I of Silesia set about founding a few towns. Deliberately, it would seem, he located them all at some distance from the ancient centers of the country, as though he were reluctant to involve the latter in radical change. The first of the old Slav centers of royal residence where formal privileges were granted to Germans as citizens was Rostock in Mecklenburg, a few years later. Not until 1230 did the King of Bohemia permit Germans to colonize the market of Prague. From then on towns gradually come to be accepted as part of the regime of the Slav countries.

There was thus a lag of from 60 to 80 years before the Slav princes recognized the advantages of German organization. Why so long a delay? What was going on? There was certainly time enough for the Slavs to observe the enterprise of their German neighbors and to begin to imitate it. Why was the Slav market not developing the German type of urban economic activity? Why did the Slav princes follow a policy of inaction for so long and then suddenly decide to let the Germans pour in and build towns? Surely they must have had good reasons for their initial conservatism: the old Slav market organization must have had special functions in the traditional regime. If it could not develop along German lines, it must have been because it was designed in the main to serve different needs.

III

The key concept for understanding the economic structure of the Slav markets is that of royal monopoly rights. It is true that territorial princes in the West, too, and the lords on whom they conferred market rights, had considerable interests in trade. Not as being large-scale entrepreneurs, but as drawing handsome revenues from trade—in the case of the princes, through regalian rights, in the case of the lords, through the rent of market sites. Princes did more than merely lay claim to market tolls. It was they who established markets. They received sums of money for so doing and retained special advantages in them. When the Western Slav states were being consolidated, between the 10th century and the 12th, they took as their model the Franco-German state of the earlier middle ages. They borrowed its great court offices, its system of local administration, and also its system of regalian rights. In regard to this last, the Bohemian state of the Přemyslides probably took the lead, as it certainly did in the other matters. The Polish Piasts followed suit, influencing the administrative institutions also of Pomerania, which then included the region of the lower Vistula. Indeed, in the first half of the 12th century Pomerania had to recognize the sovereignty of the Piast dynasty, though it freed itself very quickly when the Polish kingdom disintegrated. Hence in the 12th and 13th century we find virtually identical regalian rights in all of the independent principalities of the Western Slav world.

Regalian rights were especially well defined in Silesia. This country had originally formed part of the Piast kingdom, separating in 1163 under a cadet line of that dynasty. Shortly after this it split into the two autonomous kingdoms of Breslau and Ratibor-Opeln. Royal jurisdiction over markets is very well documented for Silesia. The charters of urban *locatio,* that is, the privileges granted the entrepreneurs to whom the prince entrusted the foundation of towns, are especially interesting. It was through these charters that German law was introduced into the towns. Yet a good deal of the ancient Pomeranian Slav law was retained. The royal rights that are set out in the charters, and also some of the rights that the prince granted to the provost (*Vogt*), come from this older system of law. Comparison with German legal institutions west of the Elbe proves that these regalian rights could not possibly have come from the law of any self-governing German town. In regard to market dues a *locatio* instituted a compromise between prince, provost, and townspeople. In this way the charters reveal the nature of the old ducal regalian rights.

The princes' market monopolies fall into three groups, each having a different juridical and economic basis.

The first group included the more general revenues arising from a market—those due to the prince for ceding the market site, for protecting it, and for staffing it with officials to enforce its regulations. These revenues were collected through tolls and similar payments, such as the *targove* mentioned in Polish sources, the market "ninths" and "tenths" due in Silesia and Bohemia, and the shares of merchandise and money paid by the colonist-tenants (*hôtes*) of the Teynhof at Prague. They were monopolistic only to the extent that any royal claim arising out of a grant may be so described. On the other hand, the use of legal tender (money) in trade was subject in Bohemia and under the Piasts to a genuine commercial monopoly. At fixed times, before the market opened, dealers were obliged to hand over all money in their possession to the duke's master moneyers and to buy it back from them.

The monopoly rights in the second group were purely economic and far more profitable. The sovereign did not attempt to control all production for the market, or all its trade. He ingeniously limited himself to control over the commodities that visitors to the market consumed.

Above all, he exploited the drink trade. The prince's tavern figures in innumerable documents, from Bohemia to Pomerania. Did a prince wish to endow a church? He would cede it his wine-shops and their keepers, or assign it regular income from his wine-shops. It is not clear whether the wine-seller was a tenant, paying a fixed rent, or whether he owed a certain percentage of his take. But the documents from Silesia and from the lower Vistula speak of a weekly accounting. This proves that taverns were an official princely enterprise. There is evidence also that the bulk of their sales were of drinks brewed from the produce of seigneurial land (honey or cereals).

The prince further reserved for himself certain market stalls. Like taverns, though less frequently, they were the object of gifts. In Poland they were implicitly included in seigneurial grants of the *utilitates* of the market, and both here and in the Přemyslid kingdoms there were also express gifts of butchers' stalls (*macella*). Charters that record the sovereign's gift, for example, of a butcher in the local market to the church of Olmutz or of 300 pence a week from the sale of meat in the shops of Breslau to the monastery of Trebnitz, prove that the meat trade was handled in the same way as the drink trade. The same was true of bakeries and shoe shops. Records of the foundation of towns and agreements with town provosts show that the three trades of the butchers, bakers, and shoemakers were always singled out for special regulation, not only in Bohemia but also in Poland and Moravia. A lord will cede the rent due him from the stalls of these three trades to the *locator* who has become provost or bailiff of a town he founded; or the lord and the provost may divide this revenue.

Now this custom cannot have come from German town law. It is true that certain practices in France and Southern Germany, at first sight, appear to be analogous. One will find taverns, bakeries, and butcheries there described as *banales* (subject to seigneurial rights). These were survivals of the lordship once exercised over the town; they date from a time when the market was not yet freed, was not really a townspeople's market. But these archaic institutions could not have influenced those of the East. In the 12th century, town law gave possession of the entire site of the market and its shops to the community or to citizens. For colonists, it was unwarranted for the sovereign to claim such sites as his own; they did not introduce the notion. It was a part of the native tradition that they had to accept.

Like the ancient seigneurial rights in German markets or the Slavic regalian right over taverns, the monopoly rights over particular trades were linked with the rural economy. The ducal lands supplied bakers, butchers, and shoemakers with their raw materials—wheat, livestock, and hides; they probably also sent bread to the market and ready-made shoes. In Silesia the sale of meat gave rise to a special seigneurial institution—the market slaughterhouse (*Kuttelhof*). Like the stalls, it was assigned by charter sometimes to the sovereign, sometimes to the provost. It had no doubt existed, as a monopoly of the prince, in the ancient Slav markets.[1]

In Silesia and in Moravia we find the profits of another institution, that of the bath-house (*stuba balnearia*), regularly assigned to the provost. It too was part of the organization of the Slav market. There was no German market institution of this kind to provide a precedent.

On the other hand, in the *Kaufhaus* designed for the sale of cloth or other costly merchandise, such as spices,[2] we are on the familiar ground of German and generally Western commercial tradition. These halls appear in the new towns, in Moravia and in Pomerania, very soon after their foundation. Neither in Germany nor in the colonial towns did the "better" burghers feel that any shame attached to retail trade in these relatively expensive wares. The halls of the merchant drapers of the West are famous from the 12th century on, for example, that of Cologne. Yet in the East these market halls had one characteristic which could not have been imported from Germany: their establishment depended on a ducal privilege. Often enough the ruler reserved the right to build and rent them, for himself. The magistrates of Magdeburg once ruled that such a claim ran counter to the traditions of urban law, at least in their city. Consulted as to whether it was in accordance with justice that Duke Henry I "is erecting a house and letting it" room by room, at Goldberg, to increase his income, they replied that it would be impossible for the lord of their city, the Archbishop of Magdeburg, to do so.

Goldberg was a town of recent foundation on a site where there had never been a Slav market. If the duke was reserving for himself the right to set up a market hall, he was undoubtedly drawing on ancient traditions of his other markets. We have direct information on only one such hall, antedating the colonization movement, that of the *Teynhof* at Prague. This, like the *Fondaco dei Tedeschi* at Venice or the Hanseatic halls in North and Northeastern Europe, was not only a market place but also a hostel for foreign merchants. Was the same true of the other halls which presumably existed in the more developed markets of the rest of the Slav countries? It is difficult to tell. Like the Teynhof, however, they were undoubtedly intended for foreign merchants. This above all marks them off from the *halles* of the Western type. This is well illustrated by a Silesian juridical document, referring to the recently founded town of Neisse, which belonged to the Bishop of Breslau. In 1245 the duke gave him permission both to institute a fair and to build a market hall. When the fair was not in session the hall was to be at the disposal of the citizens of Neisse for the sale of merchandise "which formerly they sold in their own house", cloth alone excepted. Neither citizens nor non-citizens were to sell cloth there except during a fair. It is thus clear that the commerce of a fair was originally in the hands of foreign merchants who visited only at that season. It was for them, at first, that the prince built a hall. Urban colonization introduced German customs, the citizens wanting sale rooms primarily for the benefit of the inhabitants of the town. At Neisse they were obliged to compromise with ancient custom, having to share the hall with foreigners and to let its cloth trade retain the seasonal character of a fair.[3] The reason for this was the duke's overriding concern with exploiting the influx of strangers, both as sellers, by obliging them to use his hall, and as consumers, through his tavern and his other monopolies.

We can now understand why the lord selected these particular monopolies. It was not merely to have an outlet for his own produce. If that had been his sole aim, he could simply have obliged artisans to use his raw materials, leaving them otherwise at liberty. And again, how would this motive account for the bath-house? Instead, think how a merchant coming to the market from a distance would spend his day. He has to buy meat and bread, he has to go to the tavern not only for drink but to find a lodging; after his long country journey he wants a bath, and he needs new shoes. Shoemakers were always in the trinity of trades monopolized, along with butchers and bakers, for the reason that constant travel wore out the merchants' shoes. In short, the effect of the ruler's monopolies was to compel foreigners attending the market to become his paying guests. For everything they needed they had to apply to one of his enterprises— for space to display their merchandise, and to refresh themselves. The monopoly system was undoubtedly designed to this end.

Somewhat similar thinking lay behind a second group of princely privileges, in the sale of fish and salt. But these were on a different juridical footing and their economic function was different. Juridically, they were based on the sovereign's right to the natural products of earth and water. Here again the regalian rights of the Franco-German state—in mines and fisheries—had furnished the model. In the Slav world, as in the West, the prince exploited his fishing rights through the market; this was, so to speak, in the nature of things. In places where trade took on some importance, families of fishermen organized hereditary gilds to which the prince, in return for regular but fixed payments, would cede the fisheries of a certain district and the right to sell the catch. Some of the Slav fishing gilds held on to their privileges even long after a German town had been founded in their district. At Danzig and Glogau they had their own communities, and at Breslau the members of the gild all lived in the same quarter.

But the Slav prince did not limit his interest in fisheries to the fees from these local concessions. His regalian right gave him a monopoly that he could exploit commercially. Slav princes obviously tended towards this as a matter of general policy. The herring was a "ducal fish" not only on the shores of the Baltic, where it was caught, but also in Silesia, where foreign merchants bought it for export. The same principles were applied in the salt trade. At Plock the prince in 1237 had the right to seize salt aboard the boats of the Vistula.

IV

We have seen that the prince's monopolies enabled him to exploit the market so widely as to leave little opportunity for private enterprise on the part of native merchants and artisans. The prince had almost complete control over the chief trades catering to the daily needs of market crowds. It is true that we sometimes find a group of merchants living near the market, but only a very small group. It consisted of the few men who went in for wholesale trade in staple products and the purchase of luxury items. They dealt with the Western merchants who came to sell cloth and other wares and to buy the local products that were highly prized in the West—wax, honey, furs, wood ash. Country traders who collected these products also lived in the neighborhood. The prince, the nobles, and the Church also needed merchants to procure arms, jewels, and sacred vessels that they could not obtain locally. Both the import and the export trade could generate business in loans. It is obvious that merchants would have to spend a great deal of time travelling, with very brief periods of fixed residence, and that foreigners could carry on these activities just as well as natives.

This general picture of commercial life is based on a good deal of evidence. For example, when Bishop Otto of Bamberg arrived at Kolberg on missionary work, he found the place quite empty and learned that the inhabitants were all away travelling. This was near the seacoast, where maritime trade was still rather closely connected with war. To my knowledge it was the only place where the trade of a Slav province was entirely controlled by Slavs. In Bohemia and Poland commerce was exclusively in the hands of Jews and Germans, with a few Italians. There were no native merchants or artisans domiciled in the market. At Prague, too, the well-known privilege granted the Germans—the *Sobislavum*—refers to these same three groups of foreigners. From 1100 on we have direct proof of the presence of the German element and indirect evidence of the Jewish element.

Indeed, the very notion of a merchant or a financier was equated with that of a foreigner. This is nowhere better illustrated than in a story told by the contemporary chronicler, Cosmas. In the story, Watislav II of Bohemia leaves Prague to visit his brother, Conrad of Moravia, taking along a retinue of soldiers. There are quarrels; the visit soon threatens to degenerate into an invasion. Conrad's wife, Wirperk, tries to pacify her brother-in-law by reasoning with him. If he allows his soldiers to despoil his brother, she argues, he will be despoiling himself: the property of a close relative deserves the same protection as one's own. She tries to drive the point home by slipping a rather strained analogy into a long, ironic speech: "In your own kingdom you will find immensely richer booty than here on your far-away frontiers. Nowhere could you seize a greater treasure than in your own castle in Prague and in the colony of the Wischehrad. There, there are Jews stuffed with gold and silver; there, there are the most affluent merchants; there, the master moneyers are gorged with wealth. There, there is the market, with piles of plunder for your warriors. If you want to re-enact the burning of Troy you have only to set fire to your two Prague castles. But perhaps you will say, 'All that belongs to me.' Surely. And do we not belong to you too, we and our property that you are starting to lay waste?" In describing the market of Prague, the duchess speaks only of foreigners; if to attack it had meant attacking native sons, she would have had to think of some other argument. Her whole discourse turns on the fact that the market is in the hands of foreigners. She is saying, "We here in your brother's duchy are as much yours, indirectly, as the foreign merchants and their goods."

The foreigners quartered near the market must have been engaged in the large-scale commercial enterprises we described above. They were probably also lending money, and farming the mint. They were excluded from the monopolized trades. According to the *Sobislavum,* the Germans at Prague were not allowed to run taverns on their premises. At Plock, the Duke of Masovia made two concessions to the Germans who in 1237 founded a "new town" at the market. He renounced his right to seize salt on boats lying in the harbor, and he agreed not to oblige his new *hôtes* to buy cloth for him. Like our other evidence from Neisse, these concessions show what conditions of trade had been like in earlier times.

Despite these restrictions, the markets of the East had a great attraction for foreign *hôtes.* By 1100 there were Jewish communities in the chief trading centres both in Bohemia and in the lands of the Piasts. An early document refers to Jews owing tithe to the Church from lands in their possession near the castle of Beuthen on the Oder, in lower Silesia. About the year 1200 two villages near Breslau were said to belong to the Jews, although perhaps this was only a matter of a temporary mortgage following a loan. The oldest traditions of German commercial settlement are at Prague. In Pomerania they date from shortly after the arrival of Christianity. The first German community we meet was founded in 1187 near the burg of Stettin. In Poland, Silesia, and Moravia German communities appear near the old territorial centers only as the colonization movement begins, although they antedate the foundation of towns. They may have been very old, merely receiving a new influx of colonists at this time.

V

Our sketch of the economic and social structure of the Slav market needs to be rounded out by a picture of its physical layout. What did a market look like? More exactly, when did it become, if not a town—this question would lead us into delicate problems of definition—at least an agglomeration?

There is no doubt that every market lay on the edge of some agglomeration. The great markets of the East were near *castra.* These were fortified places, built of wood and divided into quarters, with a princely "palace" in the center. We meet these from Bohemia to Pomerania. At the close of the pagan era, the Pomeranian *castra* seem to have been primarily places of residence for the aristocracy. In Bohemia and Moravia, as also in Poland and Silesia, and on the lower Vistula, the *castra* were inhabited by the prince's officials and had a garrison always readied for war. Now the market was never placed inside these great wooden fortresses; it always lay outside. At Prague it was some distance away from Wyschehrad, and faced Hradschein across the Moldau; at Olmütz it lay at the foot of the little hill on which the fortress stood; at Cracow it was below the Wawel. In Silesia the planning at Breslau, Glogau, and Opeln was apparently copied from Prague, the Oder running between the fortress and the market. In short, the market not only did not even adjoin the fortress but was so located as to leave a clear space between them. In Poland, the same is true of little rural markets; they lie at an appreciable distance from the village from which they take their name.

The requisite buildings—a church or a chapel and a few taverns were the indispensible minimum—stood either on the market space or very close by. The principal markets boasted also a counting house, slaughter house, bath-house, and shops for the sale of meat, bread, and shoes. But were there dwelling houses in the market, and if so, who lived in them? This brings us back to the question raised already, was the market an agglomeration?

There are three possibilities. First, the sovereign might have a dwelling house and barns adjoining the market, and ecclesiastical foundations endowed by him might also be adjacent. Artisans working under the seigneurial monopolies might live in the market. Foreigners—Germans, Jews, Italians—might also have houses there.

The first of these probably held true at Prague, at least as regards the clergy. Indeed, numerous churches arose on the market site itself. A charter—of doubtful authenticity—states that there was a "court" belonging to the monastery of Trebnitz, on the Breslau market.

Presumably the taverners lived in their taverns, but we know nothing about the living arrangements of the artisan butchers, bakers, and shoemakers. There was no necessity for them to live in the market; they could just as well have lived in the nearest village. Or, like other "sergeants" of the sovereign, notably the artisans who worked for the garrison, they may have lived in the *castrum*.

As to foreigners, the situation in Prague is clear. The oldest German colony mentioned in the documents was set up some distance to the east of the Old Market, near the church of St. Peter at Pořic. The Jews probably always lived to the north of the market where one may still see very fine remains, though relatively modern, of their quarter.

In short, we see that the market contained only such buildings as were essential to its functioning, that is to say, those necessary to the sovereign's monopolies. It was not a place to live in. No one lived there but the few families who had to be there even when the market was not open.

Contemporary descriptions confirm this impression. How do the companions of Bishop Otto describe the missionaries' arrival at a market or a burg? The market is always described as a place that people visited. We hear of crowds going from the fortress to the market or from the market to the fortress, never of people who lived in the market itself. The well-known verses by a monk of Leubus say of Silesia, at the time of the arrival of the Cistercians, "In this whole country there were no towns, neither large nor small, but only near the fortress a field where the market was held, with a tavern and a chapel." [4]

The truth of this description has been contested, for our monk was concerned to represent the conditions that his brethren found on their arrival as particularly hard. Certainly his picture would apply only to the poorest of the markets. Yet it is valuable in describing a typical form. To call it a *forum campestre,* a great space, open and empty, characterizes the Slav market well. And taverns are its typical buildings. The verses remind one of the formula found in donations of a market to monasteries—*forum et taberna*—referring to the site and the buildings on it. This traditional planning of the market as an empty site outside an inhabited place is attested also in Silesia and Poland by two suggestive terms, *ring* and *schroda* (*środa*). The first was the original German term for a Slav market, the second is the Polish word for a German market, seen as something new and strange.

Ring came to be the term applied in Bohemia, Silesia, and Poland to markets with an urban character. The corresponding Polish term is *Rynek*. The etymology of this is not Slavic; the word evidently came from the German. Yet there is something paradoxical about its use, in German, to designate the urban market, for a town market-place is almost always rectangular and is never round. Besides, the word *Ring* was never used of the market in Western Germany, where the bourgeoisie of the colonial towns were recruited. The name must therefore go back to a period when German merchants used it to characterize Silesian and Polish markets. We are thus brought back to the market on an open space. On market-days this space would have to be bounded in some way, either by marks or by the posting of guards. The prince's officials had to keep watch over it, if only to determine the limits within which the sovereign's regalian rights were in force. The *Ring* was this clearly defined space, under special authority, subject to the lord's monopolies, and more or less enclosed. To visiting German merchants, who at home were used to seeing markets surrounded by buildings, the erection of a barrier to delimit the sphere of the sovereign's rights made the Slav market strikingly distinctive. This is why they called it a *Ring,* and since they dominated the market, the word passed into Slav usage. Later, when the urban market surrounded with houses replaced the ducal market in its open field, the term *Ring* had become so popular that it was applied also to the new form.

The Poles, however, had invented another name for some of the new urban markets. A very old charter from Neumarkt in Silesia, dating from 1223, speaks of "Duke Henry's new market, which is called *szroda*". The same term was used of the market near the fortress of Poznan, and clung to it for some time. German merchants lived in this market until 1253, when the town of Poznan was built, a little distance away, on the left bank of the Vistula. There is actually a town called Schroda, in the western part of Great Poland, though the name is not attested until a later period. The word means "environment". Why would the Poles apply this to a German market? Because, contrary to Polish tradition, it was set up in an environment of houses. Slav markets required more space, for the foreign merchants who attended them arrived with wagons. Often these served as their lodging. The great spread of the market site has left its trace in the German colonial towns. In Western Germany the rectangular markets occupied a much smaller proportion of the town. In the East the colonial towns could at first almost be contained within their *Ring:* the site of the old *forum campestre,* with a little land added, sufficed.

VI

Let us sum up. The market was a great enterprise of the prince for the periodic organization of assemblies attended by foreigners and by the local population. The technical equipment with which it was provided belonged to the prince and was exploited for his benefit by his officials and his serfs. The market was not located within a settlement; it was not surrounded by the dwelling-houses of merchants or artisans. In the vicinity of the more important markets there were a few houses, but only for the use of great foreign merchants; these were the markets within easy reach of the *castra,* the military and administrative centers of the country-side.

How did this system develop? Why did the Slav princes maintain it for so long, while in the West a market civilization was developing along altogether different lines—bourgeois and urban? Finally, why did they gradually renounce their traditional system, in the course of the 13th century, and cede their markets to German townsmen?

To the first question there is no satisfactory answer. The genesis of the Slav market organization is no doubt bound up with that of the Slav state; as to this, we are still groping in the dark. Neither the evolution of the market system nor its diffusion throughout the Slav countries is documented. But it is virtually certain that the fundamental principle, the establishment of regalian rights over the markets, goes back to the rise of the Přemyslid and Piast monarchies in the 10th century. And if this is so, we have to admit that in its formative period the organization of the Slav market was not very different from that of Western markets; the diver-

gence came later. We have seen that the Slav rulers borrowed the principle of sovereign regalian rights from Franco-German public law. In Germany, too, in the 10th century, these rights were often exercised over
markets held in an uninhabited open space. For at that period, there
were few merchants or artisans with a fixed residence. Germs of the bourgeois town were rare, and it seems that in the West too it was chiefly foreigners who had quarters by the market. The Greek or Frisian quarters in
Cologne, the *burga* of the towns of Burgundy give us a fair idea of the
foreign quarters that were to grow up in the Slav countries. In the West,
too, these ancient merchant quarters were not located in the market itself,
but a little way off.

However, from the mid-10th century, the principles that were to become the basis of the bourgeois town were spreading in Western Europe.
Two above all must be regarded as fundamental. One was juridical in
nature. The market gives rise to a group whose members form a definite
community within the framework of the State. These associations of
mercatores, endowed with jurisdictional powers of their own, everywhere
become a corporate element of the nation, from Spain and England to
Saxony. The second principle expresses itself topographically: the market
becomes an inhabited place, and inhabited places become markets. And
though the market-place remains the center of commercial life, even after
it has become a place where people live, trade overflows into the adjacent
streets.

It is on these principles that the social and economic freedom of the
market-dweller rests; they define the "bourgeois collectivity". They give
the town its power to attract population; they facilitate the growth of a
varied and independent artisanry, producing for the market. Yet this development had no influence on the Slav peoples, despite their proximity.
Instead of following the example of the West a little further, by encour-
aging the growth of free and active market communities, recruited from
the indigenous population, the princes let their regalian rights crystallize
into monopolies. What did they gain by taking this attitude? Obviously
the traditional system assured a constant flow of foreign money into the
princes' coffers. The sole effort required to procure this steady revenue
was to provide the market buyers with provisions from the surplus of
seigneurial lands. The prince tapped the profits of trade through miscel-
laneous tolls and taxes and through the daily expenditures that foreign
merchants had to make for the necessities of life. Revenue from these latter sources accrued without the delay that collection of fees from native
merchants and artisans would have entailed. The prince's treasury was
thus assured of a steadier revenue and of revenue that was always largely
paid in money, much of it in foreign coin, which was always coveted.

A large part of the revenues went to the burg which had the duty of
protecting a market of any size. Sometimes all revenues had to be paid di-

rectly to the master of the mint. Sometimes they were assigned to a particular burg, generally that of the *châtellenie* in which the market lay. In the 12th century the princes increasingly assigned them for the endowment of churches. When the master of the mint collected the market revenues he had summary powers to enforce payment, but often he farmed the revenue, becoming an intermediary agent between the debtor and the prince or the burg.

Dues and corvées to which the prince had rights (*jus ducale*), the *vexationes* or *fatigationes* of his subjects, were also assigned to the administration of the burgs. These were almost always paid in kind, and they served to provision the fortress. Market revenues, on the other hand, were earmarked for the pay of troops. Ibrahim ibn Ja'kub tells us, in his travel memoirs of the year 965, how the first Piast prince, Mesco, supplied his soldiers with clothing, horses, arms, and everything they needed, in addition to a monthly wage in Byzantine money. The historian of Bole-Slav III, in the 12th century, also mentions the great gifts (*donativa*) of the Piasts. Money payments were continued into the 13th century, though no longer as a monthly wage but merely as gifts by which the prince was expected to reward his nobles for military service.

Under the first Piasts and Přzemyslides, that is to say, in the formative period of the great Slav states, military service, among the nobles, was still based on *compagnonnage*. This Germanic institution retained its vitality in the Slav states long after it had given way, in Western Europe, to feudalism. It was tied into the organization of the burgs, the prince's companions dividing among themselves the various forts in which their master would reside for a part of the year. Later the nobles acquired lands. At least among the higher nobility, military service then came to be extended. But the conditions of the first period survived in two institutions. The *castra* continued to be great fortified camps where troops were stationed, and the nobility, at least in Poland, kept the right to a money reward for their services. This probably explains the maintenance of the system of monopolies; it furnished the money that was required to supply the burgs and to pay the nobles.

Once established, the system was most tenacious. It undoubtedly retarded the economic development of the country. But it left the duke no way of promoting indigenous economic growth. If he wanted to keep his monopolies intact, he could not afford to give free artisans access to the market nor allow them to live in it to ply their trades. Nor could he renounce his monopolies in the interest of promoting a free market economy, for in the period of transition to a new economy and new fiscal policies his finances would have been gravely imperilled. There was, however, a way out. But it was the West, not the Slav countries, that found it. The effects could be observed in the immediate vicinity of the Slav principalities, in Germany. Trade and the artisanry could usefully replace the system of monopolies and even raise the prince's income, if the new social groups would give him an advance guarantee of full compensation by buying out his monopolies. It was impossible to copy the economic organization of the Germans. But the princes could summon it to their aid, could make use of it to rid themselves of their ancient irrational involvement in economic activity. Their plan was to hand over their markets to the Germans to be transformed into bourgeois institutions. By 1200, German citizens were successfully carrying out this task.

VII

It remains to study the transition from the old territorial market to the new German urban system.

The colonization of the Slav regions of Eastern Germany was a complex process; research has emphasized now one aspect of it and now another. But there is no doubt that one of its most important features is the financial aspect. The prince gives up part of the revenues due him as sovereign in return for rents paid by the colonists. In agriculture, these rents take the place of corvées; in trade, they replace monopoly income. This latter principle is found not only in the towns but in the countryside. The foundation of a town is the starting point of a colonization movement in which the townsmen acquire lands. This is nowhere clearer than in the Piast states, especially in Silesia. As we have shown, it was Henry I who first opened the ancient Piast kingdom to German urban colonization, about 1210, and his example was soon copied in neighboring territories. The Bishop of Breslau and the Přemyslides of Moravia welcomed agrarian colonization in their mountainous land and forests. In Great Poland Vladislav Odonisez tried to colonize the land lying between the Warthe and the Netze with the help of the Cistercians, though this aim was never realized. A popular plan in other regions was to enlarge the merchant colonies near the principal burgs, or to relocate them, as in the *novum forum* at Breslau. Organized merchant colonies appear between 1210 and 1230 at Opeln and Ratibor in Upper Silesia, at Brno in Moravia, at Cracow and Poznan in Poland. It was during this period that German bourgeois organization reached Danzig and, a little later (1237) Plock in Masovia. The new Dominican order quickly appreciated the importance of the leading markets in Slav countries, and acquired control of the churches adjacent to the German colonies at Prague, Cracow, Breslau, and Danzig.

Two words in use at this time, one German, the other Polish, are significant. We have already met the Polish word *Schroda*, applied to the market bounded by houses at Neumarkt in Silesia and at Poznan. The German word which similarly reveals the spread of the urban movement is *Burg*. Although the word was applied to a fortified place, there is another semantic tradition in which it signifies a continuously built-up section of a center of population, that is, a quarter. It is in this sense that the name Freiburg, given to the market founded by the Duke of Zator in 1120, is to be understood. The German and Italian colonies of Brno, after they were reinforced about 1220, were described as *in burge bronnensi*. Neumarkt in Silesia was also sometimes called Burgum; so was the German colony in the *châtellenie* of Milistch on the Silesian frontier. German colonists were known as *burgenses* even in tiny places like Skarzeszow.

As a general rule, the colonists of this period were granted either a new market or else privileges in some old princely market. But such grants, and enlargements of colonies, did not yet amount to a transformation of the old system. In the chief centers, the sovereign still clung to his monopolies. In the newly founded towns they were surrendered only hesitatingly and partially. Several documents relating to the merchants' halls at Neisse and Goldberg testify to the prince's anxiety lest he jeopardize his revenues. At the same time they show the citizens making headway. We have seen the men of Goldberg appealing to city officials of Magdeburg to help them protect their liberties against the monopolistic claims of the sovereign. We see the men of Neumarkt successfully appealing to the magistrates of Halle on the Saale for authority to convert the old market trades controlled by the princes into citizen gilds. The Halle decision in their favor came in 1235. The principle of this decision was rapidly diffused in Silesia and Poland alongside the earlier market law of Neumarkt itself. This contains several clauses (nos. 36–42) relating to the entry fees that bakers, butchers, and shoemakers had to pay to the town and to their gilds, and specifying also the gifts that the latter were obliged to make to the lord of the town and to his judges. These rules are given only for these three trades which, as we know, were those formerly under ducal monopoly. The fixing of these taxes at a set sum, following the Halle custom, was no doubt inserted in the charter to make it clear that these were now citizen gilds. The aim was to prevent the ducal administration from treating these artisans like their predecessors, who had been subject to the seigneurial court.

But these isolated successes were only the beginning of larger-scale efforts. The Slav regions were, so to speak, being opened up to German commercial and industrial enterprises. A final obstacle remained: it had to fall. German merchants made greater and greater efforts to conquer the great old princely markets themselves. They scored a strategic victory in 1230, when the Old Market beside the Teynhof, at Prague, was ceded to them. Breslau followed suit in 1241–42, after the retreat of the Mongols. The Old Market and the recently established German market there were united into a town. This was a signal for all the Piast countries to go ahead in the same direction, just as the square form of the Breslau market was very quickly and widely imitated. After this, the transformation of ancient markets into German towns and the founding of new urban markets went on continuously. The system of monopolies collapsed. Regalian rights over markets and mints were preserved in principle, but in practice were mitigated. Colonists were generally allowed to farm the customs and market taxes and in return for an annual payment the old obligation to hand over their money to the mint was abolished.

The monopoly that was completely destroyed by colonization was that over taverns. To be able to sell drinks without a grant from the lord was one of the fundamental articles of the new urban liberty. Often the prince found himself facing demands that he recompense churches which had been endowed by grants of tavern revenues. Almost everywhere the lord had to guarantee that no taverns would be permitted in the vicinity of the town. On the other hand, the lord's other industrial establishments —the shops of bakers, butchers, and shoemakers, the slaughterhouse, the bath-house, and the trading halls—continued to be subject to certain taxes deriving from the ancient monopolies. Deeds of sale of such buildings invariably specify the payment that is due as indemnity for the ancient monopoly.

Thus colonial towns arose where once there was only an empty market space and a tiny colony of foreigners. The towns were modest in scale but it was in the interest of lord and colonists alike that they should grow. Some of the princes' grants of privilege are most emphatic about this desire for growth. Such an attitude was in itself a reform; it was good for all concerned and did no one any harm. After the sovereigns had used their power for so long to impede indigenous economic growth, the innovation of admitting foreigners *en masse* was perhaps a necessity; certainly it was the least painful way of change open to them.

(Koebner's lengthy bibliography of the original sources has been omitted. Editor.)

NOTES

1 In Silesia there were still hop-breweries and tanneries belonging to the prince, and his assent was required for setting up such enterprises, long after the colonization period. He also retained the *Schrotamt*, a monopoly of the transport of beer kegs to the market. All these were relics of the old Slav system of monopolies.

2 In this last case, the halls were called *crami* (*Krambuden*).

3 At Glogau the bailiff long levied dues on the hall and on the cloth trade there, a custom surviving from the original foundation.

4 "Civitas aut oppidum per terram non fuit ullum—Sed prope castra fora campestria, broca, capella". See *Monumenta Lubensia*, ed. Wattenbach, p. 16. The word *broca*, for taverns, occurs also in the decisions of the general chapter of the Cistercian Order in 1134, C. LII.

Reformers

4

Gregorian Reform in Action
Clerical Marriage in England
1050-1200[1]

C. N. L. BROOKE

FEW MEN have ever shown a more sublime faith in the divine origin of
their mission than the papal reformers of the eleventh century. They set
to work with a 'modest proposal' to destroy two of the most intimate and
powerful foundations of clerical society: they aimed to abolish simony
and with it the lay control of patronage; they tried to destroy the family
life of the clergy. From one point of view they were doing only what every
policeman does—they were trying to enforce the established law. From
another point of view their platform was a devastating social revolution.
If we may admire the high idealism of Leo IX, Humbert, Hildebrand
and Peter Damian, we must also concede that their work had many victims; the legislation of the eleventh-century Popes on clerical marriage
must have produced as many broken homes and personal tragedies as the
morals of Hollywood. Both Damian the ascetic and Heloise the deserted
wife have a claim on our sympathy as historians; and both found their
supporters in their own day. Between the unbending demand for the enforcement of celibacy and the view of the Anonymous of York that it was
entirely proper for the clergy to be married there were many possible
positions. The Anonymous (writing at the turn of the eleventh and twelfth
centuries) was propounding opinions already obsolescent; and clerical
marriage found few defenders in the middle and late twelfth century. But
if the field narrowed, the subtleties of the problem were more fully appreciated. The twelfth century was an age of growing sophistication in lay
circles as well as clerical. Nowhere was this more true than in the world
of love and of marriage; in that century (whatever the lot of womankind
as a whole) the romantic ideal was born, under whose spell we still live. It
is the variety and the subtlety of the view-points which give my subject

its interest, and also its intractability. Clerical marriage is an exceedingly delicate topic, though it has not always been delicately treated.[2]

It appears that Pope Leo IX was more troubled by simony than marriage. He made some effort to reform the morals of the Roman clergy, and may have done something more; but the two contemporary accounts of his great councils north of the Alps do not suggest that clerical marriage was even discussed: the target was simony.[3] One of these accounts was written by the great Cardinal Humbert of Silva Candida, whose principal literary effort was the *Libri tres adversus simoniacos*. But if simony had first place, clerical marriage was not far behind. Subdeacons and above had been forbidden to marry since the fifth century; and married men who entered orders had been forbidden to sleep with their wives since the fourth.[4] For centuries the attempt to keep the clergy in higher orders away from the weaker sex had been a favourite activity with all kinds of reformers; and as recently as 1018 one of the last of the Tusculan Popes had insulted his ancestors by reviving the ancient decrees. The reformers regarded simony, the sin of Simon Magus, as an attempt to sell the Holy Ghost, a conception so blasphemous as to be evidently the fruit of error, and hence a heresy. Soon they erected by its side the heresy of Nicholas the deacon of Antioch, who was by a confusion supposed to be the author of the heresy of the Nicolaitans.[5] Cardinal Humbert is the first person known to have applied the title Nicolaitans to all married clergy. But their greatest enemy among the reformers was Peter Damian, who stated the case against them in four of his most eloquent epistles.[6] It is impossible to do justice in a sentence to the wealth of rhetoric, of argument, of biblical and patristic learning which this great ascetic poured out in the most cultivated Latin of the century. He took his stand on his own sacramental theology and on the law of the Church. He cited a chain of texts to show that clerical marriage was forbidden; and he built up a vision of the sacred nature of the Eucharist and of the office of the priest who celebrates the Eucharist. Just as Jesus was born of a chaste Virgin, so his re-birth in the blessed sacrament must be solemnized by a priest sworn to chastity. The attack on clerical marriage was closely associated with the new sacramental theology, with its growing emphasis on the objective nature of the Real Presence, and the growing sense that the priesthood and all who stood by the altar at mass were a race apart, 'separated for the work'. This sense made the reformers all the more aware that clerical marriage tended to assimilate the clergy to their lay surroundings. Marriage produced children and the desire for hereditary succession; and a benefice became more and more like a lay fee, passing from father to son. It may well have been this consideration which produced the law forbidding the ordination of the sons of priests, a law made definitive by Urban II at the end of the century. But the relation of marriage and inheritance cannot be simply expressed; and an attenuated form of hereditary benefice survived the onslaughts of the reformers.

When Peter Damian treated clerical marriage as heretical, that is, as a matter of faith, he erred. It could not be, and has not usually been regarded as more than a matter of discipline; such it was seen to be so soon as the Papacy won the allegiance of any part of the eastern church, in which marriage for the lower clergy became not merely pardonable but compulsory in the later Middle Ages. But as a matter of discipline celibacy has been strictly maintained for all but a small minority of the Roman Catholic clergy from that day to this; and the law has been very little altered since the twelfth century. Indeed, to anyone who has toiled with the incoherent complexities of the law of marriage in the eleventh and twelfth centuries, there is a simplicity and consistency about the laws of celibacy which is wholly admirable.

Before 1059 it was already the law that no sub-deacon or above might marry and that everyone entering these higher orders must take an oath of chastity; but a married man who was ordained did not put away his wife—he was still married, but must live with his wife as though she were his sister.[7] Underlying these provisions were two vital principles, which did not always live together in perfect harmony; the sanctity of marriage and the sanctity of orders. Some reformers might regard woman as man's worst enemy, and there was plenty of anti-feminism in all the circles in which it customarily flourishes; but the rights of a properly married wife were carefully safeguarded. It was always maintained that ordination did not dissolve a marriage and that a husband could only be ordained with his wife's consent. In earlier centuries it had been common for a married man to enter orders late in life. But in the twelfth century it came to be thought that marriage was not a suitable foundation for a clerical career; that a married clerk was too likely to lapse and commit fornication with his wife; in general that the arrangement put too great a strain on both parties. Alexander III (1159–81) laid down, first that the vow of chastity necessary to the ordination of a married man must be taken by both parties, and then that while the wife lived no married man might be promoted to a bishopric unless his wife took the veil.[8]

So far the defence of marriage; but from another angle the fortress of matrimony had already been breached and the status of a married woman undermined. Hitherto the normal doctrine had been that if a clerk married, the marriage was valid; but if he persisted in leading the life of a married man, he forfeited his orders and his benefices. Thus the marriage of Abelard and Heloise was perfectly valid, although it was illegal and should have entailed for Abelard the loss of his benefices; [9] and as Heloise pointed out when opposing the marriage, it ended Abelard's chances of clerical promotion. But in 1123 it was decreed not merely that all clerics in higher orders were debarred from marriage, but that any marriage they entered was to be broken.[10] Thus, one by one, the doors were closed; and if we meet a subdeacon, deacon, priest or bishop after 1123 with a lady on his arm, we guess that she is probably not his wife. The decree of 1123 has come in for much criticism, and it undoubtedly contributed to the confusion in the order of matrimony so conspicuous in the mid-twelfth century: it added greatly to the number of unofficial liaisons which might be felt by the partners to be marriages, but were not recognized by the law and could be broken at will. But it was the natural culmination of the attempt to make full celibacy the unambiguous law of the Church; and it had more effect than all the enactments and endeavours of the preceding half century.

In Gratian's *Decretum* (*c.* 1140) there is collected a great deal of ancient lumber on this subject; so much so that he at one moment arrives at the triumphant (and characteristic) conclusion that marriage is permitted for priests! [11] But the dead wood is swiftly dispersed by the application of principles unusually sound for Gratian: some of the authorities which seem to permit marriage are disposed of on the historical ground that at one time celibacy was not enforced, and others because the discipline of the eastern church differs from the western. The full law of celibacy is established, and only one serious obscurity remains. A famous decree of Gregory VII of 1074 (itself a repetition of decrees of 1059 and 1063) [12] had ordained that the faithful were not to attend the masses of clergy known to have intercourse with women. The original meaning of the decree is not certain. It was written when there was much controversy about the validity of sacraments administered by heretics, and Urban II had to explain that Gregory's decree did not mean that the masses of married clergy were invalid. Urban's exposition is far from clear, but it ought to have meant—and was taken to mean—that the faithful laity were to be enrolled as allies against the delinquent clergy. If the clergy were contumacious, their congregations were to strike.

In the second half of the twelfth century and the early thirteenth the laws of celibacy were little altered. Alexander III narrowed the entry of married clergy to higher orders; he and his successor dealt with individual cases as humanely as was compatible with complete rigidity on the basic principles. Thirty decretals of the twelfth-century Popes (prior to Innocent III) found their way into the *Decretals* of Gregory IX; and without making a comprehensive search I have found about thirty-nine more dealing with celibacy cases.[13] A high proportion of surviving decretals on any subject refer to England, but in this instance the proportion is remarkable: of the sixty-nine decretals counted, forty-four certainly deal with English cases,[14] twenty with continental, and the remaining five cannot be located. One of these five is a remarkable letter of Alexander III of more than doubtful authenticity, granting a personal privilege to some unnamed clerk in higher orders to marry and retain his benefices.[15] The forger might evade the law by such means as this, and its rigour could on occasion be relaxed by papal dispensation. But when Innocent III breathed new life into the campaign for celibacy in 1215 the battle had already been waged for 150 years with remarkable vigour and consistency.

My interest in this campaign and its results in England are with clerical marriage as a social institution which, however illicit, was recognized as such. I am not interested in what would be regarded in any age as immorality. For this reason I shall make little use of the evidence of penitentials, moral reformers and satirists. The perennial aberrations of mankind are of little concern to the historian, and every medieval poet had read the sixth satire of Juvenal. Clerical marriage has suffered by being studied too little concretely, and I aim to make it as concrete as I can. This involves a certain amount of self-denial. In particular, I must confine my attention mainly to the upper clergy, and leave the lower to students of episcopal registers and Gerald of Wales.[16]

The division into upper and lower clergy is fundamental, though the distinction can be exaggerated and the line too clearly drawn. Bishops, archdeacons, canons and all the regular clergy lie above it; the rank and file of the parish clergy lie below. But a member of the upper clergy—a clerk possessioner in the Lollard phrase—might reside on his cure and lead the life of the lower clergy; and there is no way to decide where to place the highly educated parish priests who wrote *The Owl and the Nightingale* or (possibly) the *Cloud of Unknowing*. For our purpose, however, the distinction is necessary.

How far the lower clergy were affected by the Gregorian reform is hard to say. Kings and churchmen had legislated with vigour against clerical incontinence in the early eleventh century.[17] In the second half of the twelfth (when the married bishop was scarcely to be met and even the married archdeacon was becoming rare) Pope Alexander III was forced on numerous occasions to denounce the frequency not merely of married clergy but of hereditary succession in the English Church. Papal decretals had a particularly good chance of survival in this country and the English bishops were particularly active in submitting their problems to Rome; but even so the proportion of English cases among the decretals of this period suggests that the problem here was particularly acute.[18] Cases of marriage and inheritance recur throughout the Middle Ages. But by the second half of the thirteenth century married clergy seem to be an exceptional problem; and the bulk of the evidence is for clerical immorality of a kind normal in a world very prolific in untrained clergy.[19] I imagine, then, that if married clergy were common in eleventh-century England, the Gregorian reform had, over two centuries, a considerable effect. There is no doubt that some clergy were married in the eleventh century—but we can be confident that the number was large only if we rely on gossip and hearsay. It may be true that 'there is no smoke without fire', but a mountain of smoke can be raised by the feeblest of fires. Among the lower clergy the effect of the reformers' work is very difficult to gauge.

It is estimated by Professor Knowles and Mr. Hadcock that there were a little more than 1000 monks in England in 1066; by 1200 the number of regular clergy had probably increased more than ten-fold.[20] The figure cannot be exactly proved, but it cannot be far wrong; and this is the most concrete indication of the success of the campaign for celibacy. The English population itself may have increased, but not on this scale. Peter Damian and Hildebrand had founded a movement designed to sweep all religious communities and all clergy who could live in a community into institutes based on a recognized rule of life, founded on vows of chastity and obedience and lived in common. Their efforts led to the formation of numerous houses of Augustinian canons all over Europe.[21] In England we know of sixty-six houses of canons at the time of the Conquest—living a life based on a rule, on misrule, or on no rule at all. By 1200 nearly half (including three cathedral chapters)[22] had been swept away, virtually all being translated or absorbed into a regular establishment, thirteen specifically becoming houses of canons regular.

The greatest change in the regular population, however, came from another quarter: well over half the English regulars of the late twelfth century were Cistercians. And their enormous numbers (estimated at over 6000 in 1200, apart from lay-brothers) raise a problem of great complexity. There can be little question that the number of upper clergy in England had multiplied many times between 1050 and 1200. The increase of regulars had not been made entirely at the expense of the seculars; indeed, it is probable that the upper secular clergy were more numerous in 1200 than in 1050, and certain that there were royal clerks and cathedral prebendaries in far greater profusion. Where, then, did the increase come from? Was the clerical profession more popular, or was it easier to rise from the ranks of the lower clergy? The answer is that both forces must have been at work. When we estimate the effect of the Gregorian reform on the quality and the morals of the lower clergy, we must remember that it is probable that the cream of the profession was being skimmed—more than ever before or since, save possibly in Counter-Reformation Spain—for the benefit of the royal service, the cathedral chapters, and, above all, the monastic houses. But in the main, the increases probably came from the upper classes: the appeal of the clerical profession was very powerful in a century under the spell of St. Peter Damian and St. Bernard, when standards of education and learning were undergoing revolutionary advances, and when it was fashionable to be a monk or a learned clerk.

Within the ranks of the secular clergy the century following the Conquest saw changes as momentous as those in the monastic orders. The novelty of the institutes founded by Damian and his followers does not mean that formal rules for canons were unknown before the papal reform. The rule of St. Augustine itself (however much altered or interpolated since it left the master's hand) was of great antiquity; and many houses of canons were nominally subject in the eleventh century to rules compiled or devised by the reformers of the eighth and ninth centuries.[23] All the English cathedrals and some proportion no doubt of the lesser minsters were subject to a communal rule with strict enforcement of celibacy in 1066. But not all the communities adhered to these rules, and some (even of the cathedrals) were so small and poor as scarcely to be able to maintain their status as communities at all. The bulk of the cathedral chapters of post-Conquest England were in every sense entirely new foundations.[24]

Just as every subaltern is supposed to have a field-marshal's baton in his knapsack, so every member of the upper clergy was a potential bishop. Only a few attained to the office; but if a section of the clergy were debarred from promotion, we should feel doubtful if they were properly called 'upper clergy' at all. Between the translation of St. Dunstan to Canterbury in 959 and the Accession of Cnut in 1016 a majority, and probably nearly all the English bishops, were drawn from the monasteries; [25] the upper secular clergy, if such a body may properly be said to have existed, are buried in total obscurity. Under Cnut and the Confessor a rapidly growing number of bishops were drawn from the royal service, from the clerks who provided the staff of the king's chapel, of his 'chancery' and 'chamber'. The royal clerks throw a remarkable light on the condition of the English secular clergy in the early eleventh century. We know at least thirty-four by name, and of these some seventeen won bishoprics. Of the thirty-four, there is reason to suppose that fifteen or eighteen were not of English origin; of these, the majority came from France and Lorraine, and three were Normans. Even allowing for the Confessor's partiality for the associates of his exile, it does not look as if the English church was organized to support on its own resources a distinguished secular clergy. Nor was it economically organized for the purpose. A century later Thomas Becket largely maintained the 'port' of royal chancellor out of the numerous benefices which he held in plurality, with a nucleus of prebends and cathedral dignities. The prebendal system was not in existence under the Confessor; and although there were some cases of scandalous pluralism, it was probably commoner for royal clerks to be supported by grants of land, like the grants from which Leofric was later able largely to endow the bishopric of Exeter.[26] The English secular clergy of the twelfth century was in most respects the creation of the Norman Conquest.

Archbishop Stigand was as good an abuse as a usurper with re-
forming pretentions like William I could wish to find at Canterbury.
He had preyed on the Confessor with even greater success than the
Kemps and the Booths later preyed on Henry VI. He held two bishoprics
and allegedly some abbeys besides; his translation to Canterbury was
uncanonical for almost as many reasons as the law could devise. He was
the very image of Simon Magus. But one crime was never laid to his
door; there is no early evidence that he was either married or incontinent.[27] Indeed, it is remarkable how little evidence of this particular
abuse can be found before the Conquest. One of Cnut's chaplains had a
son who became abbot of Winchcombe; Stigand's brother Aethelmaer
had a wife; so apparently had the bishop of Lichfield; and Albert of
Lorraine founded a dynasty in the chapter of St Paul's.[28] But both
Albert's son and his prebend may well have come to him after the
Conquest.

If we add to this picture of the English clergy evidence drawn from
the periphery, the vision is less innocent. At St. David's and Llandaff in
the late eleventh century we find dynastic bishoprics, archdeaconries and
every kind of family influence in cathedral chapters and in the surviving
remnants of the great Welsh monasteries.[29] At Durham, in the early
eleventh and again in the early twelfth century, we find a bishop who
could marry his daughter into the local nobility; in the late eleventh
century, the dean and treasurer of Durham at least were married men.
But before the century was out the Durham chapter had been ousted by
monks; and in 1114 the treasurer's son, Eilaf, was attacked in the last
stronghold of the family, the church of Hexham, of which they were
hereditary priests, by the arrival of Augustinian canons. But Eilaf retained
a life interest in the church, and lived to see his son Ailred a monk at
Rievaulx.[30] How far these conditions were peculiar to the north and
west of Britain, we cannot tell.

In 1076 Archbishop Lanfranc passed his first decree against married
clergy. It was a kindly answer to a difficult situation. For the future, no
clergy are to marry, no priests or deacons to be ordained without a pledge
that they are not married. The parish clergy who are married are permitted to keep their wives; only to canons are wives entirely forbidden.[31]
This has usually been taken to reflect the English scene, and it may be so.
But in some respects Lanfranc and his colleagues were none too sensitive
to the special needs of their new subjects, and it is equally likely that the
decree was as much the fruit of Norman as of English experience; it was
undoubtedly based on the Norman legislation of the preceding decade.
The one distinguished English bishop of native origin active in 1076,
Wulfstan of Worcester, made no use of the escape clause in his treatment of the married clergy of his diocese.[32]

The Norman clergy were by repute among the most uxorious in

Europe.[33] Even here the extent of clerical marriage and hereditary succession cannot be at all exactly estimated. We cannot trace in detail the succession to any office lower than bishop, and the office of bishop was too important to become hereditary in eleventh-century Normandy. There is an isolated case of a man who granted his hereditary archdeaconry to the abbey of St. Evroul in the middle of the century; [34] and there is a great deal of evidence to show that the upper clergy formed a more normal part of the Norman aristocracy than Gregory VII and his associates would have wished. Robert, son of Richard I duke of Normandy, was count of Évreux, and in that capacity had a wife and at least three sons. He was also archbishop of Rouen.[35] In three ways he represented characteristic features of the Norman church. He was of the ducal family, and the genealogy of the Norman dukes in the eleventh and early twelfth centuries includes seven Norman bishops, three of them archbishops of Rouen.[36] He was count as well as bishop, and so reminds us of Ivo, bishop of Séez and lord of the notorious house of Bellême for over thirty years in the middle of the century, and Odo of Bayeux, the Conqueror's half-brother and earl of Kent.[37] Archbishop Robert was married, and so takes his place with about a dozen other distinguished Norman clerics of whom we are informed.[38] This number is not excessively large; and the evidence is very fragmentary—in some respects the Normans showed their characteristics most clearly only after crossing the Channel. But we have evidence of two striking phenomena: first, of family groups within the chapter of Bayeux (the only cathedral of whose personnel we are at all well informed),[39] and secondly of the existence of certain powerful and purely ecclesiastical families—the family of Radbod, bishop of Séez, father of an archbishop of Rouen; of Sampson, treasurer and possibly dean of Bayeux, later bishop of Worcester, brother of one archbishop of York, father of another, father also of a bishop of Bayeux; and of Norman, dean of Séez, father of a bishop, grandfather of two more, great-grandfather of a fourth.[40]

Before we can compare these conditions with the affairs of the Normans in England, we must remove two of the difficulties and misunderstandings raised by problems of this kind. To us, as to Gregory VII, it makes little difference whether Sampson was subdeacon or bishop when he begat his children.[41] But in contemporary eyes it made a world of difference: the special stigma which attached to the son of a priest (and by that much the more of a bishop), was rarely transferred to any lower order.[42] I know of no case of a bishop having children after his promotion in England or Normandy in the eleventh or twelfth century, save Robert of Normandy as count of Évreux—and perhaps, though I cannot prove it, Ranulph Flambard of Durham. Thus, when I talk of a bishop as father of a family, the family is presumed to have been conceived before the bishop's consecration.

The papal reform and the investiture contest produced a number of pamphlets, and in reply to the abuse poured by reformers on married clergy and the stringent demands of the canons several treatises were written on their behalf. At least four were written in Normandy—two anonymous defences of marriage written in the 1060's and 1070's; a defence of the right to ordination of the sons of priests by a canon of Bayeux; and a pair of treatises, one on each of these issues, by the brilliant writer commonly known as the Anonymous of York.[43] The Anonymous may have visited England, though his connexion with York is pure hypothesis; his background and his milieu lay certainly in Normandy. In his writings the traditional attitudes and customs of the Norman church were defended with all the panoply of the new logic. Old-fashioned views dressed up in novel dogmatic forms produced opinions of an extreme and startling nature. But the Anonymous' defence of clerical marriage is among the least eccentric of his writings, because he was defending a position which other contemporaries did not hesitate to defend. It was widely held that sons of priests should not suffer for their parents' supposed delinquency.[44] But the Anonymous presently became entangled in his doctrine of predestination, where neither we nor his contemporaries can follow him. Similarly the text 'melius est enim nubere, quam uri' was the conventional foundation for the defence of marriage: to refuse the clergy the right to marry was to invite those who had no vocation to celibacy to far worse crimes. 'The apostle laid it down that "a bishop should be the husband of one wife". He would hardly have made this ruling,' commented the Anonymous, 'if it were adultery, as some assert, for a bishop to have at one time both a wife and a church—two wives, so to speak. . . . For Holy Church is not the priest's wife, not *his* bride, but Christ's.' [45] Along these lines the institution was defended; and if the defence was not always coherent and sometimes led plainly to heresy, the defenders can hardly be blamed. Like the men who supported lay power against the papal onslaught, they were defending deeply felt but often incoherent attitudes against a coherent ideological system many centuries old.[46] If clerical marriage was undoubtedly illegal at the turn of the eleventh century, both a married clerk and his wife could feel that they had some noted thinkers on their side, and the support of a considerable body of public opinion. But their days were numbered. The defenders of clerical marriage were so active in Normandy partly for the very reason that the reformers were active there too.

Between the Conquest and 1123 a number of canons were passed in England against the married clergy. Lanfranc's comparatively mild decree was followed by more stringent attempts to enforce the law in Anselm's two councils of 1102 and 1108.[47] To set beside the Norman Anonymous we have little overt polemical literature, save the fierce defence of priests' sons by the Oxford lecturer Theobald of Étampes; but Theobald's

writing presupposes that the clerical father had been at fault.[48] Nevertheless, the concrete evidence for the behaviour of the higher clergy shows
clearly that a substantial section followed the practices noticed among the
Norman clergy; and the English evidence reveals with greater clarity than
the Norman the connexion between clerical marriage, the inheritance of
benefices and the social structure of the Church.

For the English church as a whole, the evidence is almost as fragmentary as the Norman. Occasional cases of incontinence in high places
may be found in any century, and it is difficult to pin-point the moment
when clerical marriage became really exceptional. A large majority of the
upper clergy known to have had children between 1050 and 1200 had had
their families, at latest, by about 1130; by the middle of the century there
is a noticeable falling off.[49] What was happening can be gauged from
three of the most celebrated cases of the second half of the century. Two
letters written by John of Salisbury in 1156 describe the case of the scandalous Walkelin, archdeacon of Suffolk. They were addressed to Pope
Adrian IV:

He has ordered that a bastard whom his concubine bore while he was on his way
back from you, should be called by your most sacred name of Adrian. He, the
father of this child, has now left the lady pregnant, but has made a most provi-
dent disposition for the future, to wit that, if the child happens to be a boy he
shall be called Benevento, because his father has gone on a pilgrimage to that
place, while if it is a girl, she is to be called Adriana.[50]

This is an isolated scandal; though, if we may believe John of Salisbury's
letters, Walkelin was not the only incontinent archdeacon in the diocese
of Norwich. At about the same time Osbert of Bayeux, archdeacon of
Richmond, was deposed from his archdeaconry for the murder of St. William of York.[51] Osbert became a layman, and founded a knightly family.
It is possible that as archdeacon he was already married, since he sprang
from one of the most celebrated clerical families of the early twelfth century. He was nephew to Thurstan, archbishop of York from 1114 to 1140,
a prelate of considerable distinction. Thurstan's brother was bishop of
Évreux, and his father, Anger or Anskar, was a distinguished married
clerk from the Bessin who settled with his wife Popelina in London, and
became (with both his sons) a canon of St Paul's.[52] Anskar was married;
Thurstan and Audoen evidently not; and Osbert, if married, was also a
miscreant. The habit of marriage died more slowly in the great curial
family of Roger, bishop of Salisbury. Roger's wife or concubine, Matilda
of Ramsbury, was still active at the time of her husband's death in 1139.
Their son became for a time King Stephen's chancellor. Of Roger's
nephews, two were bishops; and Nigel of Ely himself had a son, Richard
fitzNeal or Richard of Ely, royal treasurer and bishop of London from
1189 to 1199. Richard's successor as treasurer was his kinsman William of

Ely, the last of the family known to have achieved distinction, and the last clerical member of the family known to have been a father. William died in 1222.[53]

About nine years earlier, in 1213 or 1214, occurred the death of Richard Junior, canon of St Paul's, last of the most prolific of all the clerical families of twelfth-century England.[54] Its founder, Richard de Belmeis I, had been bishop of London from 1108 to 1127. As bishop he had control, though not undisputed control, of appointments to the thirty prebends of his chapter. Two of his sons and four of his nephews at least were promoted by him; and the glory of the family was maintained by his nephew Richard de Belmeis II, who was bishop from 1152 to 1162. By a strange irony, Richard II's successor was also related to him, though not closely; but the family connexion of Gilbert Foliot was untainted by any suspicion of clerical marriage. 'The Lord deprived bishops of sons, but the devil gave them nephews.'[55] The decline of clerical marriage did not mean the end of nepotism or even of inheritance. Both found pastures new in a world of celibate clergy. When we witness the pathetic struggles of Peter of Blois and Gerald of Wales in their grey hairs to prevent their nephews securing their choicest benefices,[56] we can see that already, by the end of the twelfth century, the technique of succession and exchange was firmly established, by which the younger members of a clerical family obtained possession of the family heirlooms throughout the later Middle Ages.

Peter and Gerald had both written love lyrics in their youth, like every good scholar of the day; but in the long run they were strict upholders of celibacy.[57] The clerical element in their families was by no means based on clerical marriage; and in this it is in marked contrast with the episcopate of Richard de Belmeis I. Only two of the Belmeis promoted by him were his own children; but in return for his share of the spoils, he permitted a number of benefices to pass to the sons of canons. We know that at least a quarter of the canons were married in the period 1090–1127; that at least eight dignities and prebends passed from father to son. This information comes almost entirely from the St. Paul's prebendal catalogue, which must have been carefully kept at this period; and its authors showed no scruple about entering in the successions to various prebends: 'Albert of Lorraine, Hugh his son', 'Quintilian archdeacon, Cyprian his son', 'Roger archdeacon, son of Robert archdeacon' and so forth. Most of these men are little more than names, but there is no reason to suppose that many were disreputable; in the case of the family of Thurstan of York, quite the contrary. The chapter had its black sheep, among whom the family of Ranulph Flambard, bishop of Durham and dean of St. Paul's, was conspicuous. But there is nothing to suggest that the canons of St Paul's were exceptionally domestic among English chapters at this time. Nor can we tell whether the convention had its roots in England or in Normandy, since both races were represented among the married canons. Unfortunately this early prebendal list is the only oasis of light in the general obscurity.[58]

By the time of Richard's death in 1127, the halcyon days when nepotism and heredity could flourish side by side were drawing to a close. Of hereditary succession there are seven or eight cases known at St. Paul's before 1127, two between 1127 and *c.* 1150, and only one—and that a Belmeis—thereafter. No doubt local conditions, in the shape of ascetic bishops and an obscure but evidently powerful ascetic movement within the chapter,[59] contributed to this comparatively speedy uprooting of an established custom. But the date fits so well with the other evidence about when celibacy became fashionable throughout the upper clergy that we may take it that in this respect St. Paul's accurately reflected the state of things throughout England, and perhaps in many corners of Europe besides.

Our view of the English scene has shown that in many ways the assimilation of social arrangements lay and ecclesiastical is much as the more fragmentary Norman evidence might lead us to expect. We have few parallels for Archbishop Robert the count of Évreux, though many clerics were engaged in very secular pursuits—one canon of St. Paul's was sheriff of eight counties, and Thomas Becket led an army in the campaign of Toulouse.[60] But the great clerical families (always with some lay members, but often owing their power wholly to their grip on the Church) and the hereditary benefices flourished in the English Church between the Conquest and the Anarchy. There were many celibates; but clerical marriage was sufficiently common to be safe and even respectable. In the middle of the century—among the higher clergy—it died; more swiftly where ascetic ideals won a firm foothold, more slowly in families with a long tradition of the clerical paterfamilias.

My last word must be some brief appraisal of why the institution died when it did. In part it was simply because of the passage of time and the impact of the reformers' attack. A social revolution takes time to accomplish, and two generations had to be born under the stigma of illegitimacy before the attack could have its effect. The attack came to a crescendo in the 1120's, with Celestine II's degree making invalid all marriages contracted by clerks in higher orders. This decree was solemnly repeated in three English councils in the same decade.[61] Chroniclers like Henry of Huntingdon (himself a hereditary archdeacon) might sneer at these decrees and tell stories about the legate and the archbishop who promulgated them,[62] but there is no doubt that their impact was felt. They were repeated in later councils in various forms, and the first and most elaborate decree of the great council of Westminster of 1175 was directed against married clergy and hereditary benefices.[63] But by then the offence was rank only among the lower clergy.

The formal campaign is the first and most obvious cause, but I doubt if it was—directly—the most important. Celibacy had been the law of the Church since the fourth century, and it is far from clear why the mere reiteration of the law, however powerfully supported, should have been so startlingly successful. Decrees enjoining celibacy, indeed (as Prof. Darlington has shown), were almost as common in England before the Conquest as after.[64] Rather we must look at the situation of Western Europe as a whole in the early twelfth century. The revival of learning and all that went with it—the movement we call the twelfth-century renaissance—owed much to the stimulus of the papal reformers; but even more conspicuously, it was the papacy's most potent ally. To take an obvious example, the revival in the study and technique of law enabled the papacy for the first time to operate through a network of courts enforcing a highly wrought and sophisticated legal system. The world in which Gratian floated his astonishing *Concordia discordantium canonum* about 1140 was ripe to receive it. The generation which witnessed its appearance had been brought up to accept the standards of their schools, where they learnt to know and respect the law of the Church, and so the law of celibacy. In St. Paul's in the second and third decades of the century, the married clergy still flourished, though in decline. In contemporary Paris, Heloise and Abelard both reckoned already that their marriage would be the end of Abelard's career.

So far I have spoken from the point of view of the Church or of the clerical husband; finally, and more speculatively, we must consider the lady's point of view. There was a poetical genre of some popularity in the twelfth century which took the form of a debate as to whether a clerk or a knight was the better lover; since the authors were mostly clerks, the victory usually went to the clerk. But in one poem in which a clerk woos a lady, his hopes are most rudely dashed. 'Respuo moechari; volo nubere', says the lady, with a rare attack of brevity.[65] 'Adultery I repudiate: I want to get married'—we can never know how many potential wives of clerics answered their suitors in this manner after the decree of 1123. It must certainly have made it increasingly difficult for the upper clergy to find mates in their own class. It is a misfortune that we know so little of the class known in happier days as the 'priestesses'.[66] We know a little of Matilda of Ramsbury, the name only of the illegitimate Percy who consented to live with Hugh du Puiset when he was treasurer of York.[67] But for more personal evidence we have to turn to the continent and to Heloise, and Heloise—though she points to many of the problems in the case—was so exceptional a person as to be the worst possible basis for any generalization.[68]

One of the most startling changes in European society in the twelfth century was the rise of the Romantic ideal, the appearance north of the Pyrenees, in European dress, of the Arab and Spanish conventions of ro-

mantic love.[69] In the wake of courtly love came a more refined appreciation of the relations of men and women, higher regard for the strength
and the sanctity of the weaker sex; and in collaboration with the efforts
of the Church and the civilizing influences of the age, a strengthening of
the bonds of marriage. It may seem a paradox to associate the higher view
of marriage with courtly love; since the orthodox opinion of the more
extreme adherents of the 'religion of love' was summed up in the famous
judgment attributed to the countess of Champagne, Queen Eleanor's
daughter, that love and marriage are incompatible.[70] But powerful as was
the notion of love as adultery in the more artificial courtly circles, its importance has probably been exaggerated. In every age and every stratum
of courtly literature there are hints that the union of love and marriage is
both possible and desirable; it is surprising in how many romances it is a
married couple who live happily ever after; and the greatest of all, Wol-
fram's *Parzifal,* is the most powerful story of married love which the Middle Ages produced. The truth is that in a world in which Christian sentiment and courtly love both flourished—even if a full conceptual synthesis
had to wait for Dante or beyond—every possible view of the relations of
courtly love and married love, of the love of man and the love of God,
was possible and likely to be held. The priest's concubine might be
decked out in jewels from the altar, she might have a measure of security
with a good husband; but from the mid-twelfth century on, her position
was neither dignified nor romantic. As the Church's doctrine of marriage
became clearer and saner, the difference between marriage and concu-
binage became lucid,[71] and marriage based solely on comfort and appetite
found other competitors: a new and more lofty attitude to marriage
found classical expression in Peter the Venerable's letter to Heloise. It is
easy to exaggerate the swiftness and the extent of the change; but it is
easy, too, to understand why the ladies of the later twelfth and thirteenth
centuries were inclined to say 'volo nubere'.

NOTES

[1] A paper read at the Anglo-American Conference of Historians on 8 July 1955. I
have to thank my wife, who read the paper at an early stage, improved it with
her criticisms, and provided me with evidence from her transcripts of unprinted
Norman material.

[2] This is certainly true of H. C. Lea's great *History of Sacerdotal Celibacy in the
Christian Church* (3rd ed., 2 vols., London, 1907), which, with all its faults, remains
the only general account of the subject on a broad scale. There is an immense literature on the origins and the law of celibacy. Vacandard's account (*Études de critique
et d'histoire religieuse,* I (Paris, 1905), pp. 69–120) is still valuable; for the law, see
also A. Esmein, *Le mariage en droit canonique,* I² (Paris, 1929), pp. 313–41; J.
Dauvillier, *Le mariage dans le droit classique de l'Église* (Paris, 1933), pp. 162ff.;
Dictionnaire de droit canonique, III (Paris, 1942), pp. 132ff. For a general account
of the reformers' campaign for celibacy, see A. Fliche, *La réforme grégorienne,* I
(Louvain-Paris, 1924), pp. 30ff., 190ff., 335ff., etc.

3 Anselm's *Historia dedicationis ecclesiae Sancti Remigii* and Cardinal Humbert's *Vita Leonis IX* (ed. I. M. Watterich, *Pontificum Romanorum* . . . *Vitae*, I (Leipzig, 1862), pp. 113ff., 127ff.—especially pp. 155-7). Humbert's authorship of the *Vita* has recently been established by two scholars working independently, Dr H. Tritz in *Studi Gregoriani*, IV (Rome, 1952), pp. 194–286, and Dr Richard Mayne in an unpublished Cambridge Ph.D. thesis. Leo IX dealt with the problem of celibacy in two surviving letters (Jaffé-Löwenfeld, *Regesta Pontificum Romanorum*—henceforth JL.—nos. 4279, 4308; and he prescribed celibacy for the clergy of Rome in 1049 (C. J. Hefele-H. Leclercq, *Histoire des Conciles*, IV, ii (Paris, 1911), pp. 1007–8 and notes). There is some later evidence that clerical marriage was dealt with at Rheims in 1049 and elsewhere in Leo's pontificate (ibid. pp. 1023–4n., 1031); and Bonizo of Sutri attaches the decrees of 1059 and later (below, n. 12) to the Roman synod of 1050. Some or all of this evidence may be authentic; but it is in marked contrast to the strictly contemporary evidence, and Bonizo is inclined to read back later developments (such as the personal influence of Hildebrand) into the pontificate of Leo IX. For the canon of 1050 we have only Bonizo's word, and the unsupported testimony of Bonizo is scarcely evidence.

4 For the legal authorities, cf. n. 2 above: the bulk of them are laid out in Gratian, *Decretum*, D. 27, cc. 1, 8; D. 28, 31, 32, *passim;* D. 81, cc. 15–34; D. 82, cc. 2, 5; D. 84, cc. 3–5; cf. also C. 15, q. 8, *passim;* C. 27, q. 1, c. 40; for sons of priests, D. 56, *passim;* for hereditary benefices, C. 8, q. 1, c. 7 (cf. cc. 3–6). These include many of the decrees of papal councils from 1059 onwards, as well as the earlier material; decrees not in Gratian were issued at the papal councils of 1096 (cc. 7, 12, Mansi, *Concilia*, XX, coll. 935–6), 1099 (c. 13, ibid. col. 963), 1107 (c. 4, ibid. coll. 1223–4), 1119 (Toulouse, c. 8, ibid. XXI, col. 227), 1123 (c. 3, ibid. col. 282), 1131 (cc. 4, 15, ibid. coll. 458, 461; cf. Gratian, D. 28, c. 2), 1148 (cc. 3, 7, ibid. coll. 714, 715). The decrees of 1018 are in Mansi, op. cit. XIX, col. 353 (cf. Hefele-Leclercq, op. cit. IV, ii, p. 919). I have nothing to say in this article of the more abstruse matrimonial impediments to ordination, e.g. 'bigamy'. It is impossible to discuss here to what extent this material was known throughout Europe. It is certain that the main lines of the law of celibacy were widely known in England throughout the period (see below, pp. 7, 19); and the fresh developments were repeated in Norman councils of the mid-eleventh and in English councils of the early twelfth century. From the middle of the twelfth century both Normandy and England were beginning to be plentifully supplied with expert lawyers to interpret the law. Furthermore, even before Gratian, the outline of the law could easily be reconstructed from the popular collections of Burchard of Worms and Ivo of Chartres.

5 Nicholas of Antioch is mentioned in Acts vi. 5, and the Nicolaitans in Rev. ii. There is no reason to suppose that there was any connexion between them. Rev. ii. 14, 15 hint that fornication was one of the sins of the Nicolaitans, and in course of time the title came to be attached to almost any sect liable to this kind of error (cf. Hastings' *Encyclopaedia of Religion and Ethics*, IX (Edinburgh, 1917), pp. 363–6).

6 Humbert, *Adversus Nicetam*, ed. C. Will, *Acta et scripta* (Leipzig-Marburg, 1861), cc. 25ff., pp. 147–50; Damian, *Ep.* v, 13, *Opuscula*, XVII, XVIII (Migne, *P[atrologia] L[atina]*, CXLIV, coll. 358ff.; CXLV, coll. 379–424), and cf. also *Epp.* v, 4, 14–15 (*PL*, CXLIV, coll. 344ff., 367ff.). For the development of sacramental theology, see R. W. Southern in *Studies in Medieval History presented to F. M. Powicke* (Oxford, 1948), pp. 36ff. and references there given.

7 Gratian, *Decretum*, D. 28, cc. 1, 5, 14; D. 32, c. 18; etc.

8 JL. 14,104, also in the *Decretals* of Gregory IX—henceforward X—III, 32, 5–6.

9 It used to be argued that if Abelard was not yet a subdeacon, the marriage was not only valid but legal. This can no longer be maintained, for two reasons:—1. He was certainly a canon (*Historia calamitatum*, ed. J. T. Muckle, *Mediaeval Studies*, XII (1950), p. 188), and there is some evidence that he was a canon of Sens; there is no evidence that he was a canon of Paris, though it is quite likely that he was (ibid. n. 81 and the passage from Rémusat's life there quoted). Canons were forbidden to marry by the English council of 1076, and by a Norman council of 1080 (below, n. 31; T. P. McLaughlin, *Mediaeval Studies*, III (1941), p. 94)—decrees given

general validity at Clermont in 1095 (ibid. pp. 95ff.), and subsequently repeated by further English and French councils. These decrees condemned canons who married to forfeit their benefices (indeed, they seem to have applied to all who committed fornication). That this rule was known in the diocese of Paris is certain: Ivo of Chartres had stated it in a letter to the bishop of Paris only a few years before Abelard's marriage. 2. In any case, there is no reason to doubt that Abelard was in higher orders. He himself assures us that it was an abuse for a canon not to be (*Ep.* 8, cit. E. Gilson, *Héloïse et Abélard*, English trans. (London, 1953), p. 172). The word 'clericus' on which M. Gilson bases his view that Abelard was not at this time in orders at all was used in a variety of ways: in the passage in question it is contrasted, not with 'presbiter', but with 'laicus'—it is being used in the broadest (and commonest) sense, 'a member of the clerical order'. We do not know what his orders were, but he may well have been a priest, as he certainly was within a few years of becoming a monk (ibid. p. 67). M. Gilson has argued (ibid. chs. 1–2) that legal impediments and the threat of deprivation were not of major consequence to either party in their discussion whether to marry; and this we may (in the main) accept.

10 I Lateran, c. 21 (Mansi, op. cit. xxi, col. 286).

11 D. 28, *dictum post* c. 13.

12 Mansi, op. cit. xix, coll. 897–8, 978, 1023–5 (cf. Hefele-Leclercq, op. cit. iv, ii, pp. 1167–8, 1230, v, i, pp. 90–1). The authenticity of the decree of 1063 is not quite certain. Urban's solution is in Gratian, *Decretum*, D. 32, *dictum post* c. 6.

13 The decretals on this subject in X are in i, 17; i, 21; iii, 2–3; iv, 6; cf. also iii, 32, 5–6; v, 31, 4. I have no space here for full references to those not in X.

14 Of the decretals listed in n. 13, the following were addressed to England: X, i, 17, 2–11; iii, 2, 4–6; iii, 3, 1–2; iv, 6, 3 (there is a critical edition of X, i, 17, 2 in *Papal Decretals relating to the Diocese of Lincoln*, ed. W. Holtzmann and E. W. Kemp, Lincoln Record Society (1954), no. 5; X, i, 17, 3 is a part of an important decretal addressed to the bishop of Worcester, which is printed in full in *Gilberti Foliot Epistolae*, ed. J. A. Giles, ii (London, 1846), no. 368—it later formed the basis of the first canon of the council of Westminster of 1175, for which see below, n. 63; X, iii, 2, 4 and iii, 3, 1 formed part of a single decretal, JL. 13,813). The proportion of English cases in X, i, 17 is especially striking—this title deals with the sons of priests and problems of inheritance.

15 *Collectio Brugensis*, xxii, 3 (ed. E. Friedberg, *Die Canones-sammlungen zwischen Gratian und Bernhard von Pavia*, Leipzig, 1897, p. 152). In the same collection (xxxvii, 1) is a decretal about a forger who was a priest's son, and claimed to have a papal letter declaring this no impediment from orders.

16 For the English lower clergy in later centuries, there is a useful catena of references collected by H. G. Richardson in *Trans[actions of the] R[oyal] Hist[orical] Soc[iety]*, 3rd ser. vi (1912), pp. 120–3; cf. also J. R. H. Moorman, *Church Life in England in the Thirteenth Century* (Cambridge, 1945), pp. 63–7. For the twelfth century the *locus classicus* is Gerald of Wales, *Opera*, ii (ed. J. S. Brewer), pp. 168ff., iv, pp. 313ff. (and cf. the references in J. Conway Davies, *Episcopal acts relating to Welsh dioceses*, ii, Historical Society of the Church in Wales (1948), pp. 459f., 465ff.); but Gerald's charges are exceedingly confused and the value of his evidence very difficult to assess.

17 The legal and other evidence about the attitude to celibacy in England in the early eleventh century is fully discussed by R. R. Darlington in *E[nglish] H[istorical] R[eview]*, li (1936), pp. 404–7, 411.

18 For the proportion of English decretals see W. Holtzmann, *Papal Decretals relating to the Diocese of Lincoln*, p. xvii. The reason for the high proportion in general has been much discussed: it is due in part at least to the work done by English canonists in collecting decretals—perhaps mainly, as is argued by Dr C. Duggan in an unpublished Cambridge Ph.D. thesis on *Twelfth-Century Decretal Collections*. There is certainly no reason to suppose that the proportion of surviving decretals which are directed to England reflects at all closely the proportion originally sent.

19 Cf. the studies referred to in n. 16: the evidence has not yet been sifted by regions or in closely circumscribed chronological periods—and only thus can any conclusions

be drawn from the scandals recorded in bishops' registers or the papal dispensations granted for the ordination of the sons of priests.

20 M. D. Knowles and R. N. Hadcock, *Medieval Religious Houses* (London, 1953), pp. 359–65, esp. p. 364.

21 Cf. J. C. Dickinson, *The Origins of the Austin Canons and their introduction into England* (London, 1950), esp. ch. I.

22 Durham, Norwich and Rochester (1083, *c.* 1094, 1080).

23 I hope to give full grounds for these statements elsewhere. Cf. K. Edwards, *The English Secular Cathedrals in the Middle Ages* (Manchester, 1949), pp. 8ff.

24 St Paul's is the only English cathedral which provides any real evidence of continuity through the Conquest.

25 M. D. Knowles, *The Monastic Order in England* (Cambridge, 1940), pp. 697–701. There is no known case of a non-monastic bishop in this period; but the origins of a certain number are not known.

26 Albert of Lorraine and Regenbald were certainly holding parish churches in plurality, though whether as quasi-lay proprietors or as rectors or both is not clear (for Albert, see J. H. Round, *Commune of London* (Westminster, 1899), pp. 36ff.; *C[ambridge] H[istorical] J[ournal]* x (1951), pp. 122, 124–5; for Regenbald, Round, *Feudal England* (London, 1895), pp. 421ff.; F. E. Harmer, *Anglo-Saxon Writs* (Manchester, 1952), pp. 59–60; etc.). The greatest single landholder was Stigand, whose fabulous possessions have been indexed by O. von Feilitzen, *The Pre-Conquest Personal Names of Domesday Book* (Uppsala, 1937), pp. 374–5. For Edward's grant(s) to Leofric, see *The Exeter Book of Old English Poetry*, ed. R. W. Chambers, M. Förster, and R. Flower (London 1933), pp. 5, 15. Guibert de Nogent takes it as a matter of course that a man should make his pile as chaplain to the Confessor (*PL*, CLVI, col. 909). In addition, the perquisites of office may have been as profitable as royal gifts.

27 That Stigand was married is asserted in a long footnote in E. L. Cutts, *Parish Priests and their People* . . . (London, 1898), pp. 262–3, which lists cases of married bishops, etc. There are some errors and almost no references given for this catalogue, which must be treated with the utmost caution; I have found no support for the statement about Stigand.

28 For Godmann, Cnut's chaplain, see T. J. Oleson, *The Witenagemot in the reign of Edward the Confessor* (Oxford, 1955), p. 125; for Aethelmaer, *Domesday Book*, II, fol. 195; for Leofwine, bishop of Lichfield, Lanfranc, *Ep.* 4 (cf. J. Tait in *Essays in History presented to R. L. Poole*, ed. H. W. C. Davis (Oxford, 1927), pp. 155ff.); for Albert of Lorraine, above, n. 26. A list of benefactors of New Minster, Winchester, of the early eleventh century contains the name of a priest's wife, but her husband's standing in the church is quite uncertain (*Liber Vitae*, ed. W. de G. Birch (London-Winchester, 1892), p. 58).

29 For married clergy in the Welsh church, see the remarkable tables of succession to the churches in Archenfield (Herefordshire, on the Welsh border) in the *Liber Landavensis* (ed. J. G. Évans (Oxford, 1893), pp. 275ff.); for a general account of the evidence, see J. Conway Davies, op. cit. II, pp. 457–60, 464–8, 491–537; see esp. p. 535 (of the bishopric of Llandaff): 'For more than a century after the Norman Conquest the bishopric was reserved for the family; for more than a hundred and fifty years after the Norman Conquest the archdeaconry was reserved for the family. The chapter of Llandaff seemed almost a closed corporation reserved for the Llancarfan family.' There is exaggeration in this, and some of the evidence for family relationships is tenuous; but what can be established is striking enough.

30 J. Raine, *The Priory of Hexham* (Surtees Society, 1864), pp. l–lxvii; F. M. Powicke, *Walter Daniel's Life of Ailred* (Nelson's Medieval Texts, 1950), pp. xxiv–xxxvi; *Symeon of Durham*, ed. T. Arnold (Rolls Series), I, pp. 122–3, 215ff.; II, 316.

31 D. Wilkins, *Concilia Magnae Britanniae*, I, p. 367. For Lanfranc's treatment of celibacy, cf. his *Epp.* 21, 62.

32 *The Vita Wulfstani of William of Malmesbury*, ed. R. R. Darlington (Camden 3rd ser. XL, 1928), pp. xxxiv, 53–4. An enactment similar to that of 1076 had been made in the Norman council of Lisieux (*c.* 1064, cc. 2–3, ed. L. Delisle, *Journal des Savants* (1901), p. 517), condemning priests married since the council of Rouen (1055–63; *PL*,

CXLVII, col. 278). A more stringent canon was passed at Rouen in 1072 (Mansi, op. cit. xx, coll. 33ff.).

33 Gaufridus Grossus, *Vita Bernardi Tironiensis*, c. 6, §51 (*PL*, CLXXII, col. 1397), written after 1116, but referring to the period *c.* 1100, gives a circumstantial account of clerical marriage as a normal element in the social scene in Normandy, and relates how Bernard of Tiron, preaching continence in Normandy, was nearly lynched by the wives of the clergy; Orderic tells the same tale of John of Avranches, archbishop of Rouen, when he promulgated the decree of 1072 (ed. Le Prévost-Delisle, II, p. 171). We shall presently see how high a proportion of the controversial literature in favour of marriage was written in Normandy (above, p. 58 and n. 43).

34 'Archidiaconatum quoque, quem in feudo ab antecessoribus suis de archiepiscopo Rotomagensi tenebat . . . dedit', Orderic, II, p. 132. The phraseology is very strange, but there is no obvious way of emending the text.

35 Ibid. II, p. 365; cf. the *Acta* [*archiepiscoporum Rotomagensium*], *PL*, CXLVII, col. 277.

36 (1) Robert, archbishop of Rouen (989–1036 or 7), son of Duke Richard I (*Orderic*, IV, p. 294, etc.; *Acta*, loc. cit.). (2) Mauger, archbishop of Rouen, son of Duke Richard II (William of Jumièges, *Gesta Normannorum ducum*, ed. J. Marx (Ruen-Paris, 1914), p. 119; *Acta*, loc. cit.; etc.). (3) Hugh bishop of Lisieux (*c.* 1050–77), grandson of Duke Richard I (cf. *Orderic*, II, p. 39, 71, and D. C. Douglas, *E.H.R.* LXI (1946), pp. 154ff., 140). (4) and (5) Hugh bishop of Bayeux (died *c.* 1049) (William of Jumièges, p. 102; *Orderic*, III, pp. 416, etc.) and John of Avranches, bishop of Avranches (1061–68/9) and archbishop of Rouen (1068/9–79) (William of Jumièges, p. 137; *Orderic*, II, p. 374, etc.), sons of Rodulf, count of Ivry, half-brother of Duke Richard I. (6) Odo, bishop of Bayeux (1049/50–97), half-brother of the Conqueror (see n. 37). (7) Richard of Kent, bishop of Bayeux (1135–42), grandson of Henry I (*Orderic*, V, pp. 31, 45).

37 For Ivo, see G. H. White, *Trans. R. Hist. Soc.*, 4th ser. XXII (1940), pp. 81f., 88; for Odo, D. C. Douglas, *The Domesday Monachorum of Christ Church Canterbury* (London, 1944), pp. 33ff., etc., and the study by V. Bourrienne, 'Odon de Conteville évêque de Bayeux . . .', *Revue catholique de Normandie*, VII–IX (1897–1900).

38 Hugh and Roger, bishops of Coutances (L. C. Loyd, *Yorks. Arch[aeological] J[ournal]*, XXXI (1932–4), pp. 99ff.; *Orderic*, IV, p. 415); Radbod, bishop of Séez (see n. 40); Sampson treasurer of Bayeux (see n. 39); Norman, dean of Séez (see n. 40); Anger of Bayeux (see p. 16); Fulk, dean of Évreux (*Orderic*, II, pp. 20, 397; Robert, archdeacon of Évreux and Adelis his wife had a son Gilbert, who occurs in 1099–1100 (J.-J. Vernier, *Chartes . . . de Jumièges*, I (Rouen-Paris, 1916), no. 40); Gilbert d'Évreux, precentor of Rouen and chaplain of Henry I had at least four sons, including William prior of Ste.-Barbe-en-Auge (chronicle of Ste.-Barbe, ed. R.-N. Sauvage in *Mémoires de l'Académie . . . de Caen* (1906), pp. 19ff.); the son of an archdeacon and of the dean of Coutances witness a charter of *c.* 1140 (*Cartulaire des îles normandes*, Société Jersiaise (Jersey, 1924), no. 175). The last three are the only instances in which it is not certain that the family was raised in the eleventh century. For other cases, see next note.

39 A witness list of 1092 contains a large number of canons of Bayeux, including Ralph de St Patrick and John his son, Anschetil de St Vigor and Ralph his nephew (V. Bourrienne, *Antiquus Cartularius ecclesiae Baiocensis*, I (Rouen-Paris, 1902), no. 22); also Ranulf, son of Thurstin and Osbert, son of Thurstin (just possibly Ranulf Flambard and his brother: cf. *C.H.J.* x (1951), p. 130 and n. 18); Odo, son of Oger, who was father of Matthew, archdeacon of Worcester (Bourrienne, op. cit. I, no. 22; II, no. 362)—and Odo's father may have been Oger, precentor of Bayeux (Bibliothèque nationale, MS. Latin 5423, p. 144). The list contains six other men with patronymics, but there is no evidence that their fathers were canons or clerics. Apart from the list, Serlo, canon of Bayeux, poet and controversialist, was son of a priest (see n. 43); and it is possible, though not certain, that Anger of Bayeux held a position in the chapter there (cf. below, p. 16). But the most distinguished family group was that of the brothers Thomas and Sampson, successive treasurers of Bayeux. The children of a priest (William of Malmesbury, *G[esta] P[ontificum]*, ed. N. E. S. A. Hamilton, p. 66) called Osbert, and Muriel his wife (*Liber Vitae ecclesiae Dunelmensis*, ed. J. Raine,

Surtees Society (1841), pp. 139–40), both the brothers won English bishoprics. Thomas
I became archbishop of York (1070–1100; cf. *Hist[orians of the] Ch[urch of] York*,
ed. J. Raine, II, p. 99); Sampson, like his brother, was chaplain to the king and
treasurer of Bayeux (*Orderic*, II, p. 249, III, p. 266; H. W. C. Davis, *Regesta Regum
Anglo-Normannorum*, I (Oxford, 1913), no. 147; cf. Bourrienne, op. cit. I, no. 23),
and also possibly dean (William of Malmesbury, *GP*, p. 289) before he became bishop
of Worcester (1096–1112). Sampson had at least two sons, Thomas II, archbishop of
York (1109–14; Eadmer, *Hist[oria] Nov[orum]*, ed. M. Rule, p. 208; Malmesbury,
GP, pp. 289–90) and Richard de Douvres, canon and bishop of Bayeux (*c.* 1107–33;
Bourrienne, op. cit. I, no. 23; *Hist. Ch. York*, II, p. 124). Humphrey (two of the
name), Hugh and Roger Bovet were canons of Bayeux in the mid and late twelfth
century: Hugh and Roger held the prebend of Cartigny (Bourrienne, op. cit. I, nos.
96, 124ff., 283–4, etc.). Hugh Bovet also claimed a canonry at Salisbury by hereditary
right, but since he was only seven when his father died, he had some difficulty
making good the claim (JL. 14,098). Some of these families may have been reared
before the fathers were ever in orders.

40 Radbod, bishop of Séez in the 1020's and 1030's, was father of William Bonne-Ame,
archbishop of Rouen 1079–1110 (*Orderic*, II, pp. 64, 213, etc.); for Sampson of
Worcester, see above; for Norman, dean of Séez, F. Barlow, *Letters of Arnulf of
Lisieux* (Camden 3rd ser. LXI (1939), pp. xi–xii and notes).

41 Sampson was a subdeacon when he became bishop in 1096 (Eadmer, *Hist. Nov.*,
p. 74), and was presumably such throughout his career as a canon and dignitary at
Bayeux. The first certain evidence of Norman canons being forbidden to marry is in
1080 (cf. n. 9 above); but in any case a canon in lower orders was an abuse.

42 The prohibition against the ordination—outside a monastery—of a priest's son was
extended to all illegitimate children in the council of Poitiers of 1078 (Mansi, op. cit.
xx, coll. 498–9). But this local decree never became the law of the Church. 'Son of a
priest' was a recognised term of abuse, against which it seems to have been regarded
as sufficient defence to show that the father was not in *priest's* orders. Cf. Herbert
of Bosham's brilliant repartee to Henry II in *Materials for the History of Thomas
Becket*, ed. J. C. Robertson, III, p. 101. Becket must have been retailing current
gossip when he so described Reginald fitzJocelin (M. D. Knowles, *Episcopal Colleagues of Archbishop Thomas Becket* (Cambridge, 1951), p. 19—where for twenty-
three read thirty-three). Jocelin, his father, was either an archdeacon when Reginald
was conceived, and so most probably a deacon (all the English archdeacons of this
period whose orders are known were deacons) or already bishop of Salisbury—the
former is more likely! But it is possible that we take these stories too pedantically,
and that 'priest' in this context was popularly taken to mean a clerk of any kind,
like OE. 'preost'.

43 For these writings (mostly printed in *Libelli de Lite*, III) see H. Böhmer, *Kirche und
Staat in England und in der Normandie* (Leipzig, 1899), pp. 168ff.; A. Fliche, *La
réforme grégorienne*, III, pp. 13–38. For Serlo of Bayeux (himself the son of a
priest) see H. Böhmer, *Neues Archiv*, XXII (1897), pp. 722–38. The most recent study
of the Anonymous, his origin and his thought, is by G. H. Williams, *The Norman
Anonymous of 1100 A.D.* (Harvard Theological Studies, XVIII, 1951); cf. R. W.
Southern, *The Making of the Middle Ages* (London, 1953), p. 93 n. Williams does
not seem to realize how eccentric and how heretical the Anonymous' thought was,
and so makes him out to be a more responsible and influential person than he can
possibly have been (he even suggests that he was an archbishop). His defence of
clerical marriage is in *Libelli de Lite*, III, pp. 645ff.

44 The Anonymous' tract on priests' sons is in ibid. pp. 649ff.; see also the approximately contemporary works of Serlo of Bayeux (pp. 579ff.) and Theobald of Étampes
(pp. 603ff. and below, n. 48.)

45 Op. cit. p. 646. In the text I have omitted his characteristic 'Quod quia de scripturis
sanctis non habet auctoritatem, eadem facilitate contempnitur, qua dicitur.'

46 For the defence of lay power, see W. Ullmann, *The Growth of Papal Government in
the Middle Ages* (London, 1955), pp. 344–58, 382–412.

47 The decree of 1076 (Wilkins, *Concilia*, I, p. 367) appears to have been preceded by a

decree from the council of 1070 (c. 15, ibid. p. 365); it was followed by canons 5–8 of the council of 1102 (ibid. p. 382; for the attempt to enforce these canons, cf. the letters in Anselm, *Opera Omnia*, ed. W. S. Schmitt, IV (Edinburgh, 1949), pp. 165–70; V (1951), p. 287), and by the council of 1108, the whole of whose canons were devoted to the subject (Wilkins, op. cit. I, p. 388). For later councils, see nn. 61–3.

48 *Libelli de Lite*, III, pp. 603–7; for Theobald, cf. Oxford Historical Society's *Collectanea*, II (ed. M. Burrows, 1890), pp. 140–2, 151–9.

49 See Appendix (to be published in the next number of this *Journal*).

50 *Letters of John of Salisbury*, ed. W. J. Millor, H. E. Butler and C. N. L. Brooke, I (Nelson's Medieval Texts, 1955), nos. 14–15; cf. nos. 78–9 for the archdeacon of Norfolk.

51 For Osbert see C. T. Clay, *Yorks. Arch. J.* XXXVI (1944–7), pp. 277–9; Dom Adrian Morey, *C.H.J.* X (1952), pp. 352–3; *Letters of John of Salisbury*, I, pp. 261–2.

52 *C.H.J.* X (1951), p. 124.

53 For Roger himself, Nigel, bishop of Ely, Richard fitzNeal and Alexander, bishop of Lincoln, see *D[ictionary of] N[ational] B[iography]*; for Richard, see also *Dialogus de Scaccario*, ed. C. Johnson (Nelson's Medieval Texts, 1950), pp. xivff. and *passim*; H. G. Richardson, *E.H.R.* XLIII (1928), pp. 161ff.; for William of Ely, Richardson, *Trans. R. Hist. Soc.* 4th ser. XV (1932), pp. 45–90, esp. pp. 47, 60, 90. Matilda of Ramsbury is mentioned by name in *Orderic*, V, pp. 120–1; for her son Roger le Poer, see ibid. and *Gesta Stephani*, ed. K. R. Potter (Nelson's Medieval Texts, 1955), p. 52. On the strength of his name 'le Poer', a connexion has been conjectured between Roger and Herbert and Richard Poore, successive bishops of Salisbury at the end of the century; it has further been suggested that the Poores were sons to Richard of Ilchester, a leading exchequer clerk and bishop of Winchester 1174–88 (cf. Stubbs, introduction to Howden's *Chronica*, IV, p. xci n; *D.N.B. s.v.* Poor, Richard of Ilchester, etc.). There is plausibility in these suggestions, but no solid evidence on which to support them. Matilda of Ramsbury may well have been connected with Azo of Ramsbury, archdeacon of Wiltshire (*Register of St Osmund*, ed. W. H. R. Jones (Rolls Series), I, pp. 215, 351) and probably dean of Salisbury from before 1139 to *c.* 1145 (*Notes and Queries for Somerset and Dorset*, XXIII (1942), p. 319f.) and his brother Roger, canon of Salisbury and archdeacon of Wiltshire after Azo (*Register of St Osmund*, I, p. 351, cf. p. 349, etc.; *Historia et cartularium mon. Gloucestriae*, ed. W. H. Hart (Rolls Series), II, p. 106).

54 For what follows, see C. N. L. Brooke, *C.H.J.* X (1951), pp. 111–32, especially pp. ff. 124; for the Belmeis family, see Stubbs' introduction to Ralph de Diceto, I, pp. xxiff., xxviiff., and Brooke, art. cit., pp. 125–7.

55 This celebrated dictum is assigned to Alexander III by Gerald of Wales, *Opera*, II (ed. J. S. Brewer), p. 304.

56 Two letters of Peter of Blois relating to his nephews are preserved in a manuscript at Erfurt (Amplonian MS. F. 71, fos. 190r–v, 196r–v. I owe these references to Mr R. W. Southern, who kindly lent me photostats of the MS.). For Gerald of Wales' troubles with his nephew Gerald, see *Opera*, III, p. 325, and especially the *Speculum Duorum* (of which there is an account by W. S. Davies in *Archaeologia Cambrensis*, LXXXIII (1928), pp. 111–34; an edition by the late H. E. Butler and Dr J. Conway Davies is promised).

The exchange of benefices in later centuries (of which this is only one aspect) is discussed by A. Hamilton Thompson in *The English Clergy and their Organisation in the later Middle Ages* (Oxford, 1947), pp. 107–9, but both the phenomenon in general and its use to further family interests in particular await a full critical study.

57 For Gerald and Peter's lyrics, see F. J. E. Raby, *Secular Latin Poetry in the Middle Ages* (Oxford, 1934), II, pp. 110–11, 323–4.

58 Cf. Brooke, art. cit.; and for Flambard, pp. 124, 129ff. It is probable, though not entirely certain, that he was dean; there is no doubt that he was a canon of St Paul's.

59 Cf. M. Gibbs, *Early Charters of the Cathedral Church of St Paul, London* (Camden 3rd ser. LVIII (1939)), p. xxxiii.

60 For Hugh of Buckland, cf. Brooke, art. cit. p. 124, n. 70; for Becket's part in the campaign of 1159, see especially FitzStephen in *Materials for the History of Thomas*

Becket, III, pp. 33–4, and the *Continuatio Beccensis* and Robert of Torigni in Torigni's *Chronique*, ed. L. Delisle, II, p. 174 and I, p. 325.

61 1125 (Wilkins, op. cit. I, p. 408), 1127 (ibid. p. 410), 1129 (ibid. p. 411; Henry of Huntingdon, *Historia Anglorum*, ed. T. Arnold, pp. 250–1; Anglo-Saxon chronicle E, *s.a.* 1129, followed by several later writers); cf. also 1138 (Wilkins, op. cit. I, p. 415), and below, at n. 63.

62 Henry of Huntingdon, pp. 245–6 on John of Crema; pp. 250–1 (and cf. Anglo-Saxon chronicle E, *s.a.* 1129) on the way in which Archbishop William's simplicity was duped by Henry I, who accepted fines from the married clergy and allowed them to keep their wives. The substance of the second story is very likely correct; the tale of John of Crema's incontinence is less plausible—a memory of a different kind of his important mission is given by Gilbert Foliot, writing in 1166 (*Epistolae*, ed. J. A. Giles, I, no. 194, pp. 282–3). Henry of Huntingdon was certainly the son of a cleric; the grounds for thinking that he succeeded his father as archdeacon are given by T. Arnold in his introduction to Henry's *Historia*, pp. xxxi–xxxiii and notes.

63 Wilkins, op. cit. I, p. 477 (the best text is in *Gesta Henrici Secundi* . . . , ed. Stubbs, I, p. 85); cf. also 1195, c. 17 (Wilkins, op. cit. I, p. 502) and 1200, c. 10 (p. 507), based on the Third Lateran Council of 1179, c. 11. The canon of 1175 was based on a decretal of Alexander III addressed to the bishop of Worcester, 'Inter cetera sollicitudinis', JL. 12,254 (printed in full in *Gilberti Foliot Epistolae*, ed. J. A. Giles, II, no. 368, from the *Collectio Belverensis*). Both decretal and canon make a frequent appearance in the early decretal collections.

64 See above, n. 17.

65 The poem is by Matthew of Vendôme, and is edited by W. Wattenbach, *Sitzungsberichte der k. bayer. Akademie der Wiss. zu München, Philos.-philol. und hist. Classe*, II (1872), p. 599, cited Raby, op. cit. II, p. 34.

66 This title was commonly used in the sixth century (cf. E. Vacandard, *Études de critique et d'histoire religieuse*, I (Paris, 1905), p. 110).

67 For other names, see above, notes 38, 39, Brooke, art. cit., pp. 123–4 and notes; for Matilda, above, n. 53. For Alice de Percy, see William of Newburgh, ed. R. Howlett, *Chronicles of the Reigns of Stephen, etc.*, II, pp. 440–1, *Complete Peerage*, revised ed. X, p. 442 n.; for their son Henry du Puiset, *Historiae Dunelmensis scriptores tres*, ed. J. Raine (Surtees Society, 1839), p. 18, and *The Priory of Finchale* (Surtees Society, 1837), pp. x, 46. William of Newburgh implies that Hugh had liaisons with more than one lady, and lists three sons; but it is probable that Bouchard du Puiset was Hugh's nephew, not his son (cf. *Gesta Henrici Secundi*, II, p. 85; Roger of Howden, *Chronica*, ed. Stubbs, III, p. 16, etc. Howden, the author of both these works, was a well-informed Northerner who, unlike William of Newburgh, preferred sound information to gossip as evidence). Alice de Percy subsequently—but still during Hugh's lifetime—married Richard de Morville (*Complete Peerage*, loc. cit.). This shows that she did not regard her liaison with Hugh du Puiset as a binding marriage.

68 For the Heloise of history, see the brilliant book of E. Gilson, op. cit., and the brief but profound appraisal by Dom David Knowles in *Studies* (1941), pp. 43–58, esp. pp. 48ff. In the light of Professor Gilson's study, it is no longer necessary to defend the authenticity of Heloise's letters. Out of the many ways in which Heloise illuminates our problem, I select two. Whoever her father may have been, she was brought up in a cathedral close, and thus gives us a rare glimpse not only of a clerical wife, but also of a child of that lost society. More important, her genius elicited from Abelard himself (in his letters to her), and more particularly from Peter the Venerable (in the letter he wrote to her after Abelard's death), two of the very few really lofty statements of the doctrine of Christian marriage written at this time.

69 It seems to me highly probable that Hispano-Arab influences played a decisive part in the origin of the European tradition of courtly love; but I am aware that it is most imprudent for a historian to express an opinion on this much-vexed question.

70 The judgment is given in Andreas Capellanus, *De Amore*, ed. E. Trojel (Copenhagen, 1892), pp. 152–5 (English trans. J. J. Parry (New York, 1941), pp. 106–7). It

has been suggested that the English romances are more moral in their attitude to love and marriage—by and large—than the French (cf. M. A. Gist, *Love and War in the Middle English Romances* (Philadelphia, 1947), pp. 1ff., esp. p. 8).

71 The way in which the canonists solved the problem of what constituted a valid marriage is shown in detail by J. Dauvillier, *Le mariage dans le droit classique de l'Église* (Paris, 1933).

5

Economic Conservatism, Papal Finance, and the Medieval Satires on Rome

JOHN A. YUNCK

THE SATIRE OR DIATRIBE on the Court of Rome and its vices is a widely recurring type in the moral-satirical literature of the Middle Ages. It has been well-known for centuries: examples were anthologized by 16th century Protestant reformers for their own purposes,[1] and became relatively popular among the learned in Protestant Europe. But though poems, sermons and parodies on the theme have continued to find their way into print in large numbers and have attracted the occasional notice of scholars,[2] little has been done to elucidate them or to inquire into their causes. The purpose of this paper is to show, especially in the light of Lunt's valuable studies in papal finance,[3] that these satires have their roots in phenomena more significant than mere palm-greasing and tip-scavenging on the part of minor officials. They seem rather to be clear testimony to a widespread and often angry conservative reaction to economic changes not clearly understood by the moralists and satirists who wrote them. They arose with the expanding activities of the papacy as the Hildebrandine ideal took root, and increased in numbers and intensity as the consequent papal financial requirements increased. It may be suggested too that these satires provide a kind of documentation for aspects of papal taxation in a period for which no more reliable documents are available.

One of the most widespread and popular of all satirical themes from the 11th century to the close of the Middle Ages was the theme of human venality and fiscal corruption in general, of the power of the purse, the Almighty Denarius. It appears first and most widely in the clerical Latin literature, but is plentiful in the vernaculars, in German, French, English and Italian. Dante's treatment of the sins of the Wolf and his comments on venality throughout the *Comedia* are familiar. A large portion of the inhabitants of his *Inferno* are drawn from among the venal. In Middle English the long episode of Lady Meed in *Piers Plowman* is only the best-known example of the theme. Lady Meed, remarks R. W. Chambers, "is gifts, Rewards, this world's treasure. 'The Lady Meed is nothing more or less than the power of the purse,' says Mr. Christopher Dawson. Another *alias* (she has many) is 'The Almighty Dollar.' Langland's outlook is conservative; he believes in the old world of feudal obligations. He hates the 'cash nexus.' " This view of the venality theme as a conservative satirical device seems to touch the heart of the matter.[4]

The theme is characteristically directed against those groups whose natural responsibilities to society were considered great, and whose income came at least in part from sources other than the usual feudal channels. Venal, sacrament-selling priests and worldly, simoniac bishops were favorite subjects as well as (later) lawyers. Physicians too were included, though less frequently than the others. But the favorite target for its venality was the papal curia, the Court of Rome, including the Roman citizens in general, the cardinals and their minions in particular, and sometimes the pope himself. *Roma caput mundi* was almost universally described by moralists and satirists as also the headquarters, the *fons et origo,* of the venality of Christendom. So widespread were these attacks on Roman venality that the *Romdiatribe* achieved almost the status of a literary genre, and by the 14th century had become a conventional part of almost every *cursor mundi,* every moral-satirical survey of human society, whether or not the writer had had any direct experience with his subject. Lady Meed, it will be recalled, is as familiar as Holy Church herself at the pope's palace (B text, II, 23).

A mere bibliography of the printed items which touch on the theme in Latin and the vernaculars, in prose and verse, would fill many pages. Some of the satires are parodies, one of the best and earliest being the *Tractatus Garsiae* (ca. 1100), an earthy and hilarious work which pretends to be a description of the translation of the relics of St. Albinus and St. Rufinus to Rome, on the occasion of the consecration of a new Archbishop of Toledo.[5] The relics of these saints, as their names suggest, are merely silver and gold, and the author is indicating that the whole transaction was simony. Far better known is the brief "Gospel According to the Silver Mark," which appears in various forms in 13 extant manuscripts.[6] It is a pastiche of scriptural echoes set in the form of the gospel extract read in the mass, and may have been part of a lost "missa de muneribus" or "missa secundum simoniacos." Its oldest and shortest form is brief enough to translate here in full:

The beginning of the Gospel according to the Marks of Silver: At that time the pope said to the Romans: "When the son of man shall come to the seat of our majesty, first say to him 'Friend, whereto art thou come?' Yet if he shall continue knocking without giving you anything, cast him out into the exterior darkness." And it chanced that a certain poor man came to the court of the Lord Pope, and cried out, saying "Have mercy on me, at least you, dispensers of the pope, because the hand of poverty hath touched me. I am needy and poor; therefore I beg that you relieve my calamity and misery." And they hearing it were moved with indignation and said: "Friend, keep thy poverty to thyself, to perish with thee. Go behind me, Satan, because thou savourest not of the things that are of money. Amen Amen I say to thee, thou shalt not enter into the joy of thy lord till thou pay thy last farthing." And the poor man went his way and sold his mantle and his tunic and all that he had and gave to the cardinals and the dispensers and the treasurers. But they said: "And this, what is this among so many?" And they cast him out; and going forth he wept bitterly, and would not be consoled. But later there came to the court a certain wealthy clerk, fat and thick and gross, who in the sedition had committed murder. He first gave to the dispenser, second to the treasurer, third to the cardinals. But they thought among themselves that they should receive more. The Lord Pope, hearing that his cardinals had received many gifts, was sick, nigh unto death. But the rich man sent to him a couch of gold and silver and immediately he was made whole. Then the Lord Pope called his cardinals and ministers to him and said to them: "Brethren, look, lest anyone deceive you with vain words. For I have given you an example: as I have grasped, so you grasp also." [7]

The proverbial venality of Rome found expression, too, in other oddities, like the Rome acrostic mentioned by the sharp-tongued Walter Map:

> Radix
> Omnium
> Malorum
> Avaritia [8]

These commonplace witticisms tell us little about the actual difficulties which the clergy encountered at the Court of Rome when a case was to be heard or a bishop or an abbot consecrated or blessed. Other satires are more specific and more revealing. One poem, for example, opens by applying to the Romans the Pauline idea that avarice is idolatry. This is followed by a catalogue of the riches which the imagination of the poet pictures flowing into Rome from all over the world: fine clothes from Greece, ivory and gems from India, delicacies from France, silver and gold from England, mules from Burgundy. Money is the judge at Rome, the poor man goes unheard; the grasping doorkeeper (a standard feature of the *Romdiatribe)* awaits all visitors. Neither birth nor learning can achieve their desires; only Queen *Pecunia* reigns, supported by *Simonia* and *Giesia.* The rest of the poem is devoted to Queen Pecunia's speech, in which she catalogues with heavy irony the virtues of herself, Money. The catalogue continues at some length but Pecunia ends her speech by explaining how she has searched the world over and found no place where she is so hospitably received as is Rome. Here henceforth she will make her home.[9]

Here, then, is Lady Meed, two centuries before Langland wrote *Piers Plowman*. The ideas and the manner of expression are typical. The inferior verse is also regrettably typical but occasionally a versifier of genius handles the theme brilliantly. Such a poet was Walter of Châtillon (fl. ca. 1170), at one time a clerk in the chancery of Henry II, a friend of John of Salisbury, a teacher at Châtillon, and a student of law at Bologna. His exceptional knowledge of the classics echoes in the imagery of his satire.[10] His most brilliant poem on Roman corruption is the thirty-stanza "Propter Sion non tacebo." So Walter opens, echoing Isaiah; Rome is lowered to the slime, subjected to tribute, derelict, desolate and afflicted.

Walter dismembers the Curia, group by group. If the hounds of Scylla are the curial advocates, Charibdis is the chancery. The sirens, Walter continues, are the cardinals, who sing blandly in the poet's ear the song of friendship, and who boast their power. Though they now rule Peter's ship these cardinals are pirates, whose leader is Pilate. Without the protection of Purse the ship is dashed against the rocks until the traveller loses both his money and his clothes. The rocks are the keepers of the doors, who admit the wealthy, but like fierce beasts repel the needy. The poem closes with some conventional praise of Pope Alexander as a friend of letters, and a hint that the Pope might provide a safe haven for the storm-tossed Walter.[11]

These few examples will suffice to indicate the tone and matter typical of the satire against the Court of Rome. Behind the irony, the classical imagery and the sheer vilification of the examples there are ideas and assumptions common to virtually all the medieval satires on Rome. The complaints center about the expense for the consecration of bishops and mitered abbots by the pope, and about the costs of carrying a suit in canon law—or indeed any pressing clerical plea—*ad limina apostolorum*. The objection is not merely that the charges are too high (though this is mentioned frequently enough) but that there are any charges at all. Whatever the characters of the various satirists and whatever the individual or political axes they had to grind (they must have been multifarious), all at least pretend to be scandalized by the idea of cash transactions connected with the spiritual functions of the papacy. One concludes that the theme must have carried great weight with their readers. The apostolic privilege of consecration was a gift of the Holy Spirit, and in their eyes the enforced "gratuities" in connection with these rites were sheer simony. So at least the satirists claimed.

The fees charged by advocates and *auditores* of the judicial divisions of the Curia were equally simony, for they constituted the sale of Justice, which is the sale of Truth, also a gift of the Holy Spirit. Indeed, "he who sells the truth for money sells Christ, who is Truth." [12] Hence the name of

Judas appears beside that of Simon Magus in the moral-satirical image of Rome:

> Vendre justice est Jhesum vendre,
> Per a Judas quil seit entendre
> Qui de Jhesu velt deniers prendre,
> Peis se corut au seur pendre.[13]

Men as different in temperament and stature as Chancellor Philip, Walter of Châtillon, the unknown and impecunious goliards, Etienne de Fougeres, Langland, Peter Pictor, Walter Map, John Gower, and John of Salisbury, among others, sang the same song, and it rang out from the 11th through the 15th century. After we allow for the attractiveness of cliché and commonplace to the medieval writer, the uniformity nevertheless suggests concrete economic realities behind the complaints, and a widespread and uniformly unfavorable reaction to those realities. Commonplace content may suggest commonplace writers; it also suggests commonplace problems.

Though the satirists are agreed that the Court of Rome should not charge fees for its services, they do not demand that the Curia subscribe to the ideal of apostolic poverty. Nor do they attack the functions and services of the Curia as an institution. They seem satisfied with complaints of abuse and charges of simony, and are in fact silent on the problem of how the Court of Rome should be supported. The most attractive hypothesis is that the moralists and satirists, conservative and feudally-minded themselves, universally assumed a feudally supported and feudally oriented Curia, a court subsidized wholly by its traditional domanial revenues rather than by charges for services rendered. The latter smacked too much of the market place, especially when applied to the apostolic functions. The satirists of the 11th and 12th centuries almost never attack the Hildebrandine ideal of the freedom of the Church, or the immensely expanded activities to which this ideal committed the papacy. They merely ignore the soaring expenses caused by the expansion. The papacy had burst the bonds of feudal economics in its rapid growth, but the fact went unrecognized by the satirists, or even by those who were instrumental in the development. It is tempting to see in the repeated satirical assaults on the high cost of ecclesiastical attention at the Curia the implied contrast with a feudal court supported by its own domanial revenues. Economic theory lagged notoriously behind economic fact in the Middle Ages. I suggest that this lag lies at the heart of the medieval satire on Rome.

This is not to imply that the individual satirists themselves were all men of high, if old-fashioned ideals. Undoubtedly much of the satire reflects the petty irritations of self-seeking but highly vocal clerks. It is hard, for example, to believe that Walter of Châtillon was as much interested in the moral uplift of the Curia as he was in lining his own pockets. And much more of the satire certainly resulted from the political strife which accompanied the expansion of papal activity between the pontificates of Leo IX and Innocent III. Roman venality was a common part of the charges and counter-charges in the pamphleteering which accompanied the Investiture Contest.[14] Granting the great variety of causes which might have produced satire against the Curia, the significant point is that the satirists and moralists all find the charges attractive enough to repeat with little change. The argument must have seemed to them likely to appeal to their readers.

It seems likely, then, that the satirists are lamenting the most noteworthy and shocking example in the Christendom of their day of economic change, the defection *par excellence* from an economic way of life to which they were habituated and which they considered natural and normal. If we take the writers at their word, the fees of the Curia represented a desperate form of immorality. For the Court of Rome to finance its activities by enforced charges for services was to defile the high altar, to corrupt the very heart of Christendom. Like Langland, these early satirists too hated the "cash nexus."

It has long been commonplace that with the increasing centralization of the activities of the Church, especially after the leadership of Gregory VII, the medieval papal curia developed into incomparably the most complex court in Western Christendom. This development was in part consequence, in part cause, of the rapidly broadening activities of the papacy throughout Europe, as papal control was gradually asserted and the independent authority of the episcopacy gradually declined.[15] It is commonplace, too, that the papacy, attempting to finance this expansion of activity, found itself continually in financial difficulties, and hence was forced to resort to measures which made it a leader in the economic development of Europe. "The papacy," remarked Lunt over 50 years ago, "not only organized one of the earliest and best of the medieval finance systems, but by means of its operations influenced profoundly the general economic development of Europe . . . The Roman Church . . . with an almost modern system of taxation covering all Western Europe, furnished one of the principal sources which aided the establishment of money and credit transactions on a large scale." [16]

Lunt's subsequent studies form an admirable basis for documenting the medieval satire on Rome, though they can obviously tell us little about the personalities, the petty jealousies, the element of political pamphleteering, or even the conventionality which must have provided part of the inspiration for many satires. When Walter of Châtillon describes in vitriolic measures the suave, unctuous cardinal who addresses him at the Curia, his Latin-Italian-French jargon softened to be "sweete upon his tonge," we are in the presence of personalities beyond the province of economic history:

Dulci cantu blandiuntur
ut Sirenes et loquuntur
primo quedam dulcia:
'Frare, ben je te cognosco,
certe nichil a te posco
nam tu es de Francia.
'Terra vestra bene cepit
et benigne nos recepit
in portu concilii.
Nostri estis nostri—cuius?
sacrosancte sedis huius
speciales filii.' [17]

Such it is always with the best satire. Nevertheless, the satirical theme is most profitably approached through the larger economic realities which it reflects. "The centralization of papal power," says Lunt, "necessitated the construction of a more efficient governmental machine. Good government, it was soon discovered, was expensive. Early in the process of transformation the papacy began to look to its finances. Papal records were ransacked to discover all revenues which could be claimed, and demands for payment were pressed with vigor." [18]

We may summarize from the important recapitulations of Lunt the revenues of the papacy as they existed at the end of the 11th century.[19] The most important were the domanial revenues from the patrimonies and states of the Church, those normal feudal revenues which the papacy had already outgrown by the middle of the 11th century. A second source of income was the census of protected and exempt ecclesiastical foundations, which grew steadily during the centuries that followed. A third, if minor and highly irregular source, was the tribute paid by temporal rulers for papal protection. A fourth was the custom of Peter's Pence, which had begun very early in England and later spread to some other countries. There were also irregular income taxes levied on the clergy, but these were never levied for the use of the pope himself until 1228. Charitable subsidies, requested by the pope from his clergy, were also useful sources of income. Though they were at first voluntary (in the 11th century), the element of choice seems to have disappeared during later centuries. An ancient source of papal revenue (and for some time the most profitable) was gifts and legacies to the papacy by pious individuals. But however large this income might be, it was hardly dependable. Other sources (oblations, procurations, spoils, and fruits wrongfully received) were developed during the 12th and 13th centuries, while many others (annates, fruits during vacancies, quindennia, indulgences, the sale of offices, and compositions) were not developed until the 14th century or later.

Anyone examining the documentary evidence of this income cannot fail to be struck, first with the irregularity and undependability of almost all the sources, and second with the paucity of important sources of income at the close of the 11th century, while the papacy was taking its early, dramatic steps towards international leadership. Peter's Pence in England, for example, had quickly settled into a customary fixed annual sum just under £200 sterling, and all of the 23 exempt foundations in England brought, as late as 1327, just over £10. The result of this weakness was that the papacy began to depend very heavily on certain other revenues: services (*servitia*), visitation taxes, and chancery taxes; and these, in their rudimentary forms, are most frequently at the heart of the satirists' complaints about Roman venality.

By far the most significant and profitable of these payments was that known as *servitia*. Services are defined by Lunt as "charges paid by patriarchs, archbishops, bishops, abbots and for a period by some priors on occasion of their appointment by the pope in consistory." It should be emphasized that these payments were not established as formal taxes, prescribed, regulated and subdivided, until late in the 13th century,[20] but they clearly existed before that as customary gratuities from time immemorial. These gratuities (often referred to by papal sources as *servitia* long before their establishment as taxes) seem to have settled into *de facto* taxes whose imposition and even amount had the force almost of law. The custom of paying the gratuities was well established by the time of Justinian,[21] and was specifically recognized and accepted by Gregory the Great in 595.[22] Gregory, however, forbade outright charges for such services as ordinations and appointments. During the next four centuries the custom of gratuities apparently hardened into a rigid convention, which probably prescribed at least the minimum gratuity for receiving the pallium from the pope. In 1027 Canute complained of the high cost of these services to his bishops.[23]

Probably the amount and number of such gratuities or fees increased rapidly after the pontificate of Leo IX (1049–1055), when the great expansion of papal activity was under way, and when the number of confirmations controlled by the pope was increasing. We lack documents to show the numbers of these charges, still formally gratuities, or the amounts which were paid, but what was happening is indicated by the satirical charges of simony, some of which we have quoted. These are occasionally supported by chronicles or by letters. Early in the 12th century, for example, Bishop Ivo of Chartres replies to the papal legate, who had apparently found practices in his diocese which approached simony, that the fault lies in the example provided by Rome herself. When his deacons and cantors are accused of demanding gifts for their services, he says, they defend themselves by pointing to Rome, where the officials make exorbitant demands for consecrating bishops or abbots, which they palliate under the name of "oblations," or "benedictions." The letter suggests that Roman venality was common talk: ". . . cum nec calamus nec charta gratis ibi (ut aiunt) habeatur." [24]

It seems clear, then, that the *servitia* in their primitive and irregular form, were the major target of the earliest anti-Rome satires and the objections were probably the more shrill because the fees were large. Though records are lacking for the 11th and 12th centuries, when the Roman satires first proliferated, Lunt estimates that the total expense of the consecration of a bishop cost the new prelate almost a whole year's income, which frequently had to be borrowed, and which often placed the churchman in financial difficulties for many years in the future.[25] There are 13th-century records of large sums being borrowed to meet the expenses of confirmation by the pope.[26] Since the charges were still formally gratuities, though unavoidable, the satirists raised the cry of simony.

Visitation taxes were much lower than the *servitia* and were paid by few churchmen. The archbishops of Canterbury and York, for example, paid 300 marks once every three years. The tax provided only a minor source of income to the papal camera; yet its existence probably helped increase the satirical cry that everything at Rome had a price. The need of the expanding papacy for the taxes was unquestionable, especially in view of the irregularity of many other sources of papal income. But to those who were hurt by the payments (and they could include all the clergy of a bishop's diocese) the gratuities represented the simple sale of the gifts of the Holy Spirit, the extortion of Giezi. The satires may have reflected, too, some of the opposition by growing monarchies to the export of money from their territories.

The 11th and 12th century satirical attacks on Rome thus furnish us with interesting and useful—though vague—documentation of the development of the papal *servitia* during a period for which Lunt and Jordan can furnish no documents of a more substantial sort. They provide us with insights, often amusing, into the chaotic and haphazard growth of at least one form of papal taxation, into the disorganized and improvised efforts of the busiest, most complex, and most rapidly growing court in Christendom to maintain itself in solvency. They offer lively testimony to the gradual hardening of gratuity into formal tax, the settling of the customary into the prescriptive. The exact steps of the transformation are lost, but the anger and annoyance of clerk and prelate remain vividly recorded.

The chaotic development of the *servitia*, the haziness of its status on the borderland between gratuity and tax, and the whole informal nature of the Curia's tax structure during the period, suggest that the fees were difficult to control and to account for. They probably encouraged competition for revenue among the offices of the Curia, and acted as a blind for all sorts of minor extortion and tip-hunting. Even as early as the mid-11th century Peter Damian had attacked an unnamed bishop of the Curia, who ran about feverishly when the time for a synod approached, as if reaping time were near. "For he was girding himself to gather meed, and to reap it he was sharpening not a steel blade, but the scythe of eloquence." [27] Innocent III found the same practices and was forced to recognize them officially and take steps to stop them. One of the documents translated by Lunt suggests the practices which so irritated the satirists:

We, indeed, members of the school of the bearers of the papal tiara when he visits a church in the City, and of the school of the keepers of the napery and the chaplains . . . all alike promise by taking oath that we will not in the future exact by importunity or extort by violence from any archbishop or bishop consecrated, or abbot blessed, or any one ordained, the horse or covering or any other thing, or, on account of this, impose or cause to be imposed any injury in word or deed on any one; but we will accept with an act of thanks that which shall have been given freely to us by any of the aforesaid, or that the camerarius, having been requested, shall have been able to obtain by way of gifts . . . [28]

The satirists never distinguished this petty extortion from the taxes themselves. Indeed, during the 11th and 12th centuries there was no formally defined difference, and the complainants felt free to call their expenses simony. Their complaints increased in wrath and swelled in volume as papal demands for income increased. From the beginnings of the 11th-century reform until the Protestant Revolution financial difficulties were the chief and constant source of embarrassment to the papacy, and the wellspring of the swelling flood of satires on the venality of Rome.

One sort of expense at the Curia not discussed by Lunt but regularly reflected in the anti-Rome satires was the charges made by the law courts. Appeals *ad limina* were encouraged to increase papal control over ecclesiastical affairs, and their cost, as we have seen, became a regular refrain among the satirists. The wealthy clerk is heard, the poor one goes unsped; so sing the satirists in unison. Some of the expenses connected with such appeals were chancery taxes; others were advocates' fees; still others were no doubt fees for the *auditores* and the petty clerks of the courts. In the absence of extant records we may surmise that these law courts were essentially self-supporting, had their own treasurers and kept their own accounts. They were clearly among the chief targets of the satirists on venality for over three centuries.

Certain conclusions emerge from a review of the moral-satirical attacks on Rome in connection with the economic problems of papal finance and the economic facts of papal taxation. Because of the expansion of its activities after the pontificate of Leo IX the Curia found itself faced with financial demands far beyond the limits imposed by its older feudal and charitable revenues. By far the most complex governmental organization of its time, and the only organization whose effects—and whose taxes—could be felt in all the corners of western Christendom, it found itself unwittingly the leader in financial innovations which were ultimately to revolutionize the economy of Europe. The tangible instrument of these innovations was the papal system of taxation, and one of its earliest devices was the conversion of a charitable income, traditional gratuities, into a systematic tax for services. The change was gradual, perhaps not wholly conscious, and long before it was complete it had aroused a multitude of sharp reactions, echoed by the cries of the satirists. But while the satirists charged simony, the popes and their representatives still thought and spoke in the comfortable and familiar feudal categories, and in terms sanctioned by ancient Christian usage. The taxes were "gratuities," "benedictions," "subsidies," "obligations." They were not, when the satire first arose, formalized or regularized. Their purpose was undefined: they were described as applied to the personal use of the Lord Pope or the Lords Cardinals. And prelates were not "taxed:" rather they "paid their respects" with a certain amount of money.[29] Bureaucracy and the "cash nexus" had made their appearance, but their very originators knew no terms in which to speak of them, nor even the modes in which to think of them.

The satirists and moralists who bewailed the venality of Rome were clearly feudally-minded, and their work conservative in temper. However exalted or however corrupt the motives of the individual writers might be, the clerical ideal which their satire implies emerges as a rather uniform and distinct picture: a clergy freely devoted to the service of Justice and of Christ on earth, trustworthy custodians of the Patrimony of the Poor, freely dispensing the sacraments and carrying out the other apostolic functions, supported, perhaps, by domanial revenues, charitable donations, customary tithing. Significantly, most of the early clerical satire on Roman venality whose provenance can be determined was written in France, England, and the Empire—all areas where feudal organization remained strongest, and which were least touched by the commercial developments of the Italian city states. In the incipient taxes of the Curia the satirists saw a new world of cash payments for spiritual services, of marketable talent and learning, of the justification of office by wealth. They could hardly view it with equanimity.

The immediate cause of their satire (where it was not the outcry of the self-seeking benefice-hunter, or the conservative or imitative treatment of a popular subject) may have been the burdens which they or their acquaintances or ecclesiastical superiors felt from papal taxation. But the intense moral animus which lay behind much of their work could only have issued from the fear and dislike of an economic world new to them and alien to their modes of thought. The average sensitive and intelligent thinker had hardly adapted himself to that new world by the age of Elizabeth I. As a money economy spread to the royal courts and was felt by the other estates, they too fell under the condemnation of the conservative satirists, so that by the 14th century Langland's Lady Meed included among her followers all sorts of royal officials, justices, and civil lawyers, mayors and merchants, as well as the clergy from the highest to the lowest.

With the simple world (real or imaginary) of agrarian stability, personal relationship, and feudal obligation dissolving around them, these writers felt sufficiently bewildered and uneasy to echo the ancient cry of the Roman satirists that *Pecunia* was indeed Queen.[30] But what seemed worst of all was that the walls were crumbling not at the outposts of Christendom, but at its very heart in the sacred city of Rome. The highest spiritual functions seemed suddenly to be measurable in terms of cash, and the highest representatives of Christ on earth were venal, movable only by coin, idolaters, in Pauline terms, of gold. It must have seemed as if all the stable social and spiritual categories in the world were disappearing through the solvent powers of Queen Cash. In retrospect we can understand the outraged cries of simony and the Roman marketplace, as well as the problems of the papacy in attempting to create a new tax structure without any real awareness of the incipient economic revolution which it represented.

Our analysis of the mentality which produced the characteristic protests of the medieval Rome-satires is necessarily hypothetical. The nature of the evidence—the mask of objectivity and moral fervor on the part of the satirists, our lack of knowledge about the lives or even the identities of most of them, the absence of supporting documents concerning the rudimentary Curial *servitia* during the 11th and 12th centuries when the outcry first arose, the conflicting interests and cross-purposes of the Investiture Contest—precludes firmly established conclusions. The uniformity of the protest remains nevertheless imposing, coming as it does from a great variety of writers: *vagantes,* secular churchmen high and low, monks, and later friars and even laymen. And the early date of its origins suggests the rigor with which gratuities for papal appointments were enforced, well before they became formalized as taxes. To this extent the anti-Rome satire may be considered valuable contributory evidence to the history of one aspect of papal finance.

The difficult and ambiguous nature of the problem as it presented itself to the medieval man is reflected in some of the comments of John of Salisbury, one of the most learned and sensible men of his day. In the *Policraticus* John recounts a conversation with his friend, the English Pope Hadrian IV (1154–1159). When asked about the popular reputation of the papacy John frankly summarizes in his answer the characteristic satirical clichés about Roman avarice: "Iustitiam non tam veritati quam pretio reddunt. Omnia namque cum pretio hodie; sed nec cras aliquid sine pretio obtinebis." It would be repetitious to paraphrase them here.

When asked for his own opinion John is more circumspect; but, after remarking that he fears that the Pope will hear from an imprudent friend what he does not wish to hear, he makes his own comments on the subject of Roman venality:

> Everyone praises you, and you are called the father and lord of all . . . If, then, you are a father, why do you demand meed and remuneration from your sons? If a lord, why do you not strike your Romans with fear, repress their impudence, and recall them to the faith? But perhaps you expect to save the city for the Church by meed (*muneribus*). Did Silvester acquire it by meed? . . . What you have freely received, freely give. Justice is the queen of virtues, and blushes when she is sold for a price. If she is to be gracious, let her be gratuitous.

Hadrian laughs and thanks him, but replies with the familiar fable of the stomach and the rebellious members, who after several days of rebellion were forced to admit that their own illness arose from their failure to feed the stomach, which they had branded as lazy and voracious:

> For he from whom tribute had been withdrawn, like a public dispenser in turn withdrew support from all . . . It is far better that he receive something to distribute than that the other members go hungry through his lack . . . So it is, brother, he said, in the body of the commonweal where, no matter how much the magistrate hungers, he does not so much for himself as for others. For if he is starved he is able to give nothing to the members . . . Therefore do not measure the harshness of ourselves or of the secular princes, but pay heed to the utility of all.

The passage is a profound statement of both sides of the struggle between old feudal principle and new fiscal necessity.[31]

The largest part of the medieval satire on Roman venality is subliterary, and much of the rest belongs only to the realm of witticism or *jeu d'esprit*. But read in the light of the papacy's developing tax efforts it provides absorbing, and often lively and eloquent, documentation of the conservative unrest at the beginnings of an economic revolution which changed the face, and much of the thought, of the Western World.

NOTES

[1] E.g., M. Flacius Illyricus, *Varia doctorum piorumque virorum de corrupto ecclesiae statu poemata* (Basel, 1556).

[2] P. Lehmann, *Die Parodie im Mittelalter* (München, 1922), pp. 43–85, collects and discusses a number of the satires.

[3] Esp. *Papal Revenues in the Middle Ages*, 2 vols. (New York, 1934), and *Financial Relations of the Papacy with England to 1327* (Cambridge, Mass., 1939). These should be supplemented by K. Jordan, "Zur päpstlichen Finanzgeschichte im 11. und

12. Jahrhundert," *Quellen und Forschungen aus italienischen Archieven und Bibliotheken* XXV (1933–34), 61–104.

4 T. Wright, ed., *The Latin Poems Commonly Attributed to Walter Mapes* (London, Camden Society, 1841), p. 223. Cf., e.g., *Inf.* I, 49–60, XIX, 1–117; *Purg.* XX, 73–84; *Par.* XVII, 49–51, XXVII, 40–54, 121–123. *The Vision of William Concerning Piers the Plowman*, ed. W. W. Skeat (2 vols., Oxford, 1886), B Text, Passus II–IV. R. W. Chambers, *Man's Unconquerable Mind* (London, 1939), p. 112.

5 *Tractatus Garsiae Tholetani canonici*, ed. E. Sackur; in MGH, *Libelli de lite imperatorum et pontificum* (3 vols., Hanover and Berlin, 1891–96), II, 425–435.

6 Lehmann, *Parodie*, pp. 54–59.

7 The original is in P. Lehmann, *Parodistische Texte* (München, 1923), p. 6.

8 W. Map, *De nugis curialium*, ed. M. R. James (Oxford, 1914) II, XVII, p. 82.

9 E. Du Méril, *Poésies populaires latines antérieures au douzième siècle* (Paris, 1843), pp. 231–234. A slightly different version is printed in *Lib. de lite*, III, 706–707.

10 F. Raby, *A History of Secular Latin Poetry in the Middle Ages* (2 vols., Oxford, 1934), II, 190.

11 K. Strecker, *Moralisch-satirische Gedichte Walters von Chatillon* (Heidelberg, 1929), pp. 18–30. For other examples of Latin Rome satires cf. Strecker, *Chatillon*, pp. 75–76, 2–15; P. Leyser, *Historia poetarum et poematum medii aevi* (Halle, 1721), p. 484; *Analecta hymnica* (Leipzig, 1886–1922), XXI, 146, 151–52, 143; *Carmina burana*, I, i, 76–83, 87–89; and T. Wright, *Mapes*, pp. 7, 167–170, 229–230.

12 J. Bromyard, *Summa praedicantium* (Venice, 1586), "Advocatus," 21.

13 Estienne de Fougères, *Livre des manières*, ed. J. Kremer (Ausgaben u. Abhandlungen aus dem Gebiete der romanischen Philologie, 39, Marburg, 1887), p. 124.

14 Most of the important literary products of this strife are printed in the three volumes of *MGH, Libelli de lite*.

15 In the bulky literature on the development of papal policy during this period the most succinct and rewarding overview appears to be G. Tellenbach, *Church, State and Christian Society at the Time of the Investiture Contest*, tr. R. Bennett (Oxford, 1940).

16 "The Financial System of the Medieval Papacy," *Quarterly Journal of Economics*, XXXII (1909), 251–252.

17 Strecker, *Chatillon*, pp. 24–25.

18 *Financial Relations*, p. 31.

19 *Papal Revenues*, esp. I, 57–136.

20 A. Gottlob, *Die Servitientaxe im 13. Jahrhundert: eine Studie zur Geschichte des päpstlichen Gebührenwesens* (Stuttgart, 1903), pp. 69–100, places the establishment of the formal tax in the pontificate of Alexander V (1254–1261).

21 *Papal Revenues*, II, 233–34.

22 *Papal Revenues*, II, 234.

23 *Papal Revenues*, II, 234–235.

24 D. Ivo Carnotensis Episcopus, *Epistolae*, 133; in *PL* 162, 141–43. Part of Bishop Ivo's attitude seems to spring from his position in the Investiture Struggle; but John Bromyard's remarks (*Summa praedic.*, "Honor," 14–19) in the mid-14th century are very similar.

25 *Papal Revenues*, I, 87–89. The opening of one of Jacques de Vitry's exempla suggests the common impression of the normal state of a bishop returning from Rome: "Audivi de quodam prelato Anglico, cum a curia Romana exhaustus et sine pecunia rediret . . ." G. Frenken, *Die Exempla des Jacob von Vitry* (München, 1921), p. 140.

26 *Papal Revenues*, II, 238–239.

27 S. Petrus Domiani, *Contra philargyriam et munerum cupiditatem;* in *PL* 145, 536B.

28 *Papal Revenues*, II, 235.

29 *Papal Revenues*, II, 236, 238.

30 For *Regina Pecunia* cf. Horace, *Epistulae*, I, vi, 36–38.

31 John of Salisbury, *Policraticus*, ed. C. C. J. Webb (2 vols., Oxford, 1909), II, 67–73.

Careers, Rank, and Power

6

Gervase of Tilbury

H. G. RICHARDSON

GERVASE OF TILBURY has deserved more consideration than he has received at the hands of English historians. As Reinhold Pauli said of him, he was one with his learned fellow countrymen of the twelfth century, master Thomas Brown, master John of Salisbury and Pope Adrian IV, who sought their fortunes on the continent.[1] He was, in especial, like master Thomas who, earlier than Gervase, entered the service of the king of Sicily.[2] Pauli's examples would not, however, be the choice of everyone who wished to illustrate the cosmopolitan, intellectual society of the twelfth century. Professor Southern views it from a different angle in his recent article in *History*.[3] I myself would emphasize the dominance of the French way of life from Ireland in the West to Syria in the East, a dominance that was not necessarily dependent upon military conquest.

It does not seem to be generally realized that French influences were at work in Ireland long before Henry II landed there in 1171. The congregations of Tiron and Savigny had daughter houses in Ireland in the earlier years of the twelfth century, well before Cistercian houses were planted there under the influence of St. Malachy, the friend and disciple of St. Bernard.[4] When, at the same period, Bishop Gillebert of Limerick, a friend of St. Anselm's, drew up a constitution for the Irish Church, it was obviously based upon his knowledge of ecclesiastical organization in France and perhaps in England.[5] There were Irish monks in the greater Benedictine houses of England after the Conquest, at Canterbury, Saint Albans and Winchester, some of whom became bishops of Irish sees in the late eleventh and early twelfth centuries and were consecrated by Lanfranc and Anselm.[6] I mention these things in order to emphasize that the narrow seas were a means of communication rather than obstacles to travel. So much of Western Europe, so much of the Mediterranean, was, as it were, one vast country, where clerks and knights and merchants passed freely over great distances, however toilsome the roads, however hazardous the sea-passages. There were many difficulties to be overcome, but language seems never to present itself as one. England lay on the margin of this vast country and still further beyond, though within its borders, lay Wales and Ireland and Scotland. It is not perhaps solely on account of their remoteness that the distant provinces made so small a contribution to the general progress of European thought. The greatest intellectual effort in England appears to have expended itself in administration and law which, in their insular guise, were not exportable beyond the British Isles, however superior they may seem to anything the Continent had to offer.

And so, as Mr. Southern indicates, the cathedral schools of Northern France or, at least, the greater of them, had no comparable counterpart in England.[7] But it should be added that they attracted scholars from across the Channel. England, if I may so express it, was within their parish. It is easy to demonstrate this fact. In the account that Boso and his fellow canons from Laon gave of their begging tour through southern England in 1113,[8] they mentioned five former pupils of master Anselm of Laon, 'the fame of whose learning and eloquence was widespread throughout nearly the whole Latin world'.[9] All of the five were of English origin and all, as it so happened, were to become bishops: William of Corbeil, archbishop of Canterbury, 1132–36, Alexander, bishop of Lincoln 1123–48, Algar, bishop of Coutances 1132–51, Nigel, bishop of Ely 1133–69, Robert, bishop of Exeter 1138–55. The canons also mentioned that the sons of Ranulf, the king's chancellor, had been at Laon, not as master Anselm's pupils, but as the pupils of William of Corbeil, who had his lodging in the bishop's house. From this glimpse of the school at Laon in the early twelfth century it is evident that it was not only distinguished but fashionable, for otherwise we should not expect the justiciar of England, Roger of Salisbury, to be sending his nephews, Alexander and Nigel, there or the chancellor to be sending his sons there, presumably to learn their grammar. It is indeed evident that, while there were older students, boys were sent to Laon, as they were later sent to medieval universities, at an age when they would now be still at a preparatory school.[10]

Some explanatory sentences on the school of Laon at this early period are perhaps desirable, but of the subsequent attraction of the schools of Paris there is hardly need to adduce evidence. Schools on the Parisian model sprang up in England in the course of the twelfth century, though not in cathedral cities. Of these we are only beginning to learn a little from the obscure and scattered notices that survive. So recent is our knowledge that of Northampton, which has some claim to be considered a *studium generale* under Henry II, Rashdall and his equally learned editors knew nothing. Of Oxford in the twelfth century they knew something, but we may never recover more than tantalizing glimpses.[11] It is impossible therefore to speak with confidence of these English schools.

They may have drawn a few students from overseas, and in Geoffrey of Vinsauf Northampton did, for a brief while, have one famous master.[12] But, so far as we can tell, neither Northampton nor Oxford had the attraction for masters and students that Bologna and Paris had. They seem to have been insular schools, and it is difficult to suppose that students who had the means to go abroad would be content with them. On the other hand we may fairly call Bologna and Paris international places of learning, if we understand 'nations' in the sense given to that word at these universities in the thirteenth century, groups of students of much the same region and mother tongue. These students could not remain altogether indifferent to political boundaries and political allegiances, but they had no thought that considerations of this kind should debar them from seeking the best teachers wherever they might be or from finding a career in a land other than that of their birth. And it is because the life of Gervase of Tilbury so well exemplifies this type of man, though his was a career out of the ordinary, that it seems worth while to set down what can be told of him.

It may seem strange that the one book of his which has survived, a book that attracted the editorial labours of Leibnitz and was well known to continental scholars, should not have been included in the Rolls Series or, to give it its official title, *Chronicles and Memorials of Great Britain and Ireland during the Middle Ages*. But caprice, as well doubtless as lack of qualified editors, excluded not a few books of greater worth than the minor and (it must be added) indifferently edited works that found a place in that collection. For no evident reason Gervase failed to interest Sir Thomas Hardy. Not only is the account given of him in the *Descriptive Catalogue of Manuscripts relating to the early History of Great Britain* ludicrously misleading, but not a single manuscript of his surviving work, the *Otia Imperialia*, is particularized.[13] It is true that a few extracts from the *Otia* were included as a supplement to the *Chronicon Anglicanum* of Ralf of Coggeshall,[14] but these do not give a just idea of the nature and scope of the book. Two and a half columns are allotted to Gervase in the *Dictionary of National Biography,* but this contribution is not very helpful and it is significant that no use is made of the study by Pauli who traced Gervase's career with some exactitude and catalogued the manuscripts of his book.[15] Pauli's article, in the transactions of the Royal Academy of Sciences of Göttingen, is not easy to come by and, like Leibnitz's edition of the *Otia*,[16] is to be sought by most of us only in great libraries. Rather more accessible are the extracts Pauli edited in the *Monumenta Germaniæ Historica*,[17] and his introduction to them should, at least, save the student from grievous error. Gervase had been noticed at some length, if unsympathetically, fifty years earlier by Petit-Radel in the seventeenth volume of the *Histoire Littéraire de la France:* the summary he furnished of the first two sections of the *Otia* gives a fair idea of their contents,[18] but his patience was exhausted before he came to the third section, which has proved more attractive to later students.[19] There is, however, no informative account of Gervase in English and this is why I am attempting to tell his story here.

Gervase, in truth, tells his own story, but, apart from one anecdote which he himself related to Ralf of Coggeshall, what he tells us has to be extracted with difficulty from his book. Let us begin with some facts about which there can be no uncertainty. He was in the household of Henry II's son, also Henry, the young king as he was called from his coronation in his father's lifetime, for whom he wrote a jest-book, *Liber Facetiarum,* and for whom he planned a larger work which ultimately became the *Otia Imperialia.*[20] Gervase was a fervent admirer of the prince, and the language in which he speaks of him suggests that he was in his service for some years.[21] Elsewhere he tells us that, in the company of Philip, son of Patrick earl of Salisbury, he followed the court of Henry II as he had previously attended the 'schools'.[22] Nor can there be any doubt that these schools were at Bologna, where Gervase taught canon law.[23] Since the young king died on 11 June 1183, we can date approximately the early stages of Gervase's career. He stresses the length of his stay at Bologna, and, if the later regulations for graduation are any guide to the rules in the twelfth century,[24] he could not have incepted in canon law until he had completed at least six years of study in that discipline. We must, of course, allow for years of preliminary studies, but where these were undertaken we are left to conjecture. Since Gervase was in Venice in July 1177, when he witnessed the reconciliation between the pope, Alexander III, and the emperor, Frederick I,[25] he was presumably teaching at Bologna at the time; but he can hardly have stayed there for more than a year or two longer, for we have to account for the years he spent at the courts of Henry II and the young king. In any case he must have passed twelve years or so of his early life in Italy, for he tells us that he was in Rome when Alexander III was there.[26] This was possible only in the brief period, between November 1165 and July 1167,[27] after the pope's sojourn in France and before his expulsion from Rome by the Imperialists: the probable year is 1166. Since Gervase was then, in his own words, a boy, he must have been born in the early 1150s. Indeed, if he had been born as early as 1150, he would hardly have been considered a boy in 1166, for at the age of sixteen, even though he might have been *juvenis,* he would have been reckoned a man.

That Gervase's earliest years were spent in England there is good reason to suppose. There are a number of references to unimportant English places in the third section of his book and he usually gives sufficient particulars to enable the place to be identified. Thus he writes: scio in Anglia, episcopatu Lincolniensi, inter Londonias et Northamptonam, vico quem Aspele vulgus nominat, silvam . . .[28] The place is Aspley Guise in

Bedfordshire. Another passage shows his local knowledge: in regno Anglorum, episcopatu Londoniensi et comitatu Essexie, est castrum Angra nuncupatum quod bone memorie Ricardus de Luci . . . in Anglia quondam iusticiarius construxit.[29] The place is Ongar, where Richard de Luci undoubtedly had a castle, even though he may not have been the first builder. To any boy living on the western side of Essex, where Tilbury and Ongar both are, this would be well known, and it is likely that the story of the judgement of the swans,[30] which he places at Ongar, was one that was told to him at the time. Of course, Gervase may have visited a good many places in England in the train of Henry II and the young king, though much of this time, especially in the latter part, was presumably spent in France. Doubtless also we must allow for occasional visits to England during the long years that Gervase spent abroad, but he says nothing of them and it seems necessary to suppose that most of his knowledge of the country was acquired before he left for Italy.

We can thus account for the first thirty years of Gervase's life. Born about 1152, he was in Rome by 1166 and at Bologna by 1170, in the service of Henry II before 1180, when or soon after he passed into the service of the young king. After the prince's death he passed into the service of Archbishop William of Reims [31] and then into that of King William II of Sicily.[32] That he was high in the royal favour we may judge from his reference to the house at Nola which the king had appointed him as a refuge from the summer heat of Palermo. Here he entertained his friend Philip, Earl Patrick's son, whom chance had brought to Italy.[33] Of the manner in which Gervase served King William we learn nothing. That he was still in the royal service in June 1189 we may be certain, for he was then in Salerno,[34] but the king's death in November of that year seems to have led to his departure from Italy. Another king had arisen, Tancred, who had no love for Englishmen or Normans and would have been no friend of Gervase. For Gervase's loyalty was commanded by the widowed queen Joan, daughter of Henry II,[35] whom Tancred regarded with aversion and was minded to cheat over her dower. But, in any case, since Gervase makes no reference to Richard I's stay in Sicily in 1190 and the dramatic happenings then,[36] we may be reasonably sure that he was not present. We next find him at Arles, where he had married a kinswoman of the archbishop, Humbert.[37] He tells us of his friendship with King Alphonse II of Aragon, who was his guest in the palace that he had acquired with his wife.[38] Since Alphonse died in April 1196, we have another firm date for this stage of Gervase's career. His marriage seems to have taken place in 1190, and he was certainly married not much later.[39] Well-to-do and a member of the highest circles in Arles, it is not surprising that Otto IV, to whom he was distantly related,[40] should make him marshal of the kingdom of Arles.[41] The post was, in principle, a military one and Gervase was not trained in arms. But the duties seem to have been honorific, for Otto exerted little authority in the kingdom,[42] and such duties as Gervase assumed he discharged, as he was later to say he did, with his ready tongue.[43] Of the year in which he received the appointment we have no indication beyond the fact that Otto was crowned king of the Romans on 12 July 1198. Gervase appears to have been present in his official capacity on the occasion of Otto's coronation as emperor on 4 October 1209 at Rome.[44]

Gervase made Arles his home for many years. He calls the Mediterranean *mare nostrum* [45] and his familiarity with what we now call Provence is evident from numerous passages in his book,[46] much of which must have been written at this period.[47] The book was, however, still in progress in 1215, for Gervase refers to William the Lion as dead,[48] and William did not die until 4 December 1214. But it is possible that by then Gervase had left Arles. Otto seems never to have visited the kindom and if, as Gervase implies in many places, he was on terms of familiarity with the emperor, we must suppose that he followed the imperial court. Before the book was finished, Otto's fortunes had changed very much for the worse. The battle of Bouvines, fought on 27 July 1214, had ended in irreparable disaster for his cause. He died on 19 May 1218, and there is thus a very short space of years in which the book could have been brought to completion and presented to him, emperor no longer except in name. It is probable, therefore, that Gervase clung to his imperial master until the end. When that came he was an ageing and disappointed man. His wife, we must suppose, was dead and, like many another of his contemporaries, he seems to have ended his days in a religious house. Ralf of Coggeshall relates a story he had heard from Gervase 'cum canonicus esset'.[49] This language suggests that, when Ralf was writing, Gervase was already dead, and Ralf himself appears to have died by 1228.[50] We can get no nearer than that to the date and circumstances of Gervase's death.

Perhaps a note of explanation is called for at this point. I have suggested that Gervase entered a house of regular canons. The words used by Ralf of Coggeshall might perhaps be interpreted as meaning that he became a secular canon, but this seems quite unlikely in view of his age. There was no lack of houses of regular canons in Essex that might have received him: Colchester, St. Osyth's, Waltham and seven or eight others.[51] We can but speculate, though it is tempting to believe that he returned to the countryside where he had passed his childhood and where he was most likely to meet Ralf of Coggeshall.

By the standards of his day Gervase was a man of learning. The first and second sections of his book are obvious compilations. In the first his chief reliance is upon the *Historia Scholastica* of Peter Comestor, whom, however, he does not mention by name. Elsewhere he freely cites, among others, doubtless largely at second-hand, Lucretius, Vergil, Horace, Ovid, Lucan, Claudian, Sallust, Pliny, Orosius, Gildas, Bede, Paul the

Deacon.[52] Among later authors he borrows from Freculf of Lisieux, Hugh of Fleury, the pseudo-Turpin, Geoffrey of Monmouth.[53] His academic career had made him familiar with Gratian's *Decretum* [54] as well as imperial laws and constitution.[55] He professes acquaintance with the ancient registers of the Empire [56] and he was even led to explore the papal archives [57] in order to ascertain the names of the ecclesiastical provinces and episcopal sees of England, France, Germany and Poland. His third section is more largely the result of his own enquiries and gossip. Or should we say that he shows himself a collector of folk-lore? He is one of the primary authorities for the medieval legends of Vergil the sorcerer.[58] The impression left is that over a long life he had kept what a later age would have called a commonplace book, the repository of the fruits of his curiosity and reading. It is not surprising that the *Otia* was popular among the learned of the thirteenth and fourteenth centuries and that it was twice translated into French.[59]

To give an intelligible account of the book in a brief space is difficult; but one must do one's best or leave the story half-told. Gervase begins with the Creation, the process of which he describes in nine chapters. Then, after a description of the four monarchies of Adam, Noah, Alexander of Macedon and Augustus Cæsar, he passes to geography, beginning with the four rivers that flow from Paradise: the Ganges, the Nile, the Tigris and the Euphrates. Next, after explaining the formation of clouds and rain, he describes the sea and incidentally gives a receipt for rendering sea-water potable. He then returns to Paradise, original sin and the story of Adam, discussing incidentally the functions of *incubi*, fauns and satyrs. Lastly four chapters, traversing briefly, though with divagations, the early history of mankind up to the Deluge, bring the first section to an end. The second section begins with a survey of the post-Diluvian world, starting with Asia and passing to Europe, Africa and the islands of the Mediterranean. Geography gives way to history and at chapter nineteen Gervase gets on firmer ground with lists of emperors and kings of France from Charlemagne to Otto IV and Philip Augustus. Chapter twenty is devoted to the kings of England down to John, of whom he speaks in ambiguous terms. The two final chapters of this section return to ancient history and include a tract on the Holy Land.[60] The third section contains 'marvels of every province, not every marvel, but some from each province'.[61] There is no observable order in the 129 chapters, many of which are no more than jottings. It looks as though the author, in some hurry to present his book to the emperor, did not expand his notes as he had intended: he certainly did not methodize them, though some chapters on the same theme, those, for instance, on the legendary Vergil, are grouped together.

It is only by presenting examples that any clear idea can be given of this section of the book. It must suffice to translate one chapter (omitting the introductory sentences) which portrays an English archæologist excavating in Italy in the twelfth century.[62] This is a characteristic piece of Gervase's writing when he is not fettered by authority.

In the time of King Roger of Sicily there came a certain master of English origin asking the king of his bounty to make him a gift. Now the king, who was distinguished alike by birth and breeding, thought that some substantial favour would be demanded of him and he replied: 'Ask whatever gift you wish, and I will give it to you'. But the petitioner, a man of great learning, skilled and subtle in both the trivium and the quadrivium, experienced in physics and eminent in astronomy, told the king that he did not seek temporal rewards but rather what men might deem worthless, namely Vergil's bones, wherever they might be found within the confines of his kingdom. The king granted his request and, armed with a royal warrant, the master came to Naples, where Vergil had displayed his genius in many ways. After he had produced his warrant, the people, though ignorant of the place of sepulture, accorded their obedience and readily promised what, to the best of their belief, was an impossibility. In the end, however, the master, guided in the right direction by his art, located the bones within a tomb in the mountainside, although no sign of an opening could be discerned. The spot was excavated and after prolonged labour a tomb was exposed wherein was found the body of Vergil, not yet dissolved, and at his head a book. In this book the notary art was inscribed together with other diagrams relating to his science.[63] After the dust and bones had been removed, the book was taken by the master. Then, however, the people of Naples remembered the particular affection that Vergil had for their city and feared lest it should be exposed to harm if the bones were taken away. They decided, therefore, to disregard the king's mandate rather than by obedience to be the cause of the destruction of the town. Vergil, it was thought, had himself placed the tomb in the bowels of the mountain, opining that the removal of his bones would bring his artifices to naught. The master of the knights,[64] therefore, with a crowd of citizens, gathered the bones together again and, placing them in a leather bag, took them to a castle surrounded by the sea on the borders of the city, where they are shown through an iron grille to those wishing to see them.

When the master was asked what he had intended to do with the bones, he replied that, by his incantations, he would have so contrived that in answer to his questions the bones would have revealed to him the whole of Vergil's art and that he would have been satisfied if they had been given to him in their entirety for the space of forty days. Taking therefore, only the book with him, the master departed. We have ourselves seen extracts from this very book, made by the venerable cardinal John of Naples in the time of Pope Alexander, and by conducting experiments we have proved their truth.

We may think Gervase unduly credulous, but we have no reason to question his good faith. John of Naples was a very real person, cardinal of St. Anastasia from 1159 to 1179, a man whom Gervase may well have met, as he seems to imply, before he left Bologna. The castle, known later as the Castel dell' uovo, was also very real.[65] And though the story, as Geoffrey presents it, must be fabulous, it has been suggested that the English master was also a very real person, Adelard of Bath, the most distinguished mathematician of the early twelfth century.[66]

To summarize Gervase is perhaps to pillory him, and it is easy to write his book down as a farrago of fables, myths and popular traditions.[67] But he shared his tastes and beliefs with such men as William of Malmesbury, Walter Map, Alexander Neckham, Ralf de Diceto, Ralf of Coggeshall, to name only English writers who come readily to mind. The age of scepticism was not yet. Gervase's acceptance of the incredible did not obstruct his view of the world around him. 'Gervase,' it has been said, 'perhaps of all Anglo-Norman contemporaries re-creates most vividly and intimately the incidents of everyday life and the friendliness and hospitality of the south.' [68] He was a man of the world and a political realist. The society in which he moved was that of the high-born in the kingdoms of the West. In his palace at Arles he had entertained not only the king of Aragon, but also, it would seem, Eleanor of Aquitaine on her journey back from Sicily in 1191.[69] Without intention he conveys to us the atmosphere of the great family of Western European rulers, of which he was, in some sort, a member. Since he is writing for the emperor's ear, it is Otto's connections that he constantly stresses. When he mentions Henry II he adds more than once that he was Otto's grandfather [70] and he likewise qualifies the young king as Otto's uncle.[71] When Gervase mentions William II of Sicily, he recalls that he married Otto's aunt,[72] and similarly, when mentioning Earl Patrick of Salisbury, he reminds Otto that the earl's granddaughter had married Otto's uncle, the illegitimate William de Longespée.[73] These are reminders we need more than Otto, for they help to explain some aspects of twelfth-century politics, as they help to explain Gervase's own attitude. He was too closely bound to the emperor for any breath of suspicion to attach to his loyalty, but, canonist as he is, he is loyal also to the pope. His book opens with a dissertation upon the *sacerdotium* and the *regnum,* and he seeks to define the sphere of each. God is the author of both and the protector of both. Neither is greater than the other, nor should one ask which is superior but which of the two powers is the more faithful in discharging its duty. The argument cannot, however, be summarized in a few sentences and, truth to tell, it is too rhetorical to be crystal clear.[74] There is, however, no mistaking the significance of Gervase's counsel to Otto that he should seek to assert his authority in Burgundy rather than to pursue wider ambitions. The wider his territories, the less will his *imperium* be.[75] But this advice, though it seems to have been written some years earlier was, in the event, addressed to a monarch who had fallen from his high estate in his contest with the papacy. So Gervase reminds Otto that among men there is nothing but change and vicissitude. Anon the spirit rejoices in felicity; anon it meditates in sorrow. There is always movement, rarely tranquillity. He draws a parallel between the emperor and Saul, whose vexation was tempered by the sound of David's harp, and he presents his book as a more fitting distraction than the tales of jesters and minstrels.[76]

From Gervase's choice of words [77] it must be supposed that he did not imagine that the emperor, though he is frequently addressed throughout the book, would read it, but that it would be read to him. This does not mean that Otto was unable to read Latin but that, great man that he was, he would employ clerks to read to him, just as he would employ clerks to write his letters, though he himself could write in case of need. We must remember that silent reading was not commonly practised in the Middle Ages and that, if Otto had read the book, he would have read it aloud and, moreover, in the presence of others, for he would be rarely alone. We must picture the emperor then, in his hours of inactivity, surrounded by those few courtiers who remained faithful to him, listening to a clerk reading from Gervase's book, chiefly perhaps the marvels, for some of the other matter was heavy going. In reading the book ourselves we learn what was fashionable entertainment at the period, at least when that entertainment was decorous, for there were grosser forms of entertainment which Gervase despised.

So much for Gervase's book; but his story would not be complete if there were not added something he did not write but told to Ralf of Coggeshall.[78] The tale is too long to be told fully here, and to tell it briefly is to rob it of the marvellous element which, if now a weariness, then gave it a savour. The bare facts are horrifying enough. The year is 1183 or 1184 and Gervase is in the service of the archbishop of Reims. Spying a girl alone in a vineyard, Gervase went up to her and sought to seduce her; but she replied: 'It is not God's will that I should be your lover or that of any man, for if I should lose my virginity and my flesh should once be corrupted, without doubt I should be consigned irredeemably to everlasting damnation.' When he heard this, Gervase at once perceived that she belonged to that most impious sect, the Publicans,[79] and, while he was trying to confute her, Archbishop William came up with his company. Discovering what the argument was about, the archbishop ordered the girl to be arrested and taken to Reims. She was put on trial and, refusing to recant, was condemned to the stake. She died with the constancy of a Christian martyr, neither sighing nor weeping nor lamenting. That this tale was in the least shameful did not cross the mind of Gervase or of his interlocutor, for the sins of the flesh were venial, while the sin of heresy was mortal in this world and the next. The brightly coloured tapestry of the Middle Ages has its reverse, and the reverse is not beautiful to behold.

Such then is the story of Gervase of Tilbury. It is one to be remembered by all students of Angevin England. There were other subjects of the English king who passed from court to court,[80] others who studied and taught for a time at Bologna. All these men had something in common and their careers, though highly personal, illustrate an important aspect of the society of the twelfth century. Gervase's own career must, however, have been exceptional in that, although in minor orders and a canonist, he led such a life as an unusually well educated layman might have led. We may contrast him with another English canonist who taught at Bologna, Richard de Morins, who made a great name for himself in the university as Richard the Englishman. He also became a regular canon, but, on abandoning the academic life, he had no secular career. He entered religion in his prime and he ruled Dunstable Priory for nearly forty years. Like Gervase he was an author and he had to his credit both a number of legal works and a chronicle which, though not a work of art, is above the level of the minor monastic annals of the thirteenth century.[81] Richard, as a jurist, has his importance, but Gervase is, in his fashion, a humanist and has a wider appeal. Why that should be I have endeavoured to suggest. It is regrettable that few English medievalists should know scarcely more of Gervase than that he was not the author of the *Dialogus de Scaccario*.[82] It is regrettable too that, apart from Pauli's extracts, published three quarters of a century ago, there should be no critical edition of Gervase's writings. It would be fitting if an English scholar were to make the *Otia Imperialia* easily accessible to historians.

NOTES

[1] *Nachrichten von der k. Gesellschaft der Wissenkunden zu Göttingen*, 1882, p. 312. Pauli's reference to John of Salisbury is, in fact, mistaken. He held the view, current until recently, that John was in the service of Eugenius III, but this has been shown to be untenable: see the Introduction by C. N. L. Brooke to *The Letters of John of Salisbury*, i. xvi, xxiv, and A. Saltman, *Theobald, Archbishop of Canterbury*, pp. 169–74.

[2] There is a notice of him in the *Dictionary of National Biography*: see also C. H. Haskins in *English Historical Review*, xxvi. 438–43.

[3] *History*, xlv. 201–16.

[4] For details I may refer to my article "Some Norman Monastic Foundations in Ireland," in *Medieval Studies presented to Aubrey Gwynne*, pp. 35–40.

[5] *De statu/Ecclesiæ/*in Migne, *Patrologia Latina*, clix. 905–1004. Gillebert had known Anselm in Normandy and continued in correspondence with him after he became archbishop.

[6] Donat O'Haingly to Dublin, 1085; Samuel O'Haingly to Dublin, 1096; Malchus to Waterford, 1098 (Acts of Lanfranc in *A.S. Chronicles* (ed. Plummer), i. 290; Eadmer, *Historia Novorum*, pp. 73, 77).

[7] *History*, xlv. 202–4.

[8] Herman, *De miraculis S. Marie Laudenensis*, in Migne, *Patrologia Latina*, clvi. 961 sqq., lib. ii, cc. 6, 12, 13, 15. The original narrative has been interpolated by Herman: see E. Faral, *La légende arthurienne*, i. 225–33; and J. S. P. Tatlock in *Speculum*, viii. 454–65. These interpolations have given rise to different views as to the date of the journey. R. L. Poole's argument for a date after 1123 overlooks serious difficulties (*Exchequer in the Twelfth Century*, p. 55). In any case it falls to the ground if Guibert of Nogent, who describes the same journey, was writing, as is

believed, not later than 1117 (Guibert de Nogent, *Histoire de sa vie* (ed. Bourgin), pp. xlviii–xlix).

9 Vir sapientissimus magister Anselmus, tunc temporis ecclesie nostre canonicus et decanus, per totum pene orbem latinum sciencie et eloquencie sue fama notissimus (Herman, lib. i, c. i).

10 Nigel, although a pupil of master Anselm's, could not have been much above twelve years of age.

11 For Rashdall's knowledge of the English schools in the twelfth century see his *Universities of Europe in the Middle Ages* (ed. Powicke and Emden), iii. 9–33. For the study of Roman and canon law see now Kuttner and Rathbone in *Traditio*, vii. 321–7.

12 For the schools at Northampton see *English Historical Review*, lvi. 595–605. Of Geoffrey's teaching at Northampton we know little beyond the fact. But Matthew, the precentor of Rievaulx, a minor but interesting poet of the early thirteenth century, who modelled himself upon Geoffrey (*Revue Benedictine*, lii. 15–84), may have sat under him. There is some ground for believing that Vacarius taught at Northampton as well as at Oxford (*Traditio*, vii. 322): if so, this is a second eminent master.

13 *Descriptive Catalogue*, iii. 25–7.

14 Ed. Joseph Stevenson, 1875. The extracts, not in the order of the book and lacking any reference to the chapter divisions, are scattered over pp. xxix–xxxii and 419–449. The text is superior to that of Leibnitz.

15 *Nachrichten, ut supra*, pp. 312–32. On some points Pauli had been anticipated by E. Winkelmann, *Philipp von Schwaben und Otto IV von Braunschweig* (1878), ii. 502–3.

16 *Scriptores Rerum Brunsvicensium* (1707), i. 881–1004: corrections and additions in vol. ii. (1710) 751–84.

17 *Scriptores* (1885) xxvii. 359–94.

18 *Histoire Littéraire* (1832), xvii. 82–109. Louis Charles François Petit-Radel, 1756–1836, was a distinguished archæologist in his time and in charge of the Mazarine Library.

19 E.g. F. Liebrecht, *Des Gervasius von Tilbury Otia Imperialia* (1856), and D. Comparetti, as to whom see later.

20 *M.G.H. Scriptores*, xxvii. 366, 370, 375. Subsequent references to this edition are cited as 'Pauli'.

21 Coggeshall, *Chronicon Anglicanum*, pp. 447–8, and references in preceding note.

22 Pauli, p. 385: diutina in scolis et curia . . . regis vetustioris Anglie Henrici . . . commansione firmata.

23 *Ibid.*: in hospicio venerabilis auditoris mei in iure canonico apud Bononiam Iohannis Pinatelli Neapolitani archidiaconi. It is because he had been a doctor at Bologna that Ralf of Coggeshall called him 'magister Gervasius' (p. 122).

24 Rashdall, *op. cit.*, i. 220–1.

25 Pauli, p. 380.

26 *Ibid.*, p. 392: Sane temporibus nostris sub papa Alexandro III, dum puer eram, inventa et Rome . . .

27 The pope's itinerary can be deduced from Jaffé-Loewenfeld, *Regesta*, ii. 195–205.

28 Pauli, pp. 383–4.

29 Leibnitz, i. 993.

30 The unfaithful swan is condemned to death. This *exemplum* is known in more than one form.

31 Coggeshall, p. 122. W. Hunt in *D.N.B.* makes the good point that, since the archbishop is described as persecuting Albigensian heretics, this helps to fix the date, for in the Annals of Anchin his proceedings are described at some length *s.a:* 1183 (*Historiens de la France*, xviii. 536).

32 Pauli, p. 385.

33 *Ibid.*

34 *Ibid.* A precise date is not given, but 'anno quo fuit Acon obsessa, circa imminens sancti Iohannis Baptiste festum'.

35 See his references to her (Pauli, pp. 381, 383).

36 For a detailed account of the relations between Tancred, Joan and Richard see K. Norgate, *Richard the Lion Heart*, pp. 124–38.

37 Pauli, pp. 390–1.

38 *Ibid.*, pp. 389, 391.

39 As stated below, he seems to have entertained Eleanor of Aquitaine at Arles in 1191. This would seem to fix the date of his marriage in the year 1190, assuming that he left Sicily after the death of William II, unless—an unlikely alternative—he had married when he was in the king's service. How he made the acquaintance of his wife is nowhere indicated. What seems evident is that he settled at Arles because of his marriage.

40 Pauli, p. 385.

41 *Ibid.*, pp. 363, 366, 393.

42 Fournier, *Le royaume d'Arles*, pp. 95–7, where Otto's authority is minimized. That Otto exerted some authority seems clear, however, from Gervase's statement that he had made good his claim to his wife's inheritance 'per sententiam curie imperialis' (Pauli, p. 391).

43 Pauli, p. 366; et quod ex officio marescalcie sub debito armorum ministerio exequi teneor, acute lingue gladio ducam in ministerio. He is referring to his book.

44 *Ibid.*, p. 382: cum nuper Rome essem. That he was at Otto's coronation was first suggested by Winkelmann, *Philipp von Schwaben und Otto IV*, ii. 502.

45 *Ibid.*, p. 373; Leibnitz, i. 981.

46 He has a vivid description of the people (Pauli, p. 376) and he evidently knows the places he mentions: see the identifications by Pauli, pp. 384–93.

47 It would seem impossible, for example, that the twelfth chapter of Decisio II (Pauli, pp. 376–7) should have been written very long after Otto's coronation: in it Gervase urges the emperor to exercise his authority in the kingdom of Arles.

48 Pauli, p. 390.

49 Coggeshall, p. 122.

50 He intended to continue his chronicle to 11 Henry III (p. 163), though the existing text does not go beyond 1223.

51 Berden, Blackmore, Latton, Leighs, Little Dunmow, Thoby, Thremhall: these were all Augustinian, mostly quite small houses. There was also a house of Premonstratensian canons, Beeleigh.

52 For a long list of authors mentioned by Gervase see Liebrecht, *Des Gervasius von Tilbury Otia Imperialia*, pp. xi, xii.

53 Pauli, pp. 360–1.

54 *Ibid.*, pp. 364, 367, 387–8; Leibnitz, i. 973.

55 *Ibid.*, p. 379.

56 *Ibid.*, p. 376; particulars of the provinces of the kingdom of Arles are to be found 'in antiquissimis imperii registris'.

57 Leibnitz, i. 956: et Romane ecclesie registrum cuius de verbo ad verbum habuimus; Leibnitz, ii. 760: ut ex archivis domini Pape collegi (*or* potest colligi), *Cf.* Pauli, p. 372: Ex archivis domini pape.

58 D. Comparetti, *Virgilio nel medio evo* (1896), ii. 27–49, 187–91. There is an English translation (1895) of an earlier edition (1872).

59 Pauli, p. 361.

60 Based upon Theodosius, *De situ Terræ Sanctæ*, as Gervase indicates, but from a corrupt version: see the text in *Itinera Hierosolymitana*, ed. P. Geyer (1898). Much is super-added from a source I have not identified. Leibnitz's text is here particularly unsatisfactory.

61 Incipit tercia decisio continens mirabilia uniuscuiusque provincie, non omnia, sed ex omnibus aliqua.

62 Pauli, pp. 392–3. An Italian translation is given by Comparetti, *op. cit.*, ii. 45–7. Liebrecht has notes on this chapter (*op. cit.*, pp. 159–61).

63 Ars notoria . . . cum aliis studii eius caracteribus. Apparently a cabalistic work of some kind is intended. *Cf. Ars Notoria: the Notory Art of Solomon showing the cabalistic key of magical operations* . . . by Robert Turner, 1657: this purports to

be a translation from Apollonius of Tyana. Though the description by Erasmus in his colloquy *Ars Notoria* is not to be taken too seriously, it may be cited as giving a notion of what a book on the art was like: 'Quid continebat liber? Varias animantium formas, draconum, leonum, leopardorum, variosque circulos et in his descriptas voces, partim Graecas, partim Latinas, partim Hebraicas, aliasque barbaricarum linguarum.' For a similar book, but of necromancy, in 1331, see Sayles, *Select Cases in the Court of King's Bench*, v. 54.

64 Magister militum. Comparetti translates: Il duca dei napoletani. The passage may be corrupt.

65 *Cf.* Comparetti, *op. cit.*, ii. 40.

66 E. Jamison, *The Sicilian Norman Kingdom in the mind of Anglo-Norman Contemporaries* (Annual Italian Lecture of the British Academy, 1938), p. 40. For Adelard see C. H. Haskins, *Studies in the History of Medieval Science* (1927), pp. 20–42, and the extended study by F. Bliemetzrieder, *Adelhard von Bath* (1935).

67 *Cf.* Pauli, p. 361.

68 Jamison, *op. cit.*, pp. 40–1.

69 Pauli, p. 391: In pallacio nostro . . . in presentia pie memorie Ildefonsi illustris regis quondam Aragonensis et socrus vestre . . . The latter must be either Irene, mother of Otto's wife Beatrice, or Eleanor. Pauli rejects the former as hardly possible and with good reason. Irene could not, in any case, be called 'socrus vestra' before 1208, when Otto was betrothed to Beatrice, and probably not before 1212, when the marriage was celebrated. But the incident took place before Alphonse's death in 1196, and the only person who could be described as 'socrus vestra' then was Eleanor, Otto's grandmother. The only probable occasion for Eleanor's visit to Arles was either on her way to Sicily with Berengaria early in January 1191 via Mont-Genèvre and Milan or on her return journey via Rome (Easter 1191) and thence to Normandy. But if it were on her outward journey, we should expect Berengaria to have been mentioned. *Cf.* Landon, *Itinerary of Richard I*, pp. 45, 48, 192, and *English Historical Review*, lxxiv. 201.

70 Pauli, pp. 385, 390, 392.

71 *Ibid.*, pp. 366, 375.

72 *Ibid.*, p. 381.

73 *Ibid.*, pp. 383, 385.

74 *Ibid.*, pp. 363–5.

75 Pauli, p. 376: Unde est quod tibi dico, princeps sacratissime et domine, quod sacius esset, imperium minui in dimensione terrarum . . .

76 *Ibid.*, p. 366.

77 '. . . dignum duxi aliquid auribus vestris ingerere quo humana opertetur recuperacio'.

78 *Chronicon Anglicanum*, pp. 121–4.

79 One of the names given to the Albigensian heretics.

80 For the interchange between England and Sicily see C. H. Haskins in *English Historical Review*, xxvi. 437–43, where, however, most space is devoted to Thomas Brown. Miss Jamison's paper, noted above, is a useful supplement.

81 Russell, *Dictionary of Writers of Thirteenth-Century England*, pp. 111–13; Kuttner and Rathbone in *Traditio*, vii. 329–39; *Annales Monastici*, iii. 3–158 (*cf.* pp. x–xi).

82 Owing to a mistaken attribution in some manuscripts, Gervase was long credited with the authorship of the *Dialogus*. That this was impossible was demonstrated by Thomas Madox, *History of the Exchequer*, ii. 338–44. The reiteration of Madox's conclusion has brought this fact about Gervase, but little else, to the notice of students.

7

The Laicization of French
and English Society
in the Thirteenth Century

J. R. STRAYER

STUDENTS OF MEDIAEVAL SOCIETY have long been aware of a sharp change in attitudes and values which took place in the thirteenth century. During that period, while Europe remained sincerely and completely Catholic, the church lost much of its influence. Though it perfected its organization and carried on its religious activities with great energy, the standards which it had set for secular activities were increasingly disregarded. The forces released by the great revival of civilization in the twelfth century could no longer be controlled by the church. They broke out of the old channels and either found new courses for themselves or dissipated their energy in the swamps and backwaters of uncoördinated endeavor. This secularization of European society is apparent in every field of human activity, in art and literature as well as in politics and economics. But while the fact of secularization is undisputed, the reasons for this great change in European opinion and the way in which the change was brought about are not clear. It is a problem which is well worth studying, not only because it is the key to much of the later history of the middle ages, but also because it is an interesting example of the ways in which public opinion are changed.

This paper is an attempt to study one aspect of secularization, the laicization of French and English society in the thirteenth century. Laicization may be defined as the development of a society in which primary allegiance is given to lay governments, in which final decisions regarding social objectives are made by lay governments, in which the church is merely a private society with no public powers or duties. When society has been laicized leadership has passed from the church to the state. In the modern period this assumption of leadership by the state is usually manifested in attempts to control social services, such as education, to regulate family relationships, and to confiscate all, or part of the church's property. These particular manifestations of the idea of laicization should not be confused with the idea itself. There was no demand for government regulation of marriage and divorce in the thirteenth century and very little protest against church control of education. There were efforts to limit the church's acquisition of new property, but only a few fanatics advocated confiscation of what the church already possessed. Yet during the thirteenth century leadership passed from the church to lay governments, and when the test came under Boniface viii it was apparent that lay rulers, rather than the pope, could count on the primary allegiance of the people.

Laicization is the political aspect of secularization. As such, it cannot be wholly explained by purely economic factors. I am quite willing to accept the conventional view that the economic changes of the twelfth and thirteenth centuries made society more worldly, but worldliness is not the same thing as laicization. One is negative, the other positive. Worldliness made the leadership of the church less effective but it did not necessarily create a new leadership to supplant that of the church. Gothic art, for example, did not express religious ideas as well in 1300 as it did in 1200, yet it was still an art dominated by the church. Society was more worldly everywhere in 1300 than in 1200, yet the church did not lose political power to the same extent everywhere. Germany was fully as worldly as England, yet England was far more independent of the papacy. It took strong lay governments to challenge the leadership of the church, and economic change by itself does not explain the development of such governments. For example, throughout Europe the new economic forces were concentrated in the towns, but outside of Italy the towns were not the dominant factor in creating the new leadership. In England and France the royal officials who were most active in pursuing the policy of laicization were not exclusively, or even primarily, bourgeois. In short, while economic changes created an atmosphere in which it was easier for lay governments to assume leadership, they did not ensure the creation of lay governments which could make the most of the opportunity.

A discussion of laicization really should be prefaced by a discussion of the way in which the church had obtained the leadership of society. For the church's leadership was not unquestioned in the earliest centuries of the middle ages. It may even be argued that the complete predominance of the church was attained only as a result of the great revival of civilization which began in the latter part of the eleventh century. Limitations of space forbid the discussion of this problem; at least we can assume that in the twelfth century the church's control of society reached its highest point. Disregarding the endless variations of a pattern which was everywhere fundamentally the same, we can say that political units of the twelfth century fell into three classes. First, there were the local units, the feudal baronies and the towns. Then there were the intermediate units, the kingdoms, and the great feudal states which were practically independent. Finally there was the great unit of Christendom, headed nominally by the emperor and the pope, but which, as an effective political force, was almost wholly controlled by the pope. All men were subject to at least three governments, which represented these three types of political organization. No government had a monopoly of power, each had its own work to do and each was supposed to give the other governments a free hand to do their work. In practice there were endless quarrels, especially among the local and intermediate units, but for a long time these quarrels led to no decisive changes. This was a situation which, from a political point of view, was wholly favorable to the church. Loyalty to lay governments was divided between the local and intermediate units. In many cases the greater loyalty was to the small local unit, for it was the local unit which controlled economic and social status. Far more important than this divided allegiance to lay governments was the loyalty to the great undivided unit of Christendom. The scale of allegiance of most men would have gone something like this: I am first of all a Christian, second a Burgundian, and only third a Frenchman. The emphasis on Christianity as the most important bond between men meant that there was a real European patriotism, expressed in the armies of the Crusade. It means that there was such a thing as European citizenship or nationality, shown by the fact that a well-trained clerk or knight could find employment anywhere in Christendom, regardless of his origin. And the pope controlled the citizens of Europe and through this control he could exercise decisive influence on all aspects of European society.

From a political point of view this situation was satisfactory to the church. From the point of view of morality there was less reason for complacency. The division of responsibility between governments meant that none of them did their work very well. The quarrels between lay governments created a chronic state of warfare. This was intolerable to a church which had been preaching the ideals of peace and justice for centuries. The church was bound to support, or at least to look favorably on any reforms which would make lay governments more capable of enforcing peace and dispensing justice. Here the contrast between political and economic change is most apparent. From the very beginning the church was suspicious of the increase in business activities, and did nothing to aid it. On the other hand the church wanted more efficient lay governments, and was of great assistance in the development of such governments. Yet stronger lay governments proved to be at least as dangerous to the church as the increase in trade and the growth of urban settlements.

Efficient lay governments were dangerous to the church because they could become efficient only by obtaining a practical monopoly of political power in the districts which they controlled. Then the mere exercise of this power, even without a deliberate plan, would tend to transfer primary allegiance from the church to the state. Finally, as lay officials became aware of what was happening they could make deliberate efforts to secure the allegiance of the people. These three tendencies led to the laicization of society.

During the latter part of the twelfth and the first half of the thirteenth centuries the old mediaeval hierarchy of governments broke down in many regions. The old division of responsibility and power ended. In each region affected by these changes one government became dominant, and gained control of political activities. The dominant government was not always that of a king—in Italy, for example, it was that of the town—but whether king, count, or commune came out on top the result was the same. Only one government was left which was strong enough to inspire loyalty.

The monopoly of power secured by the dominant government was, of course, not complete. It was a *de facto* monopoly, which would not meet the tests of later political theorists any more than our present economic monopolies meet the tests of the lawyer or the economist. The political monopolies of the thirteenth century worked very much as our economic monopolies work today. Other units were tolerated, and were allowed a certain share of the business of government, as long as they recognized that they held this share only by grace of the dominant power. This is the policy of Edward I in the *Quo Warranto* proceedings, and of Philip the Fair in his *pariages* with the semi-independent feudal lords of southern France.[2] Only admit that you hold your power from us, that you exercise it subject to our correction, and we will let you retain a large degree of jurisdiction. It was a policy which could be applied to the church fully as much as it was applied to competing lay governments. A direct attack on all ecclesiastical jurisdiction would have been futile and dangerous. Minor officials who were tactless enough to make such attacks were always disavowed by their superiors. The inner circle of royal advisers wanted to weaken the church courts, but they knew that a head-on collision of authorities was not the best way of securing this result. They never denied that the church courts should have a certain amount of power. But they were going to define that power; ecclesiastical courts were to retain only the jurisdiction recognized by the royal council. The first example of this policy is found in the reign of Henry II of England, and while his attempt at definition was not completely successful, the precedent was not forgotten. By the end of the thirteenth century royal governments in both France and England were regularly defining the powers of church courts. The excesses of minor officials were a useful weapon in establishing this power of the central government. When the church was annoyed by such officials its only recourse was to beg the royal government to define and defend ecclesiastical jurisdictions.[3] As Professor Graves has shown, this is the story behind *Circumspecte Agatis* in England.[4] In France, even so powerful a prelate as the bishop of Toulouse had to seek the intervention of the royal council almost every year in order to preserve the most elementary rights.[5] The effects of this policy on public opinion are obvious. If the church's rights of government were dependent on the good will of lay rulers, if the church could maintain its jurisdiction only through the aid of the state, lay governments must be more powerful and important than the church.

Then, as certain governments obtained a *de facto* monopoly of political power they began to do more work. Their courts met more frequently, they heard more cases, they welcomed appeals from subordinate jurisdictions. These governments began to tax and to legislate, even though taxation was at first considered little better than robbery and legislation was felt to be sacrilegious tinkering with the sacred and unchangeable law. In order to perform this increased amount of work they multiplied the number of their officials. All this meant that they had more contacts with the mass of the people, that they touched at some point on the life of every man. No one could be ignorant of the fact that he was subject to one of these dominant governments. No one could fail to realize that the activities of his government were important, perhaps more important than the activities of the church. This sense of the increasing importance of lay governments was not the same thing as loyalty to those governments, but the first sentiment could very easily lead to the second. Men respect what is powerful and they can easily become loyal to what they respect.

The multiplication of the number of lay officials is one of the most striking phenomena of the thirteenth century. In every country the conservatives protested again and again that there were too many officials, and in every country the number of officials went right on increasing in spite of the protests. This increase had important effects on public opinion. It was not only that officials, with their friends and families, formed a large group which would support any action of the government. More important was the fact that every official, consciously or unconsciously, was a propagandist for his government. He had to spread the government's explanation of its policies; he had to enforce decisions which showed the government's power. Many officials, especially those of lower rank who were in direct contact with the people, were openly anticlerical. The fact that such men could brutally disregard the church's rights and still keep their positions must have convinced many people that lay governments were going to be supreme. Finally, with the steady increase in the number of government jobs a new career was opened up for able men of all classes. The church could no longer count on securing the services of the great majority of educated and intelligent men. Many laymen who might have entered the church chose to serve the king instead. Many churchmen entered the service of lay governments and became so absorbed in that service that they forgot their duty to the church. And as the church lost exclusive control of the educated class it lost much of its ability to control public opinion.

Fully as important as the increase in the number of permanent lay officials was the increase in the number of men who were not officials, but who were forced to aid the government in its work from time to time. Professor A. B. White has shown how much of the work of local government in England was performed by juries, or selected knights of the shire.[6] France had a much larger paid bureaucracy, but even in France the royal government could not function without requiring the services of its subjects. In France, as in England, local notables were associated with royal officials in administrative investigations or judicial inquests.[7] In France, as in England, thousands of men were forced to aid the government in the wearisome work of assessing and collecting taxes. For example, when the aid for knighting Louis of Navarre was collected in 1314, there were 322 collectors in the viscounty of Paris alone, excluding the city proper and the castellany of Poissy.[8] It seems unlikely that many people enjoyed dropping their own work in order to spend days and weeks in serving the government for little or no pay. Yet the men who performed these expensive and burdensome tasks did not become disloyal to the government which imposed them. Rather they became increasingly conscious of the dignity and power of secular government. They acquired the habit of obedience to lay authorities, they accepted the point of view of the permanent officials with whom they had frequent contacts. A modern parallel to this process would be found in the results of military conscription. Most men who are drafted into an army regard military service as a burden. Yet compulsory military service has proved one of the most successful means for building up fanatical loyalty to the state. Just so the compulsory civil service of the thirteenth century created loyalty to the governments which imposed it.

The processes discussed so far worked indirectly, and almost automatically, to build up loyalty to lay governments. It was natural for any ruler to try to increase his power in a given area. As he gained a virtual monopoly of power it was necessary for him to add new functions to his government and to increase the number of men who assisted him in governing. There was little theorizing behind these developments, merely the desire to gain power and to use that power effectively. But the result of this drive for power was the creation of something very like a sovereign state. There was no place for such an entity in the old mediaeval system; it was absolutely opposed to the belief in the unity of Christendom and the hierarchy of political organizations. It had to be justified, explained, sold to the people. As a result, toward the end of the thirteenth century a definite theory to justify laicization appears.

This theory, like so many other things in the thirteenth century, was the work of lawyers. This new class of men, produced by the increased activity of twelfth-century governments, set the tone of the thirteenth century even more than the new class produced by increased business activity. The thirteenth century was a legalistic century, a century in which men sought exact definitions of all human relationships, a century in which men wanted to work out the logical implications of all general ideas and projects, a century in which men wanted to complete and to justify the work of their predecessors. And because the thirteenth century was legalistic, because it was a period of definitions and detailed explanations, it was a much less tolerant century than the twelfth. It was no longer possible to harmonize divergent views by thinking of them as merely different aspects of universal truth. Thus definition of the doctrines of the church forced many reformers into heresy. Definition of the rights of the state forced many men to choose between loyalty to the state and loyalty to the church. It was only when a choice had to be made that laicization was possible.

The definition of the powers of the ruler worked out by thirteenth-century lawyers developed into something which was almost a theory of the sovereign state. Such a theory could not be reconciled with the old mediaeval system; it forced a choice between loyalties. Briefly, it ran something like this. First, there are definite boundaries to all states. The twelfth century had known spheres of influence rather than boundaries; power decreased in proportion to the distance from the ruler until a region was reached in which his authority was counterbalanced by that of another lord. In the thirteenth-century theory the power of the dominant government was to extend, undiminished, to a precise frontier. This idea may be seen especially clearly in the south of France, where royal officials worked steadily to fix an exact boundary with Aragon; [9] where they insisted again and again that the eastern boundary of the realm was the Rhone; where they flatly denied that there could be a no man's land of independent bishoprics,[10] in which the king's authority was neutralized by that of the emperor. Then, within these precise boundaries there is to be a definite superior, who can supervise and correct the work of all subordinate governments. This idea may be found in England earlier than in France,[11] but it was most clearly expressed by Beaumanoir: 'The king is sovereign over all, and has as his right the general guardianship of all the realm . . . There is none so great beneath him that he cannot be haled to his court for default of justice or for false judgment.' [12] Moreover, this definite superior, if he observes certain formalities, may issue orders which are binding on all men in the realm. As the *dictum de Kenilworth* says: 'The king, and his legitimate orders and instructions, must be fully obeyed by each and every man, great and small, in the realm.' [13] Guillaume de Plaisian is even more emphatic: 'All those in the realm are ruled by the king's authority; even prelates and clerks, in temporal matters, are bound by the laws, edicts, and constitutions of the king.' [14] The central government may state the law, or make special rulings where the laws fail to give a solution to a problem. This was recognized in England as early as Glanvill's time, when it was said that laws for the entire kingdom might be made 'in doubtful cases by the authority of the prince with the advice of the magnates.' [15] It took somewhat longer for this power to be recognized in France, but by the end of the thirteenth century Beaumanoir could say: 'The king may make such establishments as please him for the common good, and that which he establishes must be obeyed.[16] For the common good taxes may be imposed on all property in the kingdom. The most extreme statement of this right was made by Guillaume de Plaisian: 'Everything within the boundaries of his realm is the lord king's, at least as to protection, superior jurisdiction, and lordship. Even as property it is the king's, for he can give, receive, and use any property, movable and immovable, in his realm for the public good and defense of the kingdom.' [17] An English lawyer would not have said this, but the English government did insist that all property could be taxed for defense of the realm.[18] Finally, while no lesser political authority can be exempt from, or control the decisions of the king, there is no higher political authority which can interfere with the king's powers of government. Here English and French lawyers are equally emphatic. Bracton's 'the king has no equal, much less a superior' [19] is matched in a letter sent by the French government to the Emperor Henry VII: 'Since the time of Christ the realm of France has had only its own king, who never recognized nor had a temporal superior.' [20]

These ideas add up to something very like the theory of sovereignty. Within fixed boundaries there is a definite superior who has the final decision regarding all political activities. It is not quite the theory of sovereignty, not only because the word is lacking, but also because it is a theory of comparative rather than absolute power. The words which the French lawyers use show this: the king has 'superioritas,' he has 'majus dominium,' he has 'altior dominatio.' His power is greater than that of any subject, but it is not a different power; he makes the final decisions, but he does not make all the decisions. But, sovereignty or not, this theory clearly conflicts with earlier mediaeval ideas. It sets up the kingdom as the most important unit of government and demands that all subjects give their primary allegiance to the kingdom.

Moreover, these ideas were not the work of isolated theorists. Every quotation which has been given was written by a high royal official. Most of them were taken from official documents,—laws, pleas in royal courts, or letters written in the king's name. Innumerable statements of a similar sort could be found in official records. This means that everyone who attended a royal court, everyone who did business with the government, was exposed to the new theories. This must have done a great deal to spread the idea of the supremacy of royal government, and hence, to make laicization easier. Even this was not enough, and at the end of the century deliberate propaganda in favor of the new theories was begun in both France and England. Local and national assemblies were called, at which royal officials could expound their new doctrine. It has long been apparent that the Estates-General and local assemblies held in France at the time of the quarrel with Boniface were called solely for purposes of propaganda. In a book recently published, Professor C. H. Taylor of Harvard has given strong reasons for believing that the French assemblies which met to consider taxation were called primarily to create a public opinion favorable to taxation. They did not consent to taxation; in 1314, for example, the tax was already ordered before the assembly met.[21] But they could be impressed by arguments showing the necessity for taxation, and they would report those arguments to their constituents. I feel that the same thing is true of the English Parliament, as far as the knights and burgesses were concerned. True, they were asked to assent to taxation, but their assent was, at first, a matter of form. Much more important was the fact that they could be harangued by royal officials, that they could be used to spread propaganda which would make the work of the tax-collector easier.

At the same time the governments of France and England began to encourage nationalism in order to gain support for their policies. There had always been a certain amount of latent nationalism in Europe; the French had sneered at the drunken English and the Italians had despised the boorish Germans. But this early nationalism had not been very strong in comparison with provincial loyalties and it had been frowned on by lay and ecclesiastical rulers alike. It was contrary to the basic principles of Christianity and it was dangerous to lay rulers whose territories seldom coincided with national units and whose policies were not always nationalistic. The concentration of political authority in France and England encouraged the growth of nationalism by decreasing the differences between provinces and increasing the differences between countries. But even in the middle of the thirteenth century nationalism was not yet respectable. Nationalism was associated with rebellion against constituted authority, with such movements as the protests of the English clergy against papal exactions, or the opposition of the English baronage to Henry III. Men like St. Louis and Henry III, who believed sincerely in the old international ideals, could not follow a nationalistic policy. In fact, many of Henry's troubles were caused by his unwillingness to accept the nationalistic ideas of his selfish and narrow-minded barons. About

1300, however, the governments of France and England began to see that nationalism could be useful to them, and once the idea was supported by a recognized authority it grew rapidly. At one point in the war over Gascony, Edward I accused the French of wishing to annihilate the English race [22] and the anti-clerical legislation of his reign shows a tacit acceptance of nationalistic ideas. In France, the government appealed even more openly to nationalism. During the struggle against Boniface VIII repeated efforts were made to convince the country that the pope was anti-French, and that he was threatening the independence of France.[23] In the same way when the French clergy were asked for money to carry on the war with Flanders, they were reminded of the pre-eminence of France as a Christian country and were told that it was their duty as Frenchmen to defend their native land.[24] In 1305 the king wrote to the clergy of the province of Tours: 'You should realize that all the clergy and laity of our kingdom, like members of one body . . . are bound to give each other spiritual and temporal aid to preserve, defend, and protect the unity of this realm.' [25] The extremes to which French nationalism could go appear in the ingenious schemes of Pierre Dubois for subjecting all Europe to French rule. It is true that Dubois was only a minor official, and was never promoted, but that does not mean that his views were not in harmony with those of the central administration. Generally speaking, minor officials spoke more bluntly, and acted more brutally than the immediate advisers of the king, but the basic ideas of the two groups were the same. A tactless minor official, such as Dubois, might not be promoted, but neither would he be discharged. And the views of such a man, since they were never expressly repudiated, might be very influential with certain groups.

When Boniface VIII, alarmed by the growing power of lay governments, tried to limit their authority, he found that he was too late. The people of France and England remained loyal to their kings; there was not even a half-hearted rebellion in favor of the pope. In France the government had such control of public opinion that it was able to seize the church's own weapon of a charge of heresy and turn it against Boniface. A few years later it succeeded in ruining the Templars by the same method. This perhaps marks the extreme limit of mediaeval laicization —a secular ruler determines the policy of the church and uses the church for his own ends. This feat was not immediately repeated, but from the time of Boniface on there was no doubt that lay rulers had the primary allegiance of their people. Society was controlled, as far as it was controlled at all, by lay governments and not by the church. It is true that during the fourteenth and fifteenth centuries this lay control was not always very intelligent, nor very effective. During these years there was a reaction against central governments; a reaction caused, at least in part, by the fact that they had gained power by a mixture of blackmail,

chicanery, and bullying and that a generation educated in these techniques began to use them against their rulers. But this very period of weak
lay government showed how effective the work of laicization had been.
The church could not regain its old power in spite of the opportunity
afforded by a new period of anarchy. There was no substitute for centralized, lay government in France or England, however weak that government might be.

The reaction against central governments after 1300 may explain why
laicization went no further; why education, and care of the sick and
poor remained in the province of the church. But it should also be remembered that mediaeval governments were satisfied with relative,
rather than absolute power. Totalitarianism was foreign to their ways
of thinking—it would also have been too expensive. Police work cost
money—so there was no objection to letting the barons do much of it.
Education was expensive—so there was no objection to letting the church
do it. Some townspeople in England and France did object to church
control of education and tried to set up their own schools, but as far as I
know the count of Flanders was the only lay ruler who gave any support
to this movement.[26] As for social service work, the whole tendency was
to make the church do more of it, rather than less. Anyone who has
studied grants to the church must have been struck by the great increase
in the number of gifts made specifically to hospitals, poor-houses, and
university colleges after the middle of the thirteenth century.[27] The old
unlimited grant for the general purposes of the church almost disappears
in the fourteenth century. This may be, indirectly, a form of laicization;
the church is to be made to do 'useful' work instead of spending its
money on purely religious purposes. But there is no hesitation in allowing the church to perform these services; rather it is encouraged to do so.
Not until the next great wave of laicization in the sixteenth century is
there an attempt to deprive the church of its educational and philan-
thropic functions. Once the leadership, the 'superiority' of mediaeval lay
governments was recognized, they had no further quarrel with the church.

NOTES

1 This paper was read, in a somewhat abbreviated form, at the 1938 meeting of the
American Historical Association. An excellent discussion of the topic, from a
somewhat different point of view, may be found in G. de Lagarde, *La naissance
de l'esprit laïque* (Saint-Paul-Trois Châteaux et Vienne, 1934).

2 *Ordonnances*, VII, 7, in a compromise with the bishop of Viviers the king insists
only on recognition of his "superioritas," his right to hear appeals from the bishop's
court, and his power to punish temporal officials of the bishopric. 1308.

3 *Ibid.*, XVII, 221. The monastery of St. Saturnin surrenders many of its rights in a
pariage after being harassed by local officials, 1302; *Gallia Christiana*, I, *Instr.* 33, the
bishop of Cahors made a *pariage* for the same reason in 1307; *Archives Nationales*,

JJ 45 nos 88 and 90, similar transactions with the chapter of Rodez and St. Papoul, 1309 and 1310.

4 *English Historical Review*, XLIII (1928), 1.

5 Ad. Baudouin, *Lettres inédites de Philippe le Bel* (Paris, 1887), nos. 1, 6, 10, 11, 12, 13, 14, 22, 24 and *passim*.

6 A. B. White, *Self-Government at the King's Command* (Minneapolis, 1933).

7 P. Guilhiermoz, *Enquêtes et procès* (Paris, 1892), p. 605, ordinance for Parlement of 1278. In order to obtain auditors to hold inquests "baille chascuns des bailliz les nons en escrit jusques a. x. personnes aus clers des arrès, lesquiex personnes soient souffisables a faire ce que l'en leur commandera en droit . . ." *Archives Nationales*, J 237 no. 120, J 208 no. 6, J 292 no. 9¹⁰, examples of the use of local notables in appraising and assigning land.

8 *Bibliothèque nationale*, Clairembault 228, pp. 929ff.

9 *Archives nationales*, J 1029 no. 9; JJ 42 A no. 110. Cf. F. Kern, *Die Anfänge der französischen Ausdehnungspolitik* (Tübingen, 1910), p. 17ff. for similar efforts on the eastern frontier.

10 *Ordonnances*, VII, 7; *Bulletin de la Société d'Agriculture, Industrie, Sciences et Arts du Département de la Lozère* 1896–97, 'Mémoire relatif au Paréage de 1307,' p. 520. Guillaume de Plaisian argued that 'fines Francie usque ad flumen Rodani extenduntur' and that 'omnia que sunt infra fines regni sui sint domini regis, saltim quoad protectionem et altam jurisdictionem et dominationem . . ." The bishop of Mende stated the older point of view when he replied 'non sequitur quod infra fines regni non possit aliquid esse liberum a jurisdictione regali . . .' It is unfortunate that this important document, which contains the fullest summary of the theories of Philip's officials, is available only in this rare and incomplete edition.

11 Glanvill (ed. Woodbine), pp. 149ff.; Bracton, *de legibus*, II, 24, all justice is held of the king, and power of supervising it remains with him.

12 Beaumanoir (ed. Salmon), XXXIV, 1043. 'Voirs est que li rois est souverains par dessus tous, et a de son droit la general garde de tout son roiaume . . . Et si n'i a nul si grant dessous li qui ne puist estre tres en sa court pour defaute de droit ou peur faus jugement. . . .'

13 *Statutes of the Realm*, I, 12. '. . . atque ab universis et singulis majoribus et minoribus ipsius regni hominibus, ipsi domino Regi et mandatis ac preceptis suis licitis plene obediatur et humiliter intendatur.' Edward I's lawyers said that the king's orders could override even the common law. *Rotuli Parliamentorum*, I, 71, 'dominus Rex, . . . pro communi utilitate, per prerogativam suam in multis casibus est supra leges et consuetudines in regno suo usitatas.' 1292.

14 'Mémoire relatif au paréage,' p. 521. 'Item, quod dominus Rex sit imperator in regno suo, et imperare possit terre et mari, et omnes populi regni sui regantur imperio, et omnes etiam prelati et clerici quoad temporalia legibus et edictis et constitutionibus suis ligentur. . . .'

15 Glanvill (ed. Woodbine), p. 24. English laws are 'eas quas super dubiis in consilio definiendis procerum quidem consilio, et principis accedente auctoritate, constat esse promulgatas.' By the time of Edward I general laws were made by the central government without hesitation. For our purposes, the question as to who controlled the central government is unimportant. The barons claimed the right to be consulted, but they did not deny that the central government could make law.

16 Beaumanoir (ed. Salmon), XXXIV, 1043, '. . . il [li rois] puet fere teus establissemens comme il li plest pour le commun pourfit, et ce qu'il establist doit estre tenu.'

17 'Mémoire relatif au paréage,' p. 521, '. . . omnia que sunt infra fines regni sui sint domini Regis, saltim quoad protectionem et altam jurisdictionem et dominationem et etiam quantum ad proprietatem omnium singularum rerum mobilium et immobilium regni sui, quas idem dominus Rex donare, recipere et consumere potest, ex causa publice utilitatis et deffensionis regni sui . . .' This doctrine was repeated in a letter to the clergy of Tours in 1305, cf. *Archives Nationales*, J 350 no. 5.

18 Bartholomaeus Cotton, *Historia Anglicana* (Rolls Series 16), p. 317, in asking the clergy for a grant in 1296, after the pope had forbidden taxation of the Church, Hugh le Despenser said: 'Ego ex parte domini regis, comitum, baronum, militum

et aliorum domini regis fidelium vobis dico, quod de tali subsidio per quod terra defendatur de bonis ecclesiae provideatis, ne dominus rex, comites et barones de rebus vestris ecclesiasticis ordinent et disponant pro suae libito voluntatis.' *Parliamentary Writs* (London, 1827), I, 393, the clergy were outlawed until they paid.

[19] Bracton III. 9. 3 '[Rex] parem autem habere non debet, nec multo fortius superiorem . . .'

[20] K. Wenck, *Philipp der Schöne* (Marburg, 1905), p. 72, '. . . quod a tempore Christi citra regnum Francie solum regem suum sub ipso Jhesu Christo . . . habuit, nullum temporalem superiorem cognoscens aut habens . . .'

[21] J. R. Strayer and C. H. Taylor, *Studies in Early French Taxation* (Cambridge, 1939), p. 151.

[22] *Parliamentary Writs*, I, 30. The king of France, 'praedictis fraude et nequitia non contentus . . . linguam Anglicam . . . omnino de terra delere proponit.'

[23] G. Picot, *Documents relatifs aux Etats Généraux* (Paris, 1901), p. 37, Boniface was accused of saying 'se magis velle esse canem vel asinum . . . quam Gallicum,' that 'ad deprimendum regem et Gallicos, si aliter non posset fieri, precipitaret se, et totum mundum et totam Ecclesiam,' and that no scandal was too great 'dum tamen Gallici et eorum superbia destruantur.'

[24] *Archives Nationales*, J 1035 nos 36, 37, 39; J 259 Cluny 3.

[25] *Ibid.*, J 350 no. 5. 'Novistis plenius qualiter omnes et singuli clerici et laici regni nostri tanquam membra simul in uno corpore vere vivancia sibi debent ad invicem compati, mutuumque sibi prestare teneretur auxilium spiritualiter et temporaliter ad conservationem, deffensionem, et custodiam unitatis ipsius regni . . .' 1305.

[26] H. Pirenne, 'L'Instruction des marchands au moyen âge,' *Annales d'histoire économique et sociale*, I, 24–26; C. Stallaert and P. Van Der Haeghen; *De l'instruction publique au moyen âge* (Brussels (1850), extract from vol. XXIII of *Mémoires couronnés et mémoires des savants étrangers publiés par l'académie royale de Belgique*), pp. 101, 107–108, 109.

[27] Powerful communes, such as those of the Rhineland and the Low Countries, did place certain hospitals under lay control, cf. *Hist. littéraire*, XXXV, 120, and de Lagarde, *op. cit.*, I, 220. But while there are no statistics on the subject, my impression is that the church gained more hospitals through new foundations than it lost through such acts of secularization.

8

The State and Landed Interests in Thirteenth Century France and England

EDWARD MILLER

I

BEFORE COMING TO the substance of this paper, I feel that I must define its purpose somewhat more closely than I have done in the title which I have given to it. A study of the state and landed interests, of course, could embrace most of the domestic and much of the external histories of France and England in the thirteenth century. I shall be concerned with much less than that—with a problem which nevertheless seems to me to be of the first importance in any study of the social and economic policies (if that phrase be not too anachronistic) of medieval governments. I mean the break-up and alienation of feudal tenements in the thirteenth century, some of the causes and consequences thereof, and some of the attempts made to deal with the difficulties thereby occasioned. This still remains a large subject, and at best this paper is an attempt at synthesis, even of *vulgarisation*, which rests, in the main, upon the work of others. In particular, I have drawn heavily upon Professor Plucknett's study of the legislation of Edward I, and I was encouraged to venture upon some comparisons with France because he has also shown, I feel, that such comparisons may not be without value.

Before coming to my subject proper, however, I should like to say a word about the changes which were going on in the social order on the eve of, and during, the thirteenth century. A rapid transformation was taking place in the economic organization of rural society: the contraction of demesnes, 'the prodigious attenuation of agricultural services',[1] the development of the landlord into a rentier drawing his income mainly in the form of cash renders from the peasantry.[2] Such a generalized picture, of course, requires every sort of qualification. In France, these tendencies may have gone far by the time of Philip Augustus; but in England they had made less progress in the twelfth century, though Professor Postan has shown that they were not absent.[3] In both countries, furthermore, there was much variation between different districts and, in all probability, between different types of estate.[4] So far as these changes had gone, however, they had important consequences. The capacity of custom in medieval times 'to transform precedents into rights'[5] tended to perpetuate the seignorial concessions of the twelfth century. The semi-proprietary rights of many of the peasants were consolidated, and twelfth century contracts between them and their lords became hard to alter. In consequence, an element of growing importance in seignorial incomes was stabilized; and this was a serious matter in the thirteenth century when rising prices were reducing its real value. Doubtless attempts were made to check this tendency for real incomes to fall; and efforts in that direction may partly explain the 'manorial reaction'[6] in thirteenth century England, the development of new and more economic types of rent,[7] and the systematic exploitation of the incidental profits of lordship (tallages, mainmortes, wardships, judicial profits, and so on). Nevertheless, the tendency for real incomes to fall seems to have persisted, and was probably one cause of the beginnings of a 'crise nobiliaire', of which the signs are clearest in France but not entirely absent in England. There were, of course, other reasons for this crisis: an aristocratic way of life which made prodigality a virtue, wars and crusades and pious gifts, and the partition of inheritances.[8] But the economic difficulties of lords helped to bring fiefs into the market in the thirteenth century, and multiplied concessions to the peasantry in return for cash down. The nobility, or at least some sections of it, were driven progressively further along a spendthrift's path.[9]

To these changes in the social order must be added others of a political nature. The decline of the feudal army, the inroads of royal courts and royal officials into the administrative immunities of great lords, were part cause, part symptom of the disintegration of feudal communities, also attested by the multiplication of the homages into which tenants entered. This had already gone very far when, in 1224, the lord of Noyers became the man of Theobald of Champagne for certain lands. He saved the fealty due to those other lords into whose homage he had entered previously; and of these there were no less than nine.[10] As the personal bond of vassalage was in this way drained of its meaning, only those territorial dispositions, which had been in origin merely a condition for the performance of vassalic duties, were left behind. Consequently, the right of the tenant in the land tended to assume a more unconditional character; tenant-right made progress amongst the feudal tenants as well as amongst the peasantry. This, combined with the economic circumstances of the thirteenth century, stimulated a traffic in feudal tenements which it was difficult for lords to control. Thus lords were faced increasingly, not only with a crisis of revenues, but also with a crisis of control.

These, then, were some of the problems which faced landowners in the thirteenth century. The rulers of the nations could hardly ignore them; for they, with their subjects (in Professor Powicke's phrase), 'lived in a social system of land-management, wardship and marriage, according to rules . . . which they observed . . . like serious children playing an intricate parlour game'.[11] The seriousness of the game, even for kings, needs little explanation. Despite the fertility of Angevin England in new fiscal devices, the exploitation of the royal demesne remained an important activity of the revenue departments; [12] and Edward I can still be found acquiring lands for the crown 'as a landowner with capital to spare rather than as a King'.[13] Of course, these private preoccupations easily acquired a political character; indeed, the progress of the French monarchy can almost be measured in terms of the extension of the royal demesne, and it was his achievements in this direction which, according to a contemporary, won for Philip II the title of Augustus.[14] Furthermore, some part of the authority of thirteenth century monarchs was derived, in the last resort, from the superiority over the territorial order which feudalism, in fact or in theory, had vested in the monarchy. The exploitation of that superiority remained an essential part of the art of government, for so many rights were attached to land that the devolution of property still determined the distribution of much political power. At the same time the kingship carried obligations as well as authority. It was a *ministerium ad dispensationem reipublicae et utilitate ecclesiarum*,[15] an office burdened with the duty of safeguarding the rights of subjects and making justice prevail. In this connection again the monarchy was brought face to face with the problems of landowners; it had to seek to remedy their grievances. This task was the work of the king as judge and legislator; and perhaps most of all of the king as a judge. Statutes and ordinances were becoming commoner; but it was still in the courts that the most continuous effort was made to adjust customs to changing facts.

II

Amongst the many influences destroying the integrity of fiefs, I should like to say something first of family laws and customs. These became forces of increasing importance as feudal tenants acquired a more proprietary right in their holdings. Superficially, perhaps, they are relatively unimportant in England. The partition of inheritances here was confined to the peasantry of certain peripheral areas of the country.[16] The following of such a custom, indeed, according to an early fourteenth century lawyer, put a man 'clean outside the common law'.[17] Amongst military tenants the custom of male primogeniture was general; and it was probably pushed down the social scale as socage tenements were burdened with scutage and to that extent assimilated to military tenements.[18] Nevertheless, as Professor Plucknett says, 'the system of male primogeniture is quite unworkable under the normal conditions of family life',[19] and it was much modified in practice by the almost inescapable duty of fathers to make some sort of provision for their daughters and younger sons. Such provision might take the form from the beginning of an outright conveyance of some part of the family estate; or, more commonly perhaps, of a conditional gift which did not give the donees full freedom of disposition over the land so granted for three or four generations. In the interval, failure of heirs (often of a specific class prescribed in the deed of gift) would involve the reversion of the estate to the donor or his heirs. But daughters and younger sons seem to have been impatient of these restrictions designed to maintain the integrity of patrimonies; and the common law courts apparently showed some sympathy for their endeavours to turn these imperfect gifts at the earliest possible moment into holdings over which they had free disposition.[20] Opposition to these breaches of the dynastic principle was perhaps but natural in the heads of families, and in lords desirous of keeping fiefs intact. Doubtless, these feelings provoked the enactment of the statute *De Donis* in 1285. That statute, however, made a sorry mess of things. It is unintelligible as it stands, probably because it was amended at the last moment in order to concede the detachment of such gifts from the ancestral estate at the end of a single generation. This was a blow to the dynastic principle which, in its original shape, the statute may have been designed to reinforce. The reason may well have been, as Professor Plucknett has suggested, that Edward I was afflicted with last-minute fears of the support that principle gave to the power of close-knit baronial families.

Still, the primogenitary rule predominated in England and helped to keep fiefs together, despite that fondness of fathers for their younger sons which Glanville deplored.[21] In France it was otherwise. Customs were various,[22] but most of them gave a specific share of the patrimony to younger sons, and often daughters as well.[23] Leaving aside the customs of the Midi,[24] two types of provision common in the north raised special problems. The eldest son might provide for his younger brothers by enfeoffing them in portions of the patrimony, thus creating rear-fiefs. Alternatively, the younger sons might hold in parage with the first-born— i.e. receive each a portion of the fief, but do no homage to the eldest who remained responsible to his lord for the whole service of the fief. In this way the creation of rear-fiefs was avoided at first; but after the fourth or seventh generation the heirs of the younger brothers did homage to the heirs of the eldest, thus creating rear-fiefs in the long run.[25]

In these ways, then, the operation of family custom made for the break-up of fiefs and, through the creation of rear-fiefs, the removal of parts of them from the direct control of their lords. This, naturally enough, encountered opposition from the crown and the greater feudatories, concerned for their control, the services due to them, and the casual profits to be derived from the feudal relationship. Attempts to introduce the primogenitary rule, therefore, appear early in seignorial legislation.[26] Such attempts, however, were sometimes (as in Normandy [27]) limited to the more important fiefs; and the spread of parage tenure may even have been a way of getting round the rule.[28] Thus, the persistence of families in partitioning their inheritances was attacked from another angle in the Ordinance of 1210. This provided that, where a fief was divided between heirs, each partitioner should hold directly of the chief lord.[29] In this way the control and profit of lords would have been preserved; but, though some lords (like the bishop of Beauvais in the 1250's [30]) invoked the act against their tenants, its effect outside the royal demesne was very limited.[31] Impartibility was the rule in the thirteenth century only in the great principalities and the baronies, where royal insistence and dynastic ambition combined to effect this end.[32] Even here there were exceptions,[33] and the battle was often slowly won. As late as 1243 the Lusignan inheritance seems to have been partible to some degree,[34] and in the sixties Simon de Montfort and his widow were endeavouring to assert their right to a portion of it.[35] They secured no more than a life interest in certain revenues arising from the inheritance; but the principle of impartibility here can hardly be said to have been finally settled until 1298, when a younger brother's claims to a moiety of the heritage were rebutted, and he was told to rest content with the 1,000 livres of annual rent assigned to him for his life.[36] In other provinces, however, even such life interests as these were by this time regarded as hardly permissible. Duke Robert of Burgundy certainly claimed in the 1280's that such a provision for his younger brother was an intolerable dismemberment of his duchy and contrary to the custom of France.[37] But meantime, in many places, the partition of lesser properties went on, producing 'a dismemberment of middling fiefs ruinous to the feudal edifice'.[38]

Thus, to some extent in England and to a greater extent in France, family settlements were destructive of the feudal territorial order. Younger sons and daughters seem to have prevailed against their elder brothers, so that even a father's or donor's express intention to limit their expectations was often nullified;[39] and tenants, in this as so many other ways, seem to have prevailed against their lords. In these tendencies the king's courts in France seem often to have acquiesced; while the English com-

mon law courts, and Edward I himself in 1285, supported them. Doubtless the division of patrimonies which resulted was one cause of an impoverished nobility, whose cries become obvious at this time in France,[40]
and whose existence in England can be discerned in the rolls of the
Jewish exchequer.[41]

III

Meantime, other forces were working in the same direction as family
custom. Old motives for the devise of land to vassals, servants and
churches had not entirely lost their force. Further, as land began to be
looked upon as an investment, traffic in it became keener, and the creation of new wealth brought new classes of men into the investor's market. All the time, too, the circumstances and way of life of many of the
nobility made financial embarrassment a recurring experience. Everything combined, in fact, to make the alienation of fiefs one of the problems of the age.

Before turning to the manner in which the problem was tackled,
there are certain distinctions to be kept in mind. Alienation might affect
the whole fief or only a part. It might merely substitute one tenant for
another; or, in the case of subinfeudation, set an intermediate tenant between the lord and the holder of the land. Finally, the beneficiary might
be a layman or an ecclesiastical corporation. The latter eventuality raised
special problems and must be reserved for special treatment.

Even transactions between laymen, however, involved a complex
nexus of interests. In general, perhaps too much freedom on the part of
tenants to dispose of their land betrayed a weakening of the power of
lords. In this connection the Crown was concerned, not only as a landowner, but also because the power of lords to exact service from their
tenants on the king's behalf was imperilled. At the same time, it was not
a simple matter of two classes—lords and tenants—with conflicting interests. The very traffic in land itself might make lords into tenants and
tenants into lords, so that there was a 'conflict of views in the mind of
every magnate.' [42] Finally, not only kings and lords and tenants were concerned, but also families. There was a varying range of heirs naturally
concerned that their expectations should not be disappointed. In these
circumstances the development of the law and custom touching the alienation of fiefs could hardly be a straightforward one.

In the twelfth century, fiefs had not been entirely inalienable in
either country, although some restriction was placed upon the tenant by
varying needs to procure the concurrence of his heirs [43] and his lord.[44]
In thirteenth century England, on the other hand, it seems that fathers
had freedom enough with their property to disinherit their heirs by selling part or all of it; [45] and even in France the power of the heir to consent

or forbid had been whittled down into a right to exercise the *retrait lignager*—i.e. to repurchase the property from the donee at the price the latter had given for it.[46] The rights of lords in France may have been somewhat more durable. Some customs still obliged the tenant to obtain the lord's licence to alienate a fief.[47] In 1225, we even find the Emperor Frederick II insisting on this principle, after he had heard that the count of Toulouse presumed to alienate lands he held of him to the prejudice of the empire and the emperor.[48] Generally, no serious obstacle seems to have been placed in the way of alienation by substitution,[49] though various customs reserved to the lord a right of preemption, to exercise a *retrait féodale*,[50] or to receive some share of the price paid for the land.[51] These rights would be easier to safeguard to the extent that lords were able to insist that transfers of land should take place by surrender and admission in their courts.[52] Prior authorization was more likely to be demanded for alienation of parts of a fief, for that might endanger the tenant's capacity to perform the services due from it; and it might be made conditional upon the purchaser becoming the direct vassal of the overlord for his portion of the fief.[53] In general, indeed, opposition to subinfeudation hardened. In Champagne, only barons had the right to subinfeudate; in Burgundy, this power was withdrawn from all unless they procured the prior consent of their overlords. How effective these restraints were it is hard to say, particularly as their object in some cases was less to prevent alienations than to designate occasions when lords might profit by making a charge for their license. Sometimes the need to obtain consent to alienation was disappearing in the strict sense, only to be invoked when tenants failed to render the requisite payment to their lord.[54]

In all this, the state as such plays little part. It does not legislate, and the judgements of the royal courts take cognizance of local custom or refer to the demesne. It was also difficult for royal policy to be consistent, for the crown derived advantages from the alienability of fiefs. The demesne was extended by the purchase of fiefs from crown tenants lacking heirs or encumbered with debts;[55] and it was one of the grievances of the nobility that the king made similar acquisitions in fiefs and rear-fiefs held of them.[56] On the other hand, the king was as concerned as any other lord at the loss of control and casual profits he suffered from the alienation of fiefs held directly of him. He therefore imposed restraints upon them which were sometimes enforced against his greatest subjects. In the 1270's, royal officials seem to have been taking into the king's hand lands alienated by the count of Poitiers and Toulouse [57]; and in 1265 the king had compelled the marshal of France to resume a meadow sold without license to a certain knight, because in so doing he had diminished his barony.[58] Indeed, these restrictions, perhaps because they spoiled the market for noble land and almost certainly because the king's consent had to be dearly bought, became grievous, and the leagues of the early fourteenth century complained of them.[59]

This attitude to alienation is perhaps analogous to that shown towards another of the ways in which vassals dissipated their resources—by enfranchising the serfs in their fiefs. Here again the Crown imposed restrictions, though hardly out of sheer conservatism. Mass manumissions of serfs, that were essentially fiscal operations, began on the royal estates under St. Louis.[60] But if on its own lands the crown 'taxait à prix d'argent la liberté', it sought to do the same on the lands of its vassals. To free a serf was to 'abridge the fief'; it needed the consent of the lord of the fief.[61] If the fief was the king's, then his consent was needed and that might be a costly matter. The Dean and Chapter of Orléans had to promise to pay the king 200 livres in 1225 in the event of their manumitting any of their serfs.[62] If this royal consent was not sought when manumitting a serf, the serf passed, with all his disabilities upon him, to the Crown.[63] The motive was purely fiscal, and was probably similar to that which governed many other dealings of the French monarchy with the land.

Yet a further question might arise in connection with the alienation of land in France. A lord might be prejudiced, not only by the alienation of the fief, but also by the status of the recipient of the land. It was a matter of concern if the fief passed to a mere bourgeois or flourishing countryman; for such men bought for investment [64] and might be thought unfitted to assume the obligations of a fief. This purchase of fiefs by non-nobles may even have been prohibited altogether in the thirteenth century by legislation 'promulgated for the benefit of gentlemen' [65]; but the prohibition must have been impossible to enforce and, as usual, the Crown showed willingness to relax it, doubtless at a price. In 1273 the men of Toulouse were permitted to retain those fiefs they had acquired through inheritance or marriage or held for more than twenty years.[66] Casual licenses were elaborated into a system by the ordinance of 1275,[67] which legitimized past acquisitions in the king's fiefs and rear-fiefs in return for a payment to the Crown. Similar enactments were made by subsequent kings,[68] though the cost of the king's license tended to rise. Once again the situation had been turned to the fiscal advantage of the Crown.

Turning to England, there are at first sight many differences. Manumissions and the purchase of fiefs by non-nobles raise few problems. Yet the general background was very similar. In England, too, there was a busy market in noble land. A 'quiet movement towards the establishment of tenant right' was already discernible at the beginning of the thirteenth century.[69] Fees were being divided, townsmen were investing in land, and the very word *feodum* was coming to mean no more than heritable land. By 1279 subinfeudation had gone so far as to make some of the entries in the Hundred Rolls a sonorous catalogue of empty titles. The traffic in fees and the subinfeudation of feudal tenements were problems as keenly felt in this country as they were in France.

In many ways the state seems not to have been unfavourable to the feudal tenants. Most of the legislation about distress was in their interests,[70] and the courts seem to have favoured the free alienability of land. Bracton argues that a lord may not refuse a substituted tenant, and that subinfeudation docs no *injuria* to a lord.[71] Lords hardly agreed with him on this latter point. They had sought to guard against some of the consequences of unfettered alienation and subinfeudation in the Charter of 1217; and the *injurie* which might ensue were very succinctly summarized by the lord of Greystoke in 1278. He feared that, "many advantages might be lost to him and grievous prejudice ensue if he allowed a fee of his . . . to be alienated, so that he would be separated from the wardships and reliefs thereof, and likewise (the king) should the aforesaid barony fall into his hands and custody." [72]

This appeal to the royal interest was doubtless wise, for there are signs that a clear policy was consistently pursued by the Crown. Already King John had treated royal serjeanties as inalienable and impartible,[73] and instituted enquiries which extended the principle to 'knights fees and all manner of tenements which are held of us in chief'.[74] In 1256 Henry III forbade tenants-in-chief to alienate without license on pain of forfeiture, for thereby the king lost his wardships and escheats and the barons were to that extent the less able to perform the services they owed to the king.[75] It was part of the duty of the commissioners of 1274 to reveal such alienations [76]; and a few years later it was argued that 'the lord king has a special prerogative attached to his crown, namely that it is not lawful for anyone to alienate his fee without his special license.' [77] At the same time, the fact that this was a distinctive disability of tenure in chief (indeed of tenure in chief *ut de corona*) seems to be emphasized by certain petitioners in parliament in 1325. The king, they say, has been confiscating alienations in divers honours forfeited to him for rebellion, despite the fact that previously men could buy lands and take feoffments therein without permission from their lords.[78] Clearly, at least, the concern of the Crown about alienation and subinfeudation was continuously demonstrated in the thirteenth century.

In other ways, too, the Crown had shown awareness of the problems of landlords. It legislated against collusive enfeoffments which deprived lords of wardships; and lords must have derived some benefit from the actions of *cessavit* and *mesne*. But it was the freedom of tenants to subinfeudate which provoked the most radical action. The statute *Quia emptores,* in order to safeguard the right of lords to their feudal incidents, simply abolished this way of alienation.[79] By doing so, Edward met the wishes (in the words of the statute) of 'the magnates and many other

lords', whose expectations were being whittled away by the excessive freedom of tenants. Above all, he was serving the interests of the magnates,
who had most to lose, and who might expect a significant accession of
strength as the slow process of escheat and forfeiture restored to them that
direct contact with the occupying tenant which they had so often been
losing in the thirteenth century.

IV

One other type of alienation remains—alienation to churches. It was
common because it was a means to salvation. It was common, too, because
the great ecclesiastical landlords were the most efficient of their day, and
accumulated capital which could be invested in yet more property.[80] The
consequences for the lords of such property are well enough known.
These 'immortal and soulless corporations' did not die or forfeit or leave
minors; they very seldom alienated their land. Thus a whole range of
profitable incidents were lost to the immediate lord; and any lords above
him had their expectations reduced should the fief ever revert to their
hands. It was therefore reasonable to call alienation in mortmain an
abridgement of the fief [81]; and opposition to it may be found early in private contracts—in Languedocian charters before the end of the twelfth
century and in English deeds of the early thirteenth century.[82]
The problem of mortmain, however, was not left merely to private
solution. In France, the customs tackled it in a number of ways.[83] One
course was to compel churches to put their acquisitions, on pain of for-
feiting them, out of their hands within a year.[84] Alternatively, they could
obtain the consent of the lords of the fief to its abridgement. Since lords
were in a position to refuse this consent [85] and to confiscate acquisitions
made without licence,[86] they could levy a charge for their acquiescence
and increase their profit by impugning titles already venerable on the
ground that consent had not been sought for some old transaction.[87] The
cost to the churches was further enhanced by the fact that they might
have to purchase the license, not only of the immediate lord of the fief,
but also of every lord above him up to the king. Thus grievances mounted
on both sides. If the king and the lords were concerned for their services
and feudal incidents, the churches were grieved by the exploitation to
which circumstances exposed them. The situation may have been brought
to a head in the early seventies by a more than usually keen scrutiny of
ecclesiastical acquisitions in the royal domain.[88] The 'constitutio ecclesiarum utilitati' [89] of 1275 may have been in part the outcome of the political issues raised by these enquiries and the administrative experience
gained in carrying them out.
This act of 1275 provided, in the first place, that royal officers should
no longer interfere with past ecclesiastical acquisitions in territories the

lords of which had the right to amortize; or where the consent of three successive mesne lords standing above the donor had been obtained; or, in the royal domain, where titles went back thirty years or more. Secondly, more recent acquisitions in the king's lands, fiefs or rear-fiefs were to be put out of the hands of churches within a year unless they were willing to pay an indemnity specified in the ordinance. Finally, a declaration attached restricted the right of amortization to the king, the twelve peers of France, and five great counts. Two years later, the right of the episcopal peers to amortize was restricted still further to their rear-fiefs, and was not to be used in their demesnes and fiefs.[90]

In one sense these provisions were favourable to the churches. A precise figure was set upon the cost of the royal license to acquire land; some limit was imposed upon the number of lords whose compliance had to be bought; and a term was fixed beyond which no payment was required for royal confirmation of past acquisitions. On the other hand, if the king made concessions to the church, he significantly extended his interest in the demise of lands into mortmain by his subjects. This fact did not escape attention at the time. The barons and other lords of Normandy complained that they were being robbed of powers they had previously enjoyed of permitting churches to acquire lands in their territories; and the nobles of Languedoc protested at the king levying new charges in their fiefs.[91] The count of Forez even hastened to take fines from churches for their acquisitions in his domains, in order to anticipate the exercise of the royal right to do so.[92] Finally, it should be remembered that the act applied only to the past. It did not exempt churches from obtaining the consent of the lord of the fief to new acquisitions as ancient custom and royal edict decreed [93]; and such acquisitions might, as before, have to be put out of their hand.[94] But if the act of 1275 had been an act of moderation, it had also been a fiscal experiment. In 1283 at least one monastery was constrained to pay the charges for amortization on acquisitions made subsequent to the ordinance [95]; and in 1291 Philip the Fair enacted a measure very similar to that of 1275, but with higher charges for the king's license.[96] This was the beginning of a series of such acts, and the later history of royal dealings with mortmain leaves no doubt that 'it was the fiscal motive which predominated'. Yet even the ordinance of Philip the Bold, ostensibly designed in the interest of the churches,[97] had not neglected this side of the matter.

The problem of mortmain was no less acute in England. It was a grievance in 1258 [98]; and in 1259 the devise of land to churches was forbidden without the license of the lord of the fee.[99] But this prohibition was not embodied in the Statute of Marlborough; and the very terms of the baronial grievances suggest that the magnates of England had lost control of these (like other) transactions of their tenants. So the problem remained until Edward I dealt with it in that remarkable statute of 1279 which flatly forbade churches to acquire any land whatever.[100] The execution of this statute, however, as Professor Plucknett has demonstrated, makes its terms almost irrelevant. In fact it was used to confer upon the Crown the sole prerogative of amortization. Churches could still acquire lands provided they purchased a license from the king to do so. Such royal licenses, however, may not have been conceived as dispensing churches from obtaining the consent of the lords of the fee—just as, to appropriate tithes, they needed the permission of the bishop.[101] If that is so, then the Statute of Mortmain, though administered with the fiscal advantage of the Crown in view, may also have restored (like the statute *Quia emptores*) a control they had been losing to the lords of the land.

V

Finally, perhaps I may be permitted a few very tentative concluding remarks. First, there are many common features about the general direction of social evolution in the two nations. Both in France and England, family settlements and the traffic in land were causing the disintegration of feudal tenements, the units upon which at one time feudal burdens had been assessed. This in itself betrays a weakening of the power of lords, and their control over the land was further relaxed as family settlements and the traffic in tenements not infrequently interposed between the lord and the land a varying number of intermediate tenants. Indeed, there are times when one feels that lords had abandoned interest in the land their tenants held, and were seeking merely to capitalize the superiority which remained to them. Charges upon alienation and succession, escheats and forfeitures, wardships and marriages—these occasional incidents seem to be the profits of lordship which arouse concern in the thirteenth century. In some ways, it is true, the lords of France may have lost more ground than the lords of England. They had dissipated more of their rights over the peasantry before the thirteenth century began, and were less able to profit directly from the boom in agricultural profits. In consequence, the French peasant acquired a stronger proprietary right in the soil than his English counterpart,[102] and the 'crise nobiliaire' may have set in at an earlier date in France.

In other respects, however, the lords of France may have lost less ground than their English counterparts. Before the statutes of Mortmain and *Quia emptores*, the English magnates seem to have been losing rapidly all control over the devolution of their fees. Only the king had that 'special prerogative attached to his crown' which enabled him to exert such control. The lords of France had similar difficulties; but they may have been somewhat less serious because the judicial powers at their disposal to enforce control were less impaired. At the same time, they seem to have used these powers, not so much to maintain the integrity of fiefs as to exact a profit from their dissolution. This practice, combined with the fall in the real value of seignorial incomes and the partition of inheritances, seems to be destroying middling feudal property in thirteenth century France. The greatest amongst the nobility may not have been altogether the losers from this tendency. Along with the monarchy and the bourgeoisie, the close-knit dynasties ruling the provinces perhaps fell heir to some of the property dissipated in this manner by the holders of fiefs. On the other hand, the development of a squirearchy out of the vassalic ranks of French feudalism may well have been stunted. In England too, of course, men fell out of the middling feudal order in the thirteenth century; but the result was not so much the disintegration of a class as consolidation within it—a process probably aided by the general prevalence of primogeniture, and by the closer grip of English landowners on the soil in a period of high agrarian profits.

Turning to the action of the state, again there are many similarities to be noticed. There are common features in the policies adopted in the royal demesnes. Both monarchies had similar interests as feudal overlords which did something to shape the pattern of their legislation and the judgements of their courts. Both had pressing fiscal needs which helped to inspire their treatment of some of the problems which confronted them. Yet the legislation of thirteenth century France, on matters with which this paper has been concerned, has neither the scope nor the comprehensiveness of that of contemporary England. Even at the end of the century, the French monarchy was still only one amongst competing legislative and judicial authorities; and there was still much that was tentative in its incursions into the domain of private law.[103] Where it did intervene, it tended to do so very much in the manner of a mere feudal lord writ large, concerned to assert a feudal superiority and (particularly later in the century) to exploit that superiority for fiscal ends. By contrast, the statutes of Edward I have, in Maitland's words, 'a characteristic that makes them unique', in that 'they enter into the domain of private law and make vast changes in it'.[104] In some respects they halted the tendencies of a century, even where those tendencies had won the blessing of the courts of common law. They did something to restore to the lords of the land control over their property. So much may have seemed no more than necessary if the magnates were to play their proper part in an ordered community. At the same time good laws were made for the poor folk—laws which did something to consolidate the past gains of the tenant, as well as to specify ordered process as the proper recourse of all. The constructive, if not always disinterested, intervention of the state in shaping the private law of England, the curiously modern appearance of its endeavour to stabilize and direct the processes of social change, are not the least remarkable of the many remarkable features of thirteenth century English history.

NOTES

1 M. Bloch, *Les Caractères originaux de l'histoire rurale française*, p. 98.
2 M. Bloch, *Les Caractères originaux de l'histoire rurale française*, pp. 95 sq.
3 'The chronology of labour services', *Trans. Roy. Hist. Soc.*, 4th ser., xx (1937).
4 For England see E. A. Kosminsky, 'Services and money rents in the thirteenth century', *Econ. Hist. Rev.*, 1st ser., v (1935).
5 Bloch, *op. cit.*, pp. 73–4, and cf. p. 101 for champarts in which 'anciennement personne n'y avait droit d'héritage' but wherein such rights were quickly acquired.
6 I use this phrase in the sense used by Prof. Postan, *art. cit.*, p. 187.
7 E.g. the spread of leases for term of years and, in England at least, of tenancies at will: F. L. Ganshof in *Cambridge Economic Hist.*, i. 305 sqq., and E. Miller, *The abbey and bishopric of Ely*, pp. 109–11.
8 R. Boutruche, 'Aux origines d'une crise nobiliaire', *Annales d'histoire sociale*, i (1939), 161–2, and in *IXᵉ congrès international des sciences historiques, Rapports*, p. 429; A. Luchaire in E. Lavisse *Histoire de France*, iii (i), 368. For heavy reliefs as a contributory cause of 'l'affaiblissement financier' of the Poitevin nobility, see E. Lyon, 'Comment fut élaborée l'ordonnance sur les rachats en Poitou', *Bibl. de l'Ecole des Chartes*, lxxxviii (1927), 88.
9 Bloch, *op. cit.*, pp. 117 sqq.; R. Fawtier, *Hist. du moyen âge* (Glotz series), vi. 8–9.
10 E. Teulet, *Layettes du Trésor des Chartes*, ii, no. 1640.
11 *Henry III and the Lord Edward*, ii. 711–12.
12 See R. S. Hoyt, *The Royal Demesne in English Constitutional History, 1066–1272*.
13 Powicke, *op. cit.*, p. 704.
14 Luchaire, *op. cit.*, iii (i), 203.
15 J. Declareuil, *Histoire générale du droit français*, p. 183.
16 For the extent of this custom, see F. Pollock and F. W. Maitland, *History of English Law*, ii. 207; G. C. Homans, *English Villagers in the Thirteenth Century*, pp. 109 sqq. and 'Partible Inheritance in Villein Holdings', *Econ. Hist. Rev.*, 1st ser., viii (1937), 48–56.
17 *Year Books, 2–3 Edward II* (ed. F. W. Maitland, Selden Soc.), pp. 95–7.
18 Pollock and Maitland, *op. cit.*, i. 268–70. For this and what follows, see T. F. T. Plucknett, *The Legislation of Edward I*, pp. 110 sq.
19 Cf. the remarks of Boutruche in *Ann. d'hist. sociale*, i (1939), 257.
20 E.g. *Bracton's Note Book* (ed. F. W. Maitland), pl. 566, and Bracton's marginal note thereon which goes even further in allowing free disposition of the *maritagium* than the judges did in determining the case in question.
21 *De Legibus*, vii. 1.
22 For an analysis of the various customs, see E. Chénon, *Histoire générale du droit français*, ii (i), 248 sq.
23 E.g. the case between Stephen de Sancerre and his two sisters in 1268, where it was adjudged that the latter receive half the fief. This exactly follows the custom of the district which would have applied if the heritage had been partitioned between three brothers. The castle of Marcheville, however, which formed part of the fief, was not to be divided with the rest: E. Beugnot, *Les Olim*, i. 720–1; J. Boutaric, *Actes du Parlement de Paris*, i, no. 307.
24 In the south generally partition was the rule, and led to an extreme 'morcellement' of fiefs: R. Michel, *L'administration royale dans la sénéschaussée de Beaucaire*, pp. 114–15; A. Molinier, 'Administration féodale en Languedoc', in C. Devic and J. Vaissette, *Histoire générale de Languedoc*, vii (ed. of 1879), pp. 150–1.
25 For the Norman custom, see E. J. Tardif, *Très ancien coutumier*, c. xlv.
26 E.g. in Brittany (Teulet, *Layettes du Trésor des Chartes*, i, no. 337), Normandy (H. Lagouelle, *La propriété foncière dans le très ancien droit normande*, i. 227–30), and Champagne (Declareuil, *op. cit.*, p. 249).
27 Lagouelle, *loc. cit.*, and cf. F. M. Powicke, *Loss of Normandy*, pp. 68–9, 98–102. The Norman system can also be studied in practice in L. Delisle, *Recueil des jugements de l'Echiquier de Normandie*. Impartibility was the rule for baronies (nos. 137–8),

ducal serjeanties (no. 504), *feoda lorice* (no. 598) and even for the fief of quarter of a knight (no. 247). On the other hand, there are many references to heritages which are fully partible nos. 175, 587, 611, 650, 664, 698); and we even hear of a *feudum lorice* the tenant of which has *participes;* and of two such fees divided between four brothers (nos. 214, 653).

28 Lagouelle, *op. cit.,* pp. 231–3.

29 *Ordonnances des rois de France,* i. 29.

30 Beugnot, *Les Olim,* i. 47, 424.

31 Declareuil, *op. cit.,* p. 252.

32 Bloch, *La Société féodale: formation des liens de dépendance,* pp. 315–16; Esmein, *Cours élémentaire de l'histoire du droit français* (ed. of 1895), pp. 210–11. On the impartibility of baronies, see P. Viollet, *Etablissements de Saint Louis,* ii. 36; iii. 285; Boutaric, *Actes,* i, no. 1394 and Appendice, nos. 5, 170A.

33 For a royal license to partition the barony of Servye in 1268, see Beugnot, *Les Olim,* i. 706.

34 Teulet, *Layettes du Trésor des Chartes,* ii, no. 3049.

35 Beugnot, *Les Olim,* i. 263, 308; Boutaric, *Actes,* i, Appendice, no. 21.

36 *Ibid.,* i, Appendice, no. 928.

37 *Ibid.,* i, no. 2269; Appendice, nos. 545, 562.

38 Declareuil, *op. cit.,* p. 252.

39 E.g. Beugnot, *Les Olim,* i. 444, where a royal grant to X and his heir male does not defeat the expectations of that heir's younger brother.

40 Viollet, *Histoire des institutions politiques,* ii. 422.

41 Cf. my *Abbey and bishopric of Ely,* pp. 177, 185–6.

42 Pollock and Maitland, *op. cit.,* i. 331–2, and cf. Plucknett, *op. cit.,* pp. 103–4.

43 Glanville, *De Legibus,* vii. 1.

44 For France, Chénon, *op. cit.,* ii (i), 167–74; for England, Pollock and Maitland, *op. cit.,* i. 332, 346. Glanville seems to imply that a tenant was free to subinfeudate, but that he must obtain the consent of the lord to substitution: H. Brunner, "The History of English Law', *Political Science Quarterly,* xi (1896), 539.

45 Holdsworth, *History of English Law,* iii. 75, and Maitland, *Bracton's Note Book,* i. 134. In at least two of the cases Bracton collected (pl. 1054, 1102) the right of the father to alienate the heritage was supported by the courts despite the protest of the heir. This situation may even have some bearing on the early history of entails: see particularly the circumstances described in pl. 36.

46 Bloch, *La société féodale: formations des liens de dépendance,* p. 220. For examples of its use to prevent alienations in mortmain, see Beugnot, *Les Olim,* i. 444, 497. Heirs would also have the support of the courts against any attempt by donees to make a profit on the transaction, or even to recover compensation for improvements to the property while it was in their hands: Boutaric, *Actes,* i, nos. 748, 1825.

47 According to Chénon, *op. cit.,* ii (i), 168, this was the rule in Normandy, Champagne and Burgundy. In Normandy, however, a tenant seems to have had some freedom with one-third of his holding; he could mortgage it or devise it by will, give it as a marriage portion, or devise it in mortmain: Delisle, *Jugements de l'Echiquier,* nos. 595, 765, and Tardif, *Très ancien coutumier,* c. lvii. 4, lxxxix.

48 Teulet, *Layettes du Trésor des Chartes,* ii, no. 1700.

49 E.g. Tardif, *Très ancien coutumier,* c. xc.

50 Bloch, *op. cit.,* p. 324; Declareuil, *op. cit.,* pp. 259–60.

51 Viollet, *Hist. du droit civil français,* p. 652.

52 For an example of this procedure from 1226, see Teulet, *Layettes du Trésor des Chartes,* ii, no. 1745.

53 Viollet, *op. cit.,* pp. 652–3.

54 Viollet, *Etablissements de Saint Louis,* i. 162–3.

55 Luchaire, *Manuel des institutions françaises,* p. 241.

56 *Ordonnances,* i. 358 (art. viii); Langlois, *Hist. de France,* iii (ii), 268. There was a good reason for this opposition. Since the king did homage to no man, the services which vassalage entailed were lost to the lord of any fief the king acquired: L. Halphen, *A travers l'histoire du moyen âge,* pp. 266–74.

57 Boutaric, *Actes*, i, no. 1903.

58 Beugnot, *Les Olim*, i. 604.

59 Viollet, *Histoire des institutions politiques*, ii. 250.

60 M. Bloch, *Rois et Serfs*, pp. 60 sq.

61 So Odo, lord of La-Chapelle-St-Sepulchre sought the consent of Theobald of Champagne for the manumission of a serf in 1239: Teulet, *Layettes du Trésor des Chartes*, ii, no. 2762.

62 Teulet, *op. cit.*, ii, nos. 1670, 1691.

63 E.g. Boutaric, *Actes*, i, nos. 151, 1642; and on all this see Chénon, *op. cit.*, ii (i), pp. 68–70, and Esmein, *op. cit.*, pp. 247–8.

64 Ganshof in *Cambridge Economic History*, i. 291.

65 C. V. Langlois, *Philip III le Hardi*, pp. 259 sq.

66 Boutaric, *Actes*, i, nos. 1941, 1948A, Appendice, no. 159; Devic and Vaissette, *Histoire générale de Languedoc*, x (Preuves), col. 121–2.

67 *Ordonnances*, i. 303–7.

68 E.g. *ibid.*, pp. 322–4.

69 F. M. Powicke, 'Observations on the English Freeholder', *Festschrift Alfons Dopsch*, p. 384.

70 Plucknett, *op. cit.*, p. 61.

71 *Ibid.*, p. 104; Holdsworth, *History of English Law*, iii. 79. The latter also observes (p. 82) that the objection of the tenant was equally no bar to the transfer of the seignory by the lord.

72 *Select Cases in the Court of King's Bench* (ed. G. O. Sayles, Selden Soc.), i, pl. 34. It might, of course, be possible to guard against these eventualities by private agreement, and *Bracton's Note Book*, pl. 543, may indicate one of the ways of doing so. It records a declaration by Agatha, daughter of Alan of St. George, that she had made a covenant with Brian Lisle (is he her lord?) that she would not alienate any of her heritage without his consent; and that if she wished to do so, she would give him a right of pre-emption.

73 *Curia Regis Rolls*, ii. 68; iv. 34–5; Pollock and Maitland, *op. cit.*, i. 290.

74 *Red Book of the Exchequer* (ed. H. Hall, Rolls Ser.), ii, p. cclxxxv.

75 *Close Rolls*, 1254–6, p. 429. It may be that all memory of this enactment was lost until it was discovered by Mr. Turner in very recent times (*Select Cases in the Court of King's Bench*, iii, p. xlvii); but the principle which it embodied remained very much alive.

76 *Rotuli Hundredorum*, i. 13.

77 *Select Cases in the Court of King's Bench*, i, pl. 35; and cf. ii, pl. 36, and *Fleta* (ed. J. Selden, 1685), p. 198: 'Dari non potuerunt sine regio assensu tenementa que de rege tenentur'.

78 *Rotuli Parliamentorum*, i. 430.

79 Plucknett, *op. cit.*, pp. 102 sq.

80 Devic and Vaissette, *op. cit.*, vii. 157; Ganshof, in *Cambridge Economic History*, i. 285.

81 Restrictions against alienations applied, therefore, particularly to land held in feudal tenure: see the letter of St. Louis to the citizens of Tournai in R. Wauters, *Libertés communales* (Preuves), p. 129.

82 Devic and Vaissette, *op. cit.*, vii. 157; Miller, *Abbey and bishopric of Ely*, p. 130 n.

83 For what follows see Esmein, *op. cit.*, pp. 276–9; Chénon, *op. cit.*, i. 785–90; Luchaire, *Manuel*, pp. 175–7; and Viollet, *Etablissements de S. Louis*, i. 163; ii. 244–6.

84 Beugnot, *Les Olim*, i. 443, 717; Teulet, *Layettes*, ii, no. 2276; Boutaric, *Actes*, i, Appendice, no. 33. In Normandy this rule applied to all acquisitions made in the fiefs of churches, and those for which churches could not properly perform the service due: Tardif, *Très ancien coutumier*, c. lvii. 5, 6.

85 E.g. Boutaric, *Actes*, i, nos. 1503, 1836.

86 *Ibid.*, no. 1470.

87 So much is implied by the royal licence to Lagny to retain a fief given to the monastery by a certain knight forty years and more earlier: Beugnot, *Les Olim*, i. 474.

88 For the confiscation of unlicensed acquisitions see Boutaric, *Actes*, i, nos. 1820, 1821,

1831. At this stage, the king seems to have been willing to accept twenty years tenure as giving a valid title (*ibid.*, Appendice, no. 118B)—a period extended to thirty years in 1275.

89 So called in a letter to the seneschal of Toulouse: Devic and Vaissette, *op. cit.*, x (Preuves), col. 241; for the text, see *Ordonnances*, i. 303–7.

90 *Ibid.*, p. 305; Boutaric, *Actes*, i, no. 2119 and Appendice, no. 294.

91 Langlois, *Philippe III le Hardi*, pp. 206–7.

92 E. Perroy, 'Le cartulaire des amortissements de Forez', *Le Moyen Age*, 4th ser., iv (1949), 274.

93 Boutaric, *Actes*, i, Appendice, no. 701.

94 E.g. *ibid.*, i, no. 2131, and Devic and Vaissette, *op. cit.*, x (Preuves), col. 241.

95 Boutaric, *Actes*, i, no. 2501.

96 *Ordonnances*, i. 322–4. The tariff of charges, furthermore, was a minimum and not a maximum one. The commissioners were told to double them in certain districts where the price of land was high; and in all cases they were to increase them if possible and not to lower them on any account.

97 Chénon, *op. cit.*, i. 790.

98 Petition of the Barons, c. 10.

99 Provisions of Westminster, c. 14.

100 On this and what follows see Plucknett, *op. cit.*, pp. 96–102.

101 *Select Cases in the Court of King's Bench*, iii, p. xxxix. The two cases are not of course (as Professor Cheney has pointed out to me) directly comparable. The appropriation of tithes was governed by Canon Law, and not by the law and custom governing the transfer of feudal tenements.

102 Cf. Bloch, *Caractères originaux*, pp. 120–1.

103 For the limitations of the royal legislative authority, even under Philip the Fair, see Fawtier, *op. cit.*, vi. 66–7; and for its slight concern with the domain of private law, Chénon, *op. cit.*, i. 530–1 and Viollet, *Histoire des institutions politiques*, ii. 200–2.

104 *Constitutional History of England*, p. 19.

9

The Household of the Norwegian Kings in the Thirteenth Century

LAURENCE M. LARSON

THE GREAT AGE OF Old Norse literature began with the twelfth century. For more than two hundred years there was a continued production of sagas and poems, of charters and laws. Much of this literature was, it is true, the product of earlier ages now for the first time put into written form; but a large part was original. From the medieval writings of Western Europe it differs in certain important respects: it was not written in the language of the learned, but in the speech of the people, not by clerks but by cultured laymen; the clerk and the monk wrote amid cloistered surroundings and consequently the church and all its belongings occupy a prominent place in their writings; the scalds and the sagamen had other interests—their stories deal more with kings and chiefs, with warfare and politics. While these tales cannot always be relied on in matters of narrative history, the student of social and political institutions will find in them a source of much valuable information.[1] The importance of Old Norse literature for the study of early Germanic society has long been understood; but it is only within the last generation that historians have begun to realize that these writings may also be used to illustrate institutional developments that are medieval rather than Germanic. Sophus Bugge's contention that the Eddic myths are merely Norse versions of legends current in Western Europe during the Viking age may never be universally accepted;[2] but there is no doubt a large measure of truth in the statement that Scandinavian thought in the closing centuries of heathendom contained a large fund of borrowed ideas. A most favorable period for the introduction of foreign customs came in the ninth and tenth centuries when the reputed descendants of Woden were reshaping Northern society along national lines and establishing new institutions, such as a national kingship with all that the term implies. Nearly all the rulers of Norway during the tenth and eleventh centuries had spent years abroad either as vikings, mercenary chiefs or exiles before they were admitted to the kingship; and it is only natural that in the arrangement of their own courts and surroundings they should imitate the institutions of other princely households.

As the medieval Norse writers were usually men who spent a large part of their time at the royal court, they naturally allude freely to the men and the affairs of the king's garth. On the subject of court customs much information can be found in the *King's Mirror* or *Speculum Regale*,[3] a unique document dating from about 1200, the ostensible purpose of which is to instruct a youth how to demean himself in the various walks of life, especially in the royal presence. Some use can also be made of the royal charters dating from the thirteenth and fourteenth centuries of which a considerable number has come down to us.[4] But by far the best source for our present purpose is the *Court Law* of Magnus Lawmender (1263–1280),[5] a revision of an earlier law that was probably put into form in the reign of King Sverri whose rule of thirty eventful years closed in 1202.

I.

From the earliest years of the Norse monarchy the king's guard seems to have formed an organized corps subject to certain definite laws or customs. We get a glimpse of such a corps in the reign of Harold Fairhair, the first Norwegian king.[6] How complete and definite this organization was in the ninth century cannot be known; but by the thirteenth it had developed into a somewhat elaborate form. There existed then in the king's garth (the chapel service not included) four distinct but closely related guilds, all organized for the purpose of guarding or serving the king, each in its own way. Of these the king himself was only a member, though naturally the most influential and powerful one. These four groups were the "hirdmen", the "gests", the "candle-swains" and the "house-carles". Usually the complete household was spoken of as the "hird" (*hirð*), a term that suggests an Old English origin;[7] but more specifically this term was used for the most important corps, the members of which were known as "hirdmen" (*hirðmenn*).

The author of the *Speculum Regale* advises all who wish to enter the guard to appear before the king with a spokesman. On coming to the court they are told to seek out those who are in the habit of presenting such requests to the king and to cultivate their friendship. The most favorable time would be when the king was at the table, as he would then most likely be in good humor.[8] If the king agreed to receive the man, one of the higher officials of the guard, the marksman or the staller, would submit the matter to the assembled hirdmen. Should any one present object to granting the request, the matter would be laid over until the objections could be investigated; these might be based on ancestry, earlier record or the like.[9] Apparently no man could become a hirdman without the free consent of the guild membership.

The Court Law also provides for an initiation ceremony closely resembling that of homage, of which it was probably an adaptation,[10] though it is also possible that the two ceremonies may have developed independently from some ancient custom prevailing in the Germanic *comitatus.*[11] The king was in his high-seat with his guard grouped about him; across his knees lay a sword, his right hand grasping the hilt. The candidate approached, knelt, touched the sword-hilt and kissed the royal hand. He then arose and took the oath of fealty. Kneeling once more he placed his folded hands between those of the king and kissed his new lord. The officiating trencher-swain then led him to his new comrades from whom he received the hand and kiss of fellowship.[12]

While it was usual to admit only voluntary applicants to the guard, this rule was sometimes broken; the king occasionally solicited members, and at times even commanded men to join the hird.[13] On the death of the king, the men were released from their oaths; but it was customary for the new ruler to receive the former henchmen into his own guard.[14] As the Norse constitution permitted a divided kingship, it would sometimes happen that the kingdom had several courts, each of the joint rulers maintaining his own.[15] In one instance a kingsman appears to have served in two such guards at the same time.[16]

The duties of the hirdman are summed up in the oath of initiation: to be faithful to his lord in open and in secret; to follow the king at home and abroad, and never to leave his court without permission, except under stress of great necessity.[17] His particular duty was to guard the king's life and person;[18] the corps was therefore chosen from "all that was strongest and stoutest, both of folk of the land and of outlanders".[19] In battle the hirdmen were grouped about the king;[20] the bravest and strongest were with him on shipboard;[21] they sat around him and before him in the public assemblies.[22] Of the regular guards at court the sources speak of two: the day-guard or "following" (*fylgð*) and the night-guard or ward (*vörðr*).[23] Of the latter were two divisions—the inner-ward (*innvörðr*) also called head-ward (*höfuðvöðr*) and the outer-ward (*utvörðr*).[24] The head-ward was stationed near the king's person, usually outside the door of the chamber where he slept;[25] it was composed, it seems, of hirdmen only. The outer-ward was placed at a greater distance and was normally made up of gests.[26] Owing to its great length, the winter night was divided into two watch periods, the guards changing at midnight.[27] The outer-guards went to their duty heavily armed, and in times of special danger each guardsman was further provided with a trumpet.[28] All irregularities with respect to this service were heavily punished with fines or dismissal in disgrace.[29]

The day-guard was ordinarily composed of six men, one walking on each side of the king and four at a proper distance behind.[30] On certain festive occasions and when the king entertained distinguished visitors, the number was increased to twelve, and the highest dignitaries of the court and the realm were then called into service.[31] The guard reported when the chapel bell rang for matins and at once proceeded to the sanctuary to join the king in worship. During the remainder of the day they remained in the king's presence or wherever he ordered them to be. When serving in the "following" the hirdman wore his best clothes and bore his best weapons—helmet, shield and sword. As the king might have tasks to assign to those who were not acting as day-guards, it was customary for the henchmen to take a stand somewhere near the royal chambers where they might be easily be found if wanted.[32]

As the name of the guard is clearly borrowed from the Anglo-Saxon,[33] it would not be strange if the institution itself should reveal Old English influence in its general organization and character. On the make-up of the English guard, the Anglo-Saxon sources give us no satisfactory information; but there are indications that the men were grouped in day-guards and night-guards much as they were at the Norse court in later times. The Norwegian king who attended morning worship with his following of six henchmen was, perhaps, continuing an old custom that prevailed in Northumbria in the seventh century when King Oswy visited Colman's church attended by "five or six thegns".[34] Of the two forces holding night-guard, the inner-guard (head-ward) seems to be mentioned in *Beowulf*, where we are told that Wiglaf kept head-ward over his dead lord.[35] The same term (*heafodweard*) is used in the *Rectitudines* for a peculiar service that the thegn owes to the king.[36] The service reappears in *Domesday* under the name of *inguardus* (inner-ward), a duty that certain socmen of Cambridgeshire would be called on to perform "if the king should come into the shire".[37] The fact that these men were not resident at court should cause no difficulty; the Norse king also had a number of non-resident henchmen who had particular duties to perform when the king came into their part of the realm.[38] It seems probable that the mysterious term *avera*, which is coupled with *inguardus* in an entry in *Domesday* and which was also a service due "when the king came into the shire",[39] is another survival of ancient custom connected with the royal court.

The hirdmen also had a place in the council of the realm whenever the king should choose to call one.[40] They took a prominent part in coronation ceremonies and in the election of a king in cases of disputed inheritance or failure of heirs.[41] The royal council met whenever the king chose, but all matters pertaining to the installation of a new ruler had to be transacted at a grand council in Throndhjem, in which the hirdmen sat with abbots and bishops.[42]

In return for his services the henchman received a regular pay in coin or bullion paid out on the eighth day of the Yule festival. If money was lacking, dishes and jewels were broken up, weighed and distributed.[43] In addition the more favored received gifts, especially swords, arm rings and the use of royal estates.[44] In times of war extra rewards appear to have been given.[45] But, on the whole, service in the king's garth was not a very gainful occupation. To be ranked with the kingsmen was, however, a mark of great distinction, and the honor was eagerly sought.[46] When at court the hirdman ate regularly at the king's table.[47] If captured in battle or otherwise, he was generally sure of a ransom.[48] For such as were rendered completely helpless in the royal service, the king was pledged to provide a home; the very poor among the aged hirdmen were placed in some monastic institution, the king and the guard each paying half of the expenses connected with such an arrangement. To provide a fund for this purpose an initiation fee of an öre silver was collected from all who were admitted to the hird and half an öre from those who entered the corps of gests or candle-swains.[49] In 1308 steps were taken toward providing a hospital for the sick and an asylum for the aged and unfortunate in connection with the royal chapel at Oslo. For the support of this, the king donated a considerable sum and provided for fees much as before, only that greater sums were now to be collected.[50]

The business of the guild was transacted at the "hird-gemot" (*hirð-stefna*). When the signal was sounded on the trumpet, it was the duty of every hirdman to inquire as to the reason for the call and to hasten to the assembly.[51] Ordinarily the meetings were held in a hall that was used for such purposes mainly.[52] Those who were absent without good excuse were fined an öre silver; three offences meant forfeiture of membership. Each corps had its own signal and its own *gemot;* those who were not called were forbidden to attend.[53] Serious matters, such as treason,[54] riots [55] or quarrels within the guard, were brought up at these meetings. The henchmen were expected to treat each other as brethren, to assist one another in trouble and to see that justice was done to all; but the ideal of good-fellowship was hard to attain.[56] Apparently the marksman and the staller had or came to have some judicial authority at these sessions; [57] the marksman collected certain fines, perhaps he also assessed them.[58] But there is clear evidence that in serious cases some sort of a jury was employed; when a dignitary within the guard is accused of treason, says the Court Law, "there shall be named twelve of the most discreet men, who shall investigate whether the man can be rightfully convicted of the crime or not".[59] The *hirðstefna* was evidently an ancient institution in the thirteenth century; it seems to have been introduced into the English royal household in the reign of Cnut, for we find distinct traces of an organization exercising judicial authority over and among the English house-carles in the days of Edward the Confessor.[60]

Thus far we have spoken of the guard as a corps of warriors that remained continuously at the king's residence. But there were also hirdmen abroad in the realm looking after the royal interests everywhere; these spent only a part, often a very small part, of their time at court.[61] We are told that Saint Olaf kept sixty hirdmen, thirty gests and thirty house-carles continuously at his garth,[62] and that one of his successors, Olaf the Quiet (1066–1093), doubled the numbers.[63] But this total, two hundred and forty, does not represent the entire number of kingsmen; counting the candle-swains and the hirdmen whose homes were elsewhere, we should find the number much larger. Apparently there was a tendency to increase the force of absentee-henchmen with the result that the character of the corps as a whole suffered an appreciable decline.[64]

In the earlier centuries of the Norse *comitatus* there may have existed a relative equality among the henchmen, but such was not the case in the later Middle Ages. By that time a system of classes had developed within the hird, two of which stand out with some distinctness: the "landed-men" and the "trencher-swains". Just when these classes first began to appear we do not know; Snorre seems to believe that Olaf the Quiet was the first king to employ trencher-swains,[65] but it is not likely that their service was wholly an innovation of that reign. Though not hirdmen in the narrower sense, the landed-men and the trencher-swains were always classed as such; they were chosen from the hird, they retained their membership in the guild and were never wholly excused from the guardsmen's duty. In the one case the mark of distinction was social position and political influence; in the other, an important service in the king's hall.

The landed-men, as such, were neither servants nor officials. Apparently they were members of powerful families whom the king wished to bind closely to the crown.[66] To accomplish this he admitted them into his guard and endowed them with valuable fiefs. Outside the princely order they were the highest dignitaries in the land. Each landed-man was allowed to maintain a guard of forty house-carles, or more if the king permitted it.[67] As Norway rarely had a duke or an earl, the landed-men ranked next to the king in popular estimation. In return for honors recevied they assumed certain military duties, but especially did they bind themselves to watch over the king's interests in their parts of the realm. Still, they had no jurisdiction, they were not officials except when the king invested them with a recognized office.[68] Their powers were derived from wealth and family connections. Keyser believes that they were originally chiefs of the Norse hundred;[69] but this opinion can hardly be correct, as in that case the number of landed-men would have been great, while as a matter of fact the opposite seems to have been true. In the closing decades of the twelfth century there seem to have been but five men of this rank in the kingdom.[70] In the reign of King Hakon IV. (1217–1263) the saga frequently speaks of nine.[71] In all probability we have in this institution a faint reflection of feudal vassallage.

The dignity was conferred in the hirdmen's hall at one of the great festivals. Immediately after grace had been said the king would announce his intention to honor the candidate named. Two men of the highest rank present would then escort him to the high-seat; the king would rise, take him by the hand and lead him to a seat among the other landed-men.[72] At the great Christmas and Easter festivals, the landed-men were required to be present at court and serve in the day-guard.[73] At coronation ceremonies they acted a prominent and very important part.[74] But only so long as the landed-man remained faithful to his lord, could he retain his honors; treason meant a trial in the hirdmen's *gemot,* and conviction meant forfeiture of all rights.[75] In 1277 it was decreed that the landed-men should henceforth be known as barons and lords.[76] A generation later (1308) it was determined to create no more barons,[77] and the dignity gradually disappeared.

"King Olaf had these court customs, to wit, that he let stand before his board trencher-swains (*skutilsveinar*), and they poured to him in board-beakers, and also to all men of high estate who sat at his table . . ." [78] "They have the fairest service in the garth, and must be carefully trained." [79] To stand before the king's table and serve His Majesty with meat and drink was considered a great honor, and a place in this service was eagerly sought.[80] In rank the trencher-swains stood next to the landed-men.[81] In addition to their duties at the royal table, the trencher-swains had certain important responsibilities with respect to the safety of the royal person. For a week's period two of these officials had complete charge of all arrangements looking toward peace and protection, especially at night. They placed the guards and made sure that all necessary precautions were taken against possible surprise.[82] Usually the trencher-swains were excused from serving as guards-men, but in time of war or special danger they were obliged to watch with the rest in their turn, the men in charge doing guard duty during the week of their special authority.[83] Like the other members of the hird, the trencher-swains might be called upon to perform a variety of other duties both in times of peace and of war.[84]

It seems that a candidate for these honors had to serve an apprenticeship as cup-bearer in the royal hall. Appointments were always made at the close of a feast. An empty beaker was brought in and placed upon the king's table. The king handed it to the candidate who received it, kissing the royal hand; he then withdrew immediately but soon returned with the beaker filled with the king's beverage.[85] When the landed-men were given the baronial title (1277), the trencher-swains were advanced to knighthood, though it is likely that the promotion was one in title only.[86] When the baronage became extinct in the fourteenth century the knights were the highest order in the kingdom.[87]

"It is known to most men", says the scribe of the Court Law, "that in the king's guard the gests (*gestir*) stand next to the hirdmen in title dignity and privileges." [88] These formed a smaller corps, in theory half as large as that of the hirdmen.[89] As in the case of the higher guard, admission to this guild was usually on application, the procedure being much the same in both instances. The ceremony of initiation was somewhat simpler, however: the applicant would kneel, touch the royal sword, kiss the king's hand and swear everlasting fidelity; after this he was introduced to his new associates who greeted him with a hand-clasp.[90]

In general, the rights of the gests were similar to those of the hirdmen.[91] In battle they were grouped with these about the royal colors; [92] on sea they had their own ship which they sailed near to the royal dragon.[93] They had their own chief and their separate guild assembly.[94] At Yule-tide and the Easter festivals they were admitted to the king's tables, but not at other times.[95] Their wages were half as large as the hirdmen's pay,[96] and they contributed in like proportion to the fund for the sick and the aged.[97]

The duties of the gests may be grouped into two leading classes: they served as the king's spies throughout the realm and rode his errands generally; at court they served in the outer-guard. The latter duty has already been described. As the greater number of the gests might be absent on the king's errands, it was permissible to allow men who were not henchmen to share this watch, but a certain number of gests must always be present. The gests might also serve in any other form of watch except the head-ward.[98] It was as the king's spies and messengers of death that these men performed their most acceptable services. It was their duty to learn what hostile movements were abroad, to forestall treason wherever possible, to cleanse the realm of their lord's enemies. Sometimes the king would dispatch his gests to slay an enemy, in which case they were allowed half of the wealth that they could carry away; the rest, including all the gold, belonged to the king.[99] The gests might also be sent on other errands, and when necessary they could call on all the kingsmen and local officials for assistance in carrying out their instructions.[100]

As the duties of the gests were such as might involve great dangers, they were chosen, not for courtly behavior or high connections, but for personal bravery and prowess. Asbiorn, in his speech against King Sverri, speaks of the king's gests as "the worst of men, the limbs of the very fiend".[101] Though in the words of an enemy, this characterization no doubt contains a large measure of truth: to the readiness of these warriors to undertake bloody and dangerous tasks the sagas bear frequent testimony.[102] It seems exceedingly strange, that in a country like medieval

Norway, where courts were numerous and legal systems rigidly adhered to, such an institution could be permitted to exist. Realizing its seeming non-Germanic character, historians have sought its origin in Celtic and Slavic lands. A corps known as the *gosti* has been found in early Russia and some have thought that the Vikings and Verangians may have become acquainted with this on their journeys to Constantinople, where at least one of the Old Norse kings (Harold Hardrada) served in the imperial guard; but there seem to have been gests in Norway before the reign of this king. An attempt has also been made to connect the *gestir* with the twelve *gwestai* who collected the food rents of the Old Welsh kings; on the whole this seems the more plausible explanation, though in the present state of the evidence it is hardly more than a conjecture.[103]

"[King Olaf] also had candle-swains (*kertisveinar*) who held up candles before his board, and as many of them as men of high degree sat there." [104] It is natural to think of these servants as pages, boys or at least youths;[105] but the sources do not support such a view. It is probable that the candle-service came in with the other new fashions that became current in the reign of Olaf the Quiet; [106] but the Norse rulers were not mere imitators—a foreign institution transplanted to Norway soon took on a national stamp. That the Norse candle-bearers were men is evident from a variety of considerations. In addition to their regular duties in the banquet hall they might be called on to do service in the day-guard,[107] a duty that would hardly fall to a mere page; in time of war they fought with the other kingsmen; [108] they sailed their own ships, had a chief of their own appointed by the king and apparently had a guild organization like those of the higher corps; [109] in matters of household finance they ranked with the gests and shared with these in the privilege of asylum and similar benefits.[110] As the candle-swains were to serve in the royal presence on occasions when courtly behavior was a prominent virtue, they were carefully chosen from good families after a close inquiry into their social position, wealth, abilities and behavior.[111] After the tables had been cleared but before the bowl of water for the king's hands had been brought in, the seneschal (*drotseti*) led the candidate toward the high-seat. The king extended his right hand over the table; the new kingsman took it in both his own, kissed it and vowed to be faithful in every service. After the ceremony the candle-swain assisted in washing the king's hands.[112] The men who held the candles were ranked among the henchmen (*handgengnir:* men who had gone to the king's hand) but not among the sword-takers (*sverðtakarar:* men who had touched the king's sword); [113] they therefore occupied a lower place at court than gests and hirdmen.

Originally, we are told, all the kingsmen were known by the common name of house-carles (*huskarlar*); but in the thirteenth century this term was limited to the lowest class of royal servants, the men who performed the manual labor in the king's household: [114] they were "to work all needful service in the garth and at whatso ingatherings were needful".[115] They seem to have been organized like the other kingsmen with ship and chief (*ræðismaðr*) and guild laws.[116] Fagrskinna tells us that in the eleventh century the house-carles were not counted among the henchmen; [117] but a century later they had, it seems, attained to this distinction.[118] As there were absentee-hirdmen there were also house-carles who seldom appeared at court. These were often the sons of wealthy yeomen or even of landed-men who for a small fee, often for the honor merely of being known as kingsmen, or for the protection that went with this relationship, entered the royal service. Their duties were various: they might be called on to pilot the king's ship, to act as royal messengers, to serve as the king's merchants and especially to assist his majesty's local officials.[119]

Among these various corps the feeling was not always the most cordial. The difference in rank, in treatment and in fare naturally resulted in envy and jealousy which often flared up at the great festive gatherings when men had drunk too freely. King Magnus Erlingsson's gests "liked ill that the hirdmen drank mead while they were given ale"; the result was a riot (1181).[120] It sometimes happened that trouble arose between individual members of different guilds, and usually the quarrel was taken up by their comrades.[121] In such cases the king seems to have exercised extensive judicial authority, assisted, no doubt, by the staller and the marksman, whose duty it was to attend all the meetings both of hirdmen and of gests.[122]

A wholly different, though none the less important, organization centred about the royal chapel. In the first half of the eleventh century a bishop resided in the king's garth; [123] but that was while the land was still largely heathen. With the organization of dioceses the court-bishop disappears and his place is taken by the court-priest (*hirðprestr*). The Court Law provides for two such priests, one to shrive the king and his henchmen and one to have charge of the books, vestments and the like that belonged to the royal chapel. For these services the king gave them each five marks and two gowns at Yule-tide; the henchmen paid them one-thirtieth of their wages.[124] The chapel soon came to have the usual force of lower ecclesiastics,[125] and it also maintained a school of some importance.[126]

In the early years of the twelfth century King Eystein erected two new churches for the use of his court, one in Bergen and one in the old capital, Throndhjem.[127] Later kings increased the number to fourteen.[128] At first the chapel-priests were appointed by the bishops in whose dioceses the churches happened to be located; [129] but in 1308 a decree went forth from Avignon which practically separated the chapel system from the national church administration. The appointments were given to the king and at the head of the entire group was placed a *magister capel-larum,* who to all intents and purposes became a bishop. He was even allowed to wear episcopal robes, at first only when no bishop was present, but later on all occasions.[130] The significance of these arrangements is readily seen. The ambitions of the Norse episcopate had been a source of much annoyance to King Hakon's predecessors; of this the monarch would now be in part relieved. He had now his own priesthood, educated, perhaps, at his own chapel schools, appointed by himself, consecrated by his own bishop. Possibly he hoped to extend the system to all parts of the realm. But the bishops at once made war on this new organization and finally succeeded in having it condemned as contrary to canon law.[131]

II.

Of servants and officials to whom were assigned some particular line of duties or functions in the king's garth, the sources name a considerable number. Most of these were, however, servants of the lower order, such as we should expect to find in every extensive household of the age.[132] Still, there were at the Norse court six officials that took a high rank: the butler, the seneschal, the treasurer, the marksman, the staller and the chancellor. Of these, all but two were chosen from among the hirdmen, the chancellor being always and the treasurer sometimes an ecclesiastic. The seneschal (*drotseti*—the word is probably a form of the German *Truchsess*) and the chief butler (*skenkjari*) were, in the thirteenth century, household officials only. With the advice of his friends the king selected, according to the Court Law, two men from among the trencher-swains most suitable in descent and deportment to fill these offices. If the king should find more suitable candidates outside the corps of hirdmen, he might appoint them; but first he must elevate them to the dignities of henchmen and trencher-swains.[133]

The *drotseti* of the fourteenth century was, however, a wholly different official from his predecessor of the thirteenth. In 1319 Magnus, a child of three years, was chosen king of Norway and Sweden. The regency that controlled affairs in Norway did not give a satisfactory rule, and at a council held in 1323 a regent was appointed with the title of *drotseti*.[134] The seneschal was now the highest civil official in the state. In this sense the office continued till near the close of the century.[135]

The king's treasurer (*fehirðir*), though doubtless a very ancient and useful servant at court, is rarely mentioned in the sources as a prominent official. It seems that an ecclesiastic (often the king's chaplain, perhaps) usually had charge of the royal treasury; [136] but at times it was also placed in secular hands. That the office was considered important is evidenced by the fact that Anders Plytt, who held it in 1263, was classed among the landed-men.[137] During the period under survey the treasurer seems to have been with the king in the garth, but in the fourteenth century we find four such functionaries, one in each of the leading cities.[138] Whether one of these still was regarded as the regular court treasurer, as some have thought,[139] is somewhat doubtful, as all seem to have had certain duties with respect to the kingsmen that were formerly performed in the king's garth.[140]

It seems probable that in the earlier years of the Norse monarchy the marksman (*merkismaðr*) was the highest official at court. He is alluded to in the court poetry of the early eleventh century,[141] and everywhere in the sagas he appears as a warrior of great distinction.[142] The marksman was entrusted with the king's banner; [143] in naval fights he held it in the prow of the royal dragon, with the stem-men, the fiercest and mightiest of the king's guard, grouped about him.[144] The law required that he should always be near the king; he was always to sleep in the king's garth, on the king's ship or wherever the king might be. At court he acted as judge or arbitrator,[145] and the tendency seems to have been to increase his judicial functions.[146] In the thirteenth century, however, the marksman's dignity was evidently passing; he still ranked with the landed-men, but he was no longer the first official at court,[147] the staller and the chancellor having risen above him. With the death of the last marksman in 1320 the office became extinct.

In St. Olaf's hall, as Snorre describes it, there were two high-seats, one for the king on the north side and a lower one directly across. In the lower high-seat sat the staller (*stallari*), an official of great prominence, for a time the highest dignitary at court.[148] Snorre repeatedly refers to the staller in his history, and he is also alluded to in the verses of the eleventh century scalds.[149] Usually the sources speak of but one staller, though at times there might be several.[150] In the poems the staller appears mainly as a war-chief; but in the sagas we find him performing certain important civil duties as well. At great public gatherings, such as the national assemblies, he acted as an intermediary between the king and the yeomanry, presenting the requests of the populace and urging the wishes of the ruler. He performed similar functions in the king's garth.[151] "At every 'thing' Biörn stood up and spake the king's errand", says the Icelandic historian in speaking of St. Olaf's famous staller.[152] Elsewhere we read of this same Biörn as being sent to Sweden on a diplomatic mission.[153] He was also a warrior as all the stallers were.[154] In battle they frequently commanded a division of the royal host[155] or one of the principal ships of the king's fleet.[156] When the king travelled by land the staller had some duties with regard to the stable service: he saw that horses and other equipments were properly provided.[157] The staller's connection with this service has led historians to believe that there is a direct connection between his office and that of the Frankish constable. The title itself seems to point to the same origin, though it appears more likely that *stallari* is derived from Old Norse *stallr* than from Latin *stabularius*. But even if we grant that the staller's title and certain of his functions were introduced from abroad, the probabilities are that these were applied or added to an office that was already enjoying a vigorous existence. The sister kingdoms of Denmark and Sweden each had a marshal (*marsk*, clearly derived from some form of O. H. G. *marashalh—mariscalcus*, marshal) who served as the highest military functionary in the realm and thus corresponded to the constable of Capetian France; but Norway never had such an official. The staller's chief and characteristic duty was to act as the king's spokesman. A glance at the medieval Norse constitution will reveal the importance of this function. The early Norwegian kings were not absolute monarchs; they had to consider public opinion and seek popular consent in all matters of consequence. The nation was divided into four grand jurisdictions, each with its own assembly; at these gatherings the king often appeared to consult with his fellow-freemen,[158] and it is readily seen that an official who possessed the gifts of oratory and diplomatic sense combined with the prestige of military leadership would be of great service to his lord.[159] It was probably such an official that the Danish conquerors introduced into England in the eleventh century.[160]

But as royalty grew stronger the usefulness of the spokesman naturally grew less prominent; in the thirteenth century the king's chief servant was not the staller but a new functionary, the chancellor. There seems to be no direct evidence for the existence of a Norse chancery before the thirteenth century; but charters and other documents were drawn up at court before that time,[161] and a royal seal was in use,[162] so there can be little doubt that the institution did have an earlier existence. The chancellor's title may have come in at a later date, but the fact that the Court Law awards this official the highest rank at court [163] suggests that the office must have existed already for a period of some length. The probabilities are that the chancery was introduced into Norway from England with the royal chapel service in the eleventh century.[164] In addition to his duties in the royal *scriptorium* and additional ones that the king might assign, the chancellor seems to have exercised those of a modern comptroller. "He shall also keep most careful accounts of the crown possessions, including such as are acquired . . . also of those lands that the king may grant to certain of his men and in what year of grace the grant be made. Further he shall make sure that the books containing the land rents due to the king are properly kept, that what should be added is added and that what should be cancelled is cancelled." [165] The office seems always to have been held by an ecclesiastic: Aki, who was

Duke Hakon's chancellor (1293–1299), was a deacon of the royal chapel in Bergen; [166] later, when his lord succeeded to the kingship, he was made dean of the royal chapel at Oslo where the king's residence now was.[167] In 1314 the chancellor's office was permanently associated with the deanship of this church. As this arrangement definitely located the chancery at Oslo and prevented the chancellor from travelling about with the king as freely as might be necessary, a vice-chancellor was provided for by the same decree, to whom were entrusted the royal seal and conscience when the king was absent from the capital.[168]

The chancellor was invested with his office at a special meeting of the henchmen; apparently all the various corps attended. "Then shall the king make known to all that he gives to the man that is named his seal with all the honors that go with it." When this had been proclaimed, the new dignitary would kneel and swear to serve faithfully, especially to conceal what the king wished to be kept secret.[169] The marksman was invested in much the same way; in his case the symbol employed was the banner.[170] The staller's office was conferred in the royal dining-hall. After grace had been said and the king's intentions had been announced, two trencher-swains led forth the chosen one; the king rose, took him by the hand and escorted him to the staller's high-seat.[171] In the cases of the other court officials the appointments appear to have been made without any accompanying ceremonial.

The rewards and privileges of these officials were first of all those that they enjoyed as the king's henchmen, as members of the royal hird. In addition there was the enjoyment of official dignity and authority, a seat among the barons when the king entertained his magnates and a certain definite income usually awarded in the form of a landed benefice. The chancellor, while not exactly a member of the hird, shared fully in these benefits. His official income was somewhat smaller than that of the staller or the marksman, but as he was permitted to collect a fee for almost every document prepared, it seems likely that his office proved to be a source of abundant revenue.[172]

The history of Norway in the fourteenth century is a record of great calamities and broken fortunes. The king's household shared in the general decline. Hakon V., the last vigorous ruler of medieval Norway, reduced the importance of the hird by abolishing the baronage: as a believer in absolutism he naturally feared an order that was rapidly developing into an aristocracy. After his death (1319) came half a century of much confusion, caused in part by the terrors of the Black Death and in part by unwise attempts to unite the crowns of Norway and Sweden. From 1380 to 1905, the country was ruled by foreign kings. After 1319 the hird gradually disintegrated. A royal household in the medieval sense could not exist without a resident king.

NOTES

[1] In preparing this paper I have made considerable use of the following sagas: Snorre's *Heimskringla*. Snorre's dates are 1178–1241. The references are to Morris and Magnusson's translation: *The Stories of the Kings of Norway* (London, 1894). *Flateyarbok* (eds. Vigfusson and Unger, Christiania, 1860–1868). The Flatey Book dates from 1370–1380 but the sagas contained are evidently of earlier origin. *Fagrskinna* (eds. Munch and Unger, Christiania, 1847). This is a briefer form of the *King-sagas* dating from the thirteenth century (1230–1240). The author seems to have used the same sources that Snorre made use of, at least in part.

[2] *Helge-Digtene i den Ældre Edda* (Copenhagen, 1896).

[3] *Kongs-skuggsio* (Soröe, 1768). Later editions by Keyser, Munch and Unger (Christiania, 1848) and by Brenner (Munich, 1881).

[4] *Diplomatarium Norvegicum* (Christiania, 1847–1871).

[5] *Hirðskraa*, in *Norges Gamle Love* (Old Norse Laws), II. Abbreviated to *N. G. L.: H.*

[6] *Corpus Poeticum Boreale* (Oxford, 1883), I. 257. See Larson, *The King's Household in England before the Norman Conquest* (*Univ. of Wis. Bulletin*, 1904), p. 157.

[7] *Hirð* is probably derived from the Old English *hired*, household, frequently a royal household.

[8] *Spec. Reg.*, 67 (xxx.).

[9] *N. G. L.*, II. 422: *H.* 30.

[10] But the two must not be confused: the kingsman was not a vassal.

[11] In the complaint of the *Wanderer*, an Old English poem from the seventh century or earlier (see Wülker's *Grundriss zur Geschichte der Angelsächsischen Literatur*), the minstrel calls to mind "how at one time his war-lord he kissed and embraced, laying his hands and his head on the chieftain's knee, when in days of yore he enjoyed the gift-seat" (ll. 41–44). There can be no doubt that the singer refers to his initiation into his lord's following. In several important particulars—the kneeling (which is implied), the kiss, the placing of the hand—this ceremony resembles the one described in the Court Law; the "sword-touching" is not alluded to, but this particular act was not required of all who entered the royal service, as will be seen elsewhere in this paper.

[12] *N. G. L.*, II. 422–423: *H.* 31.

[13] *Orvar-Odd's Saga* (Halle, 1892), c. 41; *Egil's Saga* (Halle, 1894), c. 25.

[14] *N. G. L.*, II. 399: *H.* 11. In such cases the oath alone was required.

[15] Snorre, *King Ingi's Saga*, III. 385, 387, cc. 26, 27.

[16] *Flateyarbok*, III. 126, 127. Mention is made of two brothers who were henchmen of both King Hakon and Duke Skuli. A somewhat similar case is recorded in early English history. See Larson, *King's Household in England*, p. 95.

[17] *N. G. L.*, II. 425–426: *H.* 34.

[18] *Spec. Reg.*, 63 (xxix.).

[19] Snorre, *Olaf Tryggvesson's Saga*, I. 352, c. 101.

[20] *Ibid., passim.*

[21] *Ibid.*, I. 352, c. 101.

[22] *Flateyarbok*, II. 645.

[23] *N. G. L.*, II. 414: *H.* 25; 424: *H.* 33.

[24] Snorre, *Olaf Tryggvesson's Saga*, I. 206, c. 48.

[25] *Id.*, *Saga of Magnus the Blind*, III. 342, c. 17; see also *Didrik's Saga* (ed. Unger, Christiania, 1853), c. 228.

[26] *N. G. L.*, II. 441, 442: *H.* 46.

[27] *Ibid.*, 424, 425: *H.* 33. The ringing to matins was the signal for dismissal.

[28] *N. G. L.*, II. 441–442: *H.* 46. *Luðr*, not exactly a trumpet, rather a species of Alpine horn.

[29] *Ibid.*, 424–425: *H.* 33.

[30] *Ibid.*, 423–424: *H.* 32.

[31] *Ibid.*, 414–415: *H.* 25. In no case was the following to be composed of new henchmen, and no person with whom the king was angry would be permitted to serve.

32 *Spec. Reg.*, 81 (xxxvii.).

33 See above, p. 461.

34 Bede, *Historia Ecclesiastica*, book III., c. 26.

35 *Beowulf*, ll. 2906–2910. A similar case is recorded in the Norse sources of the reign of Hakon IV., who died in 1263. It was determined to place a head-watch at his tomb and keep it there till the end of the winter. *Flateyarbok*, III, 230.

36 Liebermann, *Die Gesetze der Angelsachsen*, I. 444. The *geneat* owes the same duty to his lord.

37 *Domesday Book*, I. 190 (see Maitland, *Domesday Book and Beyond*, p. 130). "[Sochemanni in Fuleberne] reddunt . . . 12 equos et 12 inguardos si rex in vicecomitatu veniret . . ." The "inward seems to be the duty of forming a body guard for the king while he is in the shire". (Maitland.)

38 See below, p. 138.

39 *Domesday Book*, I. 139, 190.

40 Such assemblies were attended by archbishops, earls, bishops, landed-men and hirdmen. *Spec. Reg.*, 64 (xxx.); *Dipl. Norv.*, VII. 116–118. *Cf.* the Old English *witenagemot*.

41 *N. G. L.*, I. 4, 263: II. 27.

42 *Ibid.*

43 *Flateyarbok*, III. 134, 229. *Cf.* Munch, *Norges Kongesagaer*, II. 280.

44 Snorre, *St. Olaf's Saga*, II. 79, c. 60; *Harold Hardrada's Saga*, III. 86, c. 24. The arm ring was a peculiar sign of the henchman's service. See the stories of Thormod and Thorir in Snorre's version of *St. Olaf's Saga*. Thorir was accused of being Cnut's man. At a feast King Olaf stroked his arm above the elbow. Said Thorir, "Touch it gently there; I have a boil on the arm." He was forced to show the ring; it was Cnut's gift and Thorir was slain, II. 341–342, c. 175; 439, c. 246 (story of Thormod); 337, c. 172 (sword-gifts). See also *Karlamagnus Saga* (Christiania, 1860), viii, 4, 487.

45 *Fagrskinna*, p. 117.

46 *Spec. Reg.*, 58 (xxvi.).

47 *Ibid.*, 63 (xxix.).

48 *N. G. L.*, II. 448: *H.* 53. The king and the guild provided the ransom money, but the liberated kingsman was in duty bound to restore the sum, at least in part.

49 *N. G. L.*, II. 448: *H.* 53. But a part of this fund was used to provide masses for the dead.

50 The funds were placed in the hands of four men, two clerics chosen by the king and two hirdmen chosen by the hird. *Ibid.*, III. 78–80.

51 *Ibid.*, II. 437: *H.* 42. Ordinarily such meetings were called by the king, but on occasions it seems that members, perhaps the chiefs, might order the signal to be given. See *Flateyarbok*, III. 14–16. (1217.)

52 *Dipl. Norv.*, I. 104. (Bergen, 1308.) ". . . this charter was drawn up in the hall in the king's garth where gemots are held".

53 *N. G. L.*, II. 437: *H.* 42. Fines were collected by the marksman. The henchmen were also fined for neglecting to appear at funerals of comrades. The money collected was used to pay for masses for the dead.

54 *Ibid.*, II. 408: *H.* 20.

55 After a riot in which Skuli was concerned the king gave the signal for a *hirðstefna;* the henchmen demanded satisfaction and the earl submitted to the judgment of good men. *Flateyarbok*, III. 34–35. (1218.)

56 *N. G. L.*, II. 436: *H.* 41.

57 *N. G. L.*, II. 411: *H.* 22; III. 64 (decree of 1303).

58 *Ibid.* See also *H.* 42.

59 *Ibid.*, 408: *H.* 20: *cf. Flateyarbok*, III. 34–35.

60 See Larson, *King's Household in England*, pp. 165–167.

61 Such were found even in Iceland. See *Flateyarbok*, III. 205; *Laxdöla Saga* (ed. Kaalund, Copenhagen, 1889–1891), c. 20; *Sturlunga Saga* (ed. Vigfusson), II. 386. The laws suppose their presence everywhere; see *H.* 34.

62 *Fagrskinna*, p. 150; Snorre, *St. Olaf's Saga*, II. 67, c. 55.

63 Snorre, *Saga of Olaf the Quiet*, III. 194, c. 4; *Fagrskinna*, p. 150.

64 In the early years of the fourteenth century theie is much complaint that these men are neglectful of duty; they refuse to serve in the host, to attend the courts, to testify, to keep oaths, etc. See *N. G. L.,* III. 56, 66, 68, 90 (royal decrees dating from 1303 and 1311).

65 Snorre, *Saga of Olaf the Quiet,* III. 193, c. 3.

66 Sars, *Udsigt over den Norske Historie,* II. 16ff.

67 *N. G. L.,* II. 407: *H.* 19.

68 *Ibid.,* V., index: *lendr maðr.*

69 Keyser, *Efterladte Skrifter* (Christiania, 1867), II. 107–109.

70 *Historisk Tidsskrift,* second series, IV. 157–158.

71 Nine were with the king in 1235 (*Flateyarbok,* III. 111); the same number were present at the coronation in 1247 when a full attendance was to be expected (*ibid.,* 168); nine were with the king in the expedition against Scotland, 1263 (*ibid.,* 219–220).

72 *N. G. L.,* II. 406: *H.* 18. Snorre, the historian, was made a landed-man in 1220; his particular duty was to establish the king's authority in Iceland. *Flateyarbok,* III. 38.

73 *N. G. L.,* II. 407: *H.* 19.

74 *Flateyarbok,* III. 160–170, 212–213.

75 *N. G. L.,* II. 408: *H.* 20.

76 *Sturlunga Saga,* II. 382, appendix: *Islenzkir Annalar,* 1277.

77 *N. G. L.,* III. 74ff. Royal decree of June 17, 1308. King Hakon V. Magnusson (1299–1319) was a vigorous ruler and a firm believer in absolutism. The barons may also have abused their power during the minority of his brother Erik (1280–1299). See Keyser, *Efterladte Skrifter,* II. 107ff.

78 Snorre, *Saga of Olaf the Quiet,* III. 193, c. 3.

79 *N. G. L.,* II. 412–413: *H.* 24.

80 *Fagrskinna,* p. 154.

81 In the coronation procession they had a place next below the barons and above the marksman. *Flateyarbok,* III. 212–213.

82 This seems to be the meaning of the ambiguous term, *halda stöðu. N. G. L.,* II. 424, 447: *H.* 33, 51. Fritzner states in his Old Norse dictionary that some sort of a guard is meant, but this seems hardly probable. *Ordbog* (Christiania, 1867), *staða.*

83 *N. G. L.,* II. 415: *H.* 25.

84 A trencher-swain is mentioned as royal official in the Orkneys. *Flateyarbok,* III. 103–104.

85 *N. G. L.,* II. 413: *H.* 24.

86 *Ibid.,* III. 74ff.

87 I have been unable to find an institution elsewhere that exactly corresponds to the Norse table service, but the etymology of the term *skutilsvein* (from Lat. *scutella,* probably through A. S. *scutel*) would indicate a foreign origin.

88 *N. G. L.,* II. 439: *H.* 43.

89 Sixty in the days of Olaf the Quiet (1066–1093); thirty in the days of his father. *Fagrskinna,* p. 150.

90 *N. G. L.,* II. 439: *H.* 43.

91 *Ibid.,* II. 440–441: *H.* 45.

92 Snorre, *St. Olaf's Saga,* II. 409, c. 221.

93 *N. G. L.,* II. 440–441.

94 *Ibid.: gestastefna.*

95 *Spec. Reg.,* 60 (xxvii.).

96 *Flateyarbok,* III. 229.

97 *N. G. L.,* II. 448: *H.* 53; III. 78–80.

98 *N. G. L.,* II. 440–441: *H.* 45; *Spec. Reg.,* 60 (xxvii.).

99 *Spec. Reg.,* 60 (xxvii.).

100 *N. G. L.,* II. 439–440: *H.* 44. The Court Law warns against giving the gests such errands as are unreasonable, sinful or as imply the grant of too much power. The men are urged to be just and honest, to abstain from pillage, to spare the innocent and to respect the rights of women.

101 *Flateyarbok,* II. 613.

102 *Ibid.*, III. 227; Snorre, St. Olaf's Saga, II. 72, 77, 409, cc. 59, 221; *Magnus Barefoot's Saga*, III. 320, c. 5.

103 *Ancient Laws of Wales*, p. 772 and glossary: Seebohm, *Tribal System in Wales*, p. 163; Steenstrup, *Danelag*, p. 124; Larson, *King's Household in England*, p. 174. Medieval Norse writers believed that the gests were given this name because they guested the homes of so many men and not always in a friendly spirit. *Spec. Reg.*, 59 (XXVII.).

104 Snorre, *Saga of Olaf the Quiet*, III. 193. c. 3.

105 Such seems to be Keyser's view. *Efterladte Skrifter*, II. 79, 80.

106 "In the days of King Olaf . . . men began to take up new fashions, wearing pride-hosen laced to the bone; some clasped golden rings around their legs, and then men wore drag-kirtles laced to the side, sleeves five ells long, and so strait that they must be drawn by an armcord and trussed all up to the shoulder; high shoes withal, and all sewn with silk, and some embroidered with gold. Many other new-fangled fashions there were." Snorre, *Saga of Olaf the Quiet*, III. 192–193, c. 2.

107 *N. G. L.*, II. 444: *H.* 47.

108 *Flateyarbok*, III. 131, 225.

109 *N. G. L.*, II. 444: *H.* 47.

110 *Ibid.*, II. 448, 449; III. 79; *Flateyarbok*, III. 229.

111 *N. G. L.*, II. 443, 444: *H.* 47.

112 *Ibid.*

113 *Ibid.*

114 *Ibid.*, 416: *H.* 26.

115 Snorre, *St. Olaf's Saga*, II. 67, c. 55. St. Olaf had thirty house-carles.

116 *Flateyarbok*, II. 582: *Spec. Reg.*, 58.

117 *Fagrskinna*, p. 150. Olaf the Quiet had sixty house-carles.

118 *Flateyarbok*, II. 541–542. ". . . seventy men went to the king's (Sverri's) hand; some were made hirdmen, some gests, some house-carles".

119 *Spec. Reg.*, 60, 61 (XXVII.). It is possible that some of these ranked higher than the house-carles at court, but the author of the *Speculum* makes no distinction.

120 *Flateyarbok*, II. 593. The rioters were punished at the king's command.

121 *Ibid.*, III. 60–61, 97.

122 *N. G. L.*, II. 411–412: *H.* 22–23.

123 Snorre, *Olaf Tryggvesson's Saga*, I. 315, c. 71; *St. Olaf's Saga*, II. 205, 417, cc. 118, 229.

124 *N. G. L.*, II. 410: *H.* 21.

125 *Dipl. Norv.*, III. 107, 108: deans, canons, deacons, etc.

126 *Ibid.*, IV. 121 (1312–1319).

127 Snorre, *Saga of Sigurd Jerusalem-farer*, III. 263, c. 15.

128 *Dipl. Norv.*, I. 100 (1308).

129 *N. G. L.*, II. 464 (agreement of 1273).

130 *Dipl. Norv.*, I. 100–103; *Historisk Tidsskrift*, first series, IV. 267–268. The office was given to the dean of the Church of the Apostles in Bergen.

131 *Dipl. Norv.*, I. 90–91, 107, 115–117; IV. 80, 91. The pretext urged was that the king's priests interfered in the affairs of the regular parishes and deprived the parish priests of their income.

132 Such are cooks, butlers, door-wards, horse-wards, smiths, trumpeters, bed-swains, shoe-swains and the like.

133 *N. G. L.*, II. 415: *H.* 26.

134 The regent chosen was Erling Vidkunsson, a knight (hirdman) and the wealthiest man in the realm. See any good history of Norway.

135 But the office was not continuously filled. The *drotseti* ruled only when a minor held the throne or when the king was unable to reside in the kingdom. See Keyser, *Efterladte Skrifter*, II. 93. The seneschal's office was, of course, to be found everywhere in Western Europe during the Middle Ages, but the etymology of the Norse title would indicate that this office was contributed by the Empire.

136 *Spec. Reg.*, 186. Appendix.

137 *Flateyarbok*, III. 219, 225.

138 *N. G. L.*, III. 79.

139 Keyser, *Efterladte Skrifter*, II. 105.

140 The four treasurers are instructed as to the payment of fees to the henchmen, how much each shall be paid and in what. They are also told to have the Court Law read to them, but formerly the law was always read to the assembled guard in the royal hall at the Christmas festivities. *N. G. L.*, III. 79.

141 Snorre, *St. Olaf's Saga*, II. 412–413, c. 224: the poet Sighvat quoted.

142 *Egil's Saga*, c. 16, says distinctly that the marksman was the first man at court. See also Snorre, *St. Olaf's Saga*, II. 128, 430, 429, cc. 84, 238, 239, *et passim*.

143 *N. G. L.*, II. 411–412: *H.* 23. There were several banners in the host; the marksman bore that of the king. *Flateyarbok*, III. 138.

144 Snorre, *Harold Fairhair's Saga*, I. 98–99, c. 9.

145 *N. G. L.*, II. 411–412: *H.* 23.

146 *Ibid.*, III. 64: decree of 1303; this apparently made the marksman the chief judge at court.

147 *Ibid.*, II. 411: *H.* 23.

148 Snorre, *St. Olaf's Saga*, II. 67, c. 55. So splendidly was the staller attired at times that he was mistaken for the king himself. See *id.*, *Olaf Tryggvesson's Saga*, I. 374, c. 120: *Magnus Barefoot's Saga*, III. 240–241, c. 26.

149 *Id.*, *St. Olaf's Saga*, II. 93, 333–334, 433, cc. 70, 170, 240. (Sighvat.)

150 There were two in 1066. *Fagrskinna*, p. 135. The Court Law sometimes uses the plural form in speaking of the staller.

151 *N. G. L.*, II. 411: *H.* 22.

152 Snorre, *St. Olaf's Saga*, II. 88, c. 68: see also cc. 59, 91.

153 *Ibid.*, c. 67, 86. See also *Flateyarbok*, III. 118, 219.

154 He fell at Stiklestad, 1030. Snorre, II. 432, c. 240.

155 *Flateyarbok*, II. 547.

156 *Ibid.*, II. 583; *Fagrskinna*, p. 129.

157 *N. G. L.*, II. 411: *H.* 22.

158 See Keyser, *Efterladte Skrifter*, II., or any good Norwegian history.

159 The staller spoke on the king's behalf in his absence and also quite generally when he was present; the Norse rulers with the exception of Sverri do not seem to have been orators.

160 Larson, *King's Household in England*, p. 147.

161 See *Dipl. Norv.*

162 The earl of the Orkneys had a chancellor as early as 1190. *Ibid.*, II. 2, no. 2. Seals were in use when Snorre (1177–1241) wrote his history. *Magnus Erlingsson's Saga*, c. 25. Magnus ruled from 1162 to 1184.

163 *N. G. L.*, II. 410: *H.* 22.

164 Larson, *King's Household in England*, p. 197ff.

165 *N. G. L.*, II. 409: *H.* 21.

166 *Ibid.*, III. 23. (1293.) He was a canon in 1296. *Dipl. Norv.*, IV. 15.

167 *Dipl. Norv.*, II. 72; IV. 94–95.

168 *Dipl. Norv.*, I. 127. The vice-chancellor was appointed by the king from among his chapel priests, the chancellor advising; he received one-fourth of the revenues of the seal when actually serving; he was competent to act at any time and place if for any reason the chancellor could not serve.

169 *N. G. L.*, II. 409–410: *H.* 21.

170 *Ibid.*, 411–412: *H.* 23.

171 *Ibid.*: *H.* 22. *Cf.* the method of admitting hirdmen to the baronage.

172 *N. G. L.*, II. 409, 411, 446: *H.* 21–22, 49–50; III. 77–78.

The
Communication
of Ideas

10

The Influence of Islamic Culture on Medieval Europe

SIR HAMILTON GIBB

THE PROFESSOR OF ARABIC who writes or speaks about medieval Europe is certain to invite the warning *ne sutor supra crepidam*. But it is a wholesome, if often chastening, discipline for the specialist to wander occasionally far enough from home to obtain a fresh perspective of the landscape which bounds his daily labours. At least he himself should learn something from his adventure. The present subject is not, in any case, an exploration of new country, but rather an excursion into a territory whose fields and landmarks have been frequently, though sometimes capriciously, charted. The equivalent of the Ordnance Survey is that storehouse of facts, *The Legacy of Islam,* by now a little dated (it was published in 1931), but still fascinating to read in parts, and full of good guidance. No doubt some of its landmarks and dimensions are a little dubious, but most of those who contributed to it were experts who had thoroughly explored their particular regions, whether of the arts, or law, or medicine, or mathematics, or music.

It is, of course, impossible for a layman to attempt to cover more than a fraction of this ground. What I hope to do is to suggest some general principles and conclusions, within which the individual facts may find their proper place and interpretation. There is, in addition, one important field which I must leave aside altogether on this occasion, although I suspect that the same general principles apply to it also— namely, the whole range of economic and commercial contacts and the possible transference through these of agricultural, seafaring, or commercial techniques. The many Arabic terms relating to these activities which have passed into the languages of western Europe are suggestive (even excessively so for some lively imaginations), but the subject is too complicated for anyone but a trained economic historian to handle.

In limiting myself, therefore, to the intellectual aspects of Islamic culture, it may be useful to begin by defining the term a little more closely. The starting-point of this investigation is that complex of cultural achievements which found its literary expression in the Arabic language, and which is often called "Arab culture". I am not concerned here with the argument about the relative contributions of the Arabs and other racial stocks to this culture; much of this argument seems to me to be, in any case, conducted with a remarkable disregard for elementary sociological facts. The medieval Islamic culture was a collective achievement, and not only of Arabs and Persians, but also of Copts, Aramaeans, Jews, Byzantines, Turks, Berbers, Spaniards, and not even excluding contributions from Africans and Indians. But there were two factors which gave it its unity and cohesion: one was the religion of Islam, the other the Arabic language. The language furnished the instrument of intercommunication between its widely separated regions, and the influence or contribution of Islam cannot be dissociated at any point from the whole complex of cultural activities. Islam supplied the external principle of organization, which facilitated the spread of Arabic culture in space, in the sense that wherever Islam established itself this culture was introduced along with it, and maintained in time by the cultural cohesion of all the regions of Islamic obedience. It was due to Islam that Arabic Spain continued to share all the elements of Islamic culture which were developed later in the east, and as the limits of Islam shrank, the elements of Arabic culture which survived the *reconquista* were torn out of their former matrix and gradually merged into the culture of Christian Spain.

Secondly, Islam served as an internal principle of order, which set (or was regarded as setting) a scale of values, and constituted a central core of spiritual and psychological energy round which all other cultural activities revolved as satellites. It is self-evident that not all the cultural activities in Arabic-Islamic civilization owed their origin or their energy to Islam—for example, Arabic poetry (which reached one of its climaxes in pre-Islamic Arabia), or medicine and the natural sciences (which came from older civilizations), but all of these were in varying degrees attracted into the gravitational field of Islam, and affected by their interactions with the other constituent elements of the medieval Muslim civilization. The fact is obvious in the later development of Arabic poetry; and Arabic medicine, for example, had to operate within the limits of the ban placed by Islam on the dissection of human bodies.

Outside the area of Arabic-Islamic culture, the Islamic principles of organization and order were clearly irrelevant. Whether the cultural activities which will concern us owed their origin to Islam or by attraction into the energy-field of Islam acquired particular features and characteristics is, though not totally immaterial, of minor importance for us at this point; consequently the term "Islamic Culture" must, for our purposes, be quite properly interpreted in the wider sense of the whole complex of related institutions and products which constitute the medieval Arabic culture, particularly in the Mediterranean area.

It cannot be too often pointed out that in studying the development of a given activity in a given society, the extent to which it draws on new materials from outside and the way in which it modifies or adapts them are problems of great difficulty and complexity. Mere parallelism of expression or production proves nothing, especially when two cultures draw from the same roots. This warning is particularly needed in handling our present subject, since the field is already cluttered with extravagant statements and generalizations made in the past (and still being made all too often), which rest on nothing more than fortuitous resemblances and parallel constructions from common roots. We all know the ingenious efforts of amateur linguists to prove the relationship of two distant languages by casual assonances and the assumption (or neglect) of sound-changes which would make Grimm turn in his grave. One of the most fantastic examples of the same kind of reasoning is the belief firmly held in some modern Arab circles that Dante's *Divine Comedy* was imitated from or at least greatly influenced by a kind of celestial fantasy called the *Epistle of Pardon,* written in 1033 by the famous Arab poet Abu'l-'Alā al-Ma'arrī. But not a shred of evidence has ever been produced that Abu'l-'Alā's *Epistle* was translated into any western language in the Middle Ages, or even that any part of its content entered into any Arabic work which was translated and might by chance have come to the knowledge of Dante. Whether certain other elements from Arabic literature may have reached Dante is quite another question.

It is, however, true, and probably a universal phenomenon, that when, for any reason, some particular body of ideas, or technique, or theory has begun to attract men's interest, they will readily take advantage of all other sources which may be available to them for developing this particular activity. It seems to me to be in these circumstances almost exclusively that the factor of "influence" by other cultures arises. I should go so far as to say that it is rarely, if ever, that any element from a foreign culture is introduced or taken over as an entirely *new* constituent in the receiving culture. We may almost formulate it as our "First Law", therefore, that cultural influences (by which I mean, of course, not purely superficial adjuncts, but genuinely assimilated elements) are always preceded by an already existing activity in the related fields, and that it is this existing activity which creates the factor of attraction without which no creative assimilation can take place.

One of the most striking examples is offered by the instance which at first sight seems to contradict this "law"—I mean the movement of translation of Greek philosophical and scientific works into Arabic in the eighth and ninth centuries. There was nothing in the primitive Arab tradition or in the Koran, as originally understood, to account for this apparently sudden development. But the Muslim Community, in the process of expanding, absorbed large bodies of peoples whose cultural traditions were Hellenistic, and this led in time to a conflict *within* the Muslim Community between Hellenistic traditions and the primitive formulations of Islamic concepts, so that Muslim religious circles found themselves confronted by the intellectual problems raised by Greek philosophy. One of the chief functions of the schools of translators who rendered the Greek texts into Arabic was to furnish the corpus of materials required to clarify the issues and lead to a solution of the conflict. These materials were logical and philosophical (which included, in accordance with the Aristotelian tradition, natural science)—to which medicine was added, for parallel but practical reasons.

This kind of give-and-take has characterized all living societies in historic times. Not only have all cultures expanded by developing their own resources with the assistance of elements derived from other cultures, but when they cease to do so—when their peoples begin to regard their cultural achievements as self-sufficient and to imagine that they have nothing to learn from outside—then decline and stagnation set in. It is arguable, I think, that our modern western culture is already in considerable danger of stagnation, in spite of our expanding scientific techniques, because nothing or not enough is coming in to stimulate its inner growth.

In the conflict of cultures, then, it is more blessed to receive than to give; and the real quality of any civilization is shown less perhaps by its indigenous products than by the way in which it constantly grafts new shoots on to its own trunk, to stimulate further growth and to achieve richer and more differentiated products. But there must clearly be some limit or limits to this process. Every culture is a living organism, which derives its nourishment from specific roots. It does not matter very much for our present purpose how these roots are defined; one definition which seems to me adequate, and will at any rate do well enough for the moment, selects three factors as basic: its appreciation of art, its rationality (or the liberty it allows to the pursuit of thought), and its religion (or conception of the relation of man to the universe), and adds as a fourth factor the common social tradition which binds all these together. If any one of these factors is radically changed, the whole complex of culture is affected, and a new culture is created, which is quite different from the older culture. This then would seem to supply us with two further "laws", which may define the limits of cultural borrowing. Firstly, the borrowed elements conduce to the expanding vitality of the borrowing culture only in so far as they draw their nourishment from the activities which led to their borrowing in the first place. If they develop so luxuriantly as to substitute themselves, or threaten to substitute themselves, for the native spiritual forces, they become destructive, and not constructive, elements. The graft (to return to our metaphor) must not replace the original living branches. In historical terms, this means that a living culture allows the borrowed elements to develop to the extent that they are adaptable to and blend with its native forces, but resists with all its power their over-luxuriant growth. Thus the Arabic-Islamic culture, once the grafts from Greek philosophy had attained their original purpose, deliberately stabilized them at that stage of growth, and set itself to cut back all the other shoots which seemed to be developing independently and to disturb its now established constitution and balance.

The second new "law", or third of our three "laws", is that a living culture disregards or rejects all elements in other cultures which conflict with its own fundamental values, emotional attitudes, or aesthetic criteria. Attempts may be made to graft them, but the grafts do not "take" and simply die off. So the Arabic culture rejected all Greek poetry and drama (which conflicted with its appreciation of art) and Indian philosophy (which conflicted with its concepts of the relation of man to God), although it was on the other hand positively affected by Indian mysticism, which found a congenial host in the mystical tendencies already developed within the Islamic Community.

If I have insisted on formulating these so-called "laws", it is mainly because it seems to me essential to avoid a common source of loose thinking and error in this field—namely, the conception of knowledge as lumps of inert matter passed from hand to hand. The basic factor is psychological; and even if we grant the metaphor of a statement of fact or a theory as a lump of matter, the important question is what happens to it at the receiving end; and that depends on the kind of mind by which it is received. The most striking example of static reasoning is the extravagant assertion, made not only by irresponsible publicists but even by men who should have better knowledge and judgement, that the western Renaissance of the fifteenth century was largely due to the materials transmitted to Europe by the Arabic-Islamic civilization. This assertion involves a complete misunderstanding of what is implied by the Renaissance: a moral, even more than intellectual, crisis, which created a sense of total break with the past—a sudden increase of intensity and vigour in all fields of activity, accompanied by a new desire for self-expression—a rejection of old claims and standards, and the adoption of secularism in politics and economic life. These are all *psychological* facts, and without these psychological conditions there could have been no Renaissance. Knowledge—yes; but not the simple acceptance of a received body of knowledge. Where the "official" mind files its lumps of knowledge neatly in pigeonholes, where the "orderly" academic mind tries to integrate them with other lumps, the "renaissance" type of mind pokes and probes them, delighted with nothing so much as discovering how to blow them to pieces. With such an approach every "fact" becomes an adventure of ideas or an invitation to adventure.

But while the Renaissance mind, bursting out of the bounds of existing structures of knowledge, sought for new experience of every kind, it did nevertheless start from the body of knowledge and with the techniques formed and cultivated for some two or three centuries previously. In the field of the natural sciences, at least, this existing body of knowledge not only supplied materials for the inquisitive and experimental minds of the Renaissance, but must evidently have been informed with something of the same spirit as that which came to full consummation at the Renaissance. The real problem for investigation, therefore, is not what the Renaissance may owe to Arabic-Islamic culture, but in what directions and to what extent materials derived from the Islamic culture contributed to the intellectual revival of the period extending from 1050 to 1300 or so, sometimes called the "Little Renaissance".

Here, of course, there has never been any dispute as to the fact of the translation and circulation on an extensive scale of both Greek works previously translated into Arabic and original works written in Arabic. The translated works are there, in large numbers; and the medieval scholars make no secret of their regular consultation of these works, and sometimes of their fervent admiration for those Arabic writers who, by composition or commentary, had enriched the subjects of their studies. For in those centuries, when Europe was slowly rebuilding its cultural life under the aegis of the Christian Church, not only were its psychological conditions entirely different from those of the Renaissance, but in both intellectual attitudes and assumptions it stood much closer to the Muslim world. Both cultures were characterized by the same primacy of faith, which provided a defined and finite universe and allotted to reason a certain function and range of activity; and faith and reason alike in both sprang from the same roots. Both laid the same emphasis on continuity, prizing and clinging to the heritage of the past as the surest guide, and envisaged no future different from the past, except for the millennial aspirations cherished in both. These conditions supplied an almost ideal opportunity for fruitful interaction or penetration, in which elements from the one could stimulate the other by assimilation. Islam in India, during the same centuries, offers a complete and striking contrast: a situation in which, save in the one field of mysticism, there was no point at which the two cultures touched at all.

Nevertheless, the opportunity of interaction, the possibility of interchange, does not imply its actuality; and before any assertions can be made, every case must be studied in the light of its own circumstances, techniques, and instruments of transference. In some forms of cultural activity this investigation is a fairly simple and straightforward one. The clearest case of all is medicine, in which the great names of the Middle Ages are all those of Arabic writers, superimposed to some extent on Galen: Mesue (Māsawaih), Rhazes (ar-Rāzī), Haly Abbas ('Alī b. al-'Abbās), Abulcasis (Abu'l-Qāsim al-Zahrāwī), Rodoham ('Alī b. Ridwān), and above all Avicenna (Ibn Sīnā), whose authority may be said to have remained unchallenged until the time of Vesalius and Paracelsus. So also in mathematics and in the crafts—metal inlays, lustred pottery, enamelled glass, ivory carving, weaving and papermaking—the range of influences from the Mediterranean world are clearly demonstrable, even where they are combined with indigenous traditions and techniques. And in the case of paper—itself an importation into the Arab world from China—the ultimate cultural effects have, of course, been incalculable.

But the position is entirely different when we come to the three most important fields, those of natural science, philosophy, and literature —the three fields which impinge most closely on what we have defined as the three basic differentials of a given culture: its rationality, its religion, and its appreciation of art. Here there is no such simple and direct relationship between the Islamic and the evolving European culture, and the reason is clear: that since these activities were concerned with ideas and aesthetic expression, they could not be effectively taken into European culture in their Islamic contexts, but had to be adapted in some way to the intellectual and aesthetic attitudes of the recipients.

This principle might not seem, at first sight, to apply to natural science, which stands for us on much the same footing as medicine and mathematics. But natural science in the Islamic world was a Hellenistic importation, and shared the predominantly speculative character of its sources. It was a system of demonstrated proofs from given axioms or postulates, erected by Aristotle into one of the three branches of philosophy, and almost inseparable from the Aristotelian universe. This is not to say that the Greeks had no experimental science; still less, that the Arabs had no experimental science. Not only were there Arabic scientists who showed great ingenuity in the practical application of scientific theory and the improvement of scientific instruments, but their works were eagerly sought after in the eleventh and twelfth centuries. Nevertheless, these scientists (I am excluding physicians in this context) operated on the margins of Islamic society; empirical science scarcely, if ever, entered into its educational structure, and much experimental work was bound up with astrology and alchemy (though I think Mr. Christopher Dawson goes too far in identifying Arabic science as a whole with magic).[2] In both principle and method Arabic science remained throughout within the framework of the Aristotelian system.

In Europe, on the other hand, the attitude to natural science was from the first conditioned by a practical approach. The whole problem seems to me to have been immensely clarified by Dr. A. C. Crombie in his solid study of Robert Grosseteste.[3] After summarizing the technical inventions in western society between the ninth and twelfth centuries, he makes the pertinent observation that the earliest western interest in Arabic learning was directed to the acquisition of practical knowledge, and that a large proportion of the earliest translations were of works on mathematical subjects, medicine and chemistry. Furthermore, the technical arts began to be included in higher education as early as the twelfth century, when already some of the leading scholars were beginning to conceive of the study of "natural causes" as an interest in itself. Crombie has made it clear that the subsequent eagerness to study the natural science of the Greeks and their Arabic commentators was due to the need to relate the old-established western empiricism in the practical arts to the concept of rational explanation. It was out of this confrontation that there arose a new methodology, which utilized *inter alia* the observations of the Arabic physicians, but which independently laid the foundations of modern science by replacing the metaphysical question "Why things happen" with the scientific question "How things happen".

I should be straying too far from my last to pursue this topic any further, in spite of the temptations offered by the strange figure of Roger Bacon, which has also recently been elucidated afresh by Stewart Easton.[4] Enough has been said to bring out the point that, while western scholars undoubtedly read and utilized such genuinely scientific works as the optics of Alhazen (al-Haitham), their acquisitions from these sources were from the first integrated into a distinctive and developing native system of experiment and thought. Its actual progress was due neither to taking over an inert body of knowledge nor to bare experimentation, but to the rise of new concepts of scholarship, linked with the development of new craft techniques and the interplay between ideas and techniques, all of which issued in a new kind of scientific thinking.

In philosophy, it seems to me, the facts, though superficially similar, fall into a rather different pattern. Here again the starting point is an existing tradition in western Europe, or rather two traditions: the Christian Platonism derived from St. Augustine, and the Latin Aristotelian tradition based on Boethius. It looks as if the Arabic "Aristotelian" tradition [5] came in, in the first instance, almost accidentally, through its connection with the scientific and medical works translated in the eleventh century, and by contact with the old Boethian tradition produced a new spurt of intellectual curiosity. It must be remembered that Avicenna died in 1037, and that his works were translated only a century later, that Averroes' dates are 1126–98; and that already by the end of the twelfth century the works of Aristotle were beginning to circulate in translations made directly from the Greek, as well as in translations through the Arabic versions. The western scholars were not wholly dependent, therefore, on the Arabic versions for the *text* of many of Aristotle's writings (indeed, Grosseteste was already reading him in the original Greek); but the text of Aristotle (as generations of students know) is not infrequently obscure, and it was chiefly for the sake of their commentaries that the Arabic works were prized, and above all the works of Avicenna and Averroes. The consequence of this confrontation of medieval Europe with Aristotle was the creation of scholasticism, exactly as four centuries earlier the same confrontation had created Muslim scholasticism; and the first task of scholasticism was to assimilate Aristotelianism. As in Islam, so also in the west, Aristotle was inescapable, as well in theological as in philosophical thought; and the theological problem was solved (on their own ground, of course) by Albert the Great and St. Thomas Aquinas—drawing partly on the works written with a similar object in relation to *their* religious systems by the Muslim al-Ghazālī and the Jewish scholar Moses Maimonides. And all of them, Muslim and Christian alike, stand on the shoulders of those forgotten late Alexandrians and Syrians who first trimmed Aristotle into conformity with revealed theistic religion. The *Summa* (which I have not read, and do not expect ever to read) is, no doubt, a masterpiece of creative synthesis; but so, in different degrees, are the writings of al-Fārābī, Avicenna and Averroes. The differences between them are almost entirely functions of one of two things: either how much Platonism (neo or genuine) is mixed up with their interpretation of Aristotle, or where they draw the dividing line between rationality and dogma. Hence the violent conflict in the thirteenth and fourteenth centuries between the Christian Aristotelians and the Averroists—those proclaiming the dogmas of revelation, these the dogmas of reason; but both were in reality quarreling largely over the dead bones of once living thought.

I doubt whether Aristotelianism as a system has ever been congenial to the living thought of the west. It is relevant to observe, therefore, that even during this medieval interlude the Platonist and mystical tendencies in Europe also found reinforcement in Arabic learning. Not only were there the neoplatonic elements in the systems of al-Kindī and Avicenna, but in addition there was a whole corpus of neoplatonic writings recovered through the Arabic translations, notably the materials from Proclus in the version known as the *De Causis*. Furthermore, the works of the Arabic mystics, though they perhaps influenced directly only Ramon Lull, scattered their seeds far and wide, to flower not only in the religious literature of Spain, but also in the Florentine poets and perhaps even in the later German mystics. It is, I think, arguable that the contribution of Arabic Platonism to European thought at its more intimate levels was far more important than the contribution of Arabic Aristotelianism.

The conclusion that seems to emerge from this brief discussion of the two fields of natural science and philosophy is rather a curious one. The western scholars were looking for something in the Islamic culture, but what they were looking for was entirely different from what the Arabs had looked for in Greek culture. The Arabs were looking for a logical methodology to subserve the dogmatic structure of Islam, the westerners were looking primarily for a logical methodology to subserve the practical arts. Both found what they wanted, but in the process they acquired a great deal more than they bargained for. The Arabs acquired the physical and mathematical science of the Greeks, the westerners the corpus of "Aristotelian" philosophy. In both cases these additional acquisitions were able to establish themselves for a time, because of their intimate connection with the desired objects; but finally (in accordance with our third law) they either became inert or were superseded. Natural science in the Arabic-Islamic culture was pegged to that stage at which the Arabic scientists had developed the concepts and methods taken over from the Greeks. In Europe the metaphysics of Aristotle affected for a time scholastic thought, but was ultimately displaced, partly by the older and more congenial currents of Platonism, partly by newer philosophies, and survived only in those circles which carried on the traditions of medieval scholasticism.

We turn now from the world of scholarship proper to the realm of literature. And here we must begin by again emphasizing some distinctions. Firstly, there is a distinction between genuinely creative influence and what I shall call "borrowings", that is to say, the casual utilization of literary materials. Such stories as the Squire's Tale in Chaucer, isolated episodes of eastern origin in western romances, and even whole books translated from the Arabic which circulated more or less widely in the Middle Ages—all these come into the category of borrowings, and correspond in literature to the motives and elements of technique introduced from the Arabic culture into the western plastic arts. Secondly, there is a distinction to be drawn between literary productions which exercised an influence in the aesthetic sense, and those whose influence was technical rather than strictly literary. It was inevitable that the philosophical writings that we have just been considering should have produced some reflections in western literature, directly or indirectly, and that the moral and didactic writings of European scholars should have drawn on works of the same kind in Arabic. One of the most interesting examples is the Syrian work attributed to Aristotle called the *Secreta Secretorum*. It had a peculiar fascination for Roger Bacon, and it keeps turning up over and over again in medieval literature in a variety of adaptations, besides furnishing materials for such writers as Gower. One may say without much fear of contradiction that there was a kind of legacy of prose writings of Arabic provenance which entered into the common patrimony of medieval Europe and which added some touches of colour to its native hues. But whether as quarries for moral *exempla,* or as handbooks of ancient wisdom, or simply as sources of romantic anecdotes, the materials they supplied were inserted into patterns of native origin, and it was only in Spain that they exercised any determining or formative influence upon any branch of western literature.

On the whole, therefore, "borrowings" can fairly easily be established, even when the borrowed materials have been more or less adapted to a different structure. Genuinely "creative" literary influences, on the other hand, are exceptionally hard to establish. The nature of the proof does not lie, as might be imagined at first, in mere mass or quantity. The factor excluding proof of this kind is covered by our Second Law, which implies that no structural aesthetic element can be effectively transferred to another culture unless in the process of transference it is adapted to the aesthetic tastes and requirements of the recipients. This necessity of adaptation has two effects: one, that it almost always conceals the actual process, and makes it difficult to reconstruct because of the absence of detailed documentary evidence (how many, for example, would trace James Thomson's *City of Dreadful Night* to the *Arabian Nights* if they had not his own evidence for it?); the other, that *one* successful adaptation may be enough to serve as the starting-point for a whole series of new and independent developments. For the very fact of adaptation means that both in the first example and in the later development all kinds of other cultural factors are co-operating, and all of them are so intermingled that it is scarcely ever possible to make precise attributions.

There are, I believe, only two branches of medieval western literature in which any question of the creative literary influence of Arabic culture can arise. One is that of Spanish literature, which I have already mentioned. The other is the interminably-argued relation between Spanish-Arabic and Provençal poetry; and it is precisely because of the two difficulties I have just discussed that this question is a question at all. In this instance, moreover, we come up against a third problem. The most striking fact about the new Provençal lyric is the suddenness with which it emerges, not only without any known western ancestry, but with a completely developed form and technique. This is often stated as an argument for its introduction from outside; but, on the contrary, by our First Law this fact would seem to exclude the hypothesis of a creative influence from Arabic culture, if there were no already existing cultural activity to furnish the factor of attraction.

Yet there are certain unchallengeable facts, though they are sometimes obscured in the controversy. There is the parallelism of metrical techniques in some early Provençal poems of the courtly type and some Spanish-Arabic poems; there is the persistence in the same Provençal poetry of certain themes or motifs which are traditional constituents of Arabic love-poetry. These call for a reasonable explanation. Granted that no poetry of this kind is known to us from Provence or the neighbouring regions until the end of the eleventh century, are we to suppose that it had no antecedents there at all? The suggestion is clearly absurd, and is indeed disproved by the surviving traces of earlier Romance poetry. In reality, I believe, we have in this problem a situation parallel to the apparent exception which I discussed earlier, in reference to the introduction of Greek philosophy into Islamic culture. The Islamic empire of the eighth century was a crucible in which the contributions of old Arab and Persian culture were compounded with the Hellenistic culture of the Syrians and Aramaeans. Just in the same way, in tenth and eleventh century Spain, the Christians, in the north as well as in the south, intermingled with the "Moors", who themselves not only brought in and disseminated their Arabic culture, but also incorporated large numbers of the Romance-speaking population.

It would be flatly opposed to all that we know of medieval Spain to exclude exchange of aesthetic as well as other cultural elements. There is, however, no evidence at all that the Christians were attracted by the highly formalized art of the classical Arabic *qaṣīda* or ode. On the contrary, it was the Moors who—as has now been shown with tolerable certainty—were attracted to certain types of Romance popular poetry, and who developed from them the new stanza forms of the *muwashshaḥ* and the *zajal*.[6] In doing so they of course adapted them, firstly to Arabic prosodic structure, and secondly by elaborating their content and imagery with themes and motifs derived from their own courtly or popular love-poetry. There can hardly be any doubt that in the cultivated mixed society of the Spanish Marches the developing Romance poetry was in its turn affected in some degree by the Arabic techniques and themes.[7] That there is nothing improbable (still less derogatory, as some scholars still seem, curiously, to think) in the seepage of Arabic techniques into Romance literature is demonstrated by the Northern French *Aucassin et Nicolette*. Consequently, the adaptation of elements of the Arabic prosodic structure, and the transference of its traditional motifs, would conform entirely to our First Law; and in the Provençal courtly lyric both were brilliantly exploited within a new western literary art that nevertheless stood essentially on its own feet.[8]

Finally, as Christopher Dawson has shown,[9] in its Tuscan descendant it was coloured by the newer metaphysical ideas which had permeated western secular thought from the neoplatonism of the Arabic commentators and mystics, to create the almost perfect synthesis of Mediterranean romantic art in the *dolce stil nuovo*. As for the *Divina Commedia* itself, the demonstration by E. Cerulli [10] of both the extent and the limits of Islamic themes drawn upon by Dante seems to have shown that all the so-called Arabic influences are in fact "borrowings" from secondary materials, in the sense in which I have distinguished these two terms above.

To sum up this discussion very briefly, there is a fairly clear distinction to be drawn between "neutral" borrowings from the Arabic-Islamic culture and the "shaded" influences or adaptations. In the neutral sphere of science and technology, the medieval Catholic world took over everything that it could use. In the intellectual and aesthetic spheres, it is very remarkable that all the elements taken over into western culture prove to be either elements of European origin adapted into the Arabic-Islamic culture, or elements with very close relations in western culture. On the whole, therefore, the contributions to the west from Arabic sources, although at first some of them seemed to be alien and dangerous, tended ultimately to reinforce the medieval Catholic culture rather than to disturb it. I see no argument for the assumption, still fairly often made, that these importations in themselves struck at the roots of medieval thought and prepared the way for its overthrow, with the one possible exception of Averroism—but this itself had become stagnant and inert by the end of the fourteenth century.

This conclusion seems finally to conform to what may be a universal psychological law in human societies. On the one hand, natural science and technology are indefinitely transmissible, and constitute the only truly international element in human culture. On the other hand, art, aesthetics, philosophy and religious thought retain their distinguishing characteristics within each separate culture. Every society jealously guards its own, and although not wholly impermeable to influences from without, it will absorb elements from other cultures only within a limited range and in forms adapted to its own temperament and psychological structure.

NOTES

[1] A lecture delivered in the John Rylands Library on Wednesday, the 9th of March 1955.

[2] In *Mediaeval Essays* (London and New York, 1953), p. 159.

[3] Oxford, 1953.

[4] Oxford (Blackwell), 1952.

[5] I put the term "Aristotelian" in inverted commas, since the character and constituents of Arabic "Aristotelianism" are still very imperfectly known. There was certainly a considerable Platonic or Neoplatonic element in its metaphysics (as pointed out later); and I am provisionally implying by the term a system of philosophic thought based on the physics and methodology of Aristotle.

[6] Strictly speaking, it was only the stanza-form and structure of the *muwashshaḥ* that were entirely new to Arabic poetry; in the very different *zajal* the novelty lay in technique rather than in structure.

[7] On the crucial question of themes see especially the article of Father J. Denomy in *Mediaeval Studies* (Toronto), 1944, 1945, and 1949.

[8] Since preparing this article, I find a similar conclusion expressed in the detailed study of P. Le Gentil, *Le Virelai et la Villancico* (Paris, 1954), p. 249: "Je pense que ces contacts n'ont été suivis d'effet que dans le cas où un exemple étranger se trouvait rejoindre des traditions indigènes préexistantes."

[9] *Mediaeval Essays*, pp. 234–5.

[10] In the Appendix to his edition of the *Libro della Scala*, Vatican City, 1949.

The Gothic Cathedral
Design and Meaning

OTTO G. VON SIMSON

WITHIN THE LAST CENTURY the history of architecture has sought to explain the origin and meaning of the Gothic cathedral by singling out, one after the other, three of its main aspects: function (Gothic solution of statical problems), design (Gothic form as the expression of certain esthetic principles), and significance (Gothic form as the symbolic expression of certain ideas). The interpretations based upon each of these three aspects stand in a curious relationship to one another. Developed polemically and antithetically, each has sought to interpret Gothic architecture in terms of one of the three aspects, denying or belittling the significance of the two others. In point of fact, each of the three approaches has greatly advanced our knowledge; it seems to us today as if they not only complement, but actually point toward one another, encircling, as it were, a truth that lies in their midst.

Thus it is precisely to the history and analysis of Gothic form that we owe the knowledge that this form cannot be entirely understood in terms of stylistic development. Gothic architecture emerges suddenly and almost simultaneously with the great expressions of Romanesque art, not its heir or "logical sequel," but its rival and antithesis. The first Gothic art, moreover, is geographically so closely identified with one territory and its historical destinies that the late Henri Foçillon suggested, paradoxically but wisely, that Gothic be defined as the Romanesque of the Ile de France. The new style, finally, seems to have been the creation of a small group of men whose ideas we know and who were mutual friends; we are prompted to ask whether Gothic art must not be understood as an expression of these ideas.

In other words, the stylistic analysis of Gothic architecture has suggested its interpretation as the expression of certain ideas. And this second approach, the symbolic one, though long regarded with some suspicion, has recently attracted a good deal of attention. We have been reminded that the Christian sanctuary is, liturgically and mystically, an image of the heavenly Jerusalem, the eschatological vision described by the Book of Revelation. The medieval dedication rite establishes this relationship in explicit terms and the twelfth and thirteenth centuries appear singularly preoccupied with this symbolic significance of sacred architecture. May not this significance have actually determined the design of the cathedral? Indeed, a brilliant and provocative attempt has been made recently to interpret all the essential aspects of Gothic design as representations of the celestial city.[1] Such an attempt, to be sure, encounters serious difficulties.[2] But it is heuristically valuable in that it compels us to define the exact relation between the stylistic structure and the significance of the Gothic cathedral, throwing an entirely new light upon its esthetic as well as structural aspects.

The most striking feature of the new style is a new relationship between function and form, structure and ornament. In Romanesque (and Byzantine) architecture structure is a technical means to an artistic end; it remains concealed behind painted or stucco ornaments. Indeed, the entire edifice is often but an invisible scaffold for the display of great murals and mosaics. These compositions, especially the figure of Christ in Majesty surrounded by his heavenly court that usually adorns the Romanesque apse, evoke the symbolic significance of the sanctuary as an image of the celestial city. That the structure of the building is concealed by these images reveals the spiritual source of Romanesque "antifunctionalism": the celestial vision depicted is to make us forget that we stand in a building of stone and mortar. In the Gothic cathedral the relation between structure on the one hand and ornament and its symbolic function on the other is quite different. Here the design is entirely determined by the pattern of the structural members, vault ribs and shafts. It has been remarked that the flowering of the Romanesque mural was in large part due to the technical imperfections of the buildings it adorned, that wall painting declined in the measure in which these imperfections were overcome. In Gothic architecture, the wonderful precision with which every single block was shaped in the vault (leaving no ragged joints that it was necessary to conceal) suggests a new esthetic appreciation of the dignity of structural perfection.[3] This tectonic system is never concealed but rather underscored by Gothic wall painting. Even the stained glass windows submit, in composition and design, increasingly to the pattern of the stone and metal armature in which they are imbedded. The esthetic function of these windows is not only the creation of a new luminosity; the light they admit dramatically underscores the web of tracery, ribs, and shafts.

This new esthetic dignity ascribed to structure cannot be understood in terms of modern functionalism. Architectural form reveals function if it actually shows the physical interaction of weight and support as it does in the Greek temple. What concerned the Gothic builder was not such naked expression of statical function but rather the translation of function into an essentially graphic system. By concealing volume or "dissolving" it into a bundle of frail shafts, he obtained the visual effect of a geometrical grid on a two-dimensional surface.[4] With this qualification, however, Gothic architecture is indeed functionalist. And its emphatic recognition of structure is all the more remarkable if we recall the symbolic significance of the sanctuary. As we shall see, the "functionalist" aspect of Gothic art will help us understand the precise nature of its symbolic aspect, just as the latter is indispensable for a correct definition of Gothic functionalism.

It is hardly necessary today to stress the overwhelming importance of geometry in Gothic design. The reliance on geometrical formulae, apparent in every Gothic ground plan and elevation, is amply attested by medieval documents. So much research has been done in recent years on this question that I can limit myself to a brief summary. With but a single basic dimension given, the Gothic architect developed all other magnitudes of his ground plan and elevation by strictly geometrical means, using as "modules" certain regular polygons, above all the square. The knowledge of this way of determining proportions was considered so essential that it was kept a professional secret. Only toward the end of the fifteenth century—and of the cathedral age—was it made public by Matthew Roriczer, the builder of Regensburg cathedral. He teaches "how to take the elevation from the ground plan" by means of a single square. From this figure Roriczer derives all proportions of his edifice inasmuch as its dimensions are related to one another as are the sides of a sequence of squares the areas of which diminish (or increase) in geometrical progression. The proportions thus obtained the master considered to be "according to true measure." [5]

It was not only this late Gothic architect or the German lodges that made such modular use of the square. Perhaps the most important single piece of evidence regarding the principles of Gothic design is the famous model book by the Picard architect Villard de Honnecourt, who was active in the second quarter of the thirteenth century. He, too, demonstrates how to double (or halve) a square for the purpose of determining the proportions of a building, in this case the ground plan of a cloister. That this is no mere theory is shown by Villard's plan of one of the towers of Laon Cathedral, considered by him the most beautiful in the world. This plan indicates, as Ueberwasser has shown, that all horizontal subdivisions of the tower are recessed "according to true measure."

The square—along with the other polygons, such as the famous $\pi/4$ triangle, which the medieval architect derived from the square—and the proportion "according to true measure" have determined Gothic design to a remarkable extent. The façade of Notre Dame of Paris is composed of a sequence of four squares developed according to true measure. Of course geometrical formulae had been used by pre-Gothic architects too. Here, however, they were practical rather than artistic devices of which the observer usually remains unconscious. Nowhere do they determine the esthetic impression as they do in the Gothic system. One might almost say that the development of the style, from its origin to the classical maturity reached in the mid-thirteenth century, is marked by the gradual triumph of geometrical proportion. If we compare the façade of Notre Dame with the similar and earlier one of Noyon, we realize the increasing clarity with which the geometrical principle is realized in the Paris façade.

The same principle rules over all parts of the Gothic cathedral. F. Bond was struck by the tenacity with which the square is retained in the Gothic ground plan even after the advantages of oblong bays from the viewpoint of vaulting had been discovered. We shall soon return to this phenomenon. The square is equally apparent in the Gothic elevation. That of Noyon is a good starting point. The nave was built during the last third of the twelfth century. Thanks to the fine analysis of Charles Seymour, Jr., we know how the work progressed from East to West and how this progress involved stylistic changes that mark this transition from Romanesque to Gothic. In the proportions of Noyon the geometrical element is, as Seymour observes, not yet prominent. We encounter "shifts of design and alterations of proportions" in almost every bay. Even so, it is significant that only in the three Western bays, which were completed last, is the relation of the width of an aisle to that of the main vessel "brought to a ratio of nearly exactly one to two." In the elevation of the nave, moreover, the stringcourse under the galleries marks off a height equal to the distance between the main piers; and the square thus described occurs a second time since the distance from the stringcourse to the windowsills of the clerestory is again the same.

But the Gothic trend toward "geometrical functionalism" appears elsewhere at Noyon. He who designed this elevation perceived the relation of weight and support not as the interaction of physical bodies, but as an abstraction, as an interplay of lines. The columns under the nave arcades are the only architectural members designed and articulated according to their statical function; they alone unequivocally suggest volume. But they represent an old-fashioned element, doomed gradually to disappear from Gothic architecture. The main piers remain partly embedded within the wall which conceals their bulk. The intermediary shafts, slender like bamboo shoots, could not even maintain themselves were not they, in turn, braced by the walls between them. As the work progressed, the architects suppressed everything that might divert attention from the interplay of lines. Thus ornaments and even corbel rings disappear from the later sections of the nave, capitals become smaller and simpler until only the austere web of horizontals and verticals remains.

If, on the other hand, we compare Noyon with the first—and mother —of the classical cathedrals, that of Chartres, geometrical proportion suddenly seems to have come into its own. The ground plan of Noyon is Romanesque in that it suggests an additive process of composition: one could easily add or eliminate one or more of the rectangular units of which it is composed. The ground plan of Chartres presents the compact unity and cohesion of an organism. This unity is due to proportion. Dehio was the first to notice that this plan is based on the Golden Section, since the center of the crossing divides the entire edifice in the ratio 5:8. The main proportions of the ground plan, moreover, determine those of the elevation. The church is as high as is the distance from the center of the crossing to the end of the choir (excluding the apse) and of the transepts. And the great square described by the crossing and by each double bay of the nave also reappears in the elevation: the height to the first stringcourse being equal to the side of this square, the architect has created a series of "spatial cubes" that is quite noticeable to the observer. And this square reappears once again in the elevation, since its side is equal to the length of the slender shafts that support the vault ribs. If we increase this square "according to true measure" we obtain the height of the entire nave to the windowsills. Finally, the Golden Section appears in the elevation as it does in the ground plan, determining the proportion between the piers (to the arcade imposts) and the shafts above them.[6]

What matters is not only the existence of these measurements, but the way in which the architect has brought them to our attention. He has sprung his four-partite vaults over transverse oblong bays, but has not entirely sacrificed the square: Chartres cathedral presents the alternating system of supports, in some respects an obsolete feature that occurred in Sens and Noyon but had already been dropped in Notre Dame of Paris. It is interesting to see how the master of Chartres employed alternation without sacrificing the homogeneity of identical supports. His piers consist, alternatively, of a cylindrical core surrounded by octagonal colonnettes and of an octagonal core surrounded by cylindrical colonnettes. The variation is just sufficient to induce the eye to see not one but two bays as one unit and thus to notice the square in the ground plan and the "cube" in the elevation. The main proportions of the elevation are made evident by the simple grid of intersecting verticals and horizontals. And our eye is similarly directed to notice the proportion (of the Golden Section) obtaining between the main parts of the supports: only one of the shafts in each compound lacks a capital under the nave arcade; it is the one facing the nave and just beneath the respond that rises to the springing of the transverse rib. We thus see the entire vertical member as one, harmonically subdivided, unit.

It is worthwhile to compare the elevations of Noyon and Chartres. The younger cathedral is nearly fourteen meters higher, yet it conveys the impression of far greater horizontal unification. The abandonment of the four-partite elevation in favor of the three-partite one is an important means to this end. The harmony of the Golden Section welds both the vertical and horizontal system of Chartres into an indissoluble unity. These proportions strike one as necessary and definitive, whereas the master of Noyon appears to be still groping for the right ratios. Equally increased is the tendency toward the two-dimensional in Chartres. With the elimination of the galleries, the side aisles have become narrower and lighter, a luminous membrane rather than a shadowy depth enveloping the nave. The *piliers cantonnés*—which the master of Chartres, as Panofsky observes,[7] employs for the first time—further accentuate the graphic tendency, seemingly reducing the solid core of the supports and dissolving their volume into the vertical rhythm of lines.

It ought not to be assumed that the line drawings we have been studying convey an inaccurate notion. In every other architectural style they would indeed give but a faint semblance of what the architect actually intended to build. Not so in Gothic. One has to look at the architectural drawings of the age—such as Villard de Honnecourt's or those of the contemporary Reims palimpsest, or the magnificent later collections from the cathedral lodges of Prague and Vienna—to realize that for their authors these drawings were not abstractions but the ideal which the completed edifice must seek to approximate. These wonderful systems of lines suggest neither space nor volume. Not until the end of the fourteenth century is there any indication of perspective.[8] It is as if these masters, as unconcerned with physical laws as with appearance, had been preoccupied solely with the reality of geometrical proportions.

Why this submission to geometry? One reason often given is a practical one: with measuring units varying from place to place, yardsticks were unknown or unusable; hence the use of proportions, in architectural drawings or models, that could be translated into large dimensions by geometrical means only. This explanation is but partially adequate, however. Villard de Honnecourt supplies numerical indications of size in a technical drawing, but always relies on geometry in his architectural designs. The proportion "according to true measure," whatever the facility of its practical execution, occurs, as Ueberwasser has shown, in Gothic paintings and engravings where the problem of translating one dimension into another did not enter. The Gothic artist would have overthrown the rule of geometry had he experienced it as a fetter. Yet he did not use geometrical formulae for purely esthetic reasons either; they occur in places where they are invisible to the observer. In short, the alternative "practical or esthetic" does not make sense in medieval terms. Happily, at least one literary document survives that explains the use of geometry in Gothic architecture: the minutes of the architectural conferences held during 1391 and the following years at Milan.

The cathedral of Milan was begun in 1386. After a few years difficulties developed and foreign advisors were called in from France and Germany. The minutes of the discussions between them and their Italian colleagues have survived. Two aspects of the deliberations are of importance in our present context: first, the reliance on geometric figures, attested by the German architect, Roriczer, of the fifteenth century, and the French architect, Villard de Honnecourt, of the thirteenth, is emphatically confirmed by the Italian document of the intervening century. The question debated at Milan is not whether or not the cathedral is to be built according to a geometrical formula, but merely whether the modular figure to be used is the square (which had already determined the ground plan) or the equilateral triangle.[9] The second and even more significant aspect of the Milan documents is that they suggest the reason for this use of geometrical formulae. The minutes of one particularly stormy session recall an angry dispute between the French expert, Jean Mignot, and the Italians. Overruled by them on a technical issue, Mignot remarks bitterly that his opponents have set aside the rules of geometry as if science were one thing and art another. Art, however, he concludes, is nothing without science, *ars sine scientia nihil est*. The terms art and science do not mean what they mean today. Art for Mignot is the practical know-how gained from experience; science the ability to account for the reasons that determine sound architectural procedure by rational and more precisely by geometrical means. In other words: architecture is scientific inasmuch as it is based on geometry, and unless he obeys the laws of geometry the architect must fail. This argument was considered unassailable even by Mignot's opponents. They hasten to affirm that they are in complete agreement and have nothing but contempt for an architect who presumes to ignore the dictates of geometry. It is taken for granted by both sides that the stability and the beauty of the edifice are not distinct, do not obey different laws, but are both comprehended in the perfection of geometrical forms.

Thus, the Milan document answers our question regarding the function of geometry in Gothic architecture. I think it also provides the clue to the reasons underlying what seems to us an almost superstitious belief in mathematics. Jean Mignot's juxtaposition of *ars* and *scientia* recalls, like a faint echo, the distinction that occurs almost a millennium before in the most influential esthetic treatise of the Middle Ages.

In the first book of his treatise, *De Musica*, St. Augustine defines music as the "science of good modulation." Before telling us what good modulation is, he explains why music, properly understood, is a science

He does not deny that music can be produced by instinct or practical skill, just as music can be appreciated by one who just "knows what he likes." Such understanding of music, however creative or receptive, is but of a low order, according to Augustine. Vulgar performers and vulgar audiences have such an understanding; even a singing bird has. In fact, there is little difference between man and beast in regard to this kind of musical knowledge which Augustine calls contemptuously *art*. The true understanding of music, on the other hand, that knows the laws which are of its very essence, applies them in musical creation and discovers them in music, is what Augustine calls the *science* of music, and he goes on to explain the nature of this science as mathematical. The science of good modulation is concerned with the relating of several musical units according to a module, a measure, in such a way that the relation can be expressed in simple arithmetical ratios. The most admirable ratio, according to Augustine, is that of equality or symmetry, the ratio 1:1, since here the union or consonance between the two parts is most intimate. Next in rank are the ratios 1:2, 2:3, and 3:4, the intervals of the perfect consonances octave, fifth, and fourth. It is to be noticed that the pre-eminence of these intervals, for Augustine, is not derived from their esthetic or acoustic qualities. These are, rather, audible echoes of the metaphysical perfection which Pythagorean mysticism ascribes to number, especially to the four numbers of the *tetractys*. Without the principle of number, as Augustine calls it, the cosmos would return to chaos. Taking up the Biblical passage *Omnia in mensura et numero et pondere disposuisti*, Augustine applied Pythagorean and neo-Platonic number mysticism to the interpretation of the Christian universe, its creation, and its order. He shares with Plato both a distrust of the world of images and the belief in the absolute validity of mathematical truths. Platonic metaphysics is also the basis for Augustine's philosophy of art. The views he formulated, not only as regards the function of the arts in the Christian commonwealth, but also, one may say, as regards its style, have left their imprint on Christian art during a thousand years. This influence has three aspects.

1. The principles of good musical modulation and its appreciation which Augustine established in *De Musica* are mathematical principles and therefore apply, in his opinion at least, to the visual arts as they do to music. On the monochord, the musical intervals are marked off by the divisions on a string; the arithmetical ratios of the perfect consonances thus appear as the proportions between different parts of a line. And since Augustine adduces the musical value of the perfect consonances from the metaphysical dignity of the ratios on which they are based, it was natural for him to conclude that the beauty of certain visual proportions derives from their being based on the simple ratios of the *tetractys*. The place Augustine assigns to geometry among the liberal arts, like the

place he assigns to music, is due to its "anagogical" function, that is, its ability to lead the mind from the world of appearances to the contemplation of the divine order. In the second book of his treatise *On Order* Augustine describes how reason, in her quest for the blissful contemplation of things divine, turns to music and from music to what lies within the range of vision: beholding earth and heaven, she realizes that only beauty can ever satisfy her, in beauty figures, in figures proportion, and in proportion number. The esthetic implications are clear. Augustine was quite as sensitive to architecture as he was to music. They are the only arts he seems to have fully enjoyed, and he recognized them even after his conversion, since he experienced the same transcendental element in both. For him, music and architecture are sisters, since both are children of number; they have equal dignity, since architectural mirrors eternal harmony as music echoes it.

2. Augustine uses architecture as he does music to show that number, as apparent in the simpler geometrical proportions that are based on the "perfect" ratios, is the source of all esthetic perfection. And he uses the architect, as he does the musician, to prove that all artistic creation follows the dictate of number, even though the architect, if he is a mere practitioner rather than a scientist of his art, may be unable to account rationally for his instinctive use of mathematical rules. Such views, of course, confine artistic design and composition within the rigid limits of metaphysical doctrine. Along with a real appreciation of the abstract mathematical beauty that may and perhaps always does underlie artistic composition, Augustinian esthetics harbors a profound distrust and contempt of the image, the semblance of living form that may obscure the anagogical function of the work of art. And even the proportions he admits are limited to the "perfect" ratios of Pythagorean mysticism.

3. That Augustinian thought has profoundly influenced Western art during the Middle Ages, both in its recurrent iconoclastic tendencies and in its mathematical character, is beyond question. We are apt to underrate the positive consequences of this influence. While stripping the arts, and above all architecture, of much of their life, it also assigned to them an extraordinary dignity and mission. Because true beauty is, according to Augustine, anchored in a metaphysical reality, the contemplation of visual and musical harmony will actually lead the soul to the experience of the ultimate harmony and unity that is God.

The Middle Ages never questioned Augustine's authority. The passage from the Book of Wisdom "Thou hast disposed everything according to measure and number and weight," and the interpretation he had given to it, became, as has rightly been observed, the key word to medieval thought and learning until the advent of Aristotle. E. R. Curtius has recently shown how this world view, through number composition, has af fected both the content and the form of medieval poetry. It has left an even greater impact on medieval art.

Augustinian esthetics were never forgotten during the Middle Ages. In the twelfth century, however, they gain an unprecedented importance in the Ile de France, under the influence of two movements, the first intellectual and speculative, the second spiritual and ascetical. The first centers in the group of Platonists assembled at the school of Chartres, the second in the monastic reform emanating from Cîteaux and embodied by Bernard of Clairvaux. French civilization in the twelfth century is in an important sense the synthesis of these two trends which, though distinct, are yet closely interconnected by personal and intellectual ties. Their common bond is the legacy of St. Augustine, their lasting achievement the creation of Gothic art.

The Platonism of Chartres was in many respects a true Renaissance movement. The group of men who gathered there in the second quarter of the twelfth century were primarily interested in theological and cosmological questions, to be solved by means of a synthesis of Platonic and Christian ideas. These early scholastics approached their task in a spirit of tolerance and respect with regard to the thought of antiquity that often reminds one of the "universal theism" of the fifteenth century; yet, theirs was a strange Platonism indeed. It was almost entirely based on one single treatise, the *Timaeus*. Of this treatise but a fragment was available; of this fragment not the Greek original, but only a garbled translation along with two commentaries—by Chalcidius and Macrobius—that viewed Plato's cosmology through the lenses of an eclectic and confused neo-Platonic mysticism. The Platonic fragment (and the two mediocre commentaries) were approached by the theologians of Chartres with nearly the same awe and respect as was the Book of Genesis. Both works, it was believed, were in substantial agreement in what they revealed about the creation of the universe, indeed, about the Creator himself. If one considers that the theology and cosmology of Chartres resulted largely from the interpretation of two documents as different as Plato and the Bible, but approached with the notion that they must not contradict each other and that the interpreter must not contradict either, one can but marvel at the wonderful and daring speculative system that resulted.

The aspects of the theology and cosmology of Chartres that interest us most in our present context are, first, the emphasis on mathematics, particularly geometry, and, second, the esthetic consequences of this thought.[10] The masters of Chartres, like the Platonists and the Pythagoreans of all ages, were obsessed with mathematics; it was considered the link between God and world. The most influential exponent of the system, Thierry of Chartres, hoped to find, with the help of geometry and arithmetics, the divine artist in his creation; he went further and sought to explain the mystery of the Trinity by geometrical demonstration. The equality of the Three Persons is represented, according to him, by the equilateral triangle; the square unfolds the ineffable relation between Father and Son. Thierry recalls that Plato "like his master Pythagoras" identified the metaphysical principles of monad and dyad with God and matter, respectively. God is thus supreme unity, and the Son is unity begotten by unity as the square results from the multiplication of a magnitude with itself. Rightly, Thierry concludes, is the Second Person of the Trinity therefore called the first square. It has been said, that, under Thierry's influence, the school of Chartres attempted to transform theology into geometry. The attempt, which appears so strange to us, conveys a glimpse of what geometry meant to the twelfth century.

More daring than this theology, more dubious from the standpoint of orthodoxy, and more significant for the art historian is the cosmology of Chartres and the philosophy of beauty which it engendered. In the *Timaeus* Plato describes the division of the world soul according to the ratios of the Pythagorean *tetractys*. The esthetic, especially musical, connotations of this idea, barely hinted at by Plato, are underscored by Chalcidius who points out that the division is effected according to the ratios of musical harmony. He, as well as Macrobius, insists that the Demiurge, by so dividing the world soul, establishes a cosmic order based on the harmony of musical consonance.

It was easy to fuse this notion with the Augustinian idea of a universe created "according to measure and number and weight." As a result the creation appeared as a symphonic composition. It is so described in the ninth century by John Scotus Erigena, and the idea was seized upon by the school of Chartres. William of Conches, the teacher of John of Salisbury, and Abelard, who seems to have studied mathematics under Thierry and whose cosmology is that of the school of Chartres, both identify the Platonic world soul with the Holy Ghost in its creative and ordering effect upon matter; and they conceive this effect as musical consonance. The harmony it establishes throughout the cosmos is represented, however, not only as a musical composition but also as an artistic one, more specifically, as a work of architecture. The ease with which the transition from the musical to the architectural sphere is here effected must not surprise us in view of the sistership of the two in Platonic and Augustinian thought. But for the theologians of Chartres, the notion of the cosmos as a work of architecture and of God as its architect has special significance, since they assume a twofold act of creation: the creation of chaotic matter, and the creation of cosmos out of chaos. The Greek word *cosmos* signifying ornament as well as order, it was plausible to view matter as the building material, the creation proper as the "adorning" of matter by the artful imposition of an architectural order. In the Platonic cosmology, moreover, the masters of Chartres could detect the design and method according to which the divine architect had built the universe, the cosmic temple as Macrobius calls it.

In the *Timaeus* the primary bodies of which the world is to be composed are conceived as building materials

ready to be put together by the builder's hand. This composition is effected by means of fixing the quantities in the perfect geometrical proportions of squares and cubes (1:2:4:8 and 1:3:9:27)—the same proportions that also determine the composition of the world soul. According to this composition, the world's body, consisting of the four primary bodies, whose quantities are limited and linked in the most perfect proportions, is in unity and concord with itself and hence will not suffer dissolution from any internal disharmony of its parts; the bond is simply geometrical proportion.[11]

In this view, the perfect proportions, the beauty of which we may admire in musical and in architectural compositions, also acquire an explicit technical or tectonic function: these proportions chain and knit together the different elements of which the cosmos is composed. William of Conches quite correctly interprets the Platonic passage in this sense. Here, then, perfect proportion is thought to account for both the beauty and the stability of the cosmic edifice.

The significance of these ideas for the history of architecture is very real. Some years ago N. Pevsner pointed out that the term architect is rarely used in the Middle Ages and, if it is, denotes either clerics interested or experienced in achitecture, or masons.[12] Pevsner concluded that the professional architect, in the classical sense (which is also the modern one), hardly existed in the Middle Ages, and suggested that the revival of the term in the mid-thirteenth century coincides exactly with the change from the humble master mason to the architect of the thirteenth century, no longer considered as a craftsman but as the principal artist and a "theoreticus" or scientist. There may be a good deal of truth in all this, but Pevsner is surely wrong when he seeks to connect this sociological and philological development with the introduction of Aristotle's *Metaphysics* (where *architect* is defined in our sense) to Western thought after 1200. Quite apart from the writings of Vitruvius, known and studied since Carolingian times, it was Augustine who kept alive the classical definition of the architect. His distinction between the mere practitioner and the true architect who deliberately applies scientific principles occurs in at least three different treatises, all studied and admired throughout the Middle Ages. While this definition permitted the application of the term architect even to the mere craftsman, it left no doubt that only the "scientist" schooled in the liberal arts was truly entitled to it. And since knowledge of the *quadrivium* was generally the privilege of clerics, it is not surprising to find so many ecclesiastics among medieval builders and the term architect so often applied to them.

But it was the school of Chartres which dramatized the image of the architect in the classical sense (more than a century before Aristotle's *Metaphysics* could have done so) by depicting God as a master builder, a *theoreticus* creating without instrument or effort by means of an architectural science that is essentially mathematical. And not only Augustine but Boethius, the greatest mathematical authority of the Middle Ages, taught the school of Chartres how to visualize in geometrical terms the perfect consonances. He points out that the proportions of double, half, triple, and third—those, in other words, that marked the perfect ratios on the monochord—are as readily perceived visually as they are acoustically, for, he continues, echoing the *Timaeus*, "the ear is affected by sound in quite the same way as the eye is by sight." And Boethius confines this doctrine of synesthesia not only to the proportions of line or surface; he discovers "geometrical harmony" in the cube since the number of its surfaces, angles, and edges—6:8:12—contains again the ratios of the consonances.

Toward the end of the twelfth century—at a time when the first Gothic cathedrals were nearing completion—Alanus ab Insulis described the creation of the world. To Alanus, the *doctor universalis,* the Platonism of Chartres owes probably its widest influence and diffusion. To him, God is the artful architect (*elegans architectus*) who builds the cosmos as his regal palace by composing and harmonizing the different genera of created things with the "subtle chains" of musical consonance.

The impact of these views on the architecture and architectural procedure of the twelfth and early thirteenth centuries cannot be overestimated. Since art is an image of nature, Professor de Bruyne asks, "must not the ideal church be constructed according to the law of the universe?" We suddenly understand why the high Middle Ages defined and practiced architecture as applied geometry; why the experts at Milan pay such astonishing tribute to this discipline. And we also understand why the great lay architects of the Gothic period have themselves invariably depicted, ruler and compass in hand, as geometricians. With these same attributes the creator himself was represented. Only by observing geometrical principles did architecture become a science in Augustine's sense; by submitting to its laws, the human architect imitated his divine master and in doing so his calling acquired metaphysical significance.

In order to understand this significance of Gothic architecture we must bear in mind that the musical harmony which the Christian Platonists beheld in the cosmos is primarily not a physical but a metaphysical principle. Medieval man looked upon the creation as the first of God's self-revelations, the Incarnation of the Word being the second. Between the two the twelfth century perceived innumerable mystical correspondences. The theological meaning of the universe had been obscured through Adam's fall on earth. It still appeared clearly in the perfection of God's celestial palace. Hence the tendency, familiar to every reader of Dante, to link the realm of the stars with the celestial mansions; hence also the seemingly dual symbolism of the cathedral which is at once an image of the cosmos and of the celestial city. If the Gothic architect designed his sanctuary according to the laws of harmonious proportion, he did not only imitate the perfection of the visible world but also created an image, in as much as that is possible to man, of an invisible one.

The symbolic concatenation is well explained in a passage of Abelard. After identifying the Platonic world soul with world harmony, he first interprets the ancient notion of a music of the spheres as referring to the "heavenly mansions" where angels and saints "in the ultimate sweetness of harmonical modulation" render eternal praise to God. Then, however, Abelard transposes the musical image into an architectural one. He relates the celestial Jerusalem to the terrestrial one, more specifically to the Temple built by Solomon as God's "regal palace" and at once a model for the Christian sanctuary and a mystical image of Heaven. This temple, Abelard remarks, was pervaded by the divine harmony as were the celestial spheres. The passage reflects the influence of Platonic cosmology upon Christian eschatology and symbolism in the twelfth century, the notion of an ineffable harmony gradually subdues the imagery by which the celestial city had formerly been depicted. This notion goes far to explain the transition from Romanesque to Gothic, the striking rule of harmonious proportion in the new style that emerges around 1140.

It must be emphasized at this point that the musical mysticism of the Platonic tradition was by no means the exclusive property of the School of Chartres. Embodied in Augustinian thought, it influenced the spiritual formation of the monastic movement that centered in Cîteaux and Clairvaux and is personified by St. Bernard. As I remarked earlier, this movement contributed as much to the civilization of the twelfth century as did the Platonism of Chartres, and both trends are intimately related. It is time to consider Bernardine thought in its impact upon Gothic art.

Bernard's artistic views are usually described as those of a Puritan. They are in point of fact Augustinian. No other author has had greater influence upon Bernard's theological formation than Augustine. He considered the Bishop of Hippo the greatest theological authority after the Apostles; with Augustine, Bernard writes, he wants to err, as well as to know. And Augustine musical mysticism could claim as its greatest spokesman. The following passage gives an idea of the place and function of music in Augustine's theological experience. In his treatise *De Trinitate* he meditates on the mystery of Redemption by which the death of Christ atoned for man's twofold death of body and, through sin, of soul. As the Bishop of Hippo ponders this "congruence," this "correspondence," this "consonance" of one and two, musical experience gradually takes hold of his imagination, and suddenly it dawns upon him that *harmony* is the proper term for Christ's work of reconciliation. This is not the place, Augustine exclaims, to demonstrate the value of the octave which seems so deeply implanted in our nature—by whom if not by Him who created us?—that even the musically and mathematically untrained immediately respond to it. Augustine feels that the mystery of Redemption is conveyed to human ears by the consonance of the octave, the musical expression of the ratio 1:2. The remarkable passage conveys an esthetic experience radically different from our own. It was not the primary enjoyment of musical consonances that led Augustine to interpret these as symbols of metaphysical or theological truth. On the contrary, the consonances were for him echoes of such truths and the enjoyment which the senses derive from musical harmony (and its equivalent, geometrical proportion) is our intuitive response to an ultimate reality that may defy reason but to which our entire nature is wonderfully attuned.

This experience determines the medieval attitude towards music. It accounts for the emphasis on musical studies even, and especially, in the monasteries of strict ascetical observation. To take a typical example, Othlon of St. Emmeram (1032–70), in embracing the most austere monastic ideal, renounced all his former humanistic interests. But arithmetic and music retain their mystical function for him; he uses them in his writings to convey divine secrets to his fellow monks, to prepare them for the life in a world to come. Even the order prevailing among the heavenly hosts, he writes, corresponds to the intervals of the perfect consonances.

Bernard's attitude towards music was quite similar. He was profoundly musical, and, as Father Luddy observes, an Augustinian even in musical matters. Something of a composer himself, he was once invited by the abbot of another monastery to compose an office for the feast of St. Victor. Bernard's reply is noteworthy. What he demands of ecclesiastical music is, above all, that it "radiate" truth, "sounding" the great Christian virtues and kindling the light of truth. Music, Bernard thinks, should please the ear in order to move the heart; it should by striking a golden mean between the frivolous and the harsh, wholesomely affect man's entire nature.

These are not the views of a Puritan. Bernard must have responded to musical experience with unusual sensitivity. In demanding that music be attuned to the great metaphysical and ethical experiences of Christian life, he confronted music, not with an attitude restricting its creative scope, but with a challenge. The importance of Bernard's views on music for our present inquiry lies in the fact that they also provide an indispensable clue to his convictions regarding the visual arts. That the laws of music, generally understood, "embrace everything," that they extend to all the arts is a view frequently expressed during the Middle Ages.[13] And to a man steeped, as Bernard was, in the Augustinian tradition, not only the metaphysical dignity of the perfect consonances but their presence in the sister art of music, architecture, must have been self-evident.

The appraisal of Bernard's views regarding religious architecture must rely not only on the opinions he expressed in literary form but on the testimony of Cistercian architecture, the design of which was certainly determined by his views. Bernard's demand that the "monstrous" imagery of Romanesque art—and in fact all images besides the crucifixus—be banished from the Cistercian cloister and church; his attack upon the "immense" height, the "immoderate" length, the "supervacuous" width of the Cluniac churches are but a negative statement of his views. To understand its meaning we must bear in mind that the sumptuousness of Cluniac sanctuaries was considered incompatible with monastic humility. More important than this ethical consideration, however, was a spiritual one. To Bernard the life of the Cistercian cloister—the *paradisus claustralis*—was an image and foretaste of Paradise. He sought to prepare his monks, even while in this life, for the fruition of an ultimate truth which the relatively crude imagery of Romanesque art could never convey.

Its elimination from the Cistercian monastery was therefore inevitable. Significantly, however, music maintained its place. And the disappearance of figurative sculpture and painting from Cistercian churches cleared the way for a purity of proportions that is all the more remarkable in view of the role which sacred architecture played, in the mystical contemplation of the Order, as an image of Heaven. For Bernard, as for Augustine, the perfect consonances, visible or audible, were not delusions of the senses, but echoes of transcendental reality.

We do not yet know all the geometrical modules used by the Cistercian builders. Yet the use of such modules is strikingly obvious in their churches. Augustine's "perfect" ratio 1:2 generally determines the elevation. In the abbey of Fontenay (1130–47), the best surviving example of early Cistercian architecture, this octave ratio determines the proportions of the ground plan as well. Moreover, the bays of the side aisles being of equal length, width, and, up to the stringcourse, height, we obtain in each of these cells a spatial cube—the "geometrical harmony" of Boethius which, later, we also encounter in Chartres. The austere façade, if we include the buttresses and the upper stringcourse, describes a square. The distance between the upper and lower stringcourse is determined "according to true measure." Medieval preference for this proportion appears in a new light if we recall Augustinian preference for the octave and the preoccupation with the octave and with the square in the thought of Augustine on the one hand and of the school of Chartres on the other: the proportion "according to true measure" may be defined as the geometrical expression of the ratio of the octave based on the square as module. It can hardly be a coincidence. Nowhere in Western architecture are the Augustinian consonances as present as they are in the simple and solemn proportions of this Cistercian church. Its design, in any event, is singularly attuned to the musical mysticism of the twelfth century.

Thus we have seen that the use of geometrical formulae in sacred architecture—so emphatically evident and yet so surprising to the modern observer—is rooted in the very world view of the twelfth century. Such interaction between the spheres of thought and of art is, of course, most evident in the case of Cistercian architecture. But what renders this evidence important in our present context is the close relationship between Cistercian and early Gothic architecture. This relationship has often been described. It would be incorrect to define Gothic as the daughter of Cistercian architecture. In criticizing the art of the Cluniac order, St. Bernard himself had made it very clear that his views as regards religious architecture applied to monastic buildings but not to the secular cathedrals. He readily conceded that the latter, "since they cannot excite the devotion of the carnal populace with spiritual ornaments, must employ material ones," in other words, that cathedral art had to make concessions to sensuous experience which the mystic no longer required. On the other hand, St. Bernard's insistence that all religious art and music must be attuned to spiritual experience, that they are justified only inasmuch as they lead man to ultimate truth, confronted cathedral builders with the same basic challenge which monastic architecture had answered with the creation of the Cistercian style. Cistercian and Gothic may be described as two branches of religious architecture—the one monastic, the other episcopal—growing out of the same basic experience.

There is nothing surprising about this close relationship. St. Bernard was the most forceful exponent of a vision of art, the basic tenets of which had their champions in cathedral schools like that of Chartres. It would indeed be a serious mistake to consider the two intellectual movements we have studied as entirely distinct. The Platonists of Chartres and the Augustinians of Cîteaux and Clairvaux were united by innumerable personal ties as well as by a common heritage. Of particular interest in this connection are the relations between St. Bernard and the three men who commissioned the three monuments with which Gothic art begins: Suger, Abbot of St. Denis, and the Bishops Henry of Sens and Geoffrey of Chartres.

Suger's place in the history of art is mainly due to the importance of the west façade and choir of St. Denis which, for the development of architecture as well as sculpture, mark an epoch. But his fame also rests on the fact that, unlike any other medieval builder, he has, in two treatises, rendered account of the significance of his art and indeed of the spiritual motivations that prompted him to adopt a style the dramatic novelty of which he himself seems to have sensed.

The interpretation of Suger's writings—and of his art as well—has generally suffered from the assumption that "an irreconcilable contrast" existed between his artistic views and those of the Abbot of Clairvaux. In point of fact Bernard's views were from a twelfth-century viewpoint far less extreme than is usually believed and, as I hope to have shown, offer many points of contact with the esthetic convictions of his contemporaries. Suger in particular, steeped in the neo-Platonism of Pseudo-Dionysius, must have been singularly attracted by Bernard's insistence that religious art is admissible only inasmuch as it guides contemplation toward the transcendental source of all beauty. This thought is the continued theme of Suger's treatises in which he interprets his artistic creations as he believes they ought to be understood. We have no reason to doubt his sincerity in this regard. In fact, there is good reason to think that the art of St. Denis may actually reflect Bernardine influence. The same influence, as I can but mention in passing, may have inspired the building activities of Henry of Sens and Geoffrey of Chartres.

St. Denis, Sens and Chartres West mark a beginning. But the "classical" Gothic cathedrals that follow their lead embody the same metaphysics of beauty. During the second half of the twelfth century the Platonism of Chartres and the spirituality of St. Bernard lose nothing of their influence. On the contrary, this influence is consolidated through a union of the two movements that is often as intimate as is, during the same period, the fusion of Cistercian and Gothic architecture.

This fusion, and its origin in the metaphysics of musical harmony, is most clearly embodied in the work of a professional architect. I have already mentioned the model book of Villard de Honnecourt. One of his designs represents the ground plan of a Cistercian church drawn *ad quadratum*, i.e., the square bay of the side aisles is used as a module, as a measuring unit from which all proportions of the ground plan have been derived. And these proportions, as E. de Bruyne observes, correspond in each case to the ratios of the musical consonances. Thus the length of the church *in opere* is related to the transept in the ratio of the fifth (2:3); the ratio 1:2 determines the relation between side aisle and nave, length and width of the transept, and, we may assume on the basis of Cistercian practice, that of the interior elevation as well. The 3:4 ratio of the choir evokes the musical fourth; the 4:5 ratio of nave and side aisles taken as a unit corresponds to the third, while the crossing, liturgically and esthetically the center of the church, is based on the 1:1 ratio of unison, most perfect of consonances.

Villard's testimony is of great significance. He seems to have received his architectural training at the Cistercian monastery of Vaucelles and certainly was employed as an architect by the Order. His design embodies the esthetic principles of the Cistercian tradition. While it does not seem to represent any church actually built, it shows sufficient resemblances to Pontigny and other churches of the Order to warrant Hahnloser's suggestion that Villard's ground plan was designed as the ideal type of a Cistercian church.

Villard's authority and interest was not confined to the sphere of monastic architecture. Trained during the first third of the thirteenth century and active during the second, he saw, completed or in the process of building, nearly every one of the classical cathedrals of the Ile de France. He was a distinguished Gothic architect in his own right, and it is all the more significant that, not only in his Cistercian ground plan, but on nearly every page of his model book he stresses the importance of geometry for the realization of harmonical proportion.

But it is the Gothic cathedral itself that bespeaks this artistic conviction. The proportions of the great sanctuaries of the thirteenth century are based on the simple ratios of the musical consonances that also determine Gothic music. This affinity between architecture and music was an esthetic truism to an age which perceived in the "science" of music the all-embracing principle of the universe. Abbot Suger, in the opening passages of his treatise on the consecration of the church, describes the universe as a symphonic composition in terms strikingly similar to those used by Alanus ab Insulis in the passage on the work of the divine architect. Suger invokes this vision as the sublime prototype of the sanctuary he is going to erect. But if his musical phraseology suggests that he considered his architecture a "frozen music," musical writers of the High Middle Ages, conversely, compare musical composition to architecture.

To sum up: the metaphysics of "measure and number" explains the design as well as the symbolic significance of the cathedral and influenced architectural procedure itself. The observation of geometrical canons was imposed by an endeavor that had less to do with artistic invention than with science (as these terms are understood today). Designed in an attempt to reproduce the structure of the universe—not unlike the great scientific experiments of our time in this respect—the cathedral is perhaps best understood as a "model" of the medieval universe. It is the theological transparency of this universe that transformed the model into a symbol.

NOTES

1 H. Sedlmayr, *Die Entstehung der Kathedrale*, Zürich, 1950. See my review in *Kunstchronik*, IV, 1951, pp. 78ff.
2 The Book of Revelation is neither the only source on which the Middle Ages based their eschatological vision, nor is Gothic architecture a better monumental "illustration" of that source than other styles. The temple of Solomon, especially as described by Ezekiel, probably influenced ecclesiastical symbolism as much as did St. John's description of the Heavenly City. And if a contemporary writer compares the Romanesque *Trinité* of Fécamp to the celestial Jerusalem, the sanctuary evokes for him the splendor of the biblical vision by means very different from those of the

Gothic design and yet quite as effective. See V. Mortet, *Recueil de Textes*, I (Paris, 1911), p. 345.

3 See the remarks of F. Bond, *Introd. to Engl. Church Arch.*, I (London, 1913), p. 321 on French and English methods of web filling.

4 See J. Bony, *French Cathedrals* (Boston, 1951), pp. 9ff., who defines Gothic "functionalism" much as I do.

5 Cf. esp. W. Ueberwasser, "Nach rechtem Maasz," *Jahrb. d. preuss. Kunstlgn.*, 56, 1935, and P. Frankl, "The Secret of the Medieval Masons," *Art Bulletin*, 27, 1945.

6 The most exact measurements of Chartres Cathedral are still those given by Lassus, *Monographie de la Cath. de Chartres* (Paris, 1867). Measurements vary from bay to bay and the proportions given above are but approximations. Variations seem to be due partly to changes of plan and considerations imposed by the earlier building, and partly to the rather crude methods of setting out—by means of pegs and strings—employed by the medieval builder. See now J. Harvey, *The Gothic World* (London, 1950), pp. 16ff. and L. F. Salzman, *Building in England* (Oxford, 1952), p. 17.

7 *Gothic Architecture and Scholasticism*, Latrobe, 1951, pp. 74ff.; Panofsky's analysis of the elevation of Chartres is illuminating even if one does not accept the author's interpretations.

8 See O. Kletzl, *Planfragmente aus d.d. Dombauhütte von Prag* (Stuttgart, 1939), pp. 19f.

9 *Annali della Fabbrica del Duomo di Milano* (Milan, 1877–85), esp. I, pp. 68ff. and 209ff. The best discussion of the subject is that of J. S. Ackerman, "Ars sine scientia nihil est," *Art Bull.* 31, 1949.

10 The first comprehensive interpretation of the esthetic system inherent in the thought of the school of Chartres we owe to E. de Bruyne, *Etudes d'Esthétique médiévale* (Bruges, 1946), II, pp. 255ff.

11 See F. M. Cornford, *Plato's Cosmology* (London, 1948), pp. 59ff.

12 "The term 'architect' in the Middle Ages," *Speculum*, 17, 1942. On the entire question see now the very sensible remarks of Salzman, *l.c.* pp. 1ff.

13 See M. F. Bukofzer, "Speculative thinking in medieval music," *Speculum*, 17, 1942, and L. Spitzer, "Classical and Christian ideas of world harmony," *Traditio*, II, 1944, and III, 1945.

12

Quantification
in Medieval Physics

A. C. CROMBIE

A WORTH-WHILE DISCUSSION of quantification in medieval physics requires particular care in deciding what is to be talked about. The whole question is obviously much less clear and much more equivocal in this period than it became later. So it is important to begin with some distinctions. I shall distinguish first between quantified procedures and quantified concepts, and I shall take a quantified procedure in science to be one that aims at measurement, that is, any procedure that assigns numbers in a scale. To be complete such a procedure must comprise both mathematical techniques for operating the scale theoretically and measuring techniques for using it to explore the world. Technology need contain little more than procedures of these kinds, which provide for the measurements and calculations with which it is concerned. But most sciences aim beyond these at providing explanations by means of a system of theory. So a quantified science, as distinct from quantified technology, comprises not only quantified procedures but also quantified explanatory concepts, each applicable to the other within a theoretical system. The development of a science then takes place through a dialogue between its theories and its procedures, the former offering an exploration of the expected world through predictions and explanations made by means of the technical procedures, and the latter confronting these theoretical expectations with the test of quantified data.

A dialogue of this kind requires that both sides should speak the same language. We are so familiar with the close and precise adaptation of conceptual and procedural language to each other in modern physics that it may come as a surprise to find authentic scientific systems in which this is not the case. Yet we do not have to look very far to find examples. In the contemporary social sciences and in psychology, they are notorious. We do not have to go many decades back in the history of modern genetics to find a very incomplete and interrupted dialogue between theories and procedures. Somewhat earlier, in the eighteenth century, we find the same situation in chemistry. The main interest of medieval physics in this context seems to me to be that it provides the earliest example in the development of modern science in which we can study the state of affairs when the dialogue between concepts and procedures was incomplete or absent. Then we can study the difference it made when clear and exact communication was opened, as it was in the seventeenth century. I shall assume that it is my brief to discuss medieval physics as a case history of a general problem. At the same time, I shall assume that this case history has a special historical interest because of its bearing on the particular question of the origins of modern scientific thinking.[1]

I propose to pursue the inquiry through two general questions. First, what internal intellectual needs and external practical and professional pressures were felt, leading to the quantification of theoretical concepts and theoretical procedures? Secondly, what internal intellectual needs and external practical and professional pressures were felt, leading to the collecting of quantitative factual data and to the confronting of theoretical analysis with exact and repeatable measurements?

All the information about medieval physics that has been brought to light recently shows that a far greater need was felt that concepts and theoretical and mathematical procedures should be quantified than that actual measurements should be made. The choice between different possible theoretical formulations was often decided on purely theoretical grounds within a theoretical system. When we look at how the scientific and philosophical problems concerned developed historically, this distribution of interest seems natural enough. Yet it appears as something of a paradox. We seem to be dealing with philosophical decisions that did not immediately yield much in the way of quantified physics that was empirically true, yet with decisions that may seem to have been necessary for the later development of such a physics. The paradox appears when we ask ourselves, on the one hand, what the medieval physicists themselves thought they were doing, and on the other, what we ourselves may judge their contribution to have been to the later development of quantified science. So we must consider this further question: to what extent did medieval natural philosophical ideas, in advance of factual knowledge and often also of much deep understanding of the scientific use to which they could be put, suggest physical problems and methods of conceptualizing physics in what turned out to be a fruitful direction? This question must be faced by any historian of a tradition of developing truth such as Western science. I do not think that we should be bothered by the suggestion of teleology this question carries. It can be dealt with by trying first to determine what problems the natural philosophers of the past were aiming to solve in their own period and what their intentions and preoccupations were, and by trying then to see what difference their work made in the short and in the long run. It will cause no surprise that ideas and habits of thought may come to have applications undreamed of at an earlier stage of their history—so much so that an idea may generate a completely different one with a change of context.

Some intellectual need to produce some kind of quantified conceptualization of physics can be seen as early as the twelfth century, for example, in the Chartres school. The sources of this are a form of neoplatonic philosophy derived from St. Augustine and from Plato's *Timaeus,* and such scriptural texts as that from the *Wisdom of Solomon* stating that God had "ordered all things in measure and number and weight." Vague as it is, this notion suggested kinds of explanation to look for. For example, Thierry of Chartres, in attempting to give a rational analysis of the formation of the world at the creation, replaced Plato's demiurge with the Christian God. He said that God had created space or chaos and then had ordered it so as to form the universe in accordance with the mathematical ideas in His mind. So Thierry concluded that in order to understand the story of *Genesis* rationally, it was necessary to master the mathematics of the *quadrivium,* for mathematics was the key to all rational explanation of the physical world. We might perhaps call Thierry's programme "proto-quantitative." It included such elements as attempting to account for differences between qualities as observed, in terms of geometrical differences between Plato's geometrical particles. It is hopeful and for us suggestive. But it involves no numbers or measurements. It is hardly what we regard as science.

The first more seriously scientific moves towards the quantification of concepts and procedures in medieval physics were made in the course of a controversy that arose in the thirteenth century over the Aristotelian categories of "quantity" and "quality." In effect the origin of the controversy was a critique of Aristotle's qualitative physics from two other points of view also derived from Greek sources. These were first, the Pythagorean or Platonic physical concept that qualitative differences might be reducible to differences in geometrical structure, number and movement, that is to differences in quantities; and secondly, certain mathematical concepts and procedures.

The characteristics of Aristotle's conception of physics that strike us now as most alien to the thought of modern quantified physics are not only that it was explicitly qualitative, but also that it looked for its explanations in terms of a direct classification of immediate experience. Thus Aristotle's distinctions between motion up, down, and in a circle, and between natural and violent motion, were based on a direct classification of what bodies are actually seen to do. The cosmological system in which such motions were supposed to find their explanation was built up simply as a classification of these and similar directly observed distinctions. The "natures" that were supposed to be the explanatory sources of the behavior of different things were characterized simply by a direct description of what things actually did. Thus they gave no further information beyond that already obtained from direct observation. Their characterization included both quantitative and qualitative attributes. But these were irreducibly different. Certainly Aristotle's physics made use of some quantitative relationships, such as when he said that a body would move twice the distance in a given time when acted on by twice the power. But it did not aim except incidentally at measurement, calculation, and quantitative prediction. It aimed at *episteme, scientia,* true and certain rational knowledge. Aristotle held that he had found such knowledge when he had discovered the "nature" through direct observation.

The medieval critique of this conception of the aims of physics as a science certainly fell a good way short of the position Galileo was to take up. Galileo did his best to drop all the questions to which Aristotelian physics was the answer and to ask new kinds of questions. But the new elements by means of which both the medievals and Galileo introduced a new conception of physics were analogous. On the other hand, in certain fields medieval "Platonists" looked, like Galileo, for explanations not in immediate experience but in theoretical concepts at a remove from it and capable of quantification. On the other hand, both reduced the sharp distinction made by Plato and Aristotle between *episteme* and *techne, ars,* the manipulative skills, including mathematics.

This last distinction seems to me to supply one of the various keys that historians can offer to an understanding of what happened in the Scientific Revolution. Thus in Greek scientific thought Ptolemy's mathematical astronomy, which could predict the celestial motions but could not explain them, was supposed to be a distinct field of inquiry from Aristotle's physics, which was held to explain these motions. The technical mathematical devices of astronomy were *techne.* So it was possible to hold that alternative technical devices, for example, in the middle ages those of Eudoxus and Ptolemy and in the sixteenth and early seventeenth centuries those of Ptolemy, Copernicus, and Tycho Brahe, could be combined with the same system of physics, the same *episteme.* The dynamical analysis of terrestrial and celestial motion finally brought out into the open by Kepler, Galileo, and eventually Newton showed that this was a very superficial view of the matter. It showed that in so far as the "physics" of motion was left untouched by calculation and measurement, it could be disregarded. It was irrelevant. And it showed that in so far as "physics" was exposed to calculation and measurement it was subject to the same quantitative tests as the mathematical devices used in making predictions. The essence of the seventeenth-century revolution in physics can thus be seen, from this point of view, as the using of *techne,* "art," in fact the "new experimental-mathematical philosophy," to yield a true science of nature. This was not the certain rational knowledge of Plato's and Aristotle's *episteme,* but as Pascal, Huygens, and Newton pointed out it was the nearest to the physical truth that we could get.

In medieval physics the distinction between the science of "natures" and the art of applying mathematics to physical problems was certainly not abolished or reorganized as it became in the seventeenth century. But mathematical art, the so-called *scientia media,* was introduced into the science of nature far beyond Aristotle. So at the same time there were at least some quantified physical concepts, and others that were not yet quantified but were capable of being so. The weakest of the elements that have become essential to physics since the seventeenth century was measurement. I shall now consider some examples of these elements in the quantification of medieval physics.

An example of the "proto-quantification" of physical concepts, aiming to show how to express qualitative differences in terms of differences in quantities, but without yet assigning any quantities, is provided by thirteenth-century optics. Much of this is better described as a speculative program than as theory. The deductive machinery for making calculations from theory to data is largely missing. But medieval natural philosophers were certainly aware that such machinery should be supplied in a scientific system, and in optics they made some attempt to supply it. In some problems they reached a state of primitive quantification by assigning numbers.

Consider first the conception of optics as a physical science developed in the thirteenth century by Robert Grosseteste and Roger Bacon. Grosseteste conceived the "nature" that was the cause of given events as something, not open to direct inspection, in which the event was prefigured. The ultimate physical "nature" or substance in which all physical events were prefigured he held to be light (*lux*). This had the fundamental property of self-propagation which he characterized geometrically from two points of view: (1) *super lineas et angulos,* that is along straight lines that may change direction by reflection and refraction; and (2) *super figuras,* that is in a sphere from a centre or in a cone. Thus characterized, Grosseteste described how this light, from an originally created point, generated the dimensions of space and the spheres of the universe, and operated as the efficient cause in all motion. So for Grosseteste optics became the fundamental physical science, and in order to make it work as an explanatory system he said that it was essential to operate it by means of mathematics. "Hence," he wrote, "these rules and principles and fundamentals having been given by the power of geometry, the careful observer of natural things can give the causes of all natural effects by this method. And it will be impossible otherwise, as is already clear in respect of the universal, since every natural action is varied in strength and weakness through variation of lines, angles and figures. But in respect of the particular this is even clearer, first in natural action upon matter and later upon the senses." [2]

With Grosseteste, the Aristotelian "nature" or "form" thus became mathematically characterized. Roger Bacon, continuing Grosseteste's description of this program, wrote: "All categories (*praedicamenta*) depend on a knowledge of quantity, concerning which mathematics treats, and therefore the whole power of logic depends on mathematics." [3] He then used language indicating a further shift towards a quantified physics looking for its explanations not in definitions of essences or "natures" but in mathematically expressed laws. Bacon is the first writer I know to have used the term "law of nature" (*lex naturae*) in the scientific sense familiar since the seventeenth century. Thus he wrote: "That the laws of reflection and refraction are common to all natural actions I have shown in the treatise on geometry," [4] and he claimed to have demonstrated "by the law of refraction" how the image was formed in the eye.

As a piece of speculation this mathematicizing program has a number of features suggestive and interesting for us because we know what happened in the long run. In his account of *multiplicatio specierum*, Grosseteste distinguished between the physical activity by which visible light, heat, sound, and other forms of efficient causality were propagated through the medium, and the sensations they produced when they acted on the appropriate sense organs of a sentient being. This is not of course an original distinction; it was made by the Greek atomists. But in the thirteenth century it made a significant departure from Aristotle by conceiving the world of physical science as something removed from direct observation and something capable of mathematical characterization. Grosseteste himself attempted to formulate a geometrical, almost mechanical conception of the rectilinear propagation of light and of sound as a succession of "pulses" or "waves" transmitted from part to part. He tried to use this to account for reflection and refraction, and he offered a quantitative law or "rule" for determining the angle of refraction. [5] Roger Bacon, and later Witelo and Theodoric of Freiberg, made a similar distinction between directly perceived visible qualities and light as a geometrically conceived physical activity producing these qualities. They proposed that different visible qualities were effects produced by quantitative differences in the physical activity of light. Thus Witelo and Theodoric of Freiberg developed along these lines a suggestion made by Averroes giving a quasi-quantitative account of Aristotle's explanation of colour as a mixture of light and darkness. They observed experimentally that the colours of the spectrum were in an order of increasing amounts of refraction from red to blue. They attributed this to a progressive weakening of white light by refraction, so that progressively larger amounts of darkness became mixed with it. Similarly Grosseteste correlated intensity of illumination and of heat with the angle at which the rays were received and with their concentration. In the fourteenth century another Oxford natural philosopher, John of Dumbleton, speculated with the formulation of a quantitative law relating intensity of illumination to distance from the luminous source.

We might consider these speculations as part of the pre-history of a quantified conceptualization of the science of optics. If now we ask for their cash value in quantified procedures and first scientific knowledge, we get another side to the story. In the whole conceptual development of optics following Grosseteste, there was almost no attempt at precise mathematical definition, at expressing the amounts of change quantitatively in numbers, or at measurement. One reason for this was certainly that these speculations carried the subject far beyond not only the facts but also the available mathematical techniques and concepts, which did not go farther than those of elementary geometrical optics. But if we descend from high speculation closer to the world of fact and of *techne,* we still find a gap between promise and fulfillment. We find ourselves in a scientific milieu in which certainly some natural philosophers had a more or less clear idea of how to proceed in science and in which some discoveries were made. For example, Roger Bacon's analysis and classification of the refractive properties of different curved interfaces, and his use of a geometrical model of the eye to analyze how the different refracting media focused the image, are highly intelligent examples of protoquantitative scientific procedures. But in the milieu of medieval academic science neither intellectual need nor social pressure for consistent quantitative accuracy seems to have been felt strongly enough to produce reliably consistent results. In the academic science of the universities the chances of data being challenged by repetition must have been small. It was only where investigations had some definite practical value, such as astronomical observations had for the calendar, astrology and navigation, and chemical assaying had for commercial metallurgy, that there was a strong enough demand to ensure exact and repeatable measurements.

Some further examples from optics will illustrate this unreliability in measurement characteristic of medieval academic science in practice, however much quantitative procedures may have been advocated in principle. One of the most impressive pieces of quantitative academic science in the thirteenth century is Witelo's account of the measurement of the values of the angles of refraction of light passing between air, water and glass, with angles of incidence increasing by 10 degrees to a maximum of 80 degrees. Witelo described in detail the construction and use of an apparatus for making these measurements, set out the results in tables showing concomitant variations between angles of incidence and amounts of refraction, generalized these in a set of rules assigning greater or lesser amounts of refraction but not numbers, and offered a physical explanation in terms of the densities of the refracting media. But did Witelo ever actually make these measurements? Two facts raise doubts. First, the values in the tables showing refraction from air into water and into glass, and from water into glass, which are fairly accurate, are identical with those in Ptolemy's tables for similar experiments. Secondly, Witelo's tables show very inaccurate or impossible reciprocal values.[6] (Ptolemy did not include these.) It seems that Witelo derived these values from a misapplication of the law that the paths of the rays are the same whether we are considering the light passing, for example, from air into water or from water into air. He did not know that at the higher angles of incidence, all the light striking the under surface of the water will be reflected and none will be refracted into the air. If Witelo had actually made these experiments, he would have discovered this phenomenon, but it was not discovered until the fourteenth century.

Another revealing example is provided by the studies of the rainbow.[7] According to the conception of scientific methodology developed in the thirteenth and fourteenth centuries, the explanation of an event was to be sought through an analysis of the conditions necessary and sufficient to produce it. The conditions producing a rainbow were stated in the form that if there be postulated a certain refracting medium, namely rain drops, at a position at which the incident sunlight makes an angle of 42 degrees with the line connecting the rain drops and an observer, then the observer will see a rainbow. Roger Bacon states that he measured with an astrolabe this angle subtended by the radius of the rainbow. Later investigators, especially Witelo and Theodoric of Freiberg, proceeded most intelligently to try to find out what happened to the light when it struck the rain drops. They set up geometrical models, rejected models that did not yield the observed results, and Theodoric finally carried out a successful analysis showing, by means of spherical flasks of water used as model raindrops, how the sunlight, by refraction and internal reflection, produced the order and shape of the colours seen in both the primary and the secondary bows. He stated correctly that the angle between these two bows is 11 degrees. But he also stated that he had measured with an astrolabe the angle subtended by the radius of the primary bow and had found it to be 22 degrees. It is obvious that he could not have obtained by measurement this value for an angle that is approximately 42 degrees. Theodoric's work is characteristic of a large part of medieval optics and medieval physics as a whole. He had an intelligent analytical procedure. Neither his procedure nor his conceptualization of the problem were explicitly quantified, but both were a preliminary to the quantification that Descartes, for example, was to give to the problem of the rainbow by assigning numbers by means of the newly discovered law of refraction. But Theodoric was unreliable in his measurements.

It is obvious that when they were dealing with problems in academic science, the kinds of problems that might be discussed in commentaries on texts of Aristotle and other authors used in the arts faculties of universities, medieval natural philosophers suffered not simply from a lack of quantified procedures for dealing with their speculation, but also from a lack of firm intention to apply such procedures in experimental measurement. The dialogue in their own minds between concepts and procedures for measurement had not become properly established. The fact is that however much some of them may have discussed the methodology of experimental quantitative science and advocated putting it into practice, nearly all medieval natural philosophers were primarily theoreticians. They made consistent *measurements* only when some *practical* need demanded it. But they found the development of a dialogue between concepts and quantified *theoretical* procedures something that followed naturally from their academic problems. To this aspect of medieval physics, to the development of quantified theoretical and mathematical procedures and related concepts without measurement, I must now turn.

This theoretical quantification of academic medieval physics was developed out of an attempt to provide the same procedures for representing changes of any kind, quantitative or qualitative. Behind this was the conception that all real differences could be reduced to differences in the category of quantity, for example, that a change in the intensity of a quality such as heat could be expressed as a magnitude in the same way as could a change in a quantity such as length. The question was opened in a theological context by Peter Lombard's assertion that the virtue of charity could increase and decrease in an individual and be more or less intense at different times. How was this to be understood? Two schools of thought developed and their divergent principles were taken over into physics.

The conservative school supported Aristotle's principle that since quality and quantity belonged to absolutely different categories, the one could not be reduced to the other. Examples of changes in quantity were changes in length or number, which were brought about by the addition or subtraction of either continuous or discontinuous homogeneous parts. That was all the change involved. But a change in a quality such as heat was quite different. Heat might exist in different degrees of intensity, but a change in intensity was not brought about, for example, by adding one homogeneous part of heat to another. The heats of two bodies brought into contact did not make a greater heat, as the lengths of two bodies made a greater length. So Aristotle and his supporters considered that each degree of intensity of heat was a different quality, and that a change in the intensity was brought about by loss of one quality of heat and the acquisition of another. The same went for every change in quality.

The radical school aiming at quantifying physics had to make several moves in order to deal with these opposing arguments and achieve their goal. Some philosophers distinguished between a body and its qualities and said that, for example, if the heat or the weight of one body were abstracted from it and then added to another, the latter would become hotter and heavier in amounts capable of expression in numerical degrees. Following this line of thought, definitions and distinctions of quantities were sharpened. For example, in the fourteenth century the expression "specific weight" was used to distinguish density, or intensity of weight proportional to volume, from gross weight. Another problem that arose concerned the characterization of scales. Greek writers conceived of qualities as existing in pairs of opposites: hot-cold, wet-dry, heavy-light, bright-dark, and so on. Thus Galen had suggested representing both heat and cold in numerical degrees. This conception of pairs of opposites was a major obstacle to the quantification of physics until the general introduction of linear scales from the seventeenth century. For example, when Buridan, in developing the dynamical concept of *impetus,* proposed as a measure of "quantity of motion" the product of "speed" multiplied by "quantity of matter," this applied only to "heavy" and not to "light" bodies.

In the end, whatever they took of the real nature of qualities and of qualitative change, natural philosophers and mathematicians made two important contributions to the quantification of physics in the fourteenth century. They created concepts for quantifying space, time, speed, and other magnitudes. And they devised procedures for *representing* any kind of change numerically and for manipulating the quantities concerned. The best illustration of this is found in kinematics and dynamics.

The theoretical quantification of the science of local motion began with a critique of those parts of Aristotle's treatment of the subject that had themselves some implied quantification. The technical procedures were derived in the first place from the theory of proportions expounded by Euclid and Archimedes. Consider first the stages in the critique of the Aristotelian relationship making speed (v) directly proportional to the motive power (p) and inversely proportional to the resistance (r) of the medium: $v \propto p/r$. The first thing that had to be done was to put the relationship into this form, which was impossible for the Greeks because they did not consider speed (v) to be a magnitude. According to the Greek conception, a magnitude could result only from a "true" proportion, that is from a ratio of two "like" quantities such as two distances (s) or two times (t).[8] So Aristotle could express the relationship only by considering it in separate stages. Thus

$$\frac{S_1}{S_2} = \frac{t_1}{t_2}, \text{ i.e. speed is uniform, when } p_1 = p_2 \text{ and } r_1 = r_2;$$

$$\frac{S_1}{S_2} = \frac{p_1}{p_2} \quad \text{when } t_1 = t_2 \text{ and } r_1 = r_2;$$

$$\frac{S_1}{S_2} = \frac{r_1}{r_2} \quad \text{when } t_1 = t_2 \text{ and } p_1 = p_2.$$

A metric definition of speed as a magnitude determined by the ratio between two "unlike" quantities, distance and time, i.e. $v = s/t$, was foreshadowed in the thirteenth century by Gerard of Brussels but made explicit only in the fourteenth century by Thomas Bradwardine and other mathematicians at Oxford.

Bradwardine was now in a position to propose an alternative to the Aristotelian expression $v \propto p/r$, which could not apply to cases where $p = r$ and $v = o$. After considering some other proposals, he came to the conclusion that the relationship was one which we would now call exponential and which we can express as $v = \log (p/r)$. Since $\log 1/1 = o$, the condition is satisfied that when $p = r$, $v = o$, and the relationship gives a continual gradual change in v as p/r approaches 1. It is clear that Bradwardine was concerned with obtaining a relationship consistent within his theoretical system that would also describe actual motions. He also made the important and influential move of shifting the ground of the discussion from the causal "why" to the mathematical "how," that is, from the physical causes of movement to the spatiotemporal effects of movement. But he does not seem to have thought of making experimental measurements to decide whether his expression did in fact describe actual motions.

Following Bradwardine, the theoretical quantification of the science of motion was carried several stages further at Oxford and Paris, but all without experimental measurement. Bradwardine's analysis had related velocity to instantaneous changes. At Merton College, William Heytesbury, Richard Swineshead, and John of Dumbleton went on to develop a concept of instantaneous velocity and with it an analysis of various kinds of acceleration, which Heytesbury defined as "the velocity of a velocity." (I use "velocity" in this context nonvectorially as syonymous with "speed.") This analysis grew out of the problem of representing the amounts and rates of change of any quality or quantity, which was known as "the intension and remission of forms," or "the latitude of forms." A "form" in this context was any variable quality or quantity. The "intensity" or "latitude" of a form, for example velocity, was the numerical value that was assigned to it, and thus it was possible to speak of the rate at which the intensity of the variable form, velocity, changed in relation to an invariable form known as the "extension" or "longitude," such as distance or time. Velocity was said to be "uniform" when equal distances were covered in equal successive intervals of time, and "difform" when unequal distances were covered as in accelerated or retarded motion. Further distinctions were made between "uniformly difform" motion, that is uniform acceleration or retardation, "difformly difform" motion, and so on. A very important definition was that of uniformly accelerated movement as one in which equal increments of velocity were acquired in equal intervals of time.

The problem of the relationship between the categories of quality and quantity that is behind this analysis is reflected in the distinction of the intensity of a velocity as its "quality," in contrast to the distance covered which was its "quantity." In cases of acceleration, the quality of velocity was said to vary from instant to instant. Thus instantaneous velocity was the intensity or quality of a velocity at an instant. It was measured numerically by the distance that *would* be covered by a point if it were allowed to move for a given time at the velocity it had at that instant. In Paris Nicole Oresme applied a graphical method to this analysis, using two-dimensional figures to represent changes of variable forms in relation to invariable ones. Thus he represented the "extension" of time by a horizontal straight line and the intensity of velocity at each instant by a perpendicular raised at a corresponding point on the horizontal. The height of the perpendicular represented the intensity or "quality" of the velocity, whereas the area of the whole figure, which is dimensionally equivalent to the distance covered in the movement, was its "quantity" or "total" velocity.[9]

Out of this theoretical quantification and analysis of motion came a number of interesting and valuable procedures and theorems. The most significant procedures occur in the associated development of the concept of functional dependence. The best known theorem is the so-called Mean Speed Rule of Merton College. This makes an approach that has become characteristic of modern kinematics, seeing as the basic objective of analysis the representation of nonuniform velocities by uniform velocities. The Merton theorem states that a uniform acceleration produces the same "quantity of motion," as measured by distance travelled in a given time, as a uniform velocity equal to the instantaneous velocity at the middle instant of the time of the acceleration. This theorem has application to the motion of freely falling bodies, which in the fourteenth century was discussed as a case of uniform acceleration. Yet none of these academic mathematical philosophers cleared up the question whether the velocity of falling bodies increased in proportion to distance fallen or to the time. That had to wait until the sixteenth century. And none of them checked the mathematical analysis against measurements made with falling bodies. The analysis of the problem within the framework of the Greek theory of proportions made measurement largely inapplicable. That had to wait until Galileo's experiments with a ball rolling down an inclined plane. The reason for these omissions is undoubtedly that these mathematical philosophers were primarily theoreticians, interested in philosophical method and mathematics. They felt no compelling intellectual need or social pressure to take a particular interest in falling bodies or any other particular phenomena in nature.

By far the most sophisticated and exact part of physical science in the thirteenth and fourteenth centuries was based on concepts quantified in this way for theoretical and mathematical manipulation, without thought of actual experimental measurements. As a general phenomenon arising in the arts faculty, this kind of approach to physical problems represented a union of the philosophical approach of Aristotle with the mathematical approach of Archimedes. Another example is the work in statics, where, for example, in the treatises associated with the name of Jordanus Nemorarius, trajectories and levers were analyzed into the effective quantities involved—vertical rectilinear displacement, horizontal distance from the fulcrum, "gravity according to position," and so on. This analysis made implicit use of the important new principle of virtual displacements. A further example is Jean Buridan's move towards the quantification of dynamics through the concept of impetus. This was put forward as a solution of the problem, arising within Aristotelian physics, of providing a cause for the continual motion of projectiles and for the accelerated motion of falling bodies. But by giving a quantitative measure of impetus as the quantity of matter in the moving body multiplied by its velocity, Buridan provided a measure of the *effect* of motion clearly analogous to the definition of quantity of motion or momentum used in seventeenth century mechanics. Similarly his account of the production of acceleration in falling bodies by the continuous action of a *constant* gravity has analogies with Newton's definition of force. Theoretical quantification was thus taking physics out of the irreducible Aristotelian categories. Metaphysical or "physical" restrictions, for example to considering velocity a magnitude or to comparing linear and circular motion, began to be put on one side.[10] In a quantified physics, mathematics treats all quantities as belonging to the same category.

The notion of proportions used in medieval science does not lead to measurement; hence measurements were not appropriate to the inquiry being undertaken. Nevertheless the investigation of proportions in the fourteenth century did lead to the formulation of important mathematical and logical definitions and theorems that were *later* taken over into seventeenth-century mathematical physics—for example, velocity, acceleration, instantaneous velocity, the Mertonian Mean Speed Rule. Thus, although the scholastics did not have precisely the same aims and intentions as seventeenth-century physicists, they did produce results which became part of the main history of physics—especially in kinematics. But we must not forget that medieval writers on "latitude of forms" applied their quantitative methods not only to physical problems such as motion, but also to degrees of divine grace, sin and other qualities. The fact that they considered such a wide range of questions by means of their method marks an important difference between their focus of attention and that of seventeenth-century physicists. The same is true of medieval work in the field of optics. A writer might consider within the same general framework the propagation not only of the light but also of influences from the stars and even of divine grace. Yet at the same time valuable work was done in optics strictly speaking, for example on refraction and the rainbow and on the analysis of the eye as an optical instrument by imposing a geometrical model on anatomy. Some of the numerical figures given can have been obtained only by actual measurement, for example 42 degrees for the radius of the rainbow. Yet we may doubt whether many of the figures given as if they were the results of measurements were really obtained in actual experiments. Until *after* Galileo such figures were in fact usually derived from mathematical theory.

Yet although the main development of quantification in academic medieval physics was in theory divorced from actual experiment, it would be mistaken to suppose that these philosophers were totally uninterested in the application of their theoretical analysis to the observable world and in checking it by reference to observations. Buridan, for example, continually invoked common-sense observations to illustrate his conclusions. At the same time there is evidence of a general move in practical life to quantify space, time, weight, and other aspects of the world as experienced and used. For example, by the time Henri de Vick's mechanical clock, divided into 24 equal hours, had been set up on the Palais Royale in Paris in 1370, the time of practical life was on the way to becoming abstract mathematical time of units on a scale that belongs to the world of science. King Charles V ordered all churches in Paris to ring the hours and quarters according to the time by de Vick's clock. The division of hours into 60 minutes and of minutes into 60 seconds also came into general use in the fourteenth century. Space also became abstractly quantified. In painting, the symbolic arrangements and size of subjects according to their importance in the theological hierarchy began to give way in the fourteenth century to the division of the canvas into an abstract checkerboard according to the rules of perspective. And besides maps arranging the world symbolically round a heavenly Jerusalem, there appeared maps by cartographers in which a terrestrial traveler or mariner could find his position on an abstract system of co-ordinates of latitude and longitude. Similarly in commerce and fiscal administration, exchanges and obligations were estimated in abstract units of money and bills of exchange and regulated by standardized units of weight and measure. In theoretical academic science the relating of quantified theory to measurement could remain a matter of private, internal interest. But in practical life exact and repeatable measurements are of the essence and are consequently subject to external demand. My final set of examples will show that when a similar external demand was made from science, it likewise produced exact measurements. But since the demand was primarily practical and utilitarian in its bearing, its effect upon scientific theory was far less intimate than that of contemporary thoretical discussions.

The hypothesis that in the medieval period it was normally external practical demand rather than an internal feeling of intellectual need that led to the development and use of procedures and instruments for obtaining accurate and consistent measurements, and that such measurements were lacking when such a demand was absent, whatever the field, can be tested by means of some quantities that appear in more than one context. Consider the treatment of three such quantities, time, space and weight, in academic natural philosophy and the practical crafts.

Time was the principal practical concern of astronomy, a science belonging to the academic *quadrivium*. Until the seventeenth century, astronomy was far ahead of all other theoretical sciences in the extent to which it was accurately and systematically quantified with actual measurements. For the medieval astronomers, Ptolemy's writings provided an example not only of quantified mathematical theory and procedures but also of systematic numerical observational data. The reason for the early development of astronomy in these respects was certainly that from remote antiquity the various regular movements of heavenly bodies had provided the standard measures and divisions of time regulating practical affairs, and also that since the main divisions into the solar year and day and the lunar month are all incommensurable, their relation to each other in the mathematical calendars and systems available required periodic checking by fresh measurements.

There were two main practical problems in the middle ages: to get an accurate perpetual calendar, relating especially the lunar year used in calculating the date of Easter to the solar year; and to devise means for telling the time of day at different times of year and different latitudes by observing the elevation of the sun or some other heavenly body. From the time Bede wrote on the subject early in the eighth century, these problems taught medieval scholars to think in numbers and to measure, calculate, and check against further measurements. They created a demand for mathematical knowledge and skill and for measuring instruments. Thus Bede gave a table for use with a sundial showing the length of a 6-ft. gnomon at noon, 9 a.m., and 3 p.m. at intervals of about a fortnight throughout the year, at a latitude of 55°, corresponding to that of his monastery at Jarrow.[11] From the period when the full influence of Greek and Arabic astronomy was felt in the thirteenth century, a variety of instruments for making astronomical measurements and telling the time were manufactured and put into use in the West. The most important were the astrolabe, the quadrant, and the sundial, which were improved in various ways for greater accuracy and range. At the same time improvements were made in mathematical techniques for making numerical calculations. The "Arabic" numerals and positional arithmetic introduced in the thirteenth century came into wide use first in calendars and astronomical tables and then in commercial transactions. In both fields it had an obvious practical advantage over the Roman system. The development of modern trigonometry dates from mathematical work done in Oxford and France in the fourteenth century in connection with astronomy.

The practical demand for an accurate knowledge of time put a premium on the precision of instruments and calculations. For observations made with the naked eye, the limit of accuracy is about 5 minutes of arc for angle-measurements, 20 seconds of time estimated by the earth's daily rotation, and 2½ degrees of terrestrial longitude estimated by means of eclipses and other methods involving lunar positions.[12] Ptolemy's mathematical astronomical theory had in most particulars reached this degree of accuracy. But an angle of 5 minutes subtends a distance of only 1 millimetre on a divided circle of 1½ metres in diameter. So to attain the precision required by the interaction of theory and measurement, instrument makers had to develop a very refined skill. Precision was achieved by the accuracy and closeness of the divisions, by making instruments large, and by paying attention to jointing and stability. There were considerable difficulties. For example, there was no method of geometrical construction for angles less than 15 degrees; below that divisions were made by eye. Yet with an ordinary thirteenth-century astrolabe the time could be told to within 2–5 minutes. The precision attained was well sufficient to enable astronomers to recognize by the end of the thirteenth century that Ptolemy's mathematical astronomy was much more accurate than Aristotle's. For example, in 1290 Guillaume of St. Cloud determined the latitude of Paris correctly as 48° 50′ and the obliquity of the ecliptic as 23° 34′, which compares well with the modern value of 23° 32′ for the obliquity at that date.

Thus the practical demands made on them forced astronomers to achieve an accuracy that enabled them to make a choice between theories on grounds of measurement. Compared with the systematic and regular method of observing introduced in the sixteenth century by Tycho Brahe, using instruments of measured degree of error, the irregular observations made by the medieval astronomers still allowed many discrepancies be-

tween theory and fact to pass undetected. But they made measurements
to a degree undreamed-of in fields of contemporary academic physics
that had no immediate practical applications. Demands made by such
applications could lead the same scholar or group of scholars, for example, those beginning with Grosseteste who for over a century were
concerned with the reform of the Julian calendar, to recognize the decisive importance of numerical measurements in a practical problem
while showing no such awareness in their work in purely academic
physics.

The same contrast appears in a comparison of academic treatment
of space and distance, for example in discussions of motion, with the
treatment given in contemporary methods of surveying, navigation, car-
tography, and later of gunnery. Here again practical demands forced an
attention to numerical measurement and calculation and led to the development of instruments and mathematical techniques. Surveying methods were being taught in the *quadrivium* by the twelfth century, and in
the whole practical quantification of space scholarly mathematics played
an essential part in supplying mathematical procedures to the empirical
methods of mariners, instrument makers, and other craftsmen. One example will suffice. In the sixteenth century the compass-charts or *porto-
lani* used in navigating gave two essential pieces of information: the
route to follow and the angle it must make with the North-South axis as
given by a magnetized needle; and the distance to run in the direction
thus determined. Ideally the navigator went on a line at a constant angle
from the line of the magnetized needle until he reached his destination.
If this was impossible or if he went off course for a time, rudimentary
trigonometrical tables, called *martelogio,* showed how to return to his
original route. These seem to have been the product of scholarly mathematics. An early indication of them is given by Raymond Lulle in his
Ars Magna (1305–1308), where he wrote: "When a ship runs eight miles
towards the south-east, these eight miles are equivalent to only six miles
towards the east." [13] In modern terminology, $8 \cos 45° = 5.6466$. This
provided for numerical measurements and calculations such as were not
found in contemporary academic discussions of motion.

The quantification of weight by measurement likewise occurred only
when there was a practical demand, but here this was felt almost entirely
in the field of the practical crafts and not in academic science. For example, practical metallurgists wanted to be able to produce alloys of desired and repeatable properties, coins of known and honest value, and so
on. The earliest physical property of metals to be quantitatively measured was density. A table dating from the eleventh or twelfth century
gives a list of weights relative to wax to show the founder how much
metal to melt.[14] But it was in assaying that quantitative methods based
on measuring weight with a balance were most extensively developed.

Ores were assayed for economic value and coins or jewelry to determine their quality and to detect fraud. The product was put through various processes, and weighing was carried out at appropriate stages with balances of various degrees of sensitivity. The most sensitive showed about 0.1 milligram.[15] There were beam-lifting devices to protect the knife-edge from shock, and in the course of time these became more accurate with further refinements, just as was happening with other scientific instruments. In quantitative factual knowledge, practical chemistry was far ahead of theory in the middle ages and remained so until the eighteenth century. The assayer excelled the alchemist in all but the desire for a systematized philosophy. But a dialogue between them and between the two sides of chemistry they represented was virtually impossible. The assayer concentrated his attention on changes in weight, the alchemist on changes in color and appearance. The former had no theory and the latter a theory based on the wrong concepts. The predicament of medieval chemistry is the most extreme case of the whole medieval scientific predicament of intellectual aspiration failing to get into communication with practical demand and so with quantified fact.

No claim could be made that this analysis is anything more than a preliminary exploration that may raise some questions for discussion and suggests some comparisons with problems of quantification in other periods and branches of science. But this I take to be the purpose of the papers prepared for this symposium. To give openings for discussion I will conclude by setting out the main answers, suggested by my analysis, to the questions asked at the beginning.

1. The primary internal, intellectual need felt by medieval natural philosophers was for rational, theoretical clarification and understanding rather than for knowledge acquired through observation. This need arose in a desire to understand rationally and clarify (a) the features of cosmogony and cosmology accepted as having been revealed, and (b) the system of natural philosophy presented in the Latin translations of Aristotle and the other Greek and the Arabic philosophers and mathematicians.

2. Consequently, medieval natural philosophers discussed quantification and other problems of scientific method primarily as theoretical problems without systematic reference to actual scientific measurement. They directed their intellectual effort towards quantifying theoretical concepts and procedures, especially in response to problems arising within Aristotelian philosophy and out of its relationship with concepts and procedures presented by Greek mathematics. As a result, they made some useful progress with theoretical problems. But, although they made some measurements, their intellectual interests did not by themselves provide an intellectual need strong enough to ensure that measurements in academic science were in fact accurate and that decisions be-

tween different theoretical principles or concepts were always made on grounds of actual measurements.

3. This theoretical emphasis in intellectual interests was supported and maintained by the aims, content, and methods of the education provided by the medieval universities, where the basis of both the arts course and of the higher courses in theology, law, and medicine was the making of a critical study and commentary on theoretical problems raised by standard texts.

4. Departure from this purely theoretical emphasis occurred only when there was a strong external, practical demand for exact measurements. When this was present, theoretical concepts and procedures became quantified in such a way that measurement was applicable, accurate measurements were made and used to test and decide between different theories, and instruments were developed to get increasing precision. The effect of such external, practical pressure appears in both theoretical science and the practical crafts, and in the work of both scholars and craftsmen, but because of its strongly practical, utilitarian character it did not have a profound influence on the accepted theoretical concepts of physics. Medieval academic science and medieval technology were in fact two almost completely independent monologues.

5. Thus there was in medieval physics a very incomplete dialogue between theoretical concepts and procedures on the one hand, and practical quantifying procedures in contact with the data of observation on the other. As a result, medieval physics never escaped from its Aristotelian framework. Interesting quantified procedures and conclusions were formulated within these general limits, and some of these were taken over into seventeenth-century physics, but the framework of physics as a whole was never completely rethought and reconstructed by the medieval philosophers.

6. The establishment of a complete dialogue between quantified theory and quantified theoretical and experimental procedures, between *episteme* and *techne,* is one of the principal changes that occurred in the seventeenth century. Systematic measurement became the procedure both for collecting exact data and for testing theories or challenging whole systems of theory. As this complete dialogue developed it was both felt as an internal, intellectual need and also demanded by external, practical pressure. Thus it became an intellectual and practical requirement for the new scientific profession that grew up with aims that had important differences from those of the medieval scholars. Intellectual, professional, and practical pressures all now demanded a quantified study of nature and not simply of theory.

7. This case history of medieval physics seems to suggest certain analogies in other fields and periods in the history of science, which seems to be an especially suitable subject for the comparative method of analysis.

NOTES

1 I have based my discussion in this paper on information taken from the following sources, which should be consulted for further details and bibliography: Guy Beaujouan and Emmanuel Poulle, "Les origines de la navigation astronomique aux XIVe et XVe siècles" in *Le Navire et l'économie maritime du XVe au XVIIIe siècle: travaux du colloque tenu le 17 mai 1956 à l'Académie de Marine* présentés par Michel Mollat avec la collaboration d'Olivier de Prat, Paris, 1957; D. A. Callus (ed.), *Robert Grosseteste, Scholar and Bishop* (Oxford, 1955), chapter by A. C. Crombie; Marshall Clagett, *The Science of Mechanics in the Middle Ages* (Madison, Wisc., 1959); Marshall Clagett (ed.), *Critical Problems in the History of Science* (Madison, Wisc., 1959), paper by A. C. Crombie and commentary by I. E. Drabkin and Ernest Nagel; A. C. Crombie, *Robert Grosseteste and the Origins of Experimental Science 1100–1700* (Oxford, 1953) and *Medieval and Early Modern Science* (New York, 1959) (2 vols. Doubleday Anchor Books); E. J. Dijksterhuis, *Die Mechanisering von het Wereldbeeld* (Amsterdam, 1950) (German translation, 1955); Pierre Duhem, *Le Système du monde* (Paris, 1913–1916) I–V, (1954–58) VI–VIII; C. W. Jones (ed.), *Bedae Opera de Temporibus* (Cambridge, Mass., 1943); Anneliese Maier, *Die Vorläufer Galileis im 14. Jahrhundert* (Rome, 1959), *Zwei Grundprobleme der Scholastischen Naturphilosophie*, 2nd ed. (Rome, 1951), *An der Grenze von Scholastik und Naturwissenschaften*, 2nd ed. (Rome, 1952), *Zwischen Philosophie und Mechanik* (Rome, 1958); E. A. Moody and Marshall Clagett, *The Medieval Science of Weights* (Madison, Wis., 1952); Charles Singer *et al.* (eds.), *A History of Technology* (Oxford, 1957), III—chapters by Sir Harold Spencer Jones, H. Alan Lloyd, Derek J. Price, Charles Singer, Cyril Stanley Smith and R. J. Forbes, and E. G. R. Taylor; René Taton (ed.), *Histoire générale des sciences* (Paris, 1957), I.

2 "De Natura Locorum" in *Die Philosophischen Werke des Robert Grosseteste*, ed. L. Bauer (*Beiträge zur Geschichte der Philosophie des Mittelalters*, IX, Münster, 1912), pp. 59–60.

3 *Opus Maius*, ed. J. H. Bridges (Oxford, 1897), I, 103.

4 *Un fragment inédit de l'Opus Tertium*, ed. P. Duhem (Quarracchi, 1909), p. 90; cf. p. 78.

5 Cf. C. M. Turbayne, "Grosseteste and an ancient optical principle," *Isis*, 1959, *50*: 467–472.

6 Crombie, *Robert Grosseteste*, pp. 223–225.

7 *Ibid.*, pp. 64–66, 124–127, 155–162, 196–200, 226–277, 290–292.

8 See Clagett, *The Science of Mechanics in the Middle Ages*, pp. 165ff.

9 *Cf.* Clagett, *op. cit.*, pp. xxv–xxvi.

10 *Cf.* Clagett, *op. cit.*, p. 181.

11 See D. J. Price, in *History of Technology*, III, 595.

12 *Ibid.*, pp. 583–584.

13 See Beaujouan and Poulle, *op. cit.*, pp. 106–107.

14 See C. S. Smith and R. J. Forbes, in *History of Technology*, III, 59.

15 *Ibid.*, p. 60.

The Controversy Over the Alleged Sowers of the Black Death in the Contemporary Treatises on Plague

SÉRAPHINE GUERCHBERG

IT IS WELL KNOWN that the epidemic of 1347–51, known as the Black Death, led to horrible massacres of people accused of having "sown" the plague by putting poison in wells and springs. The accusations are generally regarded as an outburst of anti-Semitism. However, this is not true of the first phase of the movement, which followed the onset of plague in southern France in the spring of 1348; here the victims were Christian. It was only as the movement spread to the north (it may have reached the Dauphiné by the summer of 1348 and was certainly at work then in the Savoy [1]), especially in Germany, where it arrived several months ahead of the plague [2] and was more serious than elsewhere, that it concentrated on the Jews. Many Christians were still accused as well, but they were now believed to have been acting under Jewish orders.[3]

There is no doubt that the mass of the people believed the accusations to be true. Similar suspicions, directed against a variety of social groups, have arisen in many countries throughout history.[4] In Western Europe charges of poisoning water supplies become more and more frequent in the 14th century; they typically occur in towns, where overcrowding and poor sanitation naturally favored epidemics.[5] On account of the hostile attitude of most of the clergy towards the Jews, it is not surprising that suspicion should light on them as a group.[6] According to the chroniclers, throughout the years 1348 and 1349 rumor accused one national [7] or social [8] group after another, only to fasten finally and inexorably on the Jews.

This article will deal with the reaction of educated society to the accusations, a problem which has never been well handled. How did the medical men of the time explain the epidemic? What were their views on the alleged sowing of the plague, and what part did their science play in forming their opinion?

The Black Death was Europe's first epidemic of plague since the reign of Justinian. It is true that chroniclers of the intervening centuries often tell of *pestis* and *pestilentia*, but they probably applied these terms to any kind of epidemic.[9] The Black Death, on the other hand, is uniformly reported as an unprecedented disaster. Chroniclers' descriptions leave no doubt that the symptoms were those of bubonic plague, including those of the most deadly form of the disease, the pneumonic. Moreover, a specialized medical literature on the subject grew up; this in itself was unusual.[10] Professor Sudhoff, the German historian of medicine, has printed nearly 300 treatises on plague, of which close to twenty were written between 1348 and 1350, and the rest by 1500.[11] It goes without saying that there must be a great deal of material of the kind still unpublished, but this paper is based chiefly on Sudhoff's texts.

These treatises were not written solely for physicians but for a wider public. Two of the initial group were composed in the vernacular, a third was translated from Latin into several languages, and the fact that in several other instances a treatise has survived in numerous copies is significant. They all naturally expound the etiological theories peculiar to the medical science of the time, which, as is well known, was a product of scholasticism and Arabic science, forming a system of rational speculation dominated by logical analysis and classification.[12] As Max Neuburger has acutely remarked, medieval science formed a real union with philosophy, whereas in antiquity the union had been only a personal one.[13] Medical practice, on the other hand, was in the main an empirical art, not organically linked with theory. The age was not, however, without brilliant practitioners. The treatises with which I shall be dealing draw very largely on observation, and the authors' advice on the treatment of the sick is often quite sensible.

The medicine of the age was also characterized by a close affinity with astrology. Astrology had declined in the early Middle Ages only to reappear in the 12th century Renaissance; it made its re-entry along with Aristotelianism, from which it was indeed inseparable. One will find no point-blank attack on it in the Thomist theology of the 13th century. Yet the Church, being against all determinism, could not accept the idea of astral influence on man's will. Consequently it attacked the cult of horoscopes. Yet it fully accepted the doctrine of astral influence on the sublunary world, including man's physical nature.[14] Its attitude thus favored the use of astrology in medicine. The Church also accepted astrological meteorology, that is to say, the prediction of calamities such as earth-

quakes, famine, epidemics, and war. The plague treatises rely heavily on
this branch of astrology. Indeed, the astrological theory of the origins of
the Black Death won out over all other etiological theories. The theory
was not entirely new, and we may note in passing that Jewish learning
had contributed to it.[15]

In April 1348, when the plague was rapidly spreading north and
appeared to be threatening the whole of France—brought by merchant
galleys from the Orient, it had first broken out in the ports of Italy and
of southern France in the autumn of 1347—, King Philip VI asked the
Faculty of Medicine of Paris to make a pronouncement on the causes of
the scourge. The masters of the Faculty laid down their opinion in the
curious *Compendium de Epidemia . . . per Collegium Facultatis Medi-
corum Parisiis.*[16] They apologized for not giving the whole truth, which
according to them was beyond the grasp of the human brain. This did
not keep them from being very dogmatic about the astrological causes.
The epidemic, they say, proceeds from a double cause: the first or superior cause is distant, celestial; the second or inferior cause, which is
the consequence of the first, is near, terrestrial. The celestial cause is the
conjunction of three planets—Saturn, Jupiter, and Mars—under the moist
sign of Aquarius, which had occurred in 1345, following solar and lunar
eclipses. The conjunction of Saturn and Jupiter in general brings fatal
disaster (their authority here is Aristotle); that of Jupiter and Mars engenders plague (here they cite Albertus Magnus). Jupiter, being hot and
moist, is especially likely to bring on putrefaction. As a result of the
conjunction a mass of noxious gas had been exuded from the earth and
from bodies of water, poisoning the atmosphere. The earthquakes of 1347
and 1348 had contributed to the poisoning not only of the air, but also,
they add, of water, through releasing these subterranean vapors. Unusually hot and wet weather had also made for putrefaction, and south
winds, provoked by the influence of Jupiter, had diffused exhalations
from rotting carcasses and from stagnant marsh waters.

This alleged corruption of the air, being near and terrestrial, con-
stitutes the second or inferior cause. The authors term it the efficient
cause of the plague. In keeping with the scheme of thought of scholastic
astrology, the second cause is not directly due to the influence of the
stars but is the result of a complex of intermediate and interrelated phenomena, as well as of numerous supplementary causes which varied with
time and place. For example, an epidemic may be caused by contamination of food and drink, which is likely to occur in time of famine. But
the Faculty considered the contamination of the atmosphere to be a
greater menace because air on being breathed goes straight to the heart.
It poisons the vital spirit which is located there and the internal organs
consequently rot. Despite the gloom of the picture they paint, the authors nevertheless hastened to reassure the public by claiming that the

plague is dangerous only to those whose organism is predisposed to it.

Most writers of the time held to this astrological theory of the plague, adding their own modifications. Its acceptance was not, however, unanimous. Indeed, soon after it appeared, it was severely criticized by an eminent German cleric, Konrad of Megenberg, who was a popular writer on scientific questions. His criticism is developed with particular care in the Latin treatise known as *Utrum Mortalitas*. Sudhoff, who found a copy of this treatise made in 1395, in a codex at Erfurt containing other medical writings from that region, published it as the work of an unknown doctor of south-western Germany. I believe, however, that it is the work of Megenberg.[17]

Megenberg attacks only the first, the distant celestial cause. His chief arguments are as follows. 1) No planetary conjunction lasts longer than a year or two, while the epidemic has already gone on for five. 2) All the movements of the heavenly bodies obey a strict order, while the epidemic wanders about aimlessly. This observation probably refers to the fact that the plague moved along the great communication routes, hitting mainly towns, centers of pilgrimage, fairs, and so on, where crowds were attracted, and often sparing whole intermediate zones. The significance of this usually escaped contemporaries, although Henry of Hervordia seems to have understood what it meant.[18] In brief, it was Megenberg's belief that the earthquakes were caused by an accumulation of noxious subterranean gases; the latter, finally escaping to poison the air, became the immediate cause of the plague. Thus although Megenberg attacked the astrological theory he arrived at the same conclusion as those who upheld it, namely, that contamination of the air was the efficient cause of the plague. Moreover, in the *Buch der Natur*, he admits that the conjunction of Mars, Saturn, and Jupiter had influenced the subterranean accumulation of gas.[19]

Other writers on the problem, more independent and lucid, stressed the factor of contagion. Chief among these were the illustrious Italian Gentile da Foligno, several of whose writings preceded the *Compendium de Epidemia;*[20] Johannes della Penna, who disputed with him on the physiological cause of the plague;[21] and the great Arab physician Ibn-al-Khatib, who paid for his convictions with his life, along with his less courageous friend Ibn Khatima, who after enunciating his theory of contagion, on the order of religious authorities immediately withdrew it.[22] Although such writers were under the spell of the traditional scholastic method, they had an innovating spirit. It is curious to see how they waver between two entirely different theories.[23] In any case the fact that the disease was contagious must have been as obvious to contemporaries, whether or not they were physicians, as it is to us. The chroniclers speak of it.[24] Contagion, however, operates in disconcerting ways. Since even the discovery in 1894 of the plague bacillus in no way solved the problem of explaining epidemics, it is hardly surprising that 14th-century physicians could not solve it.[25]

Realization that the plague was contagious led immediately to a campaign for better sanitation.[26] Indeed, measures of social hygiene may be said to date from the Black Death. Medical practice, at this period, was far ahead of theory. Yet the *Compendium de Epidemia,* in which the Faculty of Paris solemnly declared the cause of the epidemic to be the planetary conjunction of 1345, had not entirely ignored the question of contagion. A section on preventive measures warned the public to keep away from the sick and went so far as to advise against nursing one's relatives because of the danger of catching the disease. Most of the plague treatises make some such reference to contagion, without rejecting the official etiological theory. One of the earliest of the treatises [27] even lists contagion as a second inferior cause of the plague (contamination of the air being the first)—quite a radical elaboration of the scholastic astrological scheme set out in the *Compendium.* The writings of the latter part of the century often mention contagion as one of the supplementary terrestrial causes.

Although it was already common knowledge that plague could be carried by infected objects, and also by people who did not themselves have the disease,[28] there seems to be no record of Jews being accused of spreading the contagion of the Black Death artificially. Yet in epidemics of plague in the 16th and 17th centuries, especially in Italy, both Jews and Christians were accused of deliberately putting articles that had been used by the sick, such as clothing, into houses, or of rubbing ointment prepared with pus and other secretions of the sick on house-walls and windows.

Some of our sources refer to the contamination of water as well as of air, and many caution against drinking stagnant water. But in theoretical discussions the stress is on air. The authors of the *Compendium de Epidemia,* for example, regard atmospheric poisoning as the efficient cause *par excellence* of the epidemic.[29] Not until the 15th century do we find causal stress on the contamination of water supply, and this is only among chroniclers, not in medical circles; the idea is still common among chroniclers in later centuries.[30]

The theories of the etiology of plague that we have surveyed so far all rest on natural factors, but two other kinds of explanation were also current. As Konrad of Megenberg notes, some people thought the epidemic was a punishment sent by God, and some that it was caused by the Jews. In the first case we have a supernatural factor, in the second an artificial, voluntary factor, that of poisoning. The various hypotheses were of course not mutually exclusive. Even the accusers of the Jews regarded poisoning as a factor merely auxiliary to that of astral influence. (Oddly enough, Konrad does not list the theory of contagion as current; he and

Alphonse of Cordova are the only writers in the early group who ignore it.)

As to the supernatural theory, Megenberg objected that the plague showed no discrimination; if it were a divine punishment, surely it would strike only sinners. Johannes della Penna dismissed it as appealing only to the ignorant and idiotic. Simon de Corvino remarked that to explain the plague by a natural factor did not necessarily exclude the role of God's will. The *Compendium de Epidemia* advises that in the event of an epidemic sent by God we should pray humbly for grace; at the same time, since it is to God that we are indebted for medical science, we should still follow a doctor's orders. It seems to be implied here that there are two kinds of epidemic, one due to the wrath of God, and the other, like the Black Death, to astrological causes.[31] It must have been a relief to be able to fall back on a supernatural explanation. As Henry Lamme, a German physician, wrote in 1411, ". . . it is better to say that the epidemic comes from God than to repeat all the opinions one hears".[32] He nevertheless raises the question, was it God or the devil who sent the plague, and argues it relentlessly.

To come now to the theory that the plague was spread artificially, we find Konrad of Megenberg protesting, "Some say that this [the plague] is caused by the Jewish people, but this opinion cannot stand". This is a very striking statement. The context makes it quite plain that the matter is raised, not as having any scientific relevance, but as relating to a practical social problem. The Jewish question was particularly acute at the time, the treatise being written only a year or two after the agitations that culminated in the Jewish massacres of 1348–49. This is why the author was so anxious to give the lie to the accusations. At this point there is a gap in the copyist's manuscript, the passage ending with *etc.* The arguments that should follow are, however, set out in the corresponding passage of the chapter on earthquakes in Megenberg's *Buch der Natur* (p. 112). Unfortunately the text is confused, though it contains a clear enough empirical argument: "But I know that there were more Jews in Vienna than in any other German city familiar to me and that so many of them died of the plague that they were obliged to enlarge their cemetery. To have brought this on themselves would have been folly on their part." This general line of reasoning was not new; indeed, Pope Clement VI had used it persuasively in his bull of September 26, 1348.[33]

One would have expected a man of Megenberg's learning to query the assumption behind the charge of poisoning, that is, to ask where is the proof that a mere poison can produce plague. Megenberg does not do so. On the contrary, he even concedes the possibility. It is not as a man of science that he condemns the accusations, but as a political man afraid of the unleashing of mob passion [34] and above all as an honest man angered by an odious calumny. As an ecclesiastic, he is conventional enough to assure his readers that he has no intention of glossing over the fundamental wickedness of Jewry, yet he does not allow this to cloud the issue.

We have another view of the matter, set down twenty years later by the celebrated French physician and surgeon, Guy de Chauliac, who had combatted the Black Death at Avignon. As he had himself seen, people were terrified and mystified by the extraordinary mortality. "In some places", he wrote, "they killed Jews, believing them to have poisoned the world, in others they drove out paupers who were deformed, in others they drove out nobles. Things finally came to such a pass that guards were posted to see that no one who was not well known would enter a city or a village. And if they found anyone carrying medicinal powders or ointments they would force him to swallow them, to prove that they were not poisonous potions." [35] Yet whatever the people (*populus*) might say, he continued, the true explanation of the epidemic is to be sought in the astrological theory of dual causation.

Unlike Megenberg, Chauliac gives a retrospective and objective account of the "sowers of plague", mentioning Jews as only one of several groups persecuted. Moreover, his reason for regarding the persecution as absurd was different: to him, it arose from ignorance of science. He was no doubt well aware that it was not only the lower classes who believed in sowers of plague; the belief had adherents in all classes of society and even within the medical profession. But Chauliac does not bother to argue about it either empirically or on the plane of theory. It is a pity that we do not know what this great physician thought about the assumption behind the accusations, namely, that plague *could* be sown by poison.

The scarcity of testimony on this point from contemporaries of the Black Death obliges us to fall back on evidence from later generations. Ideas about the plague do not appear to have changed very much; there were quite frequent outbreaks of it and they occasionally provoked anti-Semitic agitation. Let us therefore look at what the early 15th-century German physician, Henry Lamme, had to say on the matter. Sudhoff had a high opinion of Lamme's powers of observation and judgment. Lamme describes the plague of 1410 as spreading insidiously, "as though it issued from the accumulation of bodies on a battlefield, or were due to poisonous plants, or to the poison discovered by that learned Pole whose book teaches how to concoct a preparation by which one could poison a city or even a whole region." [36] This reminds him of certain trees in India which yield a poisonous flour; whoever eats of it dies instantaneously. He takes this from *The Book of the English Knight*, in all probability referring to the *Travels of Sir John Mandeville*, which were very popular at the time. Lamme goes on to give Guy de Chauliac as authority for the fact that Jews were reputed to have poisoned Christians in the first great epidemic of 1348, adding that it then invaded almost the whole world, as though serpents, dragons, and basilisks were breathing out a mortal infection. He draws here on the story of three knights who fought a basilisk and perished from the infection of his breath. The tale, he says, is doubtfully attributed to Galen. Throughout the 15th century the notion that plague was due to mass poisoning by the breath of real or imaginary venomous animals was very widespread. The treatises of this period often mention it among the supplementary causes of the contamination of the air; sometimes they add the figure of the famous maiden who was nourished on poison.[37]

Lamme clearly believed the accusations of 1348 against the Jews to be at least possibly true for two reasons, namely, that some very noxious poisons can act with miraculous swiftness, and that by such means mass poisoning can produce effects like those of an epidemic of plague. Chauliac had merely drawn an analogy with the breath of venomous beasts; Lamme tries to interpret the passage as meaning that Chauliac believed plague to be the result of mass poisoning. Lamme's vagueness on the whole point is significant. In this connection we have to remember that other epidemic fevers were thought to have some affinity with plague. For example, the eminent French physician Chalin de Vivario, who was a contemporary and collaborator of Guy de Chauliac at Avignon, taught that *epidemia* was due to astral causes and *pestilentia* to terrestrial causes, plague (*pestis*) being the intermediate form. Among the causes of *pestilentia* he included well water contaminated by the dead bodies of poisonous animals.[38]

On the other hand, we must remember that the toxicology of the period regarded all poison as having a mysterious power which could not be fully explained by the nature of its components.[39] Consequently poison was readily credited with all kinds of miraculous properties; it could, for example, act at a distance, or its action could be delayed, etc. Moreover, it was felt that all poisoning depended for its efficacy on some element of magical procedure.

In the face of these ideas, it is clear that no physician or savant of the time could really have challenged the assumption behind the accusations, namely, that plague can be provoked at will by poisoning. The question whether there could be a special poison containing a plague-like substance would hardly arise.[40] In any case, those who sought to refute the accusations did not rely on what to ourselves would have seemed the obvious argument, that is, that no poison could produce a disease of this kind with determinate symptoms.[41] Yet even though writers would have to admit, as Megenberg and Lamme do, that poisoning might have contributed to the epidemic, they would not necessarily be inclined to believe that there were really any sowers of plague.

As for Lamme, we may be sure, if only because of his reference to Chauliac, that he did not believe Jews to be guilty. He could understand accusations arising, because he believed the deed possible. It follows that he must have been well aware of the precarious position of Jews, once a credulous mob were aroused. He himself rejected the accusations, as Megenberg and Chauliac did. But he could not do so in his capacity as a man of science. Like innumerable other reasonable and honest people in other walks of life, he was guided above all by good sense.

But if a Megenberg, a Chauliac, or a Lamme could still, despite the confusion of their theoretical ideas, see the facts steadily, there were other medical writers who did not. One of these was Alphonse of Cordova, who wrote at Montpelier in 1348, that is, in the very year when the Black Death and Jewish persecution broke out.[42] Alphonse tells us that the first outbreaks of plague were caused by the eclipse of the moon, followed by the conjunction of the three planets and by earthquakes. But he asserts that an epidemic due to these factors would at most have lasted only a year and would have affected only southern Italy and the regions of the Mediterranean facing it. The fact that it had lasted longer and spread further was proof, according to him, of a plot against Christendom. The second wave of the epidemic had been produced artificially and was far more dangerous because doctors had no cure for it. His advice to his readers was to beware of all food and drink that might have been poisoned, especially stagnant water. Alphonse does not say who the criminals were, but his talk of a plot against Christendom indicates that he was thinking of Jews and perhaps also Moslems; in France the latter had already been accused of poisonings in 1321. In spite of his concern with water, the poisoning he describes is not of water supply but of the air. Nor does he identify the poison used; he says only that it is a fermenting liquid in a glass vessel. The poisoner's technique is to carry this out of the town he plans to strike, walking against the wind. When he is some distance outside the town and at a somewhat higher level, he puts the vessel on the ground, smashes it, and runs away into the wind. The wind diffuses the evaporating poison through the town and "whoever comes in contact with the vapor dies as though he had breathed air infected with pestilence."

Alphonse was not alone in mingling fantasy with logical distinctions between kinds or phases of epidemic. Other astonishingly logical formulas were devised for defining the respective roles of God, the stars, and the Jews. Chroniclers, however, were as a rule content to repeat simply that people accused the Jews "of having caused or aggravated" the epidemic, a convenient enough formula for those who did not care greatly about truth. Alphonse himself is vague about the extent of his poisoners' power: was it limited to prolonging an epidemic started by the stars, or did poisoners produce a second epidemic independently?

We know nothing of the life of Alphonse of Cordova. Yet his treatise may have had some fame, for during the 15th century an Italian physician named Berchtoldus, who was also an "accuser", copied from it without acknowledgement.[43] To plagiarize well-known authors was a common medieval practice.

Wickersheimer interprets a reference to *speyse der pestilentie*, in a plague treatise written by five Strasburg physicians in 1349, as implying a belief that sowers of plague worked by poisoning food.[44] In our opinion, no such implication was intended. Many treatises warn against eating certain fruits and vegetables in time of plague; for example, in his *Buch der Natur* Megenberg writes of the danger of eating pears. If you throw pears into the water during an epidemic, they will float, he says, proving that they are full of pestilential gas absorbed from the air. The Strasburg doctors may well have had something of this sort in mind.

On the other hand, a German physician of the next generation, Henry Ribbeniz of Breslau, makes some allusions to sowers of plague which may refer to the period of the Black Death. Ribbeniz was renowned both as a writer on surgery and as an astrologer, and in his plague treatise, which appeared around 1370, he predicted the epidemic of 1371–72.[45] He tended to believe that all men's actions were determined by the stars. According to him, the great conjunction of Saturn and Jupiter not only brings plague, but by inducing a state of disquiet and irritation which leads men to sin against God, is the cause also of war and unrest. In reference to charges against Jews, he writes, "And in truth there must be something in this, for the Jews of Milan know a mountain nearby where a plant called *napellus* grows, which is the worst of poisons. . . ." He describes this plant (aconite) as having two roots; one acts like theriac (which almost all the plague treatises recommend as a preventive against the disease), while one dram of the other is enough to bring instant death. Ribbeniz adds, "It is forbidden to pasture animals on this mountain on account of the poison, nor are Jews permitted to go there lest they collect this plant and destroy the whole world or at least many Christians with its poison." Although he does not specifically mention the Black Death, it is reasonable to suppose that he has in mind the accusations of those years. In any case it is strange that he offers nothing in support of his belief that there must be "something" in the accusations, except this rumor that the Jews of Milan knew where to find a particularly poisonous plant. And one would like to know how so convinced an astrologer could assign poisoners any important role in the origin of plague.[46]

We have now considered the work of three men—Konrad of Megenberg, Guy de Chauliac, and Henry Lamme—who might be called defenders of the Jews; at all events, they did not believe that Jews were guilty of sowing plague. To these we may add two more: Simon de Covino—insofar as he considered the Flagellants who murdered Jews to have done so because they were mad—and a 15th-century author who dismissed the rumored accusations as imaginary.[47]

To sum up, we have demonstrated that the scientific theory of the time neither helped the defenders of the Jews nor hindered the accusers. We can now go a step further. Its role was not entirely neutral: the theory did at least provide the form that the accusations took. Writing of the Black Death, the very reliable French chronicler Jean de Venette even declares that it encouraged them: "It was said that this plague was started by the infection of air and waters and because of this opinion . . . the accusation was laid against the Jews that they had infected wells and springs and poisoned the air." [48] The formal accusations, and chroniclers' reports, actually specify for the most part only poisoning of water supply. In saying that Jews were accused of poisoning the air as well, Jean de Venette may have been influenced by the emphasis that the treatises lay on atmospheric contamination as the efficient cause of the plague. He may have been trying, as it were, to bring the popular notions more into line with the learned view. Yet the latter, as we have seen, took some account of contamination of water supply.

One could object that rumors of sowers of plague flourished in other periods too, and also that conditions of urban life in the 14th century would tend to favor them. Jean de Venette is nevertheless absolutely right in suggesting that current etiological theory must have materially encouraged the rise and spread of the rumors. Indeed, all of our sources point to the same conclusion. These were indeed sad circumstances, when objective scientific thought could contribute to the worsening of a moral situation that was already highly unfavorable to Jews. But we should not blame the scientific thinkers. It was not their fault if their ideas were put to use by agitators and persecutors.

As we have seen, the authors of the treatises did their best to direct their readers' attention to those natural factors that they held to be the true causes of plague. Barring the few exceptions found among the treatises that Sudhoff printed, we are inclined to credit them with good sense: they must surely have seen the absurdity of the accusations. We must, however, remember that if the authors include only a few accusers, they also include only a handful of defenders. The great majority did not wish to speak out loud; they preferred to pass over the question.

We turn now to another aspect of the controversy, one that came much to the fore in its later phases. This is the question of predisposition and immunity. It was the accepted doctrine that an individual's degree of predisposition depends on his temperament. This in turn depends on which of the four cardinal humours in his blood and bile, corresponding to the four elements, predominate in him. There are four temperaments (sanguine, choleric, phlegmatic, and melancholic), each characterized by one or other of four combinations of the primary qualities pertaining to the four elements of air, fire, water, and earth: hot and moist, hot and dry, cold and moist, cold and dry.[49] Astrology had assimilated this doctrine to the influence of the planets and the signs of the Zodiac.[50] A man's temperament is therefore determined by the properties of the star that governs him. Saturn being cold and dry, those whom Saturn rules have a quantity of black bile, which engenders a cold and dry (melancholic) temperament. This is the least desirable temperament, because its properties are contrary to life.[51] Jews, we should note, were supposed to be under Saturn's influence.

Epidemics provoked by a particular planet are especially dangerous to organisms whose primary qualities correspond to the properties of that planet, although other astrological factors, such as planetary conjunctions and the zodiacal sign under which these occur, will affect the situation. Again, predisposition depends on the quantity as well as on the quality of the humours: an excess of either good or bad humour will make the body impure. Impurity (*immunditia*) is the chief factor in predisposition to plague. An excess of humours may be due to an unhygienic way of life,[52] to certain phenomena relating to age and sex,[53] to occupation,[54] or to nationality.[55]

In analyzing the role of each of the three planets whose conjunction provoked the Black Death, the *Compendium de Epidemia* ascribes the principal role to Jupiter, because Jupiter is hot and moist. Hot and moist organisms are very suceptible to festering and therefore to plague. People with an excess of hot and moist humours are the most susceptible of all.

On the other hand, Konrad of Megenberg (in the *Utrum Mortalitas*) assigns the principal role to Saturn and Mars, operating respectively through black and yellow bile. Simon de Covino, too, though still placing Jupiter's influence first, stresses that of Saturn, "the corrupter of human life." Although in one passage he states that the plague hit the rich and the poor indiscriminately, in another he says that the poor were more prone to die of it. He calls them "Saturn's throng." In his opinion the life of the poor was at best a kind of death (*vita talibus mors est*). Simon also associates the Jews with Saturn, writing *lex Saturna* for *lex Judaica*.[56] But he says nothing about the Jewish rate of mortality from plague.

However, Chalin de Vivario, who wrote his treatise in 1382 at Avignon, where he had been an eyewitness not only of the Black Death but also of three subsequent epidemics, had been at pains to collect data on this very point.[57] He claims that in 1382 one in five Jews died. Since the proportion among Christians was less, he concludes that Jews, along with Spaniards, had a high predisposition to plague. In trying to explain why this should be so, he stresses the fact that they lived in dirty quarters (*immunde vivunt*), like the poor. Like the poor, too, they were gluttonous and drank too much wine, habits which make for impurity of the organ-

ism. Again, they bring infection from foreign countries where the plague
is more severe.

Chalin's figures refer to the epidemic of 1382, which is known to
have been milder than that of 1348. According to him it was only a *pestilentia*, due to terrestrial causes, not an epidemic due to the stars. As such,
he believed it to be more dangerous to people of bilious temperaments
than to those of sanguine temperament. But the crucial factor was impurity within the organism. He was certain that in any kind of plague-
like epidemic people with impure bodies were the most liable to die. As
to Jewish mortality from plague, he seems to imply that it was in general
abnormally high. Chalin may thus be taken as confirming what we know
already, on the impressive authority of Pope Clement VI, and from Megenberg, that Jewish mortality from the Black Death had been very heavy.

As to the factor of temperament, it was Chalin's opinion that the
sanguine temperament was the most predisposed to the kind of epidemic
that came, like the Black Death, from astral influence. Spaniards, he says,
are of sanguine temperament. According to him, melancholics are the
least predisposed. As to the temperament of Jews, he does not commit
himself. Possibly he felt that the factor of impurity would be decisive,
even though the Jews' temperament might have been resistant to plague.

Fifteenth-century opinion took another turn, as is clearly shown in
the treatise on plague by the German physician Primus of Görlitz.[58] This
is a scholastic discussion, the author himself declaring that he is trying to
solve problems by the speculative method. Applying this method to the
proposition that Jews die of plague less than Christians, he finds the explanation in their manner of life and diet. For example, they avoid ex-
posure to morning or night air, which, on account of the evil influence of
the stars, is particularly dangerous in time of pestilence. He adds that
they are people of Saturn and therefore of a cold and dry temperament,
which is resistant to plague.

The point of view adopted here is new and directly contradicts our
evidence from defenders of the Jews in the 14th century. The very way in
which the question is posed seems to indicate that opinion on the matter
is settled. Jews die of plague less than Christians. The author appears to
be only reviewing accepted explanations as a matter of routine. Whatever
else may have helped to shape this opinion, in my judgment it may be
ascribed largely to a heightened anti-Semitism in the 15th century; in
other words there was a desire to deprive the defenders of the Jews of
their most plausible argument. We cannot prove whether any of the
astrologer-physicians—even Primus of Görlitz—actually lent themselves to
anti-Semitic propaganda, nor can we tell at what point they knowingly
shared in so mean a falsification. However this may be, the erroneous
view that Jews were relatively or even wholly immune to the Black Death
became in the course of the 15th century so rooted a conviction that later

it was accepted, from different motives, not only by Christian defenders of the Jews but even by Jewish chroniclers.[59]

NOTES

[1] Costa de Beauregard, *Notes et documents sur les conditions des Juifs en Savoie dans les siècles du Moyen-Age, Mémoires de l'Académie Royale de Savoie,* 2nd series, II (1854), p. 101, n. 24. The Savoy document published here refers to accusations against the Jews of the Dauphiné sent to the commissary in charge of proceedings against the Jews in Savoy. Since there were accusations of poisoning here, the Dauphiné document probably dealt with poisoning. The Savoy proceedings began September 15, 1348.

[2] Höniger, *Der Schwarze Tod. Ein Beitrag zur Kulturgeschichte des XIV Jahr.* (1883).

[3] See Wickersheimer, "Les accusations d'empoisonnements, portées pendant la première moitié du XIVe siècle contre les lépreux et les Juifs; leurs relations avec les épidémies de la peste", *Communication faite au 4e Congrès de l'histoire de la médecine au Bruxelles, 1922* (Antwerp, 1927), p. 8, n. 46, for a contrary view, denying any relation between movements against Christians and Jews, on the grounds that the latter could not have referred to plague until the plague arrived, but like the French accusations of 1321, refer to leprosy. The argument proves nothing; advance rumors of sowing of plague were enough to sound the alarm.

[4] See Sticker, *Abhandlungen aus der Seuchengeschichte und Seuchenlehre,* Vol. I, *Die Pest,* part 1 (1908). This is not, however, a very sound historical work.

[5] See Hansen, *Zauberwahn, Inquisition und Hexenprocesse im Mittelalter,* Historische Bibliothek, XII, 1900.

[6] On earlier charges that Jews were poisoners see Bondy-Dworsky, *Regesten zur Geschichte der Juden in Böhmen, Mähren und Schlesien,* for accusations against Jewish doctors during an epidemic in the year 1161. See G. Caro, *Die soziale und wirtschaftliche Geschichte der Juden im Mittelalter u. i. d. Neuzeit,* vol. II (1918), p. 189, for the Council of Vienna's prohibition of buying meat from Jews, in 1267, lest it be poisoned. There seem to have been no charges of Jews poisoning water supplies before 1321; see Wickersheimer, *op. cit.;* L. Lazard, "Les Juifs en Touraine", *Revue des Etudes Juives,* XV (1888), p. 234; J. Vidal, "La poursuite des lépreux", in *Mélanges de littérature et d'histoire religieuse,* t. III (1889), (anti-Semitic interpretation).

[7] See the letter of the Narbonne official, Andrew Benedict, April 17, 1348, to the magistrates of Gerona, in *Viaje litteraria a las iglesias de Espana,* XIV (1850), p. 270.

[8] See Guy de Chauliac, *Chirurgia Magna,* ed. Nicaise (1890), tract. II, cap. 5, p. 172, and *Annales Matseenses, Mon. Germ., S. S.* IX, p. 830.

[9] Haeser, *Lehrbuch der Geschichte der Medizin und der epidemischen Krankheiten,* vol. III, 1882.

[10] See Sudhoff, "Mittelalterliche Einzeltexte zur Beulenpest", in *Historische Studien, Festgabe G. Sticker* (1930), and *Archiv für Geschichte d. Medizin,* ed. Sudhoff (hereafter referred to as Sudhoff's *Archiv*), XXIII, pp. 346–48. But see L. Thorndike, *History of Magic and Experimental Science,* vol. III (1934), pp. 224–32, 669–707 for partial text of the treatise written by Augustine of Trent in 1340 which at several points anticipates the later writings.

[11] On the earlier treatises see Anna M. Campbell, *The Black Death and Men of Learning,* 1931. For the texts see Sudhoff's *Archiv,* II–XVII (1908–1917).

[12] D'Irsay, *Histoire des Universités,* t. I, 1930.

[13] Max Neuburger, *Geschichte der Medizin,* vol. II, part 2 (1911), p. 340.

[14] See Th. O. Wedel, *The Mediaeval Attitude toward Astrology* (1926) and P. Duhem, *Le système du monde: histoire des doctrines cosmologiques de Platon à Copernic,* vols. I and IV.

[15] Neither Galen nor Avicenna, who were regarded by physicians of the time as the two greatest authorities in the field, say anything about special astral influences. Yet Arabic and Jewish-Arabic physicians were much interested in the astrological factor

and they influenced the physicians of Christian lands in this direction. There is evidence in the treatise of Augustine of Trent (see n. 10, above) that astrological theory on the origin of the plague already had a following. On predictions of the plague see the work of a French physician, Simon de Covino, *De judicio Solis in convivio Saturni*, ed. Littré, *Bibliothèque de l'Ecole des Chartes*, 1840–41, 1st series, II, pp. 208ff. An allegorical poem on the Black Death, this appeared in 1350. The prologue introduces three astrologers who had been expecting the Black Death in 1345. Two were French, the third being the learned Jew, Levi ben Gerson. Other Jewish astrologers had made the same prediction: see Gilles li Muisit, *Chronique et Annales* (*Société de l'Histoire de France*, 1905), pp. 223–224, and Detmar, *Chronik der Stadt Lübeck* (*Chroniken der deutschen Städte von 14–16 Jahr.*), XIX, pp. 513–514. Simon de Covino says that the massacre of Jews by the sect of the Flagellants could also have been predicted by means of the sun. A French astrologer of the 15th century, Simon de Phares, attributes similar predictions to several other Christian astrologers, along with several who, according to him, predicted that the Jews would poison water supplies: *Recueil des plus célèbres astrologues et quelques hommes doctes faict par Symon de Phares du temps de Charles VIII*, ed. E. Wickersheimer (1929), pp. 217–218. See also Henry of Hervorda, *Liber de rebus memorabilibus*, ed. Potthast, p. 282.

16 The text (Latin MS 11227, Bibliothèque Nationale, Paris) is printed by Rebouis, *Etude historique et critique de la Peste* (1882). For bibliographical data on its translation into French, German, and Italian, see Campbell, *op. cit.*, pp. 14–16.

17 See the text in Sudhoff's *Archiv*, XI, pp. 44–51. See also Konrad von Megenberg, *Das Buch der Natur*, ed. Pfeiffer (1870), which is largely a vulgarization of Thomas de Cantimpré's *De rerum natura*, a work of the 13th century, the additions including a section on earthquakes. On Megenberg see H. Ibach, *Leben und Schriften des Konrad von Megenberg* (Leipzig, 1938). This summarizes his *De Mortalitate in Germania* (1350), which again covers earthquakes, and discusses the conflicts between Papacy and Empire as being closely related to natural disasters. Cf. Leidinger, *Andreas von Regensburg sämtliche Schriften* (1903), pp. LXVff. The two passages of the *De Mortalitate in Germania* cited by Ibach are duplicated word for word in the *Utrum Mortalitas*. We shall therefore proceed on the assumption that both are by Megenberg.

18 Henry of Hervordia, *op. cit.*, p. 277.

19 In the *Utrum Mortalitas* there is nothing about this.

20 See his *Concilia contra pestilentiam* in Sudhoff's *Archiv*, V, nos. 30–33. In no. 30 he notes that contagion can be passed not only from man to man but *de terra in terram*.

21 See Sudhoff's *Archiv*, V, pp. 341–48, and XVI, p. 163.

22 On these two men see Campbell, *op. cit.*, notes 39 and 60, also Sidel, "Die Lehre von der Kontagion bei den Arabern," Sudhoff's *Archiv*, VI. For German translations of their treatises see, for Ibn-al-Khatib, *Sitzungsberichte der königl. bayrischen Akademie der Wissenschaften zu München*, II (1863), pp. 1–28; for Ibn Khatima, Sudhoff's *Archiv*, XIX, pp. 30–81.

23 Another curious theory of contagion will be found in a treatise in verse, *Tractatus de Epidemia compositus a quodam practico de Montepessulano, anno 1349*, in Michon, *Documents inédits sur la Grande Peste de 1348* (1809), pp. 71–81. Guy de Chauliac seems to imply that a plague patient could convey the disease by a look; cf. Seligman, *Der böse Blick*, 1908.

24 On this see especially the chronicle of Gabriel de Musis, who died in 1356, in *Giornale linguistico*, IX (1883), pp. 139ff.

25 See Quintard, *Les idées modernes sur l'épidémiologie de la Peste* (Algiers, 1937). Medieval writers confused the problem of the primordial origin of the disease with that of its spread in epidemics. Ibn Khatib is the only writer to distinguish between the two questions, insisting that epidemics spread by contagion. As to the origin of the disease, he ruled out any possibility of general corruption of the air.

26 The brave Gentile da Foligno, who died at his post in the summer of 1348, was the leader of this campaign in Italy. Physicians served on a commission he set up at

Perugia. The example was followed elsewhere in Italy and similar measures were taken in Germany and France. See the very sensible regulations at Pistoia (May 2, 1348) printed in *Archivio Storico Italiano*, series IV, vol. XX, pp. 3–24; cf. Lechner, *Das Grosse Sterben in Deutschland, 1348–1351* (1884).

27 An anonymous treatise of 1349, printed in Sudhoff's *Archiv*, XI, pp. 51–55: *Quaeritur primo quae sunt aegritudines nunc currentes.*

28 Thorndike (*op. cit.*, vol. III, pp. 526–34) credits Guillaume de Marra, who wrote in 1362, with being one of the first writers on the theory of contagion. Yet he adds nothing to what was already written between 1348 and 1350 and does not really have a theory.

29 A curious variant in the Italian version of the *Compendium* warns the public against rain water, which would absorb infection in falling through pestilential air, and recommends reliance on well-water and springs.

30 For example, Tschudi, *Helvetische Chronik*, vol. I.

31 Ibn Khatima and others after him also held that there were two kinds of epidemic. Haeser refers to a curious German doctoral thesis of the 17th century on the effects of arrows shot from heaven during plague sent by the wrath of God.

32 *Collectum de peste*, Sudhoff's *Archiv*, XI, pp. 143–163, with introduction by Sudhoff, pp. 141–43.

33 Raynaldus, *Annales eccles.*, ed. Mansi, VI, p. 476.

34 He took the same position in his *Planctus Ecclesiae in Germaniam*—printed in *Historisches Jahrbuch*, XX (1901), pp. 640 and 645–46—condemning anti-Semitism but expressing conventional disapproval of Jews as enemies of Christians.

35 The passage is printed in Haeser, *op. cit.*, III, p. 179.

36 *Loc. cit.* (see n. 32 above), p. 149.

37 See Sudhoff's *Archiv*, VI, p. 352; Herz, "Das Giftmädchen", *Abhandlungen d. bayr. Akademie der Wissenschaften. Phil.-Hist. Klasse*, XX (1893) and also his *Gesammelte Abhandlungen* (1905), pp. 156–177.

38 Raymundus Chalmelli de Vivario, whose treatise was printed by Höniger, *op. cit.* (see n. 2), app. IV, pp. 157ff.

39 Thorndike, *op. cit.*, II, pp. 904–912 and III, ch. XXXI, pp. 525ff.

40 Sticker, *op. cit.* (see n. 4) draws attention to the terms *pestis manufacta* and *pestis reclusa* in certain medieval legends, which seem to show belief in poisons that had the quality of producing plague; but the terms do not occur in the sources relating to the accusations in question.

41 To my knowledge the question was clearly posed only 150 years later, and by a chronicler, not a doctor. See Spangenberg, *Mansfeldische Chronik*, p. 337a (cited by Schudt, *Jüdische Merkwürdigkeiten*, p. 261).

42 Printed in Sudhoff's *Archiv*, III, pp. 223–225.

43 See Sudhoff's *Archiv*, XVI, pp. 77–95.

44 E. Wickersheimer, "La Peste Noire à Strasbourg et le régime des cinq Médecins Strasbourgeois," in *Proceedings of the Third International Congress of the History of Medicine* (Antwerp, 1923); the text is published there and also in Sudhoff's *Archiv*, XIV, pp. 12–20. Cf. Campbell, pp. 23–24.

45 Printed in Sudhoff's *Archiv*, IV, pp. 205–222; see especially p. 215.

46 Ribbeniz names decomposing corpses and the fetid breath of the sick as two other supplementary factors in the rise and spread of plague.

47 Sudhoff's *Archiv*, XVI, p. 26, and see n. 15 above.

48 Continuation of *Chronique de Guillaume de Nangis*, ed. Gérard, Société de l'Histoire de France, vol. II, p. 213 (1844).

49 Allendy, *Les Tempéraments*, chapter 1 (1922); also von Seyfert, "Ein Komplexionentext einer Leipziger Handschrift und seine handschriftliche Herleitung aus der Zeit nach 1300", Sudhoff's *Archiv*, XX, pp. 272–301, 371–390.

50 See the article by Diepgen on Arnold of Villanova's contribution to this doctrine in Sudhoff's *Archiv*, V. pp. 102ff.

51 The melancholic temperament was also ranked lowest in antiquity.

52 Part 2 of the *Compendium de Epidemia* (see n. 16 above) sets out the rules for a healthy life.

53 Many of the treaties deal with these points.

54 See A. Campbell, *op. cit.*, pp. 28, 62–3.

55 *Ibid.*, also Chalin de Vivario.

56 Medieval astrologers commonly assigned the Jewish religion to the dominion of Saturn, Christianity to that of the Sun or Jupiter, and Islam to that of Venus.

57 *Loc. cit.* (n. 38, above, p. 177).

58 Printed in Sudhoff's *Archiv*, XVII, p. 79.

59 These chroniclers ordinarily say that the Jews, thanks to their higher cultural level, were better informed on how to avoid the plague. The first Hebrew chronicles to deal in any detail with the events of 1348–49 date from the end of the 15th century.

Money

14

Currency Depreciation in Medieval Europe

CARLO CIPOLLA

I

IN THE LONG RUN every monetary unit is subject to a process of progressive depreciation. The extent of this depreciation varies greatly from unit to unit and age to age, but the phenomenon itself is universal. Its unfailing appearance at all times and places has given it the ineluctable character of a physical law. Indeed, historians and economists do often refer to progressive currency depreciation as to a universal 'law.' But why this law should hold and how it operates have never been satisfactorily explained. When it comes to considering the causes of the phenomenon historians display an extraordinary tendency to resolve the problem by recourse to the naïve old tale of 'spendthrift and warlike princes' occasionally acknowledging in passing the phenomenon of 'wearing and clipping,' which makes possible a reference to Gresham's law. Economists too, when they find time and opportunity to mention 'historical precedents,' rarely get away from the alluring old tale of the spendthrift kings and the mismanagement of state finances.

For the medieval period, when the circulating medium was metallic, the essential aspect presented by the phenomenon which interests us here was the progressive deterioration as to fineness and weight of the coins in circulation. The question of the relation between monetary unit and goods and services was further complicated by the fact that, save for brief periods, the purchasing power of gold and silver went on increasing throughout the Middle Ages.

It is not possible to obtain precise information about all the debasements to which the very numerous monetary units were subjected during the entire course of the Middle Ages. When exact information is available about a specific debasement, its ultimate 'causes' cannot always be traced. However, despite many lacunae, the total amount of information which can be gathered on the subject is truly remarkable. We are certainly much better informed in matters of currency for the whole of the Middle Ages than in matters of production, consumption and investment.

From an analysis of all the cases of debasement which I have been able to study for the Middle Ages, I have compiled a list of the 'causes' which, singly or in various combinations, prove to have been responsible for these same debasements. The list can be broadly formulated as follows:

(a) the long-term increase in the demand for money, resulting from the long-term growth of population and/or of income and/or of the 'monetization' of the economy;

(b) the growth of government expenditure and deficits;

(c) the pressure of social groups in the direction of profit-inflation;

(d) disequilibrium in the balance of payments;

(e) the mismanagement of the mints;

(f) the wear of the existing stock of coins in circulation, occasionally aggravated by the practice of clipping;

(g) fluctuations in the market rate of exchange between gold and silver.

It is obvious that these various causes were of varying importance in different countries and in different periods. It is also obvious that they could occur in different combinations and in varying strengths. But, all allowances made, it seems possible to lay down as a very general rule that the forces which operated most strongly in the Middle Ages were those indicated under letters (a), (b), (c) and (d). With regard to (b) the point should be made that both the absolute and relative importance of this factor tended to grow continuously throughout the Middle Ages, a growth which reflects the consolidation of the centralized state and, especially from the fourteenth century onwards, the progressive increase in the cost of military operations.

At this stage it is necessary to make another series of distinctions.[1] The circumstances listed under the seven heads above can reasonably be defined as 'causes' only in an *ex-post* sense. *Ex-ante,* they are merely sundry types of problem which a given society may find itself called upon to solve, problems for which the depreciation of the currency is certainly not the only possible solution. For every one of the problems listed there exist several alternative solutions. The society could meet problem (a) by developing new credit techniques and/or by resorting to new forms of money. Or it could allow a new equilibrium to be achieved through a fall of the general level of prices. The society could meet problem (b) by an increase in taxation or reduction in expenditure. As regards problem (c), supposing the government to be controlled by groups interested in a profit-inflation, it is quite conceivable that these groups would seek to achieve their aim by imposing a reduction in wages. As regards problem (d), a new equilibrium could be achieved by means of policies of austerity and/or restrictions on imports and/or an export drive. Problems (e) and (f) could be solved if the state assumed direct control over the mints and itself undertook the task of periodically withdrawing worn and clipped coins. As for problem (g), a new equilibrium could be achieved by allowing the forces of the market to establish rates of exchange between gold and silver coins appropriate to the new situation, or by increasing the fineness of one coinage rather than reducing that of the other. To sum up, for each of the problems listed there still exist various alternative solutions. The devaluation of the currency is only one among the various possible solutions. However, it is a solution which is valid for all the problems listed. In other words, it is the common alternative solution. Furthermore, it is also the solution likely in general to encounter the least resistance, because it is the most anonymous and takes effect in the most indirect and subtle fashion. The easy way out of a number of difficult situations: this is the formula on which is founded the great law of the ineluctable depreciation of currency.

Looking at things from this point of view, it is clear that the extent of the long-term decline of any monetary unit depends, not only on the gravity of the particular crises which may arise, but also on the special conditions and on the political and social structures prevailing in a given society which encourage that society to choose the easy way out among the various possible alternatives. To use Toynbeean terminology, it is not only a matter of the challenge, it is also a matter of the response.

In the light of this scheme I think it is possible to clarify some of the most interesting aspects of the monetary history of medieval Europe.

II

In the course of the eighth century the Carolingians carried to completion in Frankish territory a drastic reform, which eventually put an end to the gold monometallism which had prevailed there in earlier Merovingian times. They introduced as a new and the only monetary unit a silver piece called the *denarius* (penny) of 1.7 grammes weight and of the fineness of about 950/1000.[2] Having defeated the Lombards and conquered part of the Italian peninsula, Charlemagne between 780 and 790 extended the reform already carried out in France to his Italian territories.[3] In England, where silver monometallism already existed, King Ethelbert II of Kent and King Offa spontaneously adopted the Frankish reforms, replacing the local *sceattas* by a new unit (penny) which was clearly a copy of the Frankish *denarius*. Actually the English penny seems to have been slightly lighter than the Continental penny. The first pennies of King Offa varied around 1.3 grammes of silver. Later, however, the weight was raised to 1.5 grammes, bringing the English penny closer to the Continental model from which it derived.[4] As a result of these de-

velopments Europe came to form a single large monetary area: the area
of the silver penny.

This was the common starting-point. Then the 'law' of monetary depreciation began to operate. Progressively and inexorably the various
pennies began to deteriorate, one after the other, both in weight and
fineness. And, since the rate of deterioration varied from country to country and from time to time, parity between the various currencies was lost.
In Table 1 I have collected the essential data concerning this progressive
depreciation of the currency in England, in France, and in North and
Central Italy.[5] The figures shown give the equivalent in pure silver
(1000/1000) of the monetary unit of each country. For greater simplicity
and to avoid too many decimals, I have given the silver equivalent of a
fixed multiple of the penny, that is of the pound (= 240 pennies), rather
than that of the penny itself. To ease the task of anyone who wishes to
translate the silver equivalents into gold equivalents, the last column of
the table shows the approximate rate of exchange which seems to have
prevailed in the Europe of the day. All the figures in the table must be
accepted with a degree of caution. But in every case the margin of error
is certainly lower than $\pm$ 10 percent. Altogether, the data of Table 1
provide, in outline, a significant index of the secular trend of monetary
depreciation in medieval Western Europe. The data show that: (1) the
currencies of the states of North and Central Italy were always in the van
of the inflationary movement; (2) the English coinage, conversely, was by
far the least afflicted by the phenomenon of debasement. Indeed, the English currency offers a marked contrast with Continental currencies, dis-
playing by comparison with them remarkable stability; (3) the French
currency (*livre tournois*) depreciated in general less than Italian currencies, but its rate of depreciation was much closer to the Italian than to the
English rate.

I would like to examine these three points in the light of the considerations put forward in the preceding section. Before doing so,
however, I think it is necessary to make some observations about the
organization and regulation of coining in England, France and Italy as it
developed during the Middle Ages.

Contrasting the English with the Continental coinage, Mr. Grierson
has lucidly written:

When we try to enumerate the features that differentiated Anglo-Norman coinage from that of the Continent, we find at once that we can make no generalizations regarding type but that we can on organization and to a limited degree
on fineness and weight. The coinage of all England was under royal control:
though the moneyers were many and coins were struck in every locality of any
importance, the types were changed punctually at three-year intervals, the
fineness and weight of each issue was regulated by the Crown and the moneyers
procured their dies from agents of the central authority and were answerable

to the King for the use that was made of them. None of this was true on the other side of the Channel.

Though individual magnates or individual towns might control their own coinage as strictly as the King of England, the coinage of France, Italy and Germany 'had lost all semblance of unity, so that type, fineness and weight varied from one principality to the next.' [6]

In France, however, among the innumerable local coinages, two predominated over all the others, at least as far as diffusion and use were concerned. These were the *parisis* coinage and the *tournois* coinage. Eventually the *tournois* coinage got the better of the *parisis,* for which reason I have referred in Table 1 only to the *tournois.*

In North and Central Italy the situation was different. While in France monetary particularism was mitigated by the predominance of one or two coinages, there was virtually no limit to the monetary particularism of Italy. After the tenth century five clearly distinct currency areas emerged in North and Central Italy, and none of the currencies dominant in these areas succeeded in assuming a position of general predominance. So I have calculated in Table 1 the metallic equivalents for four different currencies, the *lira* of Genoa, the *lira di imperiali* of Milan, the *lira di piccioli* of Venice, and the *lira di piccioli* of Florence.

III

Let us turn to the questions which I propounded before the analysis. We have seen that over the long period the currencies of North and Central Italy depreciated at a greater rate than the currencies of France and England. I believe that in trying to define the causes of this phenomenon we ought to concentrate our attention mainly on those problems which, in the scheme proposed in section I, are marked as (a), (b) and (c).

Between the middle of the tenth century and the end of the thirteenth century the Italian population increased from about 5 to 7 or 8 millions. At the same time, especially in the North and the Centre, the growth of the economy became rapid. Income increased considerably over the long period, growing faster than the population. The division of labour became more pronounced, and the country moved from an almost natural economy towards a money economy—in other words, the monetary sector of the economy expanded more than proportionally. We are not in a position to express these trends quantitatively, but that they existed is beyond all doubt.

A consequence of these fundamental movements was a decided expansionist tendency in the demand for money. The supply of precious metals proved to be relatively inelastic throughout the whole period, and the growth of the demand for silver for monetary purposes exceeded the supply. In such conditions, if prolonged deflationary pressure and a dangerous downward movement of prices were to be avoided, three solutions were available: (A) to find substitutes for metallic money in the form of 'primitive money'; (B) to find new and more advanced systems and modes of payment; (C) to reduce the fineness of the coinage and increase the number of pieces in circulation.

All three solutions were tried in practice. As regards solutions of type A we know that in these centuries, especially in the greater mercantile centres, pepper and other goods were used as substitutes for metallic money. As regards solutions of type B we know that very quickly new banking and credit practices evolved, which were destined to develop enormously in the process of time. But, in the end, the methods of type A which were devised were seen to be inconvenient and against the tendency of the times, and those of type B inadequate. Essentially, Italian society was compelled to fall back on solution C. The *denarius* was therefore progressively sacrificed.

These trends were particularly strong in the period between the beginning of the eleventh century and the middle of the twelfth century.[7] In Venice at the beginning of the thirteenth century the penny was so debased in weight and fineness that it was regarded as inadequate and inconvenient for the majority of transactions. It was then that the authorities of the Republic decided to coin a multiple of the penny (which was to be called *grosso*); and it is significant that, in determining the precious metal content of the new coin, the Venetian authorities took as their standard of fineness that of the English penny, which up to that time had remained unadulterated.[8] The approximate parity between English and Italian currency that had once existed had been destroyed, had been so completely destroyed that the amount of silver which was equivalent to a penny in England now corresponded to a high multiple of the local penny in Venice.

From the middle of the twelfth century to the middle of the thirteenth century, the downward movement of Italian currency was markedly slower. It became more rapid between the middle of the thirteenth century and the beginning of the fourteenth century, then slowed down again in the course of the fourteenth century—among other things, the drastic fall in population as a result of the Black Death must have contributed greatly to reduce the demand for money. With the fifteenth century, however, the downward movement was resumed and continued strongly throughout the century.

Among the forces which operated continuously to debase the coinage must always be counted a relatively inelastic supply of precious metals, which did not expand proportionately to the increase in the demand for money. During the whole fifteenth century the purchasing power of gold and silver in bars continued to grow. If prices expressed in the current monetary units did not in the long run fall, that was only because the monetary units were constantly and progressively reduced in fineness.

It must be recognized, however, that from the middle of the fourteenth century onwards state budgetary deficits held an increasingly important place among the causes of monetary depreciation in Italy. In particular, a notable part of the blame for budgetary deficits after the mid-fourteenth century must be ascribed to the evergrowing cost of war.[9]

The different elasticities of the demand for money and its supply and the expansion of state expenditure undoubtedly had a pronounced effect on the weight and fineness of Italian coinages. But account must also be taken of the fact that from the eleventh century onwards the governments of the Italian states were practically always controlled by the merchant class. This class obviously had everything to lose from a prolonged deflation, and everything to gain from prolonged inflationary pressure. As between an increase in taxation and a weakening of the currency, the merchant class was also obviously inclined to favour the latter solution.[10]

IV

It has long been known that the English currency, although progressively depreciated, displayed throughout the Middle Ages a remarkable degree of relative stability, in striking contrast to the rapid depreciation of Continental currencies. In 1871 C. J. Shive wrote that 'in England they went more honestly to work than elsewhere, and the coins kept their proper weight.'[11] More recently R. G. Hawtrey reaffirmed that 'of all countries England was (during the Middle Ages) the freest from illegitimate debasements'.[12] The use of such words as 'honestly' and 'illegitimate' appears to indicate that, at least in the opinion of some scholars, the question of monetary debasement in the Middle Ages was one of moral standards and that the varying rate of depreciation of the various currencies was a function of the degree of morality and thriftiness of the various rulers. It cannot be denied, indeed, that at least in the first part of the history of the English penny a certain tradition of stability was introduced by a deliberate policy of orderly administration. After the frequent but temporary alterations in the reign of Edward the Confessor (in particular in the coinage of the third issue),[13] the weight of the English penny was stabilized. 'This stabilization . . . was apparently an act of deliberate policy, contrasting with the frequent changes of Anglo-Saxon times, and the Norman kings compensated themselves for any financial loss it might involve by levying a general tax, the *monetagium commune,* which we know from the coronation charter of Henry I to have been collected *per civitates et comitatus* and to have been an innovation of William I.' [14]

Nevertheless, if the English currency in the long run depreciated at a relatively very low rate, this could be due to a concatenation of favourable circumstances.

To begin with, the long-term demand for money, at least up to the middle of the thirteenth century, must have grown relatively slowly, and certainly more slowly than in Italy, for the simple reason that the economic development of the country was less rapid than in North and Central Italy. On the supply side too, the situation was much easier throughout the Middle Ages. England benefited from the fact that she had a surplus of the most sought-after raw material of the day, wool. When in the course of time England developed a manufacturing industry on the basis of this raw material, she found an ample market on the Continent of Europe for her own cloths. Italy too exported cloth in great quantities, but she was forced to import the raw material. All things considered, it is beyond doubt that England enjoyed throughout the Middle Ages a particularly favourable balance of payments which ensured a constant and abundant influx of precious metals. From the warden's accounts it appears that the silver used in the English mint during the decade 1290–1300 was mainly silver of Ghent, Bruges and Brussels, silver of Tours and Limoges, and silver generally described as foreign silver. Only small quantities came from the Devonshire mines and a small quantity derived from silver plate melted down.[15] For a later period, we know that foreign visitors—among them, Erasmus—were impressed by the abundance of silver and silver plate that they found in England.[16]

The English situation therefore was in sharp contrast with the Italian: on the one side an economy—the Italian—characterized from an early period by rapid growth, hampered by an unsatisfactory supply of precious metals; on the other hand an economy—the English—whose growth began later and was more gradual, which at the same time disposed of an ample and elastic supply of precious metal. Nor was this the whole difference. In Italy, as has been seen, the government was controlled throughout the Middle Ages by a class with an interest in currency depreciation. In England the coinage was always under the control of the central power, that is of the King, and there is no doubt that at least from the fourteenth century onwards the King was often tempted to meet the needs of the Treasury by debasing the coinage. But every step of this kind on the part of the King encountered the effective opposition of the English baronage, which had a strong interest in the stability of the currency and which always constituted a pressure-group capable of making its views felt by the Crown. 'Nul Rei de cete reaume ne puet changer sa moneye, ne mepeirer, ne amender, ne autre moneie fere que d'argent sanz l'assent de touz ces counties.' [17] The evidence of the *Mirror of Justices* is always suspect, but on this point there is the corroboration of a clause in the Statute of Purveyors of 1352 making it illegal for the weight of the coins to be reduced any further without the consent of the Parliament.[18]

V

At first sight it might seem strange that the French currency followed the Italian more closely than the English. While it is true that France did not enjoy England's privileged position in regard to the balance of payments and the availability of precious metals, it is also true that in France coining remained under the control of the King and of the baronage, which one might suppose would have an interest in the stability of the currency in so far as its income was in the form of fixed money payments. But it must be pointed out that, as was said earlier, while the coinage of England remained under royal control and the fineness and weight of each issue was regulated by the Crown and the profits arising from coining and debasement were monopolized by the Crown, in France feudal magnates—lay as well as ecclesiastical—controlled their own coinage as strictly as did the Crown, arrogating to themselves the profits arising from coining rights. These feudal magnates initiated the practice of debasing the coinage quite early, on their own account. Often they were impelled to do so by a shortage in the supply of silver. In any event they soon learned that the operation of devaluation could yield good profits. As Monsieur H. J. Légier has observed, it is necessary to go back a long way in time to find the origin of 'la vieille pratique des mutations féodales, bien antérieures aux mutations royales . . . Le début des muta-

Table 1

Grammes of pure silver corresponding to a pound-tale (240 pennies)

Year	England	France (livre tournois)	Genoa	Milan	Venice	Florence	Market ratio between gold and silver
ca. 800	ca. 330	ca. 390		ca. 390	ca. 390		ca. 1:10–12
ca. 1250	ca. 324	ca. 80	ca. 70	ca. 70	ca. 20	ca. 35	ca. 1:10
ca. 1500	ca. 172	ca. 22	ca. 13	ca. 9	ca. 6	ca. 6	ca. 1:11

SOURCES: R. Ruding, *Annals of the coinage of Great Britain and its dependencies*, London, 1840; C. Oman, *The coinage of England*, Oxford, 1931; G. C. Brooke, *English coins*, London, 1932; R. Sedillot, *Le franc*, Paris, 1953; C. M. Cipolla, *Le avventure della lira*, Milan, 1958.

tions royales n'est donc pas une date capitale dans l'histoire du monnayage (français).'[19] When the French kings, under pressure of deficits and of ever-increasing war costs, began to have recourse more and more frequently to the expedient of debasement in order to augment their liquid assets, the French baronage, instead of opposing like the English baronage, hastened to imitate them, devaluing its own currencies in order to procure the same advantages as the Crown procured. For this was the common preoccupation of all the *barons monnayeurs:* 'éviter que le roi tire seul profit d'un empirement ou d'un renforcement.'[20]

NOTES

[1] The following considerations were suggested to me in conversation by my friend, George Richardson, of St. John's College, Oxford. Obviously, he cannot be held responsible for any errors of formulation into which I may have fallen.

[2] On the Carolingian monetary reforms and their possible relations with Arab and Byzantine monetary reforms, *cf.* P. Grierson, 'The monetary reforms of Abd al-Malik,' *Journal of Economic and Social History of the Orient,* III (1960), p. 260ff.

[3] P. Grierson, 'Cronologia delle riforme monetarie di Carlo Magno', *Rivista Italiana di Numismatica,* vol. 2, ser. 5, t. 56 (1954), pp. 65–79.

[4] *Cf.* C. Oman, *The Coinage of England* (Oxford, 1931), pp. 17–18 and G. C. Brooke, *English coins from the seventh century to the present day* (London, 1932), p. 14.

[5] South Italy always remained outside the area of the 'penny-shilling-pound' system. *Cf.* C. M. Cipolla, *Studi di storia della moneta* (Pavia, 1948), p. 77 and C. M. Cipolla, *Le avventure della lira* (Milano, 1958), p. 15.

[6] P. Grierson, 'Sterling', in *Anglo-Saxon Coins,* ed. R. H. M. Dolley (London, 1961), p. 273.

[7] Cipolla, *Le avventure della lira,* pp. 49–51.

[8] R. Cessi, *Problemi monetari veneziani fino a tutto il sec. XIV* (Padova, 1937), pp. XVIII–XXI.

[9] Cipolla, *Le avventure della lira,* p. 56.

[10] For Florence *cf.* N. Rodolico, *I Ciompi* (Firenze, 1948); for Venice *cf.* Cipolla, *op. cit.,* p. 55, n. 35. It should be added that, after the introduction of bi-metallism in 1252, the merchant class found means to guarantee itself inflationary profits by insisting that its credits should be paid in gold coin (which remained unadulterated) and its debits (especially salaries and taxes) in progressively depreciating silver coin. I have described in detail elsewhere the complicated mechanism which favoured this game—*Money, Prices and Civilization* (Princeton, 1957), chapter 3. Here it need only be mentioned as a concrete instance of the link between the dominance of the merchant class and the high rate of currency depreciation.

[11] C. J. Schive, 'Some account of the weight of English and Northern Coins in the Xth and XIth centuries', *Numismatic Chronicle,* N.S. 11 (1871), p. 47, n. 9.

[12] R. G. Hawtrey, *Currency and Credit* (London, 1923), pp. 287–8.

[13] Oman, *op. cit.,* p. 77.

[14] P. Grierson, *Sterling,* pp. 274–5.

[15] C. G. Crump and A. Hughes, 'The English Currency under Edward I', *Economic Journal,* V (1895), p. 58.

[16] J. Clapham, *A concise economic history of Great Britain from the earliest times to 1750* (Cambridge, 1951), p. 173.

[17] *Mirror of Justices,* ed. W. J. Whittaker (London, 1895), p. 11.

[18] A. E. Feaveryear, *The Pound Sterling* (Oxford, 1931), p. 30.

[19] H. J. Légier, 'Réalités monétaires, réalités économiques, réalités historiques', *Annales E. S. C.* XIV (1959), pp. 539–40.

[20] *Ibid.* p. 540.

15

Wage Labour in France in the Later Middle Ages

E. PERROY

IT SEEMS A VERY rash thing indeed to try to track down that most elusive person, the French medieval wage-earner. Ever since the venerable but antiquated works of d'Avenel and Levasseur, no single French scholar has ventured to tackle the problem as a whole or even locally. Marc Bloch, of course, was aware of the importance of the work that remained to be done, but his projected researches were interrupted in 1939, never —alas—to be taken up again. Since then, a few monographs, dealing either with one town or with one region or with one particular trade, have devoted a few paragraphs, exceptionally a few pages, more often a footnote or two, to wages. They rarely provide us with complete series, even for a short period or a single set of wages. Their data are too scattered to permit the formulation of even tentative conclusions. This article can therefore do little more than give a short review of the difficulties of the task, of what has been done, of what remains to be done, and perhaps suggest how to do it.

During the later Middle Ages—for our data are practically non-existent prior to the fourteenth century—the main difficulty is that of the currency in which nominal wages are contracted for. In France, fourteenth- and fifteenth-century manipulations have been so frequent that historians are apt to discard whatever figures they get from documents and to translate them in terms of a more stable measure. Thus, following Natalis de Wailly, they have, for a long time, converted medieval monetary figures into nineteenth-century francs: a standard which has lost its appeal to the imagination of the younger generation, since the collapse of the nineteenth-century franc during the First World War. Or again they try to find out the value of pounds, shillings and pence tournois in grammes of gold. This habit is particularly unfortunate, since weekly or daily wages were paid to workers in black or white currency, never in gold: labourers would rarely see, still less possess a gold coin. Moreover, all medieval currencies were based on silver, not on gold, and we know how the constant and sometimes wide differences between the legal and commercial prices of the gold coins were one of the main obstacles to a really stable currency.

It must, however, be pointed out that, contrary to prevalent views, the periods of great currency upheaval were few and far between. They did not upset for long the general stability of currency, and have perhaps been given undue importance by most historians. The first period of instability lasted for eight years at the beginning of the Hundred Years War (1336–43); the second period about ten to twelve years (1349–60); and the last was a longer spell of at least fifteen years, roughly from 1415 to 1430, during the worst phase of the war. In all there were 35 years at most during which currency was markedly unstable, leaving 127 years of comparative stability between 1328 and 1500.

The upheavals, while they lasted, were indeed catastrophic. At any rate, while they lasted they completely blot out for us the normal problems of prices and wages. Thus, since the French currency did collapse in 1349 to abysmal depths, it would be quite impossible (even if we had sufficient data for it) to appreciate the results of the Black Death on the labour market, for we cannot say how far the rise in wages which took place then was due to the scarcity of labour and corresponded to a rise in real wages or was in fact an adjustment of nominal wages to meet the fall in the intrinsic value of the currency. Again, M. Wolff [2] tells us that in Toulouse, during the worst spell of devaluated currencies, from 1422 onwards, wages were often stipulated and accounted for not in pounds, shillings and pence, but in groats of gold, the groat being counted as one-eighteenth of a gold *écu*. Naturally, as the groat was a fictitious accounting division of the gold shield, workers were still paid in current coins of silver, whether black or white, but according to the varying rate of exchange of silver into gold, which meant that their nominal wages were mounting as the value of the currency went steadily down. It could also be argued that although, after each of those upheavals, the currency was stabilized at a rate approaching that which prevailed before the debasements, this did not represent the same standard of measurement, since prices and wages had in the meantime known complete dislocation.

All in all, however, those periods of great monetary instability, important though they were, were not so protracted as to affect permanently the movement of wages. Having paid due tribute to them, it would be as well to take them out of our picture and to concentrate on the longer periods of stable currency. True, even in these periods the stability was never absolute, and no medieval government, confronted with what might be termed the bullionist dilemma, could adhere firmly and for long to their ideal of a completely stable currency, which was so eloquently advocated by Nicolas Oresme in the seventies of the fourteenth century. Thus, in a little over a century and a half (1313–1500), the intrinsic value of the pound tournois was gradually lowered to about 50 per cent of its original standard, but by stages more gradual and less perceptible than some of the contemporary devaluations of the pound sterling (the English debasement of 1464 being a case in point).

To cite but one instance, all modern historians have accused the Marmosets Government—those virtuous councillors of the late wise King Charles V—of having resorted to the unhealthy expedient of devaluation (on the lips of modern historians this is something of *tu quoque*). In fact, the debasement of 1390 lightened the currency to the extent of 2.2 per cent for gold and 7 per cent for silver of its previous value.[3] Apart from the fact that old coins were called in or revaluated and new coins issued, it is difficult to see how this measure, which tended to absorb a recent rise in the price of bullion, did affect commodity prices, still less wages. Money-changers and mint-farmers would be the only persons to lose or gain by such a change, which on the other hand would pass unnoticed by most merchants, artisans and above all labourers. Thus, even with a floating and finally 'melting' currency, the legal system of accounting with pounds, shillings and pence tournois was not entirely fictitious. It did mean, for the wage-earner, a real amount of fixed money and coins possessing a fairly stable buying value. Wages were a daily preoccupation in the workers' home, not primarily a matter of speculation by economists over long periods of several centuries. Let us think of them as the wage-earners did: they spoke and thought of small real coins which meant so many pence, and not so many grammes of gold. The general stability of prices and wages, during the period here under review, is a further argument which seems to prove the point.

Too much space has been given to these currency matters. But having thus vindicated the good old pound tournois, we can now turn to the different classes of wage-earning people and see how they fared during the fourteenth and fifteenth centuries.

The most elusive of all is the agricultural wage-labourer. Manorial accounts do not survive in large numbers in France, even for the later Middle Ages. Besides, to a far greater extent than in England, manorial economy was by then fast declining, and most agricultural demesnes were farmed out for shorter or longer periods, thus depriving us of any information about the cost of the labour employed on the estates. This is true of all districts for which information has been provided by recent or forthcoming monographs: Bordeaux (M. Boutruche), Toulouse (M. Wolff) or Paris.[4] In all the three regions, the only agricultural worker who left his trace in the records is the *vigneron*, for most landlords were still managing their vineyards themselves and employing hired workers in them.

The accounts of the archbishop of Bordeaux provide us with a fairly long, if not continuous, series of *vignerons'* daily wages,[5] and we can easily convert them into sterling, as the local currency was more or less pegged to sterling. They show a general tendency to rise during the second half of the fourteenth and the beginning of the fifteenth century, passing from 4*d.* or 5*d.* sterling around 1350 to 9*d.* or 10*d.* around 1430. In fact, a sharp rise took place between 1410 and 1430. Up till then, the scarcity of labour is hardly perceptible and the effects of the war on the vineyards are limited. Local conditions may explain why, after the devastations effected by the French troops of the Duke of Orléans in the early years of the fifteenth century, the labour market was suddenly depleted while the needs of landlords in manual labour increased considerably.

We should not therefore necessarily follow M. Boutruche when he asserts that the rise in the *vignerons'* wages corresponds to a general rise in prices and wages all over the country, for the data provided for other French districts will tell a very different story. If we turn with M. Wolff to the vineyards belonging to the Périgord College of Toulouse,[6] we notice first a greater differentiation of wages according to the seasonal works: the February pruning of the vine-plants and the May ploughing were done by skilled workers and therefore better paid than the autumnal grape-picking, which required more numerous but more unskilled hands. In the harvest, furthermore, women (who did the grape-picking proper) were usually paid at half the rate allotted to men, who carried the full baskets to the lord's cellar. But the main fact is the great stability of all these wages. They hardly vary at all, whether they are expressed in pence tournois, as from the middle of the fourteenth century to 1422, or—after 1422—in groats of gold according to the sliding scale to which we have already referred. It looks as if Toulouse did not experience the same scarcity of labour as did Bordeaux, and as if the influx of peasants into the town, owing to the dangers of the war, maintained a cheap and constant supply of hands to the manorial vineyards of the neighbourhood. What then about the Paris district, which is said to have suffered more than others from the devastations of the war and the economic upheavals of the first half of the fifteenth century, and about which every textbook nowadays quotes the case of the village of Magny-les-Hameaux, made famous by Marc Bloch, where in 1470 there were found living only three families of Norman settlers?

In that region the series of manorial accounts, practically non-existent for the fourteenth century, but fairly good for the first half of the fifteenth and almost continuous for the second half, show that the work on demesne vineyards was effected according to two different systems of pay. For the winter and spring works, plots were let out to workers who were paid a lump sum per *arpent* for doing all the required works. These sums varied slightly from manor to manor and from year to year. On the whole they remained fairly stable, with no marked tendency to rise or fall. Of course, the workers thus engaged were not landless labourers, but tenants who, by doing supplementary work on plots carved out of the lord's vineyard, were adding to their normal earnings from their own fields and vineyards. But the general stability of their pay shows that, however depopulated (this was the time when the same landlords were desperately trying to find new tenants for vacant holdings), the villages of the Paris suburbs had nevertheless enough tenants to carry the work on the demesne vineyards. On the other hand, grape-picking was a boon-work for which daily labourers were engaged. The canons and monks of Paris were apparently less antifeminist than the scholars of Toulouse, since they do not distinguish between feminine and masculine labour. But—what comes to the same thing—they paid two rates of wages, one for the grape-pickers (*coupeurs*) and another, about double the first, for the basket-carriers (*hotteurs*). There again, these rates varied slightly from village to village and from year to year, and even in one given year in the same village, they varied according to local conditions of labour. Thus at Meudon, in 1485, pickers were paid 12*d.* *parisis* at the beginning of the harvest, then, too many candidates having volunteered, the wages were lowered by one-fifth before the end of the work, whereas at Thiais, in the same year, owing to the necessity of attracting new hands in order to complete the job in time, wages rose from 11*d.* at the beginning to 12*d.* at the end. But there again there was no general rise or fall of wages during the whole of the fifteenth century.

Even granted that all these wages had a low purchasing value, we must not conclude that their earners led a miserable life. Boon-works are never revealing of the real trend of wages, for the labourers, if badly paid, were well fed. We have travelled very far from the frugal bread and cheese and ale of the English villeins' works of the thirteenth century. Manorial accounts tell us of the considerable quantities of meat bought to feed the harvesters, and that was no doubt washed down, as it still is in the vineyards of Southern France, with gallons of free wine. Besides, none of these workers were regular wage-earners and it would be a mistake to multiply their daily pay by the approximate number of working days in order to obtain the yearly earnings of agricultural labourers. In fact, in Bordeaux as well as in Toulouse or Paris, all hands employed on demesne vineyards were members of tenants' families. At harvest-time the manorial accounts of St. Denis and St. Germain des Prés, which list the names of the workers, enable us to trace them) wives and daughters or sons of peasants flocked to the vineyards in order to earn a little money and to have a lot of fun for a few weeks. The changes in their rate of pay may tell us of the greater or smaller abundance of labour; they have no value for an estimate of the standard of life of these workers.

In fact, the agricultural labourer proper, the man with no land of his own and no other means of living than his wages, whether he be a servant or a jobbing-worker, is conspicuously absent from our records. That such a man existed, we can hardly doubt. He may not have been found in great numbers at a time when land was cheap and abundant; or he may have been a familiar figure if lack of equipment prevented him from taking up vacant holdings. But we know nothing of him and we must, however reluctantly, leave him to his obscure fate.

Very different were the conditions of labour in the towns, for the town-labourer or 'companion' was entirely dependent on his wages. They need closer scrutiny, inasmuch as their conditions varied very much from trade to trade, and as there was a wide gap between the wages of skilled and unskilled labour. Our information about town-labourers, even if not better in quality, is at least to be had in greater quantity than that relating to agricultural labour. As scholars have as yet hardly tapped these sources of information, it is necessary to enumerate briefly the classes of records and the kind of information they are likely to provide.

Roughly speaking, records dealing with town-wages fall into three classes. First, municipal by-laws, which are fairly numerous at a time when town authorities were trying to control labour and wages and had power to enact regulations or *bans,* as they were called in Northern France and in the Low Countries. The records dealing with the textile industry and published by Espinas and Pirenne (all unfortunately prior to 1384) give an idea of what can be found in the registers of *bans,* most of which still await publication. But valuable as they are, these by-laws are of little practical use. They tell of the legal rate of wages, which is not of course devoid of interest. It is thus interesting to learn that during the year following the Black Death the textile workers of St. Omer were able to get three successive rises, on the pretext of the great rise in the cost of living, but in fact because scarcity of labour enabled them to dictate their conditions to their employers. But it still remains unknown how far the legal rates of wages were actually enforced. In general they seem to have been rarely observed. If labour was plentiful, employers would pay less than the rate, using subterfuges for not openly breaking the law. Thus at Douai, in the thirteenth century, they deducted from the salary whatever payment in kind they were supposed to provide (food, dress, a pair of shoes, lodging and so forth). This practice was several times forbidden by the municipality, which means that it could not be suppressed. The possibilities of evading the law were so numerous that at Ypres it was decided that the weekly payment of wages should take place every Saturday at noon in the Town Hall, each employer settling his debts to his employees in full view of the other artisans and workers. Therefore all we can learn from municipal by-laws is the general trend of the wages system, not its actual working.

The second class of records, which can be found only in those regions where notaries kept registers—that is, roughly speaking, the southern districts of Languedoc and Provence—consists of private deeds by which employers engaged domestic servants or workers for a period of several months or years and fixed their wages and obligations in a written contract. They concern a particularly interesting type of wage-earner, those who were paid quarterly or yearly and whose salary was a poor cash benefit, since in most cases servants and companion-workers were housed, fed and even clothed by their master. From these returns we are therefore able to get much inside information on the actual conditions of salaried labour; but, owing to the great variety and dissimilarity of the individual circumstances, we are unable to tabulate the results so as to get a clear view of the general trend of wages. Besides, even when notaries' registers survive by the hundred, wage-deeds are not numerous: in Toulouse, roughly between 1350 and 1450, M. Wolff has collected over a thousand of these wage-contracts; but as more than nine-tenths of these are in fact apprenticeship contracts, in which the apprentice's family promises to pay the employer for his upkeep, there remain barely a hundred wage-contracts proper, differing so widely one from another (in the same year, the same employer engages two workers of similar skill on two different conditions of pay) that they are useless in the aggregate.[7]

So we turn to the third class of records; back to accounts. In the case of towns, these are accounts of corporate bodies, whether municipalities or colleges of some sort. Here at last is a mass of registers which deserves study, but has so far discouraged most scholars. How tantalizing for instance is M. Marquand, who tells us that, while working on the economic life of Lille during the fifteenth century, he could not bother to go through the complete set of town accounts and only picked a few of them, one in every five years! No wonder, that in a monograph of 300 pages, he devotes in all thirty lines to wages, including half a dozen figures.[8] A point of further interest in these documents is that they may offer the possibility of a comparison, for what it is worth, between the wage-earners and such salaried people as town servants and petty officers. On the other hand, the greatest defect of town and corporation accounts is that they restrict information to those sections of the wage-earning population that were likely to be employed by a town or a corporate body: mainly all kind of domestic servants and casual hands; or else workers of the building and allied trades (masons, carpenters, tilers, street-pavers) to the exclusion of all other trades.

Research on these records having hardly begun, one can only set forth impressions on what has been found so far. In the main, these impressions are similar to those given by manorial accounts: the later Middle Ages, and especially the fifteenth century, after the temporary dislocation of the labour market due to the Black Death, were times of low and stable wages. The fact is grudgingly admitted by M. Marquand, who, working under the impression current among scholars twenty years ago that wages and prices had risen consistently during the fourteenth and fifteenth centuries, was startled to find the contrary to have been true at Lille, at least from 1403 to 1467, and could not find an explanation. Similarly, M. Mollat suggests, although the data he gives are far too scanty, that in Normandy, after a temporary rise following the French reconquest of the province (1450), wages fell sharply during the last quarter of the century.[9] More revealing facts abound about Toulouse, where carpenters were paid exactly the same nominal wages in 1388 and 1443, while the wages of women labourers remained at the low rate of 4 *oboles* a day from 1367 to 1443, during an age when it was formerly thought that scarcity of labour coupled with currency debasements were bound to have produced a constant upward movement in nominal, if not in real wages.[10] Similar figures have been adduced for the Paris suburb of St Germain des Prés.[11]

Furthermore, the poorer paid labourers were also those whose employment was the less secure, chiefly in the building industries, where work was perforce seasonal. Thanks to the minute accounts of the building of the Périgord College at Toulouse, which took nearly seven years to complete (1365–71), we know that in no year was the total of working days more than 150; that labourers employed in this work included many women, whose rate of pay was far lower than that of men; and that during the winter months when work was slack and therefore unemployment prevalent, all daily wages fell sharply—as much as from 5 to 2, and this during the season when, owing to irregular employment, the workers had to buy most of their food, since they were fed by the employer while at work.[12] Skilled workmen, master-masons or master-tilers, might survive these lean days, for their rate of pay was always more than double that of unskilled workers. But one wonders how labourers, who got only one or two groats per working day, could live during the season of unemployment.

The problem of real wages, that is of the relation of wages to prices, is too complicated to be tackled here. As, during the later Middle Ages, wheat prices seem to have diverged from other cereals and since most workers lived on ryebread, it is necessary to find out the variations in the cost of rye. It is also necessary to find out what part of the labourers' wages went on bread, and if their budgets were affected by changes of diet, such as a greater use of meat, not to speak of the other commodities which they had to acquire. There is no question of being able to compile a compound index of the cost of living, such as that to which the present-day minimum wages in France are linked and which is based on the prices of 213 commodities. A better standard of comparison might be afforded by the budgets of persons of moderate means, such as poor widows, scholars and country chantry-priests, for whom, as charters and wills of the late thirteenth century tend to show, an annual rent of 80s. tournois (equivalent to 20s. sterling) was deemed to cover all their needs.[13] We can only suggest here this line of approach to a difficult problem.

At this stage of our knowledge, we can very tentatively say that if Thorold Rogers was able, a century ago, to state that the later Middle Ages were in England the golden age of the agricultural labourer, who enjoyed high wages while agricultural prices were kept low, this cannot be said of his French counterpart, still less of the town wage-earner. Scholars have certainly laid too great an emphasis on both the depletion of the labour market owing to the Black Death and subsequent epidemics, and on currency debasements, two factors that ought to have sent prices and wages soaring. That this did not happen—or does not seem to have happened—is yet another proof that even currency manipulations or shortage of hands were unable to counteract the deflationary trend of later Middle Ages economics, a trend that it was the special aim of currency debasements to counteract. Wages were low because trade and industry were in decadence. Low wages meant small purchasing power, which in turn meant a small output of commodities—and in order to avoid further falls in prices through overproduction, municipal by-laws were trying to restrict production in all the main industries. Low production in its turn meant small employment and therefore low wages, irrespective of the fact that the available labour may have been small in absolute numbers. Thus the vicious circle was complete.

In other words, it could be said that whereas both France and England certainly witnessed a double fall of population and production, the relative importance of the two phenomena was different in each country. In England, the demographic contraction was more accentuated than the fall of production; therefore wages rose. In France, the economic disruption due to wars and other as yet unknown factors was so complete as to limit production faster than population. In spite of a great fall in the number of men the magnitude of the recession kept wages low all through our period.

Those suggestions do not pretend to be by any means final. They need to be tested by the compilation of data and the collection of series from as many accounts as may have survived. At any rate we can say that in the revision of our ideas on late medieval economy which has been going on for some years, the question of wages is of the first importance. It ought to be tackled and, if possible, answered. The question deserves to be given priority over many others but unfortunately, it is also one of the most difficult, and this is probably why it has not been given the attention it deserves.

NOTES

1 Based on a paper read at the Economic History Society Annual Meeting, Bristol, 15 April 1955.

2 Philippe Wolff, *Commerces et marchands de Toulouse, vers 1350–vers 1450* (Paris, 1954), pp. 327–34.

3 Compare with the English debasements of 1411 (one-sixth) and 1464 (one-fifth).

4 M. Guy Fourquin kindly provided me with data from the accounts of the Cathedral chapter of Paris (Archives nationales, LL 13 and 14), the abbeys of St. Denis (LL 1232–8, 1242–8, 1271–5 and 1297–1301) and St. Germain des Prés (LL 1112–6 and 1143), which he proposes to use in a forthcoming thesis on the agricultural life of the Paris region during the later Middle Ages.

5 R. Boutruche, *La crise d'une société: Seigneurs et Paysans du Bordelais pendant la Guerre de Cent Ans* (Paris, 1947), pp. 267–8.

6 *Op. cit.,* pp. 443–4.

7 *Op. cit.,* pp. 432–8.

8 R. Marquand, *La vie économique à Lille sous Philippe le Bon* (Paris, 1940), pp. 217–218.

9 M. Mollat, *Le commerce maritime normand à la fin du Moyen Age* (Paris, 1952), p. 375.

10 Ph. Wolff, *op. cit.,* pp. 439 *et seq.*

11 Francoise Lehoux, *Le Bourg de St. Germain des Prés depuis les origines jusqu'à la fin de la Guerre de Cent Ans* (Paris, 1951), pp. 323 *et seq.*

12 Ph. Wolff, *op. cit.,* pp. 441–2 and Graph XVI.

13 This assumption is made on the basis of *Chartes du Forez antérieures au XIVe Siècle* (Mâcon, 13 vols., 1933–55).

Views of Society

16

Chiliasm and
the Hussite Revolution

HOWARD KAMINSKY

IN THE YEARS following John Hus' martyrdom the movement he had led developed from a Prague University reform movement into a national reformation.[1] Ideas that had formerly existed as topics for discussion among university intellectuals were established as actual religious practice among large groups of people, of all estates and with widely varying interests and viewpoints. As each such group entered the national movement it necessarily contributed its own viewpoint, with the result that every extension of the reform involved almost as many difficulties for the Hussites as for the Catholics. Of course there had always been differences among the university masters themselves, the inevitable conservative-radical dichotomy based ultimately on differences of spiritual temperament that exist within any group. But far more significant was the *social* polarization that took form as the concept of reform held by the upper estates was opposed by programs deriving from the point of view of artisans, peasants, and "the poor."

The rejection of the Roman system by the upper orders in Bohemia involved on the one hand certain changes in religious practice (chiefly the return to utraquist communion), and on the other the secularization of church property and the replacement of the Roman-controlled hierarchy with a national church under the patronage of the feudality and bourgeoisie, and under the doctrinal authority of the University. This concept of the reform did not presuppose a formal break with Rome and certainly not a withdrawal from the European religious community; on the contrary, the conservative Hussites did all they could to stay within this community—which was their own—and win it over to reform. But when the lower orders entered the reform movement they brought with them an accumulated hatred of the Roman Church, both as a feudal lord and as a greedy and corrupt institution, ever ready to squeeze payments from the faithful to support the pomp of ritual, the luxury of prelates, and the sinful lives led by many of the clergy at all levels. The early Church had not been so exalted, so complex, or so worldly; the comparison of the Roman system with the Primitive Church, a fundamental Hussite idea, took on an almost savage quality in the minds of the lower estates. Thus even as early as 1415 we find the emergence of a context of ideas and attitudes precisely like that of Waldensianism, the popular heresy *par excellence* of the Middle Ages, and while scholars do not all agree that these tendencies can be traced to actual Waldensian influences in Bohemia, it is hard to avoid characterizing the sectarian Hussitism in question as Waldensianist in nature.[2]

For about four years the potential split between "orthodox" and sectarian Hussites was contained within the unified national movement. For one thing that movement had won the favor of leading Czech barons and the benign neutrality of King Wenceslas IV, so that the years 1415–1418 saw the establishment of reform all through Bohemia and into Moravia, the secular powers exercising their rights of patronage in favor of Hussite priests, even radical ones. At the same time, while official Hussite doctrine, under the leadership of the university master Jakoubek of Stříbro, continued to accept the basic elements of the Catholic worldview, it developed a practical radicalism that made possible the application of even sectarian reforms while the scholastic framework of University Hussitism remained intact.

But in early 1419 the conditions for this working arrangement came to an end. King Wenceslas began a new policy of Catholic restoration; utraquist communion was tolerated but there could be no Hussite agitation and no extension of the reform beyond utraquism. Those whose concept of reform was predicated on the cooperation of the secular powers felt that they had to obey the royal decree; they formed a politically conservative party which included even the religiously radical Jakoubek. But more militant radicals in Prague were unwilling to give up their gains or their freedom to propagate their ideas, while the radicals in the provinces, often unable even to enter their parish churches unless they renounced utraquism, were virtually forced to resist. In south Bohemia, long the most active center of popular heresy and then of radical Hussitism, the radical priests organized congregations outside the parish system, on open hilltops, where they gave utraquist communion and preached vigorous evangelical sermons against the Roman system. The spirit of these congregations was a conscious imitation of evangelical and apostolic Christianity, with an emphasis on Christian pacifism, brotherly love, and such practical acts as the sharing of food. As groups of regular, perhaps even permanent, congregants took shape there emerged the rudiments of a really new life, one held together by love rather than by institutions based on force. The effect was to create a new social foundation for the radical party; those who felt alienated from the established social system and whose religious ideas constituted a rejection of that system in principle had now taken the final step of building a kind of social existence wholly outside the feudal order. The center of these mass congregations was a hill near Bechyně castle that the radicals renamed "Mt. Tabor," after the mountain in Galilee where Jesus was supposed to have spoken with his disciples and to have appeared to them after his death.[3] The congregants themselves became known as Taborites.

Although the original creation of these congregations had been an expression of the sectarian spirit of withdrawal from the world, the priests and petty nobles who came to lead the movement were still thinking in terms of an established national reformation rather than some sectarian dream of perfection. Very soon, indeed, the congregations were given nationwide organization and scope, so that certain meetings took on the character of national assemblies, where religious observance was associated with political planning. Out of the separate world of the hilltops there emerged a schismatic religio-political program designed to bring about a national reformation in defiance of Wenceslas' Catholicizing policies. Even in the King's lifetime there was talk at the congregations of electing a Hussite bishop and a Hussite prince; after Wenceslas' death, on August 16, 1419, these projects became a definite political program. At the beginning of October and again in early November congregants from all over the kingdom were brought together in Prague itself, where the radical leaders urged their policies on the Hussite magistrates and university masters.

But the conservatives, still loyal to the principle of legitimacy, sought to secure the succession of Wenceslas' brother, the Emperor Sigismund, on condition that he grant freedom to Hussitism and secure a European hearing for the reform. He was indeed the only man who could conceivably do the latter. The Hussite barons joined with their Catholic colleagues to form a royalist party, committed to preserving the *status quo* while waiting for Sigismund to enter the realm, and they urged the Prague magistrates to adhere to this party. On one occasion the radicals were able to bring the city into open war with the royalists, but this success only pushed the burghers more powerfully into the arms of the party of order, and on November 13, 1419 Prague concluded a truce with the royalists, by which the latter would insure the freedom of utraquism in return for Prague's cession of the important Vyšehrad fortress south of the city, and her promise to stop radical attacks on churches, monasteries, and images, and to see that the Taborites left the city.

* * * * *

The truce of November 13, which was to last until April 24, 1420, completed the isolation of the provincial radicals, already begun with the congregations of 1419. The radicals who returned to the provinces from Prague after the truce had no political ties binding them to the national movement, no possibility of achieving political results within the framework of Hussite unity, and no reason to regard the conservatives with any emotion kinder than hatred. And if any of them were not ready to reject the Prague world of ideas, the ensuing events of the winter provided the final argument, for the truce of November 13 was the signal for a savage persecution of non-royalist Hussites throughout Bohemia. A contemporary Hussite chronicler has described it vividly: [4]

> In these times therefore the faithful Czechs, both clergy and laity, who favored communion in both kinds and devotedly promoted it, and who grieved at the unjust death of Master John Hus . . . suffered very great difficulties, tribulations, anguish, and torment throughout the Kingdom of Bohemia, at the hands of the enemies and blasphemers of the Truth, who grievously afflicted them by plundering their property, by subjecting them to hard sorts of captivity, to hunger and thirst, and by slaughtering their bodies. For these enemies of the Truth hunted down priests and laymen who ardently supported the chalice in various parts of the realm and brought them to the men of Kutná Hora, to whom they sold some for money. The Kutná Horans—Germans and cruel persecutors and enemies of the Czechs, especially of those loving the Truth of Christ —afflicted them with various blasphemies and diverse sorts of punishments, and inhumanly threw them—some alive, some first decapitated—into deep mine shafts, especially into the mine shaft near the Church of St. Martin near the Kouřim Gate, which shaft the Kutná Horans called "Tabor" . . . In a short time more than 1600 utraquists were killed by them and thrown into the shafts, the executioners often being exhausted by the fatigue of slaughter.

The radicals could either suffer themselves to be exterminated or they could resist and, by taking up arms in defense of Hussitism against the royalist feudality, create a new total situation, one in which the reform would pass over into revolution. In the course of the winter precisely such a situation emerged. By early 1420 the campaign of extermination against the "Wyclyfites"—a generic term signifying, at this point, those Hussites who did not abide by the policy of the November truce —ceased to be the affair merely of royalist barons and German burghers; Sigismund himself had turned his attention to the Bohemian problem and was directing the battle against the rebels. While Hussite Prague was deliberately humbling herself before Sigismund for the sake of her conservative concept of reform,[5] the Emperor was urging his loyal subjects to "persecute and as far as possible exterminate" all Wyclyfites.[6] The latter maintained their defiance in certain urban bastions—particularly Plzeň and Klatovy in the southwest, Písek in the south, Hradec Králové in the northeast, and, perhaps, the towns of Žatec, Louny, and Slaný in the northwest.[7]

It is precisely at this time that the sources show the beginnings of the chiliast movement. The reliable Master Laurence of Březová notes, just after his entry for January 9, 1420: [8]

During this time certain Taborite priests were preaching to the people a new coming of Christ, in which all evil men and enemies of the Truth would perish and be exterminated, while the good would be preserved in five cities. For this reason certain cities in which communion in both kinds could freely be given refused to enter into any agreement with the enemy, and especially the city of Plzeň.

For these Taborite priests in the district of Bechyně and elsewhere were deceiving the people in a remarkable way with their preaching, advancing many erroneous doctrines contrary to the Christian faith, by falsely interpreting the prophetical books according to their own heads and by despising the Catholic doctrines of the holy doctors. They urged that all those desiring to be saved from the wrath of almighty God, which in their view was about to be visited on the whole globe, should leave their cities, castles, villages, and towns, as Lot left Sodom, and should go to the five cities of refuge. These are the names of the five: Plzeň, which they called the City of the Sun, Žatec, Louny, Slaný, and Klatovy.[9] For Almighty God wished to destroy the whole world, saving only those who had taken refuge in the five cities. They alleged in support of this doctrine prophetical texts falsely and erroneously understood. Also, they sent letters containing this material through the Kingdom of Bohemia. And many simple folk, accepting these frivolous doctrines as true, and having zeal, as the Apostle says, but not acting through knowledge, sold their property, taking even a low price, and flocked to these priests from various parts of the Kingdom of Bohemia and the Margravate of Moravia, with their wives and children, and they threw their money at the feet of the priests.

Laurence's account suggests that the preaching did not at this point focus attention on the new age that would succeed the predicted Day of Wrath; arbitrarily reserving the word "chiliasm" for the whole movement, we can distinguish between an initial *adventism* and a subsequent *millenarianism*. The task of adventist propaganda was to separate the people from the established order; how difficult it was appears from a contemporary song: [10]

Faithful ones, rejoice in God! Give Him honor and praise, that He has pleased to preserve us and graciously liberate us from the evil Antichrist and his cunning army . . . .

Take no heed of the faithless ones and do not follow them for Satan draws them in his train, away from endurance. . . . Many will excuse themselves and depart from the feast, some to look at their villages, others to try out their oxen, and still others to embrace women. To such Christ has promised that . . . they will be deprived of the eternal feast. Therefore fear this and let us endure with him to the end, always keeping in mind the reward that Christ will give to the one who stays with him to the end and does not leave him on account of some

suffering, or some whim, or booty of some sort. [The faithful must not grumble.]
. . . Give us [the strength] not to look back as Lot's wife did. . . . And Christ
mentioned her when he spoke of his coming and commanded flight to the mountains; he said: Who is then on the roof, let him not come down, and who is in
the fields, let him not look back. Remember Lot's wife, that faithless daughter,
who looked at her home.
Lord Christ, make us have strong faith in you so that we may conquer, firmly
staying with you, O living and most worthy Bread, until we come into heaven,
joyfully singing Amen, rejoicing with the Lord God, and ruling with Him
forever.

The kind of battle that was being fought for the minds of the provincial radicals is more fully illustrated by the chiliast letters, referred to
by Laurence. An early example reads: [11]

Dearest brothers in God! Know that the time of greatest suffering has already
drawn near . . . the time about which Christ in his Scriptures, and his apostles
in their epistles, and the prophets, as well as St. John in the Apocalypse, have
prophesied. In this time the Lord God commands His elect to flee from the
midst of the evil ones. . . . But where are God's elect to flee? To fortified cities
that the Lord God has provided in the time of greatest suffering. . . . And there
are five of these cities, which will not enter into agreements with the Antichrist
or surrender to him. . . .
The lion has gone forth from his lair and the heathen pillager has arisen, that
is, against God and His Law; just as the King of Hungary [Sigismund], who has
plundered many pagans, has gone forth from his city, that is, from Hungary, in
order to lay waste your land. Your cities will be wiped out and remain without
inhabitants. Therefore, knowing these things, give diligent heed to the Lord
God Himself and do not be tardy; He is at the gates. . . . Do not let yourselves
be turned here and there by unbelieving seducers who say, "This will not happen in our time;" it has already been fulfilled, and God knows when it will
happen. . . . Therefore you, if you are faithful, do not scorn holy prophecies.
For the Lord God says through the prophet Amos in chapter ix [10]: "All the
sinners of my people will die on the sword who say, 'It will [not] approach and
the evil will not come on us' "—like those who say [now]: "It will not be in
our time nor in the time of our children." God's mercy be with you. Amen.

The "unbelieving seducers" included above all the Prague masters,
who naturally sought to keep the reform within their world of ideas.
Their resistance to chiliasm was undoubtedly sharpened by the fact that
the chiliasts called Prague Babylon—it was, in truth, associated with the
royalists—and urged the citizens of the capital to flee their doomed city
and join the radical congregations.[12] In letters to their provincial contacts and in official statements requested by perplexed Hussites, the university masters conducted a vigorous anti-chiliast polemic, some of the
more interesting passages of which follow: [13]

The priests should take care not to preach to the people in a presumptuous
spirit that a horrible disaster is about to visit the people, assigning a time for

it on their own and criminally keeping the people in a state of suspense, without themselves having had any certain divine revelation about this.

[The priests should] exhort the people, publicly and privately, not to leave their dwelling-places. . . . The evangelical priests would do well to live evangelically, thus teaching the people and destroying sins in them, but relinquishing these presumptions of theirs.

The common people, urged on by the priests, are taking up carnal and secular arms against the enemy. . . . Let the subject people beware, lest they usurp the sword from the higher powers, against God, not having any certain and special revelation. The *higher* powers can legitimately wage war, but they expose themselves to great perils of the soul in so doing. . . .

We affirm that the faithful are permitted to congregate [for the honor of God, etc.] . . . But as God is our witness, it is not our intention in asserting this truth to offer any occasion for rapine, plundering, or homicide, or the destruction of churches and parish-houses. . . . [The congregations should be] made in the church rather than in deserted fields or on mountains—particularly where scandal . . . and peril may probably be feared.

Another surviving chiliast letter seems to be striking back against just these arguments, which must have carried powerful weight, reinforcing as they did the natural disinclination of the people to break with not only the existing social order but also the whole past tradition of the Hussite movement. The chiliast prophet wrote: [14]

May God be with you and please to enlighten and comfort your souls in your sorrows and sufferings. Dearest brothers and sisters in God! See this hard, terrible, and dangerous time, prophesied by Christ, by the apostles, and by the holy prophets, which time is called that of the greatest wrath, and which is to be particularly known, according to Christ, by many various and concealed seductions, by battles and supposed battles. For many are now aggrieved against Christ's commands, *supposing that it is not necessary to carry on a regular fight with a physical sword* against evils and abominations, against errors and heresy. But Christ has said: do not be grieved when you hear battles and struggles; these things must be, as the holy prophets prophesied. . . . And Christ also makes this time known by conflicts, by many scandals, by the spread of evil, by many oppressions, by destruction, by abomination in the holy place—that is, sins, idols . . . and other disorders abominable to God, by torments, by imprisonment, *and primarily by the killing of God's elect.* . . . In this time Christ gives *the special command* to his faithful ones, to flee not only from sins, *but also from the midst of evil, hostile, and insincere people;* and he says: flee to the mountains, *that is, to the faithful people.* . . .

Do not say then: "What, are we to flee before God? Wherever the just man dies, there he dies well." [15] That is sometimes the truth but not always. [Lot was ordered to flee Sodom even though he was a good man.] Christ also orders us [like Lot] *not to look back on homes, on estates, on any material things,* and not to believe the seducers who say that wherever the just man dies, he dies well. For Christ says: then they will say to you that Christ is here or he is there, but do not believe it; that is, if they say that a man needs only to flee from sins for Christ to be merciful to him, in a village or in a city, that is a great deception. For Christ says, further: false prophets will arise and will give signs and miracles, so that the elect too may be led into error, if that were possible.

And what are the great signs that the false Christians and false prophets give? *These [people] can be, outstandingly, personages who are [university] masters and nobles;* it is evident that they have seemed to be something, and they are nothing. Thus they mislead God's elect, saying that the masters do not hold this, nor do the lords, only . . . those eccentrics who expound things from their own heads. And indeed they themselves mislead the simple people . . . as when they say to the people who are moved by the Word of God to abandon and take no thought for their property, "Do not leave your property, they are deceiving you." This is obviously against Scripture, which says: Whoever leaves home, brothers, sisters, father or mother, or land and field for my name, will win a hundred times more and will obtain eternal life.

[Christ's] disciples asked him. . . . "Where, O Lord?" And he said: "Where the Body will be, there the eagles will gather." Therefore brothers and sisters, *where you know Christ's Body to be given with all the pieces of God's Truths,* there gather in the time of vengeance and greatest suffering. And in that time those places cannot be in a village or elsewhere, on account of the strong and dreadful Antichrist, but *in fortified cities,* of which St. Isaiah names five. . . . Therefore it is necessary to congregate without delay, to fast and weep for your own sins and those of others, to pray day and night to the Lord God, crying out to Him that He should please to save you in the times of greatest suffering. And also to fit yourselves, with [the help of] God's Word, for good examples and counsels, and particularly in order to fill yourselves with the precious food and drink of Lord Jesus Christ. . . .

*   *   *   *   *

It is clear that this adventist preaching of the earliest period—January and February—continued the older Taborite congregation-movement in many ways: the radicals were urged to gather on the mountains to take utraquist communion and listen to the Word of God. But there were essential differences: the congregations were no longer periodic events, from which the masses might return to their villages, but permanent communities; the main purpose of these communities was not communion and preaching, nor the political aim of a national reformation, but self-preservation in an imminent period of catastrophe, the battle between Christ and Antichrist that would end the existing Age; the meetings were not to be permeated with the spirit of evangelical pacifism but with the readiness to fight with the physical sword. It is also interesting that at least some chiliast letters specifically noted that the "mountains" were to be understood as, simply, the congregations, or more specifically still, five cities.

To contemporaries the most striking change was that from pacifism to an ideology of warfare. In a letter written sometime before February 10 to the chiliast prophet Master John of Jičín, formerly a close associate of Hus' and Jakoubek's in the university reform movement, Jakoubek asked: "Did you [priests] not formerly preach against killing, and how then has everything now come to be turned into its opposite?" [16] The layman Peter Chelčický, who had probably been a Taborite in 1419 but who refused to give up his Waldensianist condemnation of violence, killing, and secular power, also addressed himself to this problem. In his *On Spiritual Battle,* written about 1421, he reviewed the whole development of Taboritism as he saw it: [17]

. . . to our great shame and sorrow, we must acknowledge how our brethren have been cleverly seduced by Satan, and how they have departed from Holy Scriptures in strange and unheard-of ideas and acts. When Satan first came to them it was not with an open face, as the Devil, but in the shining garb of voluntary poverty, which Christ commanded priests to hold to, and in the zealous work of preaching to and serving the people and in giving them the Body and Holy Blood of God. And all of this flourished to the point that a great many people flocked to them. Then the Devil came to them clothed in other garb, in the prophets and the Old Testament, and from these they sought to confect an imminent Day of Judgement, saying that they were angels who had to eliminate all scandals from Christ's Kingdom, and that they were to judge the world. And so they committed many killings and impoverished many people, but they did not judge the world according to their words, for the predicted time has elapsed with which they terrified the people, telling them strange things which they collected from many prophets.

This statement seems to mean that the earlier congregations, as blameless as their transactions seemed, were still the origin of what Chelčický regarded as the openly evil chiliast congregations. Indeed he argued generally in the tractate as a whole that man cannot do good or persist in a good course by his own virtues; as soon as he ceases to rely absolutely on divine support he lays himself open to the Devil. Chelčický thought that few men could avoid this trap,[18] and so he must have seen the fundamental fault of the congregations of 1419 in their very success as mass movements. By reaching outside of the narrow limits within which sectarian ideals of perfection can be safely pursued, the congregations degenerated morally to the point where their reaction to persecution, in the winter of 1419–1420, was not the Christian suffering of the New Testament but the self-conscious violence of the Old.

Chelčický was not the only radical to resist the new Taborite ideas. Many Hussites wondered whether the new, permanent congregations were justified at all, and they turned to the recognized arbiters of doctrinal truth, the Prague University masters.[19] Could "the faithful come together in time of persecution," "for the honor of God, the edification of the Church, and the promotion of the evangelical Truth?" To take a poignant case, could "a wife who is of the faithful leave a husband who is not, for Christ and his gospel?" And could pious Christians take the sword? And even if it was permissible for secular lords to fight in defense of the Truth, the question arose, "whether, if the secular lords are so lax that they are unwilling to defend the Truth with sword in hand, the faithful subject communities may and ought to defend that Truth with the material sword?" Obviously, those who asked such questions were torn between two desires: on the one hand was their unwillingness to step outside the main Hussite tradition and the scholastic world of ideas; on the other hand were the urgent demands of Hussite self-defense, to which only the Taborite preachers seemed to be doing justice.

The Prague masters, evidently relying on Wyclyf's doctrine of the loss of "dominion" through sin, sought to supply a doctrine of legitimate revolution:[20]

We concede that secular lords can resist God and His Law so much that their power may be removed by God Himself, and it would then be permitted to the communities, admitted to this work by God, to defend the evangelical Truth in a practical and not fantastic way.

But they at once began to pile on reservations:

But there must always be preserved the proper order, consonant with the Law of Christ, as this is indicated by divine instinct, certain revelation, or reliable evidence. Moreover, care must be taken that no one assert, forwardly and too precipitantly, that the lords have been deprived of their power just because they have refused to go along with every vagrant wind. And further, communities can and should defend the Truth by helping their lords. It is neither safe nor just that the common people take on a task that does not belong to them, particularly when they have lords in whom there is no defect so evident, notable, or incorrigible that the only way justice can be secured is for the people themselves to engage in a task that is not only difficult but full of perils and snares.

And some weeks later they warned that their justification of war should not be taken as a license, "as some now suppose," to destroy cloisters, churches, and parish houses, or to plunder.[21]

Since there did emerge various non-chiliast and non-Taborite centers of resistance to Sigismund, it may be supposed that the Prague rescripts had a certain influence in helping these Hussites pass from the older reliance on established authority to their new posture of independent action. But the Taborite movement developed its own theoretical framework, quite outside the scholastic body of thought. By virtue of the new coming of Christ and the end of the *seculum,* all aspects of the medieval order were reduced to meaninglessness; what became meaningful, concretely, was the new world of the elect. It is this world that must now be studied.

* * * * *

The first great hope of the Taborites was Plzeň, the "City of the Sun" in chiliast propaganda. The Plzeň radicals, led by the priest Wenceslas Koranda and the baron Lord Břeněk of Skála, had played the leading role in organizing the great political congregations that had met in Prague during the autumn; after the November truce these contingents returned to Plzeň. With them, however, came powerful new forces determined not to accept the truce; the combined forces were led by John Žižka, Lord Břeněk of Skála, Lord Valkoun of Adlar, and several members of the lower nobility. A typical radical program of destruction of monasteries and some churches was put into effect, and there was chiliast preaching.[22] "One day," Koranda preached, "we'll get up in the morning and see all the others lying dead, with their noses pointing up in the air." [23] But this pleasure was not enjoyed by the Plzeň Taborites; quickly attacked and then besieged by the royalists, and faced with a predominantly hostile citizenry, the Taborites in the city could hold out only until about March 20, 1420. After its surrender and evacuation by the Taborites, Plzeň became a Catholic bastion and remained so for the rest of the Hussite period.

It was in south Bohemia that Taborite chiliasm found its political success. It will be recalled that Laurence of Březová stated that in the first part of January "certain Taborite priests" were preaching adventist sermons "in the district of Bechyně and elsewhere." The Taborite center of this region, which had had a long history of sectarian heresy, had previously been the city of Ústí-nad-Lužnicí, whose radical leaders had organized the first congregations of 1419 after they had been driven out of the city. They seem to have returned, for the Taborite contingents in Prague during the autumn included one from Ústí.[24] This group may have returned to the city after the truce, but if so they were probably driven out by the anti-Hussite Lord Ulrich of Ústí as part of the royalist war on the radicals.[25] In view of the insistence of at least one adventist agitator on congregating in walled cities rather than in the open, we can probably suppose that the Ústí contingent sought such a city.

All the available evidence suggests that *the* walled chiliast city of south Bohemia was Písek, which had long been a center of sectarian radicalism.[26] In the early adventist preaching, before the "five cities" had become more than a concept, the people were urged to congregate in Plzeň and in Písek; [27] as of February 10, 1420—but doubtless long before —the latter city was the only important center of "Wyclyfite" resistance in south Bohemia.[28] And Master John Příbram, in an explicitly historical presentation of the progress of chiliast ideology, confined his account of the actual formation of the chiliast type of community to what had taken place in Písek: [29]

The Taborite priests, . . . not satisfied with having deceived such a great number of people in so ugly a way in regard to their souls, their faith, and their property, immediately thought up another disgraceful deception. They preached and ordained, in the city of Písek, to those people who had fled to them on the mountains,[30] that all the brethren should pool absolutely everything, and for this purpose the priests set up one or two chests, which the community almost filled up for them.

I suppose Laurence of Březová's statement, that the people "threw their money at the feet of the priests" in the Bechyně region, to refer to these chests in Písek, and perhaps to their prototypes which had presumably been set up on the mountains. In any case, it seems probable that the mountain congregations of the area transferred themselves to Písek.

In connection with the common chests a civil regime took shape, consisting of the priests, various officials, and at the head, the captain Matthew Louda of Chlumčany.[31] This regime distributed what was in the chests according to individual need,[32] and it also seems to have carried out a confiscation of burgage property.[33] The organization of the people into four divisions for fighting and plundering, attested at a somewhat later date,[34] may also have existed in the beginning; certainly the plundering did—the masses of uprooted poor people could hardly have supported themselves otherwise. Writing in January or early February, Master Jakoubek of Stříbro complained: [35]

The people, from your preaching and perilous interpretations of Scripture, are taking up carnal arms, abandoning the usual labor of their hands, and living in idleness from the plundering of their neighbors' substance; they kill and shed blood. . . . Many trustworthy people are complaining about you . . . calling you bloody priests.

The emergence of a new social order at Písek was only a preliminary to an even more remarkable development: the installation of that order in a totally new community. The background of this event is very unclear, although we know that it followed shortly after the predicted coming of Christ, during Carnival, had failed to take place.[36] In the early morning of February 21, 1420, "a large number of Taborite brethren and of peasants," with the help of "their brethren within the city," captured Ústí-nad-Lužnicí while the Catholic citizens were still incapacitated from their revels of the night before, Shrove Tuesday.[37] We are told that the coup was led by the priest Vaněček and the cleric Hromádka, who had one year before organized the first hilltop congregations on Mt. Tabor, in the same general region, and that they had the help of the local priests John of Smolín and John of Bydlín; they also had the help or perhaps even leadership of Lord Procop of Ústí,[38] whose anti-Hussite uncle held the city. A few days later these Taborites took possession of the nearby abandoned fortress of Hradiště, on a much stronger site, and they began to move there, renaming it Tabor. Hromádka took the further, decisive step of sending news of his action to Žižka in Plzeň, together with a request for help. Žižka, his position in Plzeň growing more and more unsafe, first sent one of his lieutenants, then came himself, with all the Plzeň Taborites, on March 25. Soon after, on March 30, the town of Ústí was burnt and abandoned.

Since Písek had fallen into royalist hands, perhaps about a week or so before,[39] Tabor emerged as *the* chiliast city of the realm, the heir of all the previous congregations and communities, and the main center of attraction for new adherents to the chiliast revolution.[40] The regime of common chests was set up in the manner described above for Písek,[41] and the people were divided into four military and political divisions.[42] A series of petty raids and more sizable expeditions smashed feudal power in the whole region, which fell under Tabor's dominion.[43] Písek was liberated and at once regained her eminence as a leading Taborite city, rivalling Tabor herself. Indeed, during the whole of 1420 and 1421, Písek and Tabor seem to have polarized the Taborite movement, the former attracting the less fanatical chiliasts and eventually emerging as the center of the Taborite reformation after the chiliast element had been destroyed.[44]

The foundation of the chiliast communities has been seen to have given rise to a new social system, one of communism, and an actively hostile, parasitical relationship to the "outside" world. The inner logic of this development was reconstructed nine years later by the rabidly anti-Taborite Master John Příbram: [45]

The people, thus seduced [by the chiliast summons to leave everything, congregate, and pool their money], saw how they had evidently been deceived and how they had been deprived of their estates. And, seeing that nothing had come or was coming of the things that their prophets had prophesied, and suffering hunger, misery, and want, they began to grumble and complain greatly against the prophets. At this point the false seducers thought up a new lie somehow to console the people, and they said that the whole Christian church was to be reformed in such a way that all the sinners and evil people were to perish completely, and that only God's elect were to remain on the earth—those who had fled to the mountains. And they said that the elect of God would rule in the world for a thousand years with Christ, visibly and tangibly. And they preached that the elect of God who fled to the mountains would themselves possess all the goods of the destroyed evil ones and rule over all their estates and villages. [They would enjoy a superabundance of wealth and would not have to pay dues or rents, or render services.]

Then the seducers, wanting to bring the people to that freedom and somehow to substantiate their lies, began to preach enormous cruelty, unheard-of violence, and injustice to man. They said that now was the time of vengeance, the time of destruction of all sinners and the time of God's wrath . . . in which all the evil and sinful ones were to perish by sudden death, on one day. . . . And when this did not happen and God did not bring about what they had preached, then they themselves knew how to bring it about and again thought up new and most evil cruelties . . . , that all the sinners were to be killed by the afflictions described in Ecclesiasticus [xxxix, 35–36]. . . . And again those cruel beasts, the Taborite priests, wanting to excite and work up the people so that they would not shrink from these afflictions, preached . . . that it was no longer the time of mercy but the time of vengeance, so that the people should strike and kill all sinners. . . . And they called us and others who admonished them to be merciful, damaging hypocrites. . . .

Except for the crude implication of conscious demagoguery, the pictured interplay of material necessity, social fantasy, and violent mass-action seems convincing. What Příbram shows is the passage of the movement from a predominantly or perhaps entirely adventist emphasis, with a fundamentally passive attitude to reality (leave the old world, congregate, and wait, fighting in self-defense), to an aggressive posture vis-à-vis the feudal order, and a new emphasis on the millennium that would succeed the Day of Wrath.[46] And it is important that all these ideas came to life as the ideology of an actual social organism.

The postulates on which the new, properly chiliast world-view was based are stated in a Latin chiliast tractate that displays all the rigorous articulation of a scholastic *questio*.[47] The author first states his four suppositions: that Apocalypse x, 7 and Daniel xii, 7 are true; that the glories of the new era will come only after the completion of Christ's (i. e., of the Christians') sufferings; that "the words of the Old and New Testaments are true as they sound and in the way they are arranged," and that they can be cited as true statements; that "nothing is to be added to or removed from the divine words." He goes on:

On the basis of these suppositions I have formed the position that is the foundation of almost all my preaching. Already now, in consummation of the Age, Christ is coming, on the day that is called the Day of the Lord, in order to prepare the consummation in the conquered House of Exasperation [Ezekiel iii, 9], and in order to renovate the Church and set it as a praise on the earth. He is coming to assume his kingdom in this world, and to purge all scandals from it, as well as all those who do iniquity; nor will he admit anything polluted to it, anything productive of lies or abomination. . . .
The glory of the Church is to be awaited in respect to the following: First that it will be gathered together; second that it will be purified; third that it will be multiplied; fourth, that it will be pacified; fifth, that it will be of greater glory than it has ever been.

Although the author took great pains to make clear his conception of "seculum" as an Age rather than as the world itself, citing various scriptural passages that he thought proved his point (e.g., Heb. ix, 26; Matt.

xii, 32; Lukc xx, 35), the Prague masters insisted on regarding his inter-pretation as an "ignorant error," showing a lack of grammatical train-ing.[48] But understood in the context of the Taborite communities' situation in the winter of 1419–1420, the author's ideas are relevant first prin-ciples, not mere speculations of doubtful accuracy. The confrontation of the Taborite congregations and the royalist butchers, with all the good apparently on one side and all the evil on the other, could easily seem like the prelude to the secular conflict awaited by many late-medieval Europeans—especially the Hussites, of all parties. All the divine promises of redemption (cf. Jeremiah xxxi ff. and *passim*) would be fullfilled in "those who have been collected," and the "consummation of the Age" was simply "the commutation of the good into better and the extermina-tion of the evil." [49]

The passage from this general picture to an actual ideology of vio-lence was effected primarily by the Taborite priest John Čapek, whose tracts—"more full of blood than a fish-pond is of water"—supplied the ideas that "almost all the Taborite priests" preached to "the simple people gathered on the mountains." [50] Starting with the postulate that "the present time is the Day of Vengeance and punishment," Čapek urged the Taborites to destroy all property, all buildings, all people of higher estate, and indeed all people of any estate who refused to join the Taborites in promoting the chiliast program—"the liberation of every truth, the increase of the praise of God, the securing of human salvation, and the destruction of sins" [51]—in other words, to adhere to the chiliast community. It was a doctrine of unlimited warfare, wholly alien to the scholastic justification of war, which insisted on certain conditions: a just cause, a valid authorization, and an upright intention.[52] Practically, these conditions meant that the sword was normally reserved to the established powers, who were to use it primarily to defend the Church or the Faith; the nature and duration of the fighting would be determined by the aim alone. The Prague masters repeated these principles again and again, but the essentially negative goals of chiliast warfare made anything short of total destruction unsatisfactory, and "legitimate, Christian warfare" was contemptuously rejected in favor of "unchristian war, based on evil and unworthy principles." [53]

This negativity of chiliast ideology lay behind even the apparently positive ideas that justified Taborite practice. Thus, according to a list of Taborite "articles" compiled in the medieval manner from the Tabor-ite literature and statements of the period,[54] the chiliasts thought that Christ had already come secretly, like a thief in the night and was work-ing through them: they were "God's angels sent to lead the good out of their cities and villages . . . onto the mountains," and to "sweep out all scandals and evils from Christ's Kingdom." [55] They were "an army sent by God through the whole world to inflict all the plagues of vengeance." [56] They were thus emancipated from all human restraints—the faithful had to plunge their swords into the enemies of Christ's Law and wash their hands in their victims' blood.[57] This punishment of sinners was "according to the will of the Holy Spirit" [58]—a very significant formulation, as will be seen. Needless to say, the only emancipation that took place was downwards, and contemporary observers saw not angels but "insensate beasts, mad dogs, and roaring lions." [59]

The social ideas of the chiliast vision were similarly subject to the contradiction between unchanging human needs and the postulated transformation of human nature that did not come about. The general principle has already been seen: the old *seculum* was being superseded by a new one which would be not just better than the old but wholly different, based on a new relationship between God and man. In this new "renovated" Kingdom, Christ himself would come down to Mt. Tabor from heaven, this time openly and in glory, and entertain his elect at great festivals on the mountains.[60] All the elect would "have the Holy Spirit fully," [61] and would hence be purged of all sinfulness; they would be brought to the innocent state of Adam in Paradise. The old sacraments would consequently lose their reason for existence, and would either be dropped or transformed.[62] The Law of God would be written on men's hearts and there would thus be no need for teaching, books, Bibles, or "worldly wisdom" in general. Indeed, "in that time the New Testament would cease and be annulled in many points." Women, finally would not have to "pay the debt" to their husbands, but would conceive without physical seed and bear children without pain.

Since the fact of original sin was supposed to be ultimately responsible for all the institutions of medieval society and all the characteristics of man's painful life on earth, the elimination of original sin would mean a life of perfect satisfaction: [63]

Those who will remain alive in that time will be brought to a state of innocence, like Adam and Enoch and Elijah in paradise, and no one will suffer hunger or thirst or have any physical pain or any sorrow, and no one will suffer any vexation.

And since social institutions as such presuppose man's sinful nature, the new society would have no need for them: [64]

In that time there will be no kingship or dominion on the earth, nor any subjection. All rents and dues will cease. No one will compel another to do anything, but all will be equal brothers and sisters.

If then we are told that the chiliasts urged that the people "do not work" but instead destroy the crops,[65] we can regard this total lack of prudence as the expression of the *true* chiliast attitude to social problems. But the new communities could hardly live by these ideals; as long as there was still a need for food and other necessities, and as long as men were of limited intelligence and morality, there would have to be social institutions. And we have seen that such institutions were set up in the form of common chests and a supervisory corps of officials. Insofar as this system was determined by something else than simple expediency, as a practical way of distributing scarcity, it must have been inspired not by the chiliast ideal of a perfect condition—which could not really give rise to any practical arrangements—but by the imitation of the apostolic Christianity portrayed in Acts ii, 44–47. In other words, the older sectarian tradition, which had animated the first hilltop congregations of 1419, pointed the way to practical action where chiliasm could not. At the same time, this communistic arrangement became a Taborite article of faith, along with the properly chiliast doctrines quoted above: [66]

Just as at Tabor there is nothing mine and nothing yours, but everything in the community is possessed equally, so everything should always be in common for all, and no one may have anything privately; if he does, he sins mortally.

Still more practical, if less pleasant, were other ideas circulating alongside the chiliast prophecies: the Taborites would become the lords of the earth, entering into all the property of the evil.[67] In the sense that these and other contradictory elements all stemmed from the rejection of the existing world, they may be regarded as parts of the same ideology, but it is correspondingly clear that the purely chiliast ideas *cannot* have had their origins as ideas in the social needs of the Taborite masses, however richly these needs nourished the ideas.[68]

* * * * *

In seeking now to determine the true origin of the chiliast world view, we are fortunately able to begin with some fairly explicit statements in the sources. At the beginning of his discussion of Taborite chiliasm, Laurence of Březová wrote: [69]

The chief author, publicizer, and defender of these doctrines was a certain young priest from Moravia, of elegant wit and with an extraordinarily good memory, whose name was Martin [Húska] and who was called Loquis. . . . His chief helpers were Master John of Jičín, Markold—a bachelor of arts, Koranda, and other priests of Tabor named previously. All of these had much respect for a certain Wenceslas, a tavern-keeper in Prague, who had a surpassingly good knowledge of the Bible, expounding the New Testament by the Old, and vice versa.

Apart from this evidence we have an excellent picture of Martin as a chiliast in Peter Chelčický's report of a long discussion he had had with Martin sometime in late 1420 or in 1421. Chelčický, in the course of a critical tractate addressed to the priests of Tabor, complained: [70]

But Martin was not humble or at all willing to suffer for Christ—even as you are not. And he declared to us his belief that there will be a new Kingdom of the Saints on earth, and that the good will no longer suffer, and he said, "If Christians were always to have to suffer so, I would not want to be a servant of God." That is what he said!

This priceless testimony clearly shows the chasm between the chiliast and the Waldensian outlooks, as well as the nature of the change that had come about in Chelčický's former associates.

But Martin's name was also associated with another heresy, which came to the surface in 1420 and 1421: the denial of a Real Presence in the Eucharist and the reduction of that sacrament to a commemoration. In Hussite Bohemia this heresy was called "Pikartism"; according to Laurence of Březová: [71]

The origin and root of this accursed heresy came to the Kingdom of Bohemia from certain Picards, who came to Prague in 1418 with their wives and children, almost forty men, saying that they had been expelled by their prelates on account of the Law of God. And they said that they had come to the realm because they had heard that in Bohemia there was the greatest liberty for the evangelical truth.

The name of "Picard" suggests an origin in northern France, and indeed one source says the group had come from "Gallia Belgica," [72] but it has been argued that the name was simply a version of "Beghard." [73] In any case these heretics soon showed that their conception of the "evangelical truth" involved the debasement of the very sacrament that the Hussites venerated above all else; but although they alienated most of their former friends in Prague they also made Czech disciples, among whom we may probably number Martin or Martin's teacher—perhaps Wenceslas the tavern-keeper and Bible expert.[74]

It has already been seen that the chiliast doctrine of a New Age implied the abolition of the existing sacraments; the infusion of the Holy Spirit would wipe out sin and hence make the Catholic sacraments unnecessary. Pikartism, in actual fact, was closely related to chiliasm. An even closer relation, which became known in 1421, was the heresy of the "Adamites," who not only claimed to be already living in the New Age but actually behaved as if they were, indulging their supposedly sinless natures in orgiastic practices that were in no way different from what unregenerated souls did, or longed to do, under the title of lust.[75] And while Martin does not seem to have preached or practiced Adamitism, his name appears as the Adamites' teacher, at least in the Pikart ideas that they held. At any rate, it is sufficiently clear that chiliasm, Pikartism, and Adamitism were in fact elements of a *single* thought-structure, capable of taking on one or another emphasis according to the situation or to the disposition of its adherents. What we call chiliasm was only the full secular development of this complex under favorable political conditions. And if Martin was chiefly responsible for bringing these ideas into the Taborite movement, those who originally introduced the heresy, "in a kind of sudden storm," were "the most faithless Pikarts, immigrants." [76]

At this point, then, the inquiry must direct itself across Europe, to "Gallia Belgica." And indeed this general area provides us with a splendid example of just the kind of heretical complex we have been discussing.[77] In 1411 the famous Pierre D'Ailly, Bishop of Cambrai, presided over an inquisitional process concerned with a Brussels sect known—to its members—as the "Homines intelligencie." [78] The resulting list of heretical articles emphasizes sex in the first place and in extremely interesting detail: it is clear that the "Homines intelligencie" and the Bohemian Adamites were enjoying pretty much the same thing in the same ways. Another Brussels doctrine, "that God is everywhere—in stores, in men's limbs, even in Hell—just as He is in the sacrament of the altar, and therefore any man has God perfectly even before he takes communion," clearly points to the common basis of both Adamistism and eucharistic heresy. But in a subordinate position in the list is still another set of ideas similar in content and even language to the ideas of Taborite chiliasm.[79] The Brussels articles, however, point clearly to the ultimate *source* of these ideas: the "Joachimite" construction of history in the sectarian form given it by the sects of the "Free Spirit." [80] Thus we read that "whatever idea came to them or suggested itself, they thought it had come from the Holy Spirit." They believed in the "end of the present law" and the beginning of the "law of the Holy Spirit and of spiritual freedom"— ideas that animated the new Taborite society that has been traced out above. With the Brussels heretics, however, these revolutionary principles could be realized only in individual behavior of a sort consonant with the sect's underground existence. Their sexual liberty was the only positive freedom that the poor could enjoy.[81]

Two qualifications, however, must be made in the above account. Although the Prague sources credit the Pikart immigrants of 1418 with introducing the heresy into Bohemia, it is also possible that there were other pathways of Free Spirit influence—particularly through contact with Catharo-Waldensian sects active generally in central Europe, including South Bohemia.[82] And in any case the Taborite chiliasts presented the Free-Spirit ideology in a form determined partly by their unique social situation, partly by their general Hussite background. The former modification needs no further discussion; in regard to the latter it is clear from the sources that the Taborites spoke only of a new advent of *Christ,* the Kingdom of *Christ,* or even the Kingdom of the Father, but never explicitly the Kingdom of the Holy Spirit. But there is no difficulty, since we read that "all in this coming are to have the Holy Spirit fully," [83] that "an abundance of the Holy Spirit will come into the hearts of the faithful," [84] that the elect "will be baptised in the Holy Spirit." [85] And Martin, the leading chiliast, wrote that "Christ is the Holy Spirit, about whom it is said in the Bible: 'And I shall give you another comforter'; that is, really himself, but different and spiritual. And so now . . . Christ is giving himself spiritually and he is with us to the end of the world . . ." [86] It is as though Martin were himself trying to demonstrate the possibility of expressing Free-Spirit doctrine within the conceptual framework of a less radical tradition.

* * * * *

Returning now to the Taborite communities, we can understand their revolutionary significance with precision. If a revolution is defined as the sudden substitution of one social and intellectual world for another, it is clear that Tabor was the first revolutionary society in Europe. The peasant or artisan who abandoned his land or sold his property, who burnt his home and left his friends and family, and who then made his way to chiliast Písek or chiliast Tabor, was truly passing from one world into another, in which neither the first principles nor the practical arrangements of the old order had validity. *In actual fact,* the Joachimite-Free-Spirit vision of the chiliast prophets, who included almost all the Taborite priests in 1420, had set the Taborites free from the feudal order. They could now build their own society.

As soon as they began to do so, however, they inevitably developed counterbalances to the chiliast influence. The standing army could support itself by plunder, and to an extent did so,[87] but in the long run it had to be based on a more certain socio-economic foundation. Thus alongside the common chests and the plundering raids there was built up a regular seigneurial relationship between Tabor as overlord and the peasants and villages under her sway.[88] (Eventually the common chests seem to have become simply the means by which Tabor supported her clergy.[89]) A system of crafts was also developed, so that Tabor soon became a "Gewerbestadt," economically similar to most of the royal towns of Bohemia,[90] except that the old guild monopolies were broken, at least in the beginning.[91] And the priests of Tabor, having done their work of fanatical chiliast preaching, had to turn their attention to the more ordinary aspects of religious practice; in September 1420 they elected a "bishop," Nicholas of Pelhřimov, who was to regulate preaching, supervise the clergy, and administer the common funds "according to the need of each brother." [92] He also addressed himself to the task of developing a systematic Taborite religion to transcend the negative or impractically perfectionist sectarianism of earlier days.[93] A Prague B. A., Nicholas, used his grasp of scholasticism to compose a body of doctrinal literature second to none in Hussite Bohemia.[94] The religio-social organism that he thus helped to create was the first reformed society in Europe.

Of great help in this general consolidation of Tabor was the renewal of the Prague connection. After Sigismund had had the anti-Hussite crusade openly proclaimed, on March 17, 1420, Prague had to reverse her policy of collaboration.[95] She summoned all good Czechs to help defend their country, and at the end of May the Taborites set out en masse for the capital. Collaboration in the *national* war, the discipline necessary to allow Taborites and Praguers to live in the same city for several months, and the accommodation of doctrine demanded by the formulation of a common Hussite program—the Four Articles of Prague [96]—all these combined to stabilize the Taborite mind.

By the end of 1420, when the Prague masters read off their list of seventy-two "heretical" articles, including the whole of chiliast doctrine as well as Pikartism, the leading Taborites paid only lip service to these ideas. Žižka was totally silent, and Nicholas of Pelhřimov, while stating his adherence to the articles of the list—except for "what was venomous in them"—took the first opportunity to shift the discussion to the wholly non-chiliast subject of mass-ritual.[97] Only Martin Húska among the priests spoke up with any vigor. And two months later Nicholas and the Taborite Master John of Jičín actually denounced Martin and the Pikarts to the Prague masters and asked the latter for help.[98] Then the Taborite leaders expelled the Pikarts from the city, and the Taborite armies, in cooperation with Prague, slaughtered both Pikarts and Adamites by the hundreds. With the cruel burning of Martin himself, on August 21, 1421, the Free-Spirit phase of Taboritism was officially ended, although chiliast tendencies evidently persisted among some Taborites well into the 1420's. It was not until 1422 and even later that the chiliast doctrine of total war was formally replaced by regulations drawn from Prague's scholastic doctrine,[99] and the blood-and-thunder Bible-preaching of the chiliast-minded priests was explicitly superseded by the principle that nothing might be preached which contradicted the life and teachings of Jesus and the Apostles.[100]

In the mid-twenties a leading Taborite, perhaps Nicholas of Pelhřimov, wrote: [101]

We do not consider as true that story which some tell, that a good age is coming, in which there will be no evil doers, and that they will not suffer at all but will be filled with ineffable joy.

Thus Martin Húska's moving declaration to Chelčický, that "if Christians were always to have to suffer so, I would not want to be a servant of God," was relegated to the Taborite attic of outmoded ideas. We know, of course, that it was precisely that "story" that had led the radical Hussite masses to give up their old life and join the new Taborite communities in the winter of 1419–1420. And we know that the chiliast ideology of unlimited war against the old world had transformed south Bohemia from a Catholic hunting-ground into a Hussite bastion, nourishing perhaps the most vital elements of the Bohemian reformation. But it was the heroic virtue of men like Nicholas of Pelhřimov and the other leading Taborite priests that they were able to sense the point at which the beautiful story had exhausted its constructive power, break with their chiliast past, and devote themselves to the much more difficult tasks of hard thinking and political action required to make the Taborite vision work. Here as always in the radical movement, intellectual nourishment was drawn from the Prague University, even while spiritual vitality was provided by the generations-old tradition of popular heresy.

NOTES

1 The following introduction is based on the author's "Hussite Radicalism and the Origins of Tabor. 1415–1418," *Medievalia et Humanistica*, X (1956), 102ff, and on an unpublished study of the events of 1419. The general background and sequence of events of the period covered by the present paper can be studied in F. Heymann's *Žižka and the Hussite Revolution* (Princeton: Princeton University Press, 1955)—hereafter cited as "Heymann."

2 The sectarian ideas amounted to the rejection of all doctrines and rites not stipulated as necessary by the New Testament. Rejected were, specifically, the cult of saints, holy images, the complexities and lavishness of mass-ritual, the doctrine of Purgatory and the consequent works for the dead, the doctrinal and ecclesiastical authority of the holding of property or regular reception of income, in any form, by the clergy. The sacramental acts of sinful priests were regarded as invalid.

3 The mountain is not so named in the Bible but only in a tradition dating from the fourth century. Cf. the sermon on Matt. xxviii, 16, preached by the Prague radical John Želivský on 21 April 1419 [ed. A. Molnár, *Jan Želivský. Dochovaná kázání z roku 1419*, I (Prague: Czechoslovakian Academy, 1953), 43]. Aeneas Sylvius, *Historia Bohemica* (Helmstadt: J. Sustermann, 1699), ch. xl, also cites the tradition as the source of Tabor's name. Cf. also Judges iv, 6ff.

4 Master Laurence of Březová, "Hussite Chronicle" (in Latin), ed. J. Goll, *Fontes rerum Bohemicarum*, V (Prague, 1893), 351f. (this work hereafter cited as "Laurence of Březová"). Laurence's chronicle is extremely reliable and is the basic narrative source for the period under discussion.

5 See Heymann, p. 105ff.

6 Laurence of Březová, p. 357 (an entry for January–February 1420).

7 On 10 February 1420 Sigismund named Plzeň, Písek, and Hradec Králové as centers of Wyclyfite resistance (*Urkundliche Beiträge zur Geschichte des Hussitenkriegs*, I, ed. F. Palacký (Prague: Tempský, 1873), 15–17). The name of Klatovy, near Plzeň, is added in an anonymous news report (*ibid.*, p. 24). Cf. also the source presented by A. Bernt, "Ein deutsches Hussiten-paternoster aus dem Stifte Hohenfurt," *Mitteilungen des Vereins für Geschichte der Deutschen in Böhmen*, XXXIX (1901), 320, which names Žatec as a center of resistance. The chiliasts at one point urged people to flee to Žatec, Louny, and Slaný (see note 9 below); these towns *may* therefore have maintained resistance during the whole period after the November truce.

8 P. 355f. The second paragraph obviously recapitulates and amplifies the first, and may therefore have been a later insertion. Laurence's dating is confirmed beyond reasonable doubt by the fact that the only exactly dated source for the early phase of the chiliast movement, an anti-chiliast letter, was written on 22 January [ed. F. M. Bartoš, "Z dějin chiliasmu r. 1420," *Do čtyř pražských artykulů* (Prague, 1925), p. 97].

[9] The idea that five cities would endure through the Day of Wrath was based on Isaiah xix, 18. No chiliast text we know names five Bohemian cities, and we know indeed that at first the cities were not named: the resultant confusion in the minds of the faithful was noted in a rescript issued by the Prague masters Jakoubek of Stříbro and Christian of Prachatice, probably written sometime in January 1420 (ed. J. Goll, *Quellen und Untersuchungen zur Geschichte der Böhmischen Brüder*, II (Prague: Otto, 1882), 52–53 (hereafter cited as "Goll"). The naming of the cities, presumably all pro-chiliast, cannot have been in vogue after Plzeň's surrender to the royalists, on 20 March 1420. On the other hand, the omission of Písek, an important Taborite city, suggests that the list had only a secondary significance.

[10] Ed. Z. Nejedlý, *Dějiny husitského zpěvu za válek husitských* (Prague, 1913), p. 800f. (in Czech). Nejedlý associates it with the early congregations, in the spring and summer of 1419 (p. 198), but on the basis of content, and in my reconstruction of Taborite history the content fits early 1420 much better.

[11] Ed. F. Palacký, *Archiv český*, VI (Prague, 1872), 43f. (in Czech).

[12] Jakoubek, writing at about this time, noted that "unus spiritus prophetat, quod rex Babilonis id est rex Ungarie . . . destruet Babilonem id est Pragam" (Goll, II, 58); later, however, the chiliasts preached "quod iam nunc in hoc anno ulcionis Pragensis civitas velut Babilon debet destrui et comburi per fideles" (Laurence of Březová, p. 455). Cf. also Master John Příbram's *Život kněží táborských* ("The Story of the Taborite Priests"), ed. J. Macek, *Ktož jsú boží bojovníci* (Prague: Melantrich, 1951), p. 263 henceforth cited as "Život"). In his Czech commentary on the Apocalyse [ed. F. Šimek, *Jakoubek ze Stříbra: Výklad no Zjevenie Sv. Jana*, I (Prague, 1932), p. 528], Jakoubek noted that the "blasphemous cry" was raised in Prague: "Flee quickly from Prague—only on the mountains is there salvation and liberation;" elsewhere he accused the Taborite Master John of Jičín of having written to the Praguers, especially to the women, urging them to leave the city (Goll, II, 60). The biblical idea of fleeing Babylon and taking refuge on the mountains was not new to the Bohemian reformers of all parties, but it had previously been understood symbolically.

[13] Taken respectively from the rescript of Jakoubek and Christian of Prachatice, Goll, II, 51–53; a letter from Jakoubek to an unnamed non-chiliast priest, Goll, II, 57–59; this letter again; a University rescript of February 17, 1420, ed. F. M. Bartoš, "Z dějin chiliasmu," pp. 97–100. All in Latin.

[14] Ed. F. Palacký, *Archiv český*, VI, 41–43 (in Czech); I have emphasized key points.

[15] The quote seems to come from Jakoubek's letter, Goll, II, 58.

[16] Goll, II, 60; the letter notes that the chiliasts had set a day between February 10 and 14 for the coming Day of Wrath. Master John Příbram compared the Taborite switch from pacifism to violence with the haphazard flight of grasshoppers (*De ritibus missae, apud* K. Höfler, *Geschichtschreiber der husitischen Bewegung in Böhmen*, II, *Fontes rerum Austriacarum*, I. Abt., Bd. VI (1865), 531–hereafter cited as "Höfler").

[17] Petr Chelčický, *O boji duchovním*, ed. K. Krofta (Prague: Otto, 1911), p. 27f. See M. Spinka, "Peter Chelčický, the Spiritual Father of the Unitas Fratrum," *Church History*, XII (1943), 271–291; Spinka regards it as almost certain that Chelčický was influenced by the Waldenses (p. 274).

[18] See his *O trojím lidu* ("On the Triple Division of Society"), ed. Krofta, *op. cit.*, p. 155ff. and *passim*.

[19] The evidence, some of which has already been noted, consists of the letters and rescripts addressed by the Prague masters to those who had asked their advice. The surviving letters were probably all written by Master Jakoubek; they include: (1) a letter to non-chiliast priests in general, January 22, 1420 (ed. F. Bartoš, "Z dějin chiliasmu," p. 97); (2) a letter to an anonymous non-chiliast priest (Goll, II, 57–59); (3) a letter to the chiliast Master John of Jičín (Goll, II, 59–60).

Of the rescripts two survive. In one case two priests, a Nicholas and a Wenceslas, had disputed the points summarized in the text below and had agreed, "before a large number of people" to abide by the decision of the masters Jakoubek of Stříbro and Christian of Prachatice, which decision survives (Goll, II, 51–53). The other rescript, anonymous but dated February 17, 1420, is addressed to a "nobilis Domine, zelator legis Christi precipue" and answers the questions whether the faithful might congregate and whether the "secular estates" might fight for the Hussite cause (ed. Bartoš, "Z dějin chiliasmu," pp. 97–100). On the assumption that the rescripts were addressed to Taborites, scholars have tried to identify Nicholas and Wenceslas and the noble lord; I believe the assumption to be flimsy and the identities of the recipients immovably lodged in obscurity (but cf. Heymann, p. 89). The quotes that follow are drawn chiefly from the first rescript.

20 Goll, II, 52–53.

21 The rescript of February 17, ed. Bartoš, *op. cit.*, p. 99.

22 Of the four chiliast priests named as most prominent by Laurence of Březová, two, Koranda and Markolt, are known to have been in Plzeň (see p. 59 above).

23 *Život*, p. 266. Cf. also p. 275f.

24 *Staří letopisové češti* ("Old Czech Annalists"), ed. F. Palacký, *Scriptores rerum Bohemicarum*, III (Prague, 1829), 29–30 (henceforth cited as "*OCA*").

25 The main body of the local Taborites captured Ústí on February 21, 1420 (see below), and had presumably been expelled some time before that date; a turbulent history of mutual expulsions by the various parties in Ústí is suggested by one source, *OCA*, p. 471f., which is unfortunately telescoped and hence not clear. See Heymann, p. 87.

26 For Písek radicalism in 1416 see J. Macek, *Tábor v husitkém revolučnim hnuti*, I (Prague: Czechoslovakian Academy, 1952), 216. Laurence of Březová, p. 347, tells of the destruction of the Dominican monastery there by the Hussites on August 20, 1419. A special study of the "Beginnings of Taboritism in Písek" has been published by J. Macek ["K počátkūm táborství v Písku," *Jihočesky sborník historický*, XX (1953), 113ff.] but is unavailable in this country; some at least of its main contributions are included in Macek's books on Tabor, which I have used and cited.

27 Jakoubek argued that salvation was not to be expected on the basis merely of a man's being in Plzeň or Písek rather than in Prague (Goll, II, 58).

28 See note 7 above.

29 *Život*, p. 264f.

30 This difficult passage reads in the original, ". . . a tomu zběhlému lidu k sobě na hory v městě Piesetským kázali a ustavili. . . ."

31 Louda had taken minor orders, studied at the Prague University, and been a notary. In the Hussite revolution, however, he emerged as a political leader [see Macek, *Tábor v husitkém revolučnim hnuti*, II (Prague: Czechoslovakian Academy, 1955), 78f]. It has been argued that Louda was with Žižka in Plzeň [F. M. Bartoš introduction to *Staré letopisy české z Vratislavského rukopisu*, ed. F. Šimek (Prague, 1937), p. vii], but the argument seems to me to be based on too many combinations to be cogent.

32 Although not attested for Písek, this principle governed the administration of the common chests later set up at Tabor: Laurence of Březová, pp. 381, 438.

33 Macek, *Tábor* . . . , II, 237.

34 *Ibid.*, 145.

35 Goll, II, 60.

36 See above note 16. According to Aeneas Sylvius, *op. cit.*, the day had been fixed at Pentecost. I agree with Macek, *Tábor* . . . , II, 54, that no great significance is to be attached to such particular dates, which were probably furnished by individual preachers *ad hoc*.

37 Laurence of Březová, p. 357f.; *OCA*, p. 33.

38 *Chronicon veteris collegiati Pragensis*, Höfler, I, *FRA*, I. Abt., II (1856), 79.

39 *OCA*, p. 34; cf. Macek, *Tábor* . . . , II, 76, n. 130.

40 See Laurence of Březová, pp. 358, 370; *Chron. vet. colleg. Prag.*, *loc. cit.*

41 We know that in the course of 1420 the chests existed in Písek, Tabor, and Vodňany (*Staré letopisy české*, ed. Šimek, p. 28). See also Laurence of Březová, pp. 381, 438.

42 Laurence of Březová, p. 362.

43 Macek, *Tábor* . . . , II, 136ff., offers by far the best reconstruction and analysis to date of Tabor's wars in south Bohemia and their relation to chiliasm.

44 Both Žižka and the future Taborite Bishop Nicholas of Pelhřimov, the two strongest forces leading Tabor towards order and national political action, chose Písek as their base. See Macek, *Tábor* . . . , II, 238 and *passim.* Macek assimilates the Písek-Tabor polarization to the split between the "bourgeois opposition" (a wholly inaccurate Marxist cliché, meaning in the present context anyone who was interested in property) and "the poor."

45 *Život,* pp. 265–267.

46 A third surviving chiliast letter seems to show this penetration of adventism with the chiliast vision (ed. F. M. Bartoš, "Z dějin chiliasmu," pp. 96–97):

. . . the sun will blaze, the clouds will disappear, the darknesses will vanish, blood will flow from wood, and He will reign who is not expected by those living on the earth. . . . Therefore let us be ready. . . . And who is ready? Only he who remains in Christ and Christ in him. And he is in Christ who eats him. But to eat Christ's Body is livingly to believe in him. And to drink his Blood is to shed it with him for his Father. And he takes Christ's Body who disseminates his gifts, and he eats his Body who livingly listens to his Word. . . . And for this eating the just will shine like the sun in the kingdom of their Father, when he comes in clouds with his glory and great power, and sends as representatives his glorious angels to sweep out all scandals from his inheritance. And then evil will be abashed, lies will perish, injustice will disappear, every sin will vanish, and faith will flower, justice will grow, paradise will open to us, benevolence will be multiplied, and perfect love will be abundant. . . .

I write these things to you as to adults, able to eat of all foods, and not as to those living on milk. . . . I admonish you in the name of God to make this letter known to the whole community.

Bartoš dates this letter at the very beginning of the movement, in early January 1420, presumably because of its vagueness. But it is obviously *advanced* in comparison to the other two letters, and gives a picture of the future Age that none of the early adventist preaching seems to have given. If the letter *did* originate in January, then it would lead us to interpret even the early adventist preaching as inspired—perhaps at one or more removes—by somebody's clear picture of the millennium.

47 The text has been preserved by Laurence of Březová, pp. 417–424. Only one other Latin chiliast tractate is known to survive, and it is more diffuse and practical than this one (ed. Bartoš, "Z dějin chiliasmu," pp. 102–111).

48 Laurence of Březová, p. 456; K. Krofta, "O některých spisech M. Jana z Příbrama," *Časopis českého Musea,* LXXIII (1899), 213.

49 Laurence of Březová, p. 418.

50 *Život,* pp. 268, 269, 282. Like most important Taborite priests, Capek had a University background. He seems to have been associated with the reform movement even in Hus' time (*Urkundliche Beiträge,* II (1873), 521f.), and he was later reminded by John Příbram that he had held orthodox views on the eucharist in 1417 (*Život,* p. 303). He was a prolific song-writer, and one of the songs definitely his ("Ve jméno božie počněme," c. 1417, ed. Nejedlý, *op. cit.,* p. 805ff.) shows a spirit and body of thought very much like Jakoubek's—limiting the cult of saints, for example, but not demanding its abolition; etc. It is instructive to note how the chiliast fever could take possession of such a man.

51 *Život,* pp. 268–270.

52 These conditions appear in Aquinas' *Summa theologica,* II, ii, 40, and in Wyclif's *De civili dominio,* ed. Loserth, II (London, 1900), p. 240ff. N. Jastrebov, *Etjudy o Petře Chelčickom i jego vremeni* (St. Petersburg, 1908), p. 92ff., shows, with parallel citations, that the masters were following Wyclyf. On the general subject of Hussite attitudes to war, particularly in the tractates and discussions of early 1420, cf. K. Hoch, "Husité a válka" *Česká mysl,* VIII (1907), 131ff., and Jastrebov, *op. cit.,* p. 33ff.

53 *Život,* p. 267.

54 The list is of the greatest importance, since it preserves Taborite ideas not otherwise attested by the sources; its authenticity is proven by the following facts: (1) the articles seem to preserve the Taborite formulations of the original texts, (2) many of the articles are to be found in surviving Taborite sources, and these in no case contradict the articles of the list, (3) the Taborite leaders themselves accepted one version of the list as substantially true, although venomously formulated in some cases (Laurence of Březová, p. 462f.). The surviving texts may be grouped as follows:

I. 1. A Czech version, ed. Palacký, *Archir česky*. III (1844), 218ff., and ed., with corrections, by J. Macek, *Ktož jsu boži bojounici*, pp. 57–66 (I cite from Macek). The MS was part of the Třebon archives of the Rožmberk family, Tabor's neighbors and greatest enemies in South Bohemia.

2. A Latin version used by Laurence of Březová, pp. 403–405, 413–416, in a systematic discussion of Tabor inserted into the course of his chronicle *ad* August 1420.

II. A Latin version read by the Prague masters at a discussion with the Taborites, in Prague, December 10, 1420 (Laurence of Březová, pp. 453–462).

III. A Latin version given by John Příbram in his *Contra errores Picardorum* [cf. F. M. Bartoš' catalogue of Příbram's works, *Literárná činnost M. Jana Rokycany, M. Jana Příbrama, M. Petra Payna* (Prague: Czech Academy, 1928), p. 64, No. 5]. It has been published by (1) J. Döllinger, *Beiträge sur Sektengeschichte des Mittelalters*, II (Munich, 1890), 691–700, and (2) F. Prochazka, *Miscellaneen der Bömische und Mährische Litteratur* (Prague, 1784), 279–293.

IV. A Czech version, evidently based on II (*via* III) but very much reworked and adding important historical and circumstantial information, in John Příbram's *Život*, p. 263ff.

Text III differs from II mainly in the arrangement of the articles; there are also some additions. I, 2 seems to be a reworking of I, 1 (or its equivalent). Thus there are basically *two* redactions known, I, 1 and II; of these II is *obviously* further away from the original Taborite sources, although possibly preserving a few elements of them not in I, 1. The purpose of I, 1 seems to have simply been to collect the articles; the purpose of II was to make clear their heretical meaning: the articles of II, as opposed to I, 1 are systematized, arranged in logical sequence, and stripped of circumstantial elements. See note 62 below.

All of the lists contain both chiliast and non-chiliast articles, the latter for the most part Waldensianist. This fact has led some scholars to regard the chiliast and Waldensianist complexes as related. Since the Waldensianist articles are attested as radical beliefs as early as 1415—and notably in the very south Bohemian area where chiliasm flourished and Tabor was founded—it has been supposed that chiliast ideas also were in vogue at that date. Thus, e.g., Heymann, p. 59, in a discussion of pre-1419 radicalism, says that "they were chiliasts." And J. Macek, who regards all the sectarian articles as part of the ideology of "the poor," expressing the poor's social aspiration and attitudes to the feudal order, does not attempt to separate out the varying parts of this ideology (cf. e.g. *Tábor* . . . , II, 89ff.). Against these loose treatments *it must be insisted* that the Waldensianist and chiliast complexes were distinct, even though co-existing in 1420 among the Taborites and, undoubtedly, in the minds of many individual Taborites. My arguments are as follows:

1. The datable sources show Waldensianist ideas among the provincial radicals as early as 1415 and up through 1418, but they do not speak of chiliasm before January 1420.

2. The Waldensianist and chiliast complexes, although alike in expressing the sectarian mind, stemmed from different orientations of that mind. See for example Chelčický's striking criticism of Martin Húska, p. 30 below. Or compare the following articles, *both* from the list in question:

[Waldensianist:]
Christians should not hold or believe anything that is not explicitly stated and written in the Bible.

[Chiliast:]
In that time [of Christ's Kingdom] . . . no one will teach anything to anyone,

nor will there be any need of books or Bibles, for the Law of God will be written in the heart of everyone. . . .
Other equally striking contradictions could be given.

3. Laurence of Březová, who did not simply give the list but used it to compose a picture of Tabor in 1420, separated the two complexes.

My reconstruction, based on the above and other evidence, is this: The basic and original *sectarian* inspiration (there were other inspirations too) of Hussite radicalism and Taboritism was Waldensianism, the ideas and attitudes of which entered the Hussite movement in 1415, if not earlier, and, fused with the scholastic mind, formed the basis of Taborite religion throughout Tabor's separate history—i.e., until 1452. For a brief time, however, the Free Spirit complex of chiliasm (see below) surged to the fore and dominated the Taborite movement, politically and doctrinally, until the latter part of 1420, when representatives of the Waldensianist-scholastic fusion progressively liberated themselves and the Taborites from Free-Spirit ideas. The latter, losing their political scope, took on more and more narrowly sectarian forms, specifically Pikartism and Adamitism (see below), the adherents of which were driven out of Tabor and exterminated in the course of 1421. By the time the Prague masters read their list, on December 10, 1420, the chiliasts had been, so to speak, bypassed as influences on the development of the Taborite organism; although no Taborites disowned the chiliast or Pikart articles of the list at the meeting, no Taborite defense of them was ever offered, and their foremost exponent, Martin Húska (see below) was almost at once imprisoned by one of Tabor's allies.

55 Macek, *Ktož jsú boží bojovníci*, pp. 58–60.
56 Laurence of Březová, p. 455.
57 *Ibid.,* p. 454; Macek, *Ktož jsú boží bojovníci*, p. 58. It is important that these bloodthirsty doctrines also appear in a *chiliast* source, the Latin tractate published by Bartoš, "Z dějin chiliasmu," p. 111: "the just . . . will now rejoice, seeing vengeance and washing their hands in the blood of the sinners."
58 *Apud* Nejedlý, *op. cit.,* p. 183 n. 40.
59 Laurence of Březová, p. 424.
60 J. Macek, *Ktož jsú boží bojovníci*, p. 60. Cf. Jakoubek of Stříbro, *Výklad*, ed. Šimek, p. lxxxvii. The chiliasts thought that Christ had already come secretly.
61 Jakoubek, *Výklad*, ed. Šimek, p. 527.
62 The chiliast tractate in Latin ed. Bartoš, "Z dějin chiliasmu," p. 110f., explains that at least some of the sacraments, especially the eucharist, will remain, but in a new form, as memorials of Christ's victory rather than his passion. The author is not sure about the others because "even now certain ones are not kept"—an evident reference to the basic Waldensianism of the Taborite movement. The Czech redaction of the list of Taborite articles, Macek, *Ktož jsú boží bojovníci*, p. 61, makes exactly the same point, but explains more precisely that the need for the old sacraments will not exist because there will be no sin in the New Age. But the Prague text, in Laurence of Březová, p. 460, says only that the Taborites believed the sacraments would not last until Christ's final coming. It is obvious that this text was formulated *ad usum inquisitionis.*
63 Macek, *Ktož jsú boží bojovníci*, p. 60.
64 *Ibid.,* p. 61.
65 *OCA,* p. 478. Macek, *Tábor . . . ,* II, 62 supposes that only work for the lords was to be stopped, but on p. 367 he interprets the source literally, evidently oblivious of his earlier improvement on it.
66 Macek, *Ktož jsú boží bojovníci*, p. 59.
67 See Příbram's testimony, above, p. 55. Cf. Laurence of Březová, p. 423f. And cf. J. Pekař, *Žižka a jeho doba,* I (Prague: Vesmír, 1927), 181f.
68 This is the main weakness that I find in J. Macek's Marxist interpretation, *Tábor . . . ,* II. Without in the least denying the correlation between the point of view of the medieval "poor" and chiliast ideology, I feel that the proper use of this insight is as a means of analysis and understanding, not as an *a priori* determination of essence. For the rest, much of Macek's brilliant work can be wholly accepted, but in reverse: for example, chiliasm was certainly not atheistic, as he says (p. 118), but

Marxism may well be called chiliastic; thus the effort to interpret chiliasm as a kind of forerunner of Marxism *can* lead to valid judgments.

[69] P. 413. Markold and Koranda were among the Plzeň Taborites; John of Jičín was probably active in south Bohemia, perhaps at Písek (cf. *OCA*, p. 471f.). Martin's pre-eminence is attested by Příbram, *Život*, pp. 290, 294.

[70] *Apud* Macek, *Tábor* . . . , II, 73.

[71] P. 431.

[72] Aeneas Sylvius, *Historia Bohemica*, ch. xli.

[73] Cf. R. Holinka, "Počátky táborského pikartství," *Bratislava*, VI (1932), 191.

[74] Laurence tells of the Czech disciples, p. 431; cf. p. 494 for the later strength of Pikartism in Prague.

[75] Laurence of Březová, pp. 517–519 (a letter from Žižka to Prague, describing Adamite practices). Cf. *OCA*, p. 476ff; Aeneas Sylvius, *op. cit.*

[76] J. Příbram, *Contra errores Picardorum, apud* K. Krofta, "O některých spisech M. Jana Příbrama," *Časopis českého Musea*, LXXIII (1899), 212.

[77] The relationship of heresy in north France and Belgium to Hussite Bohemia has been brilliantly explored by F. M. Bartoš, "Picardi a Pikarti," *Časopis českého Musea*, CI (1927), 225–250. He concludes (pp. 227, 229) that the Picards of 1418 had come from Lille and Tournai, fleeing an inquisition of that year.

[78] The record of the process is published in P. Fredericq, *Corpus documentorum inquisitionis haereticae pravitatis Neerlandicae*, I (Ghent: J. Vuylsteke, 1889) 269ff.

[79] The comparison has been made by R. Holinka, *Sektářství v Čechách před revolucí husitskou*, Sborník Filosofické Fakulty University Komenského v Bratislavě, VI (1929), 169–170. He infers not a direct derivation (see note 77 above) but an absolute agreement in substance.

[80] I follow Holinka, *Sektářství*, p. 171, in regarding the Brussels sect's fusion of Joachimite and Free-Spirit motifs as also the essential characteristic of chiliasm. (But cf. Heymann, pp. 210ff., 258ff.: the chiliast element seems to be ignored.) On Joachim of Floris and the (Pseudo-) Joachimite tradition, see H. Grundmann, *Studien über Joachim von Floris, Beiträge zur Kulturgeschichte des Mittelalters und der Renaissance*, XXXII (Leipzig: Teubner, 1927). For the Joachimitism of the Brussels sect, see p. 182 n.1. In characterizing Taborite chiliasm as basically the same as the Brussels heresy I am guided by Grundmann's formulation, p. 115.

[81] There were certain *negative* liberties: e.g., the leader of the sect walked naked through the streets one day. It is interesting that the Bohemian Adamites also practiced nudism.

[82] So J. Sedlák, *Taborské traktáty eucharistické* (Brno, 1918), introduction, and Holinka, "Počátky táborského pikartství," p. 195. There is indeed one explicit statement that ideas of the chiliast movement were derived from 14th century German heretics active around Jindřichův Hradec (Neuhaus) in south Bohemia: *Staré letopisy české*, ed. Šimek, p. 29. This area was in fact a seat of popular Waldensienism [cf. V. Chaloupecký, "K dějinám Valdenských v Cechách před hnutím husitským," *Český časopis historický*, XXXI (1925), 376]. And various central European Waldensian groups at this time did actually cultivate millenarian expectations (see the text in Döllinger, *op. cit.*, II, 363f.). Even the occasional physical violence of some of these groups may help explain the passage from Waldensianism to chiliasm at Tabor: cf. W. Preger, "Ueber das Verhältnis der Taboriten zu den Waldensiern des 14. Jahrhunderts," *Abhandlungen der königliche Bayrische Akademie der Wissenschaften*, Hist. Cl., XVIII (1889), 100f; and cf. Döllinger, *op. cit.*, II, 305.

[83] Jakoubek, *Výklad*, ed. Šimek, p. 527.

[84] *Staré letopisy české*, ed. Šimek, p. 28.

[85] Laurence of Březová, p. 416.

[86] *Život*, p. 291.

[87] The division of booty is attested by, e.g., Laurence of Březová, p. 381. Strict chiliast doctrine would demand the total destruction of all property, and this was often done after military victories. But there were innumerable petty raids that drew on local peasants, etc. for food and drink; the confessions tortured from those raiders

captured by the Rožmmberks are preserved in the *Popravčí Kniba pánův z Rožmberka*, ed. F. Mareš (Prague, 1878).

88 Laurence of Březová's chronicle contains a note, p. 438, to the effect that although the chiliasts had preached in the summer that all seigneurial dues would cease, Tabor nevertheless collected the usual dues from "her" peasants on St. Gall's Day (October 14) 1420, the regular day of collection. J. Macek, *Tábor* . . . , II, 295–298, argues that the villages later to be parts of Tabor's domains were demonstrably under rule of other lords through 1420 and in some cases later; therefore Tabor cannot have collected from them. But the argument seems to me mechanical: a Taborite force could easily have received collections from a village that also had to pay to another lord. We *know* that such cases did exist; a Taborite synod of 1422 decreed that exactions should be avoided ". . . ubi villani fideles veritati adhaerentes coguntur parti adversae censum solvere . . ." (Höfler, II, 485)—the context makes it plain that this practice had gone on. Cf. also Příbram's testimony, *Život*, p. 266, that the peasants were paying five or six rents under Tabor.

89 Aeneas Sylvius Piccolomini visited Tabor in 1451 and described the system in a letter to Cardinal Carvajal [ed. R. Wolkan, *Fontes rerum Austriacarum*, II. Abt., LXVIII (1918), 25].

90 Macek, *Tábor* . . . , I, 345ff.

91 Cf. Macek, *Tábor* . . . , II, 77 (*re* the Taborite city of Vodňany). Tabor was a new settlement and had no monopolies to begin with.

92 Laurence of Březová, p. 438.

93 Of Free-Spirit ideas only Pikart eucharistic doctrine left its mark on later Taborite doctrine, which however did not deny a kind of Real Presence—in the form of an infusion of Grace as the worthy communicant took the sacrament.

94 His greatest work was the *Chronicon causam sacerdotum Taboriensium continens*, Höfler, II, 475–820, a majestic collection of tractates and other works, many of them Nicholas' own, arranged to document the Prague-Tabor disputations that lasted from 1420 to 1444.

95 See Heymann, p. 105ff.

96 The draft was produced by discussions of all the Hussites in Prague on March 27, 1420, but the first three had already been proclaimed a month before by Prague and the Hussite barons. Thus the provincial radicals were in effect adhering to the Prague program and putting their own into the background. Very briefly, the Four Articles demanded: (1) free preaching of the Word of God, (2) utraquist communion, (3) the removal of civil ownership or dominion from the clergy, (4) the punishment of all public mortal sins. See F. M. Bartoš, "Vznik pražských artikulů," *Do čtyř praůských artykulž* (Prague, 1925), pp. 70–73: even the last article may have preceded the May meetings.

97 See Heymann's account, p. 192ff. What the Prague masters wanted primarily was to force the argument of chiliast ideas before the University community, the latter being the supreme Hussite arbiter of doctrine. Cf. Jakoubek's request that John of Jičín do just that, in January 1420, Goll, II, 60.

98 Laurence of Březová, p. 474f.

99 Höfler, II, 482ff; cf. Hoch, *op. cit.*, p. 377, Jastrebov, *op. cit.*, p. 103ff.

100 Höfler, II, 482ff.

101 *Apud* Macek, *Tábor* . . . , II, 354.

BIBLIOGRAPHICAL NOTE

The phenomenon of Taborite chiliasm has been the subject of several scholarly works since the first appearance of this article, in March 1957. The East-German Communist scholar, Ernst Werner, has discussed the Free-Spirit and Adamite elements of Taboritism in the context of related or parallel movements elsewhere in medieval Europe; he disagrees with Josef Macek in regarding this context as significant, and also in being willing to accept the evidence for Adamite orgiastic practices ("Die Nachrichten über die böhmischen 'Adamiten' in religions historischer Sicht," in T. Büttner and E.

Werner, *Circumcellionen und Adamiten* (Berlin: Akademie-Verlag, 1959), pp. 73–141). See also Werner's "Popular Ideologies in Late Medieval Europe: Taborite Chiliasm and Its Antecedents," *Comparative Studies in Society and History,* II (1960), 81–100; also his "Messianische Bewegungen im Mittelalter, II," *Zeitschrift für Geschichtswissenschaft,* X (1962), 598–605. I have taken up these problems in detail in my "K dějinám chiliastického Tábora," *Československý časopis historický,* VIII (1960), 895–904, and my "The Free Spirit in the Hussite Revolution," *Millennial Dreams in Action, Comparative Studies in Society and History,* Supplement II (The Hague, 1962), 166–186. An extraordinarily detailed and profound treatment of all aspects of Taborite chiliasm forms an important part of a recent monograph on Hussite ideology by the Czech Communist scholar Robert Kalivoda, *Husitská ideologie* (Prague, 1961), pp. 287–481, with a German summary on pp. 513–528.

17

Nationality at
the Council of Constance
An Anglo-French Dispute

LOUISE R. LOOMIS

EVERYONE IN THESE DAYS talks of nationalism and views with satisfaction or dismay the spread of the idea of nationality around the globe from Europe to Cathay. A few have the curiosity to wonder when and how this idea first made its appearance in modern Europe but find among the learned no agreed answer as yet to their question. One may recall Luther's appeals to folk consciousness as a force to array Germans against an Italian pope or look back a century earlier to the enthusiasm kindled by Jeanne d'Arc for the deliverance of France from the alien English or discover still earlier traces of discrimination between peoples on ground of differences in blood, manners, language, climate, or political allegiance and call these the beginnings of nationalism.[1]

It is doubtless impossible to name any event of which one may confidently assert that it reveals a modern nation in the very act of emerging into conscious existence, a nation, that is to say, as distinct from an earlier clan, tribe, province, or kingdom. But one may take it as presumptive proof that something at least resembling what we now call nationalism had arrived when one discovers the word "natio" defined in almost a modern sense in the course of an argument at the Council of Constance over the right of one people to rank as a nation in that international assembly. The phenomenon, one would suppose, must even have existed for a considerable time when an old word is interpreted in a new way to give it a name, especially when the phenomenon is not so much a new material creation as a new social complex of attitudes and relationships, marking a new shift in popular interests and loyalties of the sort that comes about slowly and is seldom remarked at once. A few years previously another old word had been given a fresh definition. "Humanitas" and "studia humanitatis" meant in the fourteenth century something different from what they had meant to Cicero or to the twelfth and thirteenth century schools. But the movement for the revival of classical letters was in its third generation before the old word was reinterpreted to furnish it a name.[2]

In the Middle Ages the word "natio", whether in Latin or in one of its vernacular forms, had been used in several senses, each of them simpler than the modern. At times it had merely the old Roman meaning of "gens" or "familia", family, kindred, a group of persons nearly related by blood. Hear the Wife of Bath lamenting:

> Allas! that any of my nacioun
> Sholde evere so foule disparaged be! [3]

In the plural it might take on the more comprehensive sense, in which it had been used by Cicero and St. Jerome, of "gentes", "populi", the indefinite hordes of humankind outside either the Roman state or the Jewish or Christian scheme of salvation. "Salve nos fac Domine Deus noster et congrega nos de nationibus", the Psalmist prayed.[4] Or, in a medieval context, it might denote the countryside in which a man was born, his native region, "patria". "Qui por amor de vos avoie ma terre lessiee et la douçor de ma nacion", protests the king of Sarras to Joseph of Arimathea in a thirteenth century romance of the Holy Grail.[5] Or, finally, it might mean any group of persons connected by bonds of common traits or pursuits, especially if to these were added further ties of common birthplace, language, or habitation.

> Among the gentil nacion
> Love is an occupacion,

sang Gower, with the gentlefolk of all Europe in his mind.[6] Whereas Wyclif was indubitably thinking only of men bred in England when he spoke of "gospels of Crist written in Englische, to moost lernyng of oure nacioun".[7]

The bands of foreign merchants who established themselves for trade in medieval cities and of masters of arts in medieval universities, organized on the basis of the provenance of their members, were called "nations". In both merchant community and university the primary requirement for the erection of a nation seems to have been the presence of enough men from a single locality, speaking the same dialect and addicted to the same habits, to function as a unit for the purpose in view. The relative size or importance of the locality whence they came mattered not at all. The silk merchants of Lucca had their nations in Genoa, Rome, Paris, Bruges, and London.[8] At the University of Paris the nation from the comparatively small home province of the Isle de France counted for as much as the nation that included the masters from all England and Germany. In most universities the number of nations was early fixed by custom at four, and thereafter men from regions without a nation of their own were assigned to membership in that one of the four which seemed geographically most appropriate. Once started, the life of these nations went on under their elected officers, proctors, receptors, beadles, and the like, with little or no more reference, apparently, to the home region, except when it became necessary to draw more clearly the boundary that separated one region from another in order to determine to which of two nations a newcomer at the university belonged.[9] After all, the members were in Paris or Orleans or Toulouse for their own individual advancement, and the nations existed for their convenience and for nothing else.[10]

The nations that presently appeared at ecumenical church councils, however, were from the outset a somewhat different thing.[11] We hear of them first at Lyons in 1274, when Gregory X, in order to drive through, against the resistance of his cardinals, some measures of reform relating especially to the conduct of papal elections, met the archbishops and abbots of the council "by nations" secretly between sessions and at these meetings got their written consent to his proposals. The cardinals retorted by holding meetings of nations too, but quite in vain.[12] At Vienne, in 1311–12, when the business of the Knights Templars was pending, Clement V conferred with certain archbishops whom he had caused to be elected for the purpose from several kingdoms and called for the final votes of the prelates in order of their "nations", Italians first, then Spaniards, Germans, Danes, English, Scotch, Irish, and French.[13] At both councils it seems clear that the pope utilized the deepseated differences that existed between these various groups of clergy to break up the unity that properly should have characterized an ecclesiastical assembly and impose his own will. At Vienne, certainly, the nations were divided along the main regional and political lines of Western Europe, all Italians together, and likewise all Spaniards, all Germans, all Scandinavians, and all Frenchmen. Only the delegates from the small kingdoms of the British Isles, clustering in little groups, amalgamated no further.

At Pisa, in 1409, there was but one nation from the British Isles, and the character and purpose of all the nations were still more altered. Called by the cardinals in the hope of ending the Great Schism and lacking the sanction of either pope or emperor, this council had to justify somehow its assumption of power, and to do so fell back on the theories of Marsiglio of Padua, William of Ockham, and their followers, to wit, that a general council represented the universal church and hence possessed full authority, even without a pope, to act for the good of the church, that it was, in fact, superior to a pope. Under such circumstances it was eminently desirable that the most influential peoples and governments who had sent deputations to its sessions should feel that their views were indeed represented in the conduct of proceedings. As a way to ensure this result, the envoys from Italy, France, Germany, and Britain, of their own accord, began meeting apart, each group by itself, and appointing a spokesman to present their opinions to the council. Robert Hallam, bishop of Salisbury, was the mouthpiece for "the English nation" and Simon de Cramaud, who carried the title of patriarch of Alexandria, for the French and Provençal nation.[14] There were no representatives from Spain, which still remained loyal to the pope at Avignon.

By general consent membership on important commissions was divided among these four nations.[15] They each chose deputies to attend the meetings of the cardinals, who were acting as official heads of the assembly, in order to report back what was said and done there.[16] Still sitting separately, each nation came to its own decision on the questions at issue and voted as a unit when it met the other nations in sessions of the council as a whole.[17] These nations were definitely representative bodies, basing their claim to a voice not on the number or status of the members present at Pisa but on the power and importance of the land whence they came. The English were one of the four nations, although in that gathering of over five hundred there were said to be only fifteen Englishmen.[18]

Five years later the Council of Constance was convened by a pope and an emperor-elect and attended by them both, but there was still schism and discord in Europe and no universally accepted head. Again, therefore, the authority of the council was declared to rest on its representative character, and again the four nations promptly appeared, this time as even more aggressive elements in the situation, with positive wills and policies of their own.[19] When in February, 1415, it was necessary to begin voting on a method to end the schism and Pope John XXIII's host of Italians threatened to outvote all the others, the English and the Germans proposed that each nation should again cast its vote in the sessions as a unit, no count being taken of individuals. The French nation, after some hesitation, concurred. In this way the nations at Constance became, as at Pisa, constituent parts of the council and the council itself distinctly a federation of nations under the sanction of the emperor. For a time even the cardinals were forbidden to act or vote as a college and were instructed to join their nations. The nations were formally organized, each with its president, deputies, and notaries, its seal and bank of seats in the cathedral, and its private hall of meeting, where it assembled regularly three mornings a week to discuss and vote on each question as it arose. The votes of the nations having been harmonized by the efforts of the commission of general deputies or central steering board, composed of representatives from each nation, the council gathered in stately session in the cathedral and publicly ratified the conclusions already reached by the nations in their separate meetings.[20]

As to what groups should be recognized as nations for purposes of separate participation in the council there seems at the beginning to have been no dispute. No Spaniards joined the council during the first year, and the Italians, French, Germans, and English carried over from Pisa without, apparently, much opposition. For a moment the Emperor Sigismund hoped that his Hungarians might be admitted as a fifth nation, but his wish, however it may have been expressed, was disregarded.[21] Hungarians, Czechs, Poles, Danes, and Swedes joined the German nation and made what impression they could on its proceedings. The Italian nation took in the prelates from Dalmatia, Cyprus, and Greece. Yet it was understood that, ideally at least, each nation was distinguished from the rest by some degree of homogeneity in its membership, particularly as regarded language. The French nation embraced the delegates from Savoy, Provence, and much of Lorraine, provinces of the Empire, because they spoke the French tongue and were therefore of that nation.[22] At the same time the word "nation" was frequently used to denote the people at home represented by the nation at Constance. They were also a unity of some sort, linguistic, geographic, or racial.

Contemporary writers describing the organization at Constance seem not as a rule to have remarked any particular resemblance between it and the familiar organization of the universities, beyond the fact that in both there was corporate voting.[23] On the other hand, every now and again there are references to current theories of corporate representation in law, politics, or business and to the responsibilities of the nations at the council to the greater nations at home. "As the rights of an entire college or corporation", said an English spokesman, "may be lodged, we know, in one person or two, so the rights of a whole nation may and should reside in one or two persons in a general council, for they represent not themselves alone but innumerable others." [24] The French demanded a reform of the annates system so that when they returned home "they might report the efforts they had made to the princes, prelates, and other clergy who had stayed behind and not be thought to have acquiesced tamely in abuses".[25]

The organization by nations at Constance seemed at first thoroughly successful. It reduced the Italian vote to one in four, put through rapidly the deposition of John XXIII and the execution of John Hus, received the abdication of Gregory XII, and started proceedings against Benedict XIII. In July, 1415, Sigismund left Constance on a trip to the south to win over the Spaniards, Benedict's sole remaining supporters. In Sigismund's absence the council was to take up the needed work of reform and the further eradication of heresy. And herewith began the troubles within and between the nations that reached their climax in the French attack on the right of England to retain her status as one of the four nations that made up the council.

The mood of elation that had marked the earlier months of accomplishment faded when the council was faced with issues no longer comparatively simple but complicated and distorted by every sort of prejudice and passion, political, institutional, and personal. Practically everyone but a few negligible Bohemians had agreed on the condemnation of Hus, but when it came to Jean Petit and his doctrine of tyrannicide, it was a different matter. From the outset the French nation at Constance had been the least united, reflecting, as it did, the divisions in the country whence it came and combining in one uneasy company the ambassadors of Charles VI, then under the domination of the Orleanist party, the deputies of the duke of Burgundy, himself almost an independent sovereign and the Orleanists' mortal enemy, the delegates from the nobility, clergy, and universities of the French kingdom at large, loyal for the most part to their poor, crazed king but distrustful of both the violent parties that fought for possession of his unhappy person, and, finally, the envoys from the French-speaking provinces of the empire with their varying interests and points of view. The case of Petit split the nation wide apart. The royal ambassadors, supported by Jean Gerson, chancellor of the University of Paris, and by the most eminent French cardinal, Pierre d'Ailly, called on the council to condemn the perilous and heretical theory of tyrannicide as propounded by Doctor Jean Petit in order to defend the duke of Burgundy's murder of the king's younger brother, the duke of Orleans, in 1407. The theory had already been condemned by an episcopal court at Paris. A special panel of judges from different nations was accordingly appointed, as for the case of Hus. But the agents of Burgundy, among whom was Bishop Pierre Cauchon, later to win greater notoriety at the trial of Jeanne d'Arc, resorted to every ingenious argument, counteraccusation, and threat and eventually prevailed on the court to confine its inquiry to the question of the legality of the episcopal trial at Paris and, in January, 1416, to annul the verdict as irregular and void.

This signal victory obtained by the Burgundians over the representatives of Charles VI aroused a storm of bitter discussion that raged through the following spring and summer and exacerbated many of the meetings of the council. An additional cause of French unhappiness was the news of the disaster to the king's forces at Agincourt, in October, 1415, and of the subsequent English advance through Normandy. In the summer of 1416 the French complained that business of importance to everyone was being smuggled through the commission of general deputies without the knowledge of the nations. The deputies from the French nation then on the commission happened to include several Burgundian sympathizers. Their president was known to be on close terms with Sigismund.[26] There was a feeling that French interests were being sacrificed by the treacherous Burgundians to the English and the Germans. An attempt on the part of a French contingent to join with the cardinals and the Italians to bring about the adoption of stricter rules of order, requiring open and thorough discussion of every matter by both college and nations, was foiled by English and German opposition.[27]

The resentment of the French royalist party against the Burgundians and their associates, the Anglo-German bloc, was intensified still more by the news that arrived early in the fall of 1416 that Sigismund in the course of his travels had abandoned his original notion of acting as impartial mediator between the French and English kings and had signed a treaty of active alliance with Henry V and met the duke of Burgundy in amicable conference; [28] also, that the duke had sent instructions to his subjects at Constance to co-operate in every way with the English and the Germans.[29] The one consolation lay in the arrival of a small but proportionately haughty embassy from Aragon, who demanded as the price of their joining the council a place in it suitable to their dignity, certainly not the last seats in the cathedral, below the English.[30]

In the midst of simmering agitation, on October 1, 1416, Cardinal d'Ailly read to a meeting in the parish church of St. Paul his newly finished treatise, *De ecclesiastica potestate,* which contained, along with a scholarly defense of conciliar authority in general, a short but sharp attack on the national system, which he with his nation had once accepted. It had, he announced, by this time gone far to destroy the essential nature of a church council, its unity. "Do the four nations, as distinguished in this sacred council . . . excluding the college of cardinals, in fact constitute a general council?" he asked. "Are they not rather several particular councils, very unequally and disproportionately divided, coming to separate conclusions?" Granted that under the circumstances some division of the membership had been desirable at the beginning, there were precedents to indicate how it should have been carried out. Pope Benedict XII, in his bull *Vas electionis,* had divided the Roman obedience into four parts: the first comprising France, Navarre, and Majorca; the second, Germany, England, Hungary, Poland, Norway, Denmark, etc.; the third, the Spanish kingdoms; and the fourth, Italy, Sicily, Sardinia, Corsica, Greece, Slavonia, and Cyprus. Now that the Spaniards were assuming their rightful place in the council, the reason for the continuance of England as a separate nation existed no longer. The council should be reorganized on the lines laid down by Benedict XII and England reduced to her proper position as a part of the great German nation.

As additional proof to show the subordinate place England should occupy, D'Ailly cited a second bull of Benedict XII, which divided Western Christendom into thirty-six provinces for the holding of local synods by the Black Monks of St. Benedict. One of these provinces embraced the two sees of Canterbury and York. By this ruling, then, all England constituted just one thirty-sixth of the Roman obedience. How absurd to permit her to play the part of one fourth or even, after Spain was admitted as a nation, of one fifth! If she were to continue as a separate nation, all the great nations of the council should be divided into smaller nations, each equivalent to England and each with a vote. Otherwise the ancient canonical method of voting in councils by individuals should be restored.[31]

D'Ailly's assault on the national system seems not at first to have been taken seriously by the council at large. There were more pressing subjects to consider—the tedious proceedings against Benedict XIII and the terms on which Aragon might be induced to combine with Castile, Portugal, and Navarre to form the new Spanish nation.[32] It was fantastic at this juncture to suggest upsetting the whole conciliar framework and destroying the balance of power that had lasted so long. The English, however, were outraged at what they considered a gratuitous insult to their nation [33] and were suspicious thenceforth of the slightest gesture of Frenchman or Spaniard that seemed to cast a slur upon their standing in the council. The following incident reflects their feeling. A routine document was being stamped, as usual, with the seals of the approving nations. A notary had affixed five pieces of wax to the bottom of the paper to receive the impressions of five seals, the Aragonese being invited as a matter of courtesy to add theirs. The presidents of the Italian, French, and German nations had stamped their seals on the first three bits of wax. The president of the Aragonese got the paper next and set his seal on the fourth. The president of the English had the paper last. He effaced the seal of Aragon, stamped the English in its place, and wrote above the fifth wax: "The same for Spain." The Aragonese thereupon refused to sit in the council until they were given fourth place, above the English. They talked of not regarding the English as a nation at all. For eight days business was at a standstill while desperate efforts were made to restore peace and placate the Spanish wrath.[34]

For November 1, the feast of All Saints, Cardinal d'Ailly had been appointed celebrant of High Mass and preacher in the cathedral. Bishop Hallam of Salisbury, leader of the English at Constance as at Pisa, convinced that D'Ailly would seize the occasion to repeat to a larger audience his denunciation of the organization by nations, persuaded Count Palatine Ludwig of Bavaria, whom Sigismund had left as chief lay guardian of the council, to see that D'Ailly had orders to refrain from introducing the dangerous topic into his sermon. D'Ailly obeyed as far as his cathedral sermon was concerned, though he filled it full of solemn warnings against errors of faith, scandals, and dissensions,[35] but on that same day, in another place, a substitute read for him a series of propositions, "Canones reformandi ecclesiam", in which he referred again to the defects of the system at Constance. Church councils should not be divided into nations representing kingdoms, for "such a mode of division is secular rather than ecclesiastical and foments disputes over superiority or priority". They should be divided on ecclesiastical principles, as laid down in the past; there should be no intrusion of lay politics.[36]

The interference, such as it was, with D'Ailly's right to say what he pleased in his cathedral address gave him and his supporters, the French royal ambassadors, a new grievance, the value of which they were quick to appreciate.[37] On several previous occasions the council had upheld the right of liberty of speech for all its members.[38] D'Ailly now prepared a formal protest to be read in the approaching general session of November 5, but the English and the Germans heard of it beforehand and sent notice to the college of cardinals to intervene and stop it. Otherwise, they said, neither Germans nor English would attend the session, and the scheduled steps in the case against Benedict XIII would be indefinitely delayed. The cardinals informed D'Ailly, who reluctantly agreed to content himself for the moment with reading the protest to the college alone. But the incident of the seal still rankled in the breasts of the Aragonese, and in the following session they precipitated the disturbance it had been hoped to avert by announcing positively their intention not to regard the English thenceforth as a nation. The bishops of Salisbury, London, Bath, Lichfield, and Norwich and the noble ambassadors of Henry V leaped to their feet and, as soon as quiet could be restored, registered their protests against the unwarranted aspersions of Aragon. Before the day was over there were clashes between French and English men-at-arms and belligerent parades with daggers, swords, and clubs through the cathedral and the city streets. D'Ailly and the French royal ambassadors were warned to stay indoors.[39]

Next day D'Ailly appeared in a meeting of the French nation to ask its approval of a new protest he was making in the name of the king and realm of France against the violence and intimidation to which he was subjected by the king's enemies, the English and their confederates. In his person the honor of the king and the realm of France was being assailed. He might indeed do well to stay away from the council thereafter, for in such a state of tumult and insecurity it could accomplish nothing and would probably be dissolved.[40] The French nation, however, deliberated and returned a cool and sober reply. It would have no hand in the protest, first, because it had not been consulted about the previous protest; second, because, with no special mandate from home, it disapproved thoroughly of the attempt to alter the constitution of the council at this time and deprive the English nation of its standing. Such an attempt was peculiarly ill advised at a moment when a truce had been signed between the kings of France and England, which, it was hoped, might develop into a permanent peace.[41] The English would manifestly die sooner than surrender the honor they had enjoyed so long. They would never submit meekly to such ignominy. The French nation was aware of no grievances sufficient to make it forget the solemn obligation, laid upon it by princes and superiors at home, to labor for peace and reform in the church. To join the movement started by D'Ailly would be to prepare the way for new divisions and new wars.[42]

With no large following even among the French and only the handful of fire-eating Aragonese besides to back them, D'Ailly and the royal ambassadors were in an isolated position. The Aragonese too were losing interest since the Germans, acting the part of magnanimous hosts of the council, had offered them for the time being their own place as third nation and declared their willingness to take the last place themselves.[43] Meanwhile the lay potentates in charge of the council, Count Palatine Ludwig and Burgrave Friedrich Hohenzollern of Nuremberg, with a number of prominent German bishops, had come to the college of cardinals and stated their conviction that D'Ailly's complaints of insecurity were damaging to the status of the holy council and a reflection on the honor of the serene king of the Romans and of the count palatine himself. Confronted with this formidable opposition, D'Ailly succumbed, confessed that he had no fears for his personal safety, and affirmed that he had not meant to impugn the honor of the Roman king or to imply that either the count palatine or the burgrave had failed in his duty of preserving liberty in the council.

With these admissions on D'Ailly's part the cardinals professed themselves satisfied. The count palatine, however, prompted, it was said, by the English, went on to call a large meeting of prelates and notables from every nation and lay before them the charge against D'Ailly as disturber of the peace. Deputies came to D'Ailly to discuss the situation and impress on him the necessity of allaying the excitement and allowing the council to proceed with its work unimpeded. D'Ailly irritably replied that he had already done what was asked of him to appease the count palatine and saw no more that he could do. He was sure that the bishop of Salisbury was behind the count's hostility. Everyone knew that the English had the Germans on their side.[44]

D'Ailly was thus effectively silenced, but now the ambassadors of Charles VI came forward to state with dignity that their duty to their king compelled them to make a public explanation of their position, and they secured from the count palatine permission to do so at some future session. Matters, however, temporarily went no further, although during the Christmas season feeling again ran high. Once more the count palatine was called in to calm the contestants, and Christmas mass was celebrated by the Germans and the English in one church, by the cardinals, the French, and the Italians in another, and by the Spaniards in a third.[45] At last came the long anticipated return of Sigismund to Constance, toward the end of January, 1417. Any lingering hope, however, that the French may have cherished of finding a fair arbiter in him must have been dashed by the mode of his entry into the city. He was wearing the collar of the Garter, newly bestowed on him by his beloved ally, Henry V, and he singled out the English, in the throng who went out to meet him, for handclasps and other conspicuous signs of friendship. D'Ailly had planned to deliver a speech of welcome at the cathedral, in which he might have commended himself and the French to Sigismund's kindness, but Hallam of Salisbury hurried on ahead and got possession of the pulpit for an exuberant eulogy on the text, "He shall be great in the sight of the Lord." By the time he was through, Sigismund, hungry and tired, would listen to no one else.[46]

The French ambassadors waited a few days and then, aware that a move of some sort was imperative, sent a delegation to the emperor with an offer to drop all efforts to alter the constitution of the council on condition that they be allowed to make one statement of their grievances at a public session and then refer them to the consideration of the future pope. For answer Sigismund appointed a commission, which immediately drew up a resolution for presentation to the council by the terms of which the latter pledged itself to permit no prejudice to the right of "any nation here principally represented" and no increase or diminution in their number and enjoined future councils to continue the system of organization by nations, "as the Holy Spirit hath inspired us". A copy of this resolution Sigismund himself took to the house of Cardinal d'Ailly, whom he found in conference with another French cardinal, Fillastre, and the royal ambassadors. What words D'Ailly used to the emperor on his abrupt appearance we do not hear, but Fillastre, who tells the story, says that after a glance at the paper he himself burst into a hot defense of his friends' conduct, insisting that "there had been no scandals in the council but those the English had created", that the French had never had a chance to present their case, and that it was strange indeed that the simple right of a hearing, granted to the legates of Portugal and Poland and everyone else, "as often as they chose", was denied to the reasonable and conciliatory envoys of the great king of France. Sigismund, annoyed, demanded back the paper and left the house. In dread of his anger, the French proposed an amendment to the resolution that would make it more acceptable, but Sigismund rejected this and ordered the resolution in its original form to be submitted to the vote of the nations. The Germans, English, and Italians approved it. In the debate in the French nation the royal ambassadors were silent, but the nation as a whole called it tricky and refused to pass it. The Spaniards followed the French. In consequence the affair was once more at a standstill.[47]

At length, at the session of March 3, when the business scheduled for the day had been dispatched, the advocate of the French king arose and asked permission for one of the royal proctors to speak. Master Jean Campan thereupon started to read a paper setting forth the views of his party in full but had not got beyond the first eight or ten lines when a loud groan interrupted him and then such a clamor that he could not be heard. He shouted above the tumult his protest against the injustice and his demand that a record be made of it and of the paper he had tried to read. But when the noise had subsided, Sigismund expressed his own severe disapprobation of this infraction of the conciliar rule against bringing any matter before a session that had not previously been approved by the nations as well as of all propositions that tended to throw discredit on the council. He desired that nothing more of the kind be attempted as long as the council lasted.[48] At the session of March 31 Thomas Polton, an English protonotary, delivered to the notaries of the council for record an English answer in writing to the French argument.[49] With this unsatisfactory performance the ambassadors of Charles VI had perforce to let the matter rest.

Some inkling of the feeling produced in England by reports of the incident may be gathered from an unprinted letter, written on April 23 by Chicheley, archbishop of Canterbury, to Hallam at Constance, congratulating him and his colleagues on the favor shown them by the emperor and on their victorious defense of the rights and honor of the realm and clergy of England "against the malice of the French, who have always been our enemies" and urging an unremitting vigilance "lest by their wiles they regain the control over the church which they had in times past and cunningly rob others of their rights".[50]

In these French and English memorials, presented in the third year of the council and never publicly read, we find at last a realization of the need of putting an end, for the moment at least, to the vagueness and ambiguity inherent in the various uses of the word "natio" and of clarifying the issues at stake by definitions that fitted not merely the transient groups at Constance but also the far larger, permanent associations of people at home whom the nations at Constance were there to represent. The French begin by pointing out that four of the nations at the council represent "general", not "particular" nations, that is, great divisions of the Roman obedience, that the Italian, French, Spanish, and German groups include delegates from several "particular" nations, regions, or provinces, whereas the English includes men from but one "particular" nation, since neither Wales nor Scotland and only a small part of Ireland have sent delegates or count themselves subjects of the English king. The French hark back to the four ecclesiastical divisions of Benedict XII, in which England figured as part of the German section, and to his list of thirty-six provinces, in which England appeared as one and France as six. It is not just to the others, they contend, that England should keep a position so out of proportion to her size. There have been only twelve to twenty-four voting members in the whole English nation at Constance. If they are unwilling to become one of the particular nations included in the general German nation, then the other general nations should separate into their component parts, each part with a vote. France alone would furnish six provinces, each as large as England and with a longer history of undeviating devotion to the faith. Or else the council should revive the ancient practice of voting by individuals.[51]

The English in answer carry further the process of definition thus begun by the French. They admit a distinction between general and particular nations but with no great difficulty dispose of the French argument for reorganizing the council after the pattern set by the scheme of Benedict XII. His four divisions were merely economic regions, in each of which the fee for episcopal procurations might be fixed at a uniform rate. He had no more thought of mapping out the nations of Europe in this plan than he had when he listed the ecclesiastical provinces where Benedictines might hold their synods. Rules should not be stretched to cover cases for which they have never been intended. In a soaring flight of imagination the English go on to assert that as a matter of fact they are a general nation, representing eight particular kingdoms, viz., "England, Scotland, and Wales—the three that together compose Great Britain—the kingdom of the Sea,[52] and, in Ireland, near to England, four large and notable kingdoms—Connaught, Galway, Munster, and Meath—as recorded together expressly and by seal in the catalogue of Christian kings in the registers of the Roman curia . . . . also the notable principality of John, prince of the Orkneys and other islands, about sixty in number, some as large as or larger than the realm of France".[53] They comprehend five languages, English, the tongue used by both England and Scotland, Welsh, Irish, Gascon, and Cornish. "By every law it can represent as many [particular] nations as it contains distinct languages." [54]

As for the characteristics required of an authentic nation, England possesses them all, "whether nation be understood as a people marked off from others by blood relationship and habit of unity or by peculiarities of language, the most sure and positive sign and essence of a nation in divine and human law . . . or whether nation be understood, as it should be, as a territory equal to that of the French nation".[55] The realm of England alone comprises, besides many duchies, baronies, and other domains, "thirty-two spacious counties, four or five of which are equal to the whole realm of France". The realm of France has only two archiepiscopal provinces, Reims and Sens, twenty dioceses, and six thousand parish churches, to which England can oppose the two huge provinces of Canterbury and York, twenty-five dioceses, and over fifty-two thousand parish churches, besides cathedrals, collegiate churches, monasteries, and hospitals. (One must find what excuse one can for these figures by recalling the mutilated state of France in 1417.) England has the more ancient faith, reaching back to Joseph of Arimathea, who lies buried at

Glastonbury, whereas France had to wait for Christianity until the coming of St. Denis. England has its excellent royal house that produced St. Helen and her son, the Emperor Constantine, and has never departed from obedience to Rome.[56] It has its own wide land, eight hundred miles or forty days' journey from north to south, and its numerous and mighty people.

In spite of the dangerous sea and the long distance that separate England from Constance, it has sent to the council, first and last, twenty-two bishops, abbots, and other high ecclesiastics, twenty-seven masters of law or theology, twenty-five other university graduates, over sixty proctors of prelates and cathedral chapters, and more than a hundred lesser men of letters. Even if this representation has been smaller than that of other nations, each nation should count as equal to every other, as faculties and gilds do in university and city governments. For one peer has no rights over another peer nor one superior over another. "Nations in a general council should be considered equals and each should have the same rights." God, who is the author of change, has permitted nations to come into being and the ancient method of governing councils to be superseded by one more appropriate and rational in these days when men and customs vary widely from land to land, and each land should have a voice in framing the laws to be imposed upon it.

The rest of the English argument, the proposal to disregard nations and divide Europe thenceforth for purposes of conciliar representation simply into four geographical blocks, as suggested by Albertus Magnus, a western block consisting of France and Spain, a northern block of England, Scotland, Ireland, Norway, Denmark, and Sweden, an eastern block of Germany, Poland, and Hungary, and a southern block of Italy and the other Mediterranean lands, is of little interest now. At the time, moreover, hardly anyone could have expected that it would be taken seriously. It was merely a counterblast to the bulls of Benedict XII, with the special merit of reducing the two votes of France and Spain to one.

What is of interest in all this is the English summary of the elements essential in a nation that would rank as such in an international council—a sense of race and "habit of unity, setting it off from others", a peculiar language, and an extended territory. Race, a common unity of some sort, language, territory—each of these elements in turn had been the basis of one or another of the many medieval kinds of nation. The nations that are called such at Constance must have them all. Behind the English boasts of king and church there is evident a consciousness of solidarity and character as a people. There may well have been some thought, too, of recent prowess in France, although no one in the sacred assembly alluded openly to the war. A nation, while admittedly a growth of the newer times, is already something substantial, with an existence quite apart from the royal dominion. It is not the same as a kingdom.

"Everyone knows that it matters not whether a nation obeys one prince only or several. Are there not many kingdoms in the Spanish nation that pay no obedience to the king of Castile, the chief ruler in Spain? But it does not follow that they are not parts of the Spanish nation. Are not Provence, Dauphiny, Savoy, Burgundy, Lorraine, and many other regions that have nothing to do with our adversary of France included nevertheless in the French or Gallican nation? And the like is true in other nations." [57] In the previous October the Portuguese embassy had objected to the inclusion of prelates from Sicily and Corsica with the Aragonese in the Spanish nation on the ground that, although subjects of the king of Aragon, they spoke another language and were "truly of a different nation".[58]

Every nation at Constance displayed on occasion the peculiar species of touchy conceit and bombast and the unscrupulous assertiveness that were to be symptoms of the new nationalism. The English, being the least numerous, posed as champions of the right of each nation to be counted as the equal of every other. Yet they joined with the larger nations in ignoring the rights of Hungarians, Czechs, and Poles to separate identity and a separate vote. With nearly five centuries and a quarter of nationalist history since Constance behind us, we read with a stirring of something not unlike sympathy the following remedy for international contentiousness prescribed by an anonymous observer of events at the council, though we ourselves may see no reason for limiting the ingredients to churchmen: [59] "Recipe for the stomach of St. Peter and total healing of the same, issued at the council of Constance. Take twenty-four cardinals, one hundred archbishops and prelates, the same number from each nation, and as many curials as you can get. Immerse in Rhine water [60] and keep submerged there for three days. It will be good for St. Peter's stomach and for the cure of all his diseases." [61]

NOTES

[1] For evidence of so-called German national feeling as far back as Charlemagne see K. G. Hugelmann, "Die deutsche Nation und der deutsche Nationalstaat im Mittelalter", *Historisches Jahrbuch*, LI (1931), 1–29, 445–84.

[2] Coluccio Salutati, *Epistolario*, ed. by Francesco Novati (4 vols. in 5, Rome, 1891–1911), III, 534–36.

[3] Chaucer, *Wife of Bath's Tale*, ll: 212–13.

[4] Vulgate, Psalm CV, 47; King James's version. CVI. 47.

[5] *La queste del Saint Graal*, ed. by Albert Pauphilet (Paris, 1923), 34, ll. 2–3. This reference I owe to Miss Winifred Sturdevant.

[6] John Gower, *Confessio amantis*, bk. iv, ll. 1451–52.

[7] *Select English Works of John Wyclif*, ed. by Thomas Arnold (3 vols., Oxford, 1869–71), III, 393.

[8] James Westfall Thompson, *Economic and Social History of Europe in the Later Middle Ages, 1300–1530* (New York, 1931), p. 253.

[9] See Gray C. Boyce, "The Controversy over the Boundary between the English and

Picard Nations in the University of Paris", *Études d'histoire dédiées à la mémoire de Henri Pirenne* (Brussels, 1937).

10 Boyce, *The English-German Nation in the University of Paris during the Middle Ages* (Bruges, 1927), pp. 14–15, 25–28.

11 The common practice of comparing the nations of church councils with university nations tends to obscure the difference, as, for example, in Boyce, *English-German Nation*, p. 13; A. Diehl, "Heiliges Römisches Reich Deutscher Nation", *Historische Zeitschrift*, CLVI, 461; Eustace J. Kitts, *Pope John the Twenty-third and Master John Hus of Bohemia* (London, 1910), p. 282; M. Creighton, *History of the Papacy from the Great Schism to the Sack of Rome* (London, 1899–1901), I, 318.

12 G. D. Mansi, *Sacrorum conciliorum nova et amplissima collectio*, XXIV, 66.

13 Ewald Müller, *Das Konzil von Vienne, 1311–1312, seine Quellen und seine Geschichte*, in the Vorreformationsgeschichtliche Forschungen (Münster, 1934), pp. 99, 108, 113–14.

14 *Chronique du religieux de Saint-Denis* (Paris, 1839–52), bk. xxx, ch. 3, Vol. IV, pp. 228, 230, in the Collection de documents inédits sur l'histoire de France.

15 Mansi, XXVI, 1219; XXVII, 7, 266.

16 *Ibid.*, XXVII, 7–8.

17 Anonymous letter to the Council of Constance, Heinrich Finke, ed., *Acta Concilii Constanciensis* (Münster, 1896–1928), III, 101.

18 There were but eight members in the English royal delegation, Jacques Lenfant, *Histoire du Concile de Pise* (Amsterdam, 1724), p. 26.

19 The council was opened on November 5, 1414. On December 7 there were speakers for the Italian and the English nations. A. Fillastre, "Gesta Concilii Constantiensis", in Finke, II, 17; Cerretano, "Liber gestorum", Finke, II, 197. Not long afterward Cardinal d'Ailly proposed that a committee on order of procedure be appointed, with members chosen from each nation, to prepare business between sessions. Hermann von der Hardt, *Magnum oecumenicum Constantiense Concilium* (6 vols. in 4, Frankfurt, 1700), II, 197. He repeated the suggestion in January. Finke, III, 55. On January 7 the envoys from the University of Cologne wrote of attending meetings of the German nation. Edmond Martene and Ursin Durand, *Thesaurus novus anecdotorum* (Paris, 1717), II, 1610.

20 For more details of this procedure see Louise R. Loomis, "The Organization by Nations at Constance", *Church History*, I (1932), 191–210.

21 Only one chronicler mentions this ambition of Sigismund: William of Turre, "Acta concilii", Finke, II, 351.

22 Bibliothèque nationale MS. Latin, 1450, fol. 62ʳ, quoted by Noël Valois, *La France et le grand schisme d'Occident* (4 vols., Paris, 1896–1902), IV, 283, n. 2.

23 Peter de Pulka, envoy from the University of Vienna, writes back to his colleagues that the nations at Constance vote as faculties do in universities. "Epistolae", II (Feb. 7, 1415), in *Archiv für Kunde österreichischer Geschichts-Quellen*, XV, 14.

24 Hardt, V, 97.

25 French nation, "Declaratio de annatis non solvendis", *ibid.*, I. 785. See also the unwillingness professed by the French to embark on new business that might impede their carrying out of the mandate with which they were sent to Constance, as described below, pp. 519–20. For a description of the election of representatives from the French clergy to the council see Valois, IV, 256ff.

26 The president was Jean Mauroux, patriarch of Antioch; "a snake in the grass", D'Ailly called him.

27 On this episode see Fillastre, "Gesta", Finke, II, 65, 71, 72, and Peter de Pulka's letter of August 29, 1416, *Arch. Kunde Öst. Gesch.*, XV, 48. The text of the proposed rules is in Finke, II, 742–58.

28 When Sigismund left Constance, the duke of Burgundy was his hardly concealed enemy, and Sigismund went south by way of Savoy to avoid the risk of journeying through Burgundian territory.

29 Letter of the duke of Burgundy, Aug. 26, 1416, in Joannes Gerson, *Opera*, ed. by Du Pin (5 vols., Antwerp, 1706), V, 672–73.

30 D'Ailly, "Responsiones ad quaedam interrogatoria", Gerson, V, 693.

31 D'Ailly, "De ecclesiastica potestate", Hardt, VI, 15–78; also in Gerson, II, 925–60. On the general argument of this treatise see Agnes E. Roberts, *Pierre d'Ailly and the Council of Constance*, in the *Transactions of the Royal Historical Society*, 4th ser., XVIII, 132–38.

32 Fillastre, "Gesta", Finke, II, 71–76.

33 D'Ailly, "Responsiones", Gerson, V, 693.

34 Fillastre, "Gesta", Finke, II, 77.

35 Extracts from this sermon are given by Paul Tschackert, *Peter von Ailli* (Gotha, 1877), pp. 46–50 of the appendix.

36 D'Ailly, "Canones reformandi ecclesiam", Hardt, I, 409-33.

37 D'Ailly, "Responsiones", Gerson, V, 693.

38 In his imperial writs of summons to Constance, Sigismund had promised that speech and act there should be free. Hardt, VI, 5–6. Pope John XXIII had repeated the promise in his address at the first session. *Ibid.*, IV, 16–19. In January, 1415, the count palatine himself and the bishops of Worms, Speyer, and Verdun had made the preservation of free speech a condition of their adhesion to the council. *Ibid.*, II, 207. The council had stood resolutely for the principle against Sigismund. Cerretano, "Liber", Finke, II, 202–206. One of its charges against John XXIII had been his attempts to prevent free debate. Finke, III, 61–63, 66–74.

39 *Acta* for Session XXIII, Hardt, IV, 960–61; D'Ailly, "Responsiones", Gerson, V, 693–94; Fillastre, "Gesta", Finke, II, 78–79; envoy from the University of Cologne, letter of Nov. 16, 1416, Martene and Durand, II, 1667.

40 D'Ailly, "Protestationes lectae in natione Gallicana", Gerson, V, 696–97.

41 A truce had been signed on October 3, which lasted until February 2 of the following year.

42 French nation, "Motiva propter quae regnicolae Franciae non debent adhaerere protestationibus", Gerson, V, 697–99.

43 Envoy from the University of Cologne, Martene and Durand, II, 1667; Fillastre, "Gesta", Finke, II, 81–82.

44 Fillastre, "Gesta", Finke, II, 79; D'Ailly, "Responsiones", in reply to the questioning of the deputies, Gerson, V, 692-96.

45 *Ulrichs von Richental Chronik*, ed. by Michael Richard Buck (Tübingen, 1882), pp. 96–97. Not long after this time the English must have received the letters patent issued by Henry V on December 2, appointing Hallam, two other bishops, Lords John Tiptoft and Hertonk van Clux, and Master Philip Morgan, doctor of laws, as proctors and ambassadors to treat with the clerical and secular princes and nobles of the Empire for their oaths of fealty and aid to himself, in return for annual money pensions as fiefs. Thomas Rymer, *Foedera* (London, 1704-35), IX, 412–13.

46 Letter of John Forester to Henry V, Feb. 2, 1417, in Rymer, IX, 434.

47 Fillastre, "Gesta", Finke, II, 86–88.

48 *Ibid.*, pp. 89–90; *Acta* for Session XXVIII, Hardt, IV, 1103–1109.

49 *Acta* for Session XXXI, Hardt, IV, 1196.

50 British Museum, King's MSS., 10. b. IX, f. 59, a–b. The letter bears no year date, but the contents show that it must have been written in 1417.

51 "Gallicae nationis solemnis protestatio contra Anglos", Hardt, V, 56–75.

52 The name of this fourth kingdom might, I suggest, be read as "kingdom of Man", "regnum de Man", instead of, as in the text, "kingdom of the Sea" or "de Mari". Britannia did not so early claim to rule the waves. But in the thirteenth century the Isle of Man had been held as a "regnum" in fee from the pope. In 1406 Henry IV had granted it with regalities to Sir John Stanley and his heirs, subject only to a relief of two falcons to be paid to every future king of England at his coronation. A. W. Moore, *History of the Isle of Man* (2 vols., London, 1900) I, 196–97. William E. Lunt, *Papal Revenues in the Middle Ages* (2 vols., New York, 1934), no. 226.

53 "Anglicae nationis . . . vindicatio sui juris quoad propriam nationem in concilio", Hardt, V, 86. There were in fact at this time a Patrick, bishop of Cork, a Lewis, bishop of Bangor, and several Welsh doctors and clerics in the English nation at Constance but no representatives from the Scottish or other dioceses. James I of Scotland was a prisoner in England. In February, 1416, the council had sent envoys

with a letter of convocation to the duke of Albany, acting regent for James, and to the clergy and nobility of Scotland and in January, 1417, had received the duke's promise to send a Scottish deputation to Constance as soon as he could. Fillastre, "Gesta", Finke, II, 57, 84–86. The English reply, "Anglicae nationis vindicatio", covers pages 76 to 101 in Hardt (Vol. V).

54 "Anglicae nationis vindicatio", Hardt, V. 93.

55 The Latin of this noteworthy passage runs: "sive sumatur natio ut gens secundum cognationem et collectionem ab alia distincta, sive secundum diversitatem linguarum, quae maximam et verissimam probant nationem et ipsius essentiam, jure divino pariter et humano, ut infra dicetur; sive etiam sumatur natio pro provincia aequali etiam nationi Gallicanae, sicut sumi deberet." *Ibid.*, p. 92.

56 A contrast is doubtless implied here with the French kings, who for over twenty years during the schism had supported the Avignon pope against Rome.

57 *Ibid.*, p. 87.

58 "Protestatio Portugallensium", Hardt, IV, 918.

59 *Ibid.*, I, 499.

60 The Rhine, it will be remembered, flowed by one wall of the city of Constance.

61 As I was finishing this paper, my attention was called by Professor Gray C. Boyce to an admirable article by Finke, covering some of the same material, "Die Nation in den spätmittelalterlichen allgemeinen Konzilien", *Hist. Jahrbuch*, LVII (1937), 323–38.

18

Medieval Democracy in the Brandenburg Towns and Its Defeat in the Fifteenth Century

F. L. CARSTEN, D.PHIL.

AT THE TIME OF the so-called German colonisation to the east of the Elbe, German merchants and artisans entered the Brandenburg Mark, whose rivers, woods, and marshes stretched from the Old Mark to the west of the Elbe to the New Mark to the east of the Oder. The immigrants brought with them the economic methods and social organisation of their homeland. Town life, self-government, and trade quickly developed everywhere, whether the new town was established on an uninhabited site, or on the site of a Slavonic village which gave its name to the new settlement, or a walled town or fortress of the Slavs was transformed into a German town.[1]

The towns were directly under the margrave * and, either in their foundation charters or by later privileges, were granted far-reaching rights which made them virtually independent of any outside interference. The *locatores* entrusted with the foundation of a town became its hereditary mayors and exercised jurisdiction over the inhabitants and the municipal possessions outside the town, and received one-third of the proceeds of the town's court. Only when caught red-handed could burghers be tried outside their own town, and the *advocati* and other officials were forbidden to summon them before outside courts, or to interfere in any way with the jurisdiction of the town.[2] This privilege became one of the towns' most cherished rights and was confirmed to each of them by every new margrave. Several towns even acquired jurisdiction over knights and squires who committed a crime within their bounds.[3] Later on, many towns also received the highest jurisdiction, i.e. the feudal overlordship over the mayor (an important right if his family died out) and the two-thirds of the proceeds of the jurisdiction which hitherto had gone to the margrave.[4] The margraves' castles, which had been built in or near the various towns and were a threat to their independence, were destroyed, and an assurance was given that they would not be re-built in the future.[5] After the death of Woldemar, the last Ascanian margrave, in 1319, the towns paid homage to the first Bavarian margrave, Lewis of Wittelsbach, whose father, as king of the Romans, had been able to secure Brandenburg for his house; Lewis then had to promise them that he would, with their advice and help, raze all the castles erected since Margrave Woldemar's death to the ground [6]; and the town of Prenzlau was granted the right to destroy all those fortifications within a radius of three miles round the town which had been constructed without the consent of the aldermen.[7]

While the independence of the towns was thus firmly established, their internal constitution was and remained aristocratic. The aldermen were drawn from a few leading families of merchants, clothiers, or land-owners and elected their own successors, the craft gilds and the commons having no share in the government of the town. According to the law of the town of Brandenburg, the capital of the Mark, which was adopted by many other towns, even permission for the formation of gilds had to be given by the aldermen, and they appointed the wardens.[8] According to the law of Stendal, a few of the leading burgesses were allowed to take part in the election of aldermen [9]; but it is not stated whether these were wardens of gilds or simply former aldermen.[10] In any case, this participation seems to have ceased at an early date.[11] Only the law of Seehausen allowed the election of aldermen by the burghers; but this exception, recorded only from the fourteenth century, may have been the result of a revolution against the aristocratic form of election, as it certainly was in the case from which our knowledge of this law is derived, that of Pritz-walk.[12]

This being the state of affairs at the beginning of the fourteenth century, it was only natural that inside the towns the gilds and commons should try to break the power of the aristocracy and to gain a share in the town government, and that outside the towns the margraves as well as the nobles should attempt to encroach upon the independence of the towns and to subjugate them. The margraves used the internal conflicts of the towns to establish their own rule over them and often supported the rule of the aldermen over the lower classes; and the latter were in frequent rebellion against their rulers both inside and outside the towns. These struggles are intimately connected; they lasted throughout the fourteenth and fifteenth centuries, and the final defeat both of the towns and of the lower orders in the towns marked the end of medieval democracy in Brandenburg and the establishment of the nobility as the ruling class in society.

The towns, each too weak to resist attack single-handed, sought to strengthen their position by alliances among themselves and with towns outside the country. The first 'union' of Brandenburg towns of which a record exists was formed in 1308 and comprised all the towns of the Ottonine half of the Mark,[13] among them Berlin and Cölln, the Neustadt of Brandenburg, Frankfort, and Salzwedel; they vowed mutual help against any violence or injustice.[14] It was probably the same towns which, in the following year, formed a new union; they promised to share their expenses when resisting either attempts to cite their burghers before the margrave's high court or violence done to one of the towns by any *potentes*,[15] among whom was clearly included the margrave. Many more such unions for mutual assistance in case of attack were formed between various Brandenburg towns during the fourteenth and fifteenth centuries[16]; and the margraves were obliged solemnly to declare their approval of these unions.[17]

Equally important were the alliances with foreign towns. By the second half of the thirteenth century Stendal and Salzwedel, the leading towns of Brandenburg, were already important members of the Hanseatic League,[18] which not only fostered trade and secured trade routes and privileges, but also afforded protection against the princes and nobles. Altogether seven towns of the Old Mark, four of the Prignitz, and three of the Middle Mark became direct members of the Hansa.[19] But the power of the League was strong only along the coast of the Baltic, and for this reason Stendal and other Old Mark towns concluded alliances with important nearby inland towns, such as Magdeburg, Brunswick, and Lüneburg, especially when threatened by danger.[20]

By these unions and by their membership of the Hansa the Brandenburg towns protected themselves not only against attacks from without, but also against movements of the lower classes within: a paragraph was included in the Old Mark union of 1436 saying that plotters, rioters, and rebels were to forfeit their lives and goods and were not to be admitted into other towns when fugitives.[21] Probably two years later, a clause against rebellious gilds and commons appeared in the draft of an alliance of the Old and Middle Mark towns.[22] These are indications of the growing power of the gilds and of increasing rebellion against the patricians, which was not confined to Brandenburg, but affected the towns all over Germany. In 1418 the Hanseatic League had decreed expulsion from the Hansa towns and the death penalty for burghers who conspired against the aldermen, while towns in which the commons seized power were to lose the privileges and membership of the Hansa.[23] In the leading Hanseatic towns, which lay in the colonisation area and were therefore commercial and not industrial towns, the ruling merchant aristocracies were strong enough to suppress revolutionary movements and helped each other to maintain their power.

The first recorded conflicts between aldermen and gilds, rich and poor, in the Brandenburg Mark, occurred in 1285 in its leading town, Stendal [24]; this town, with its important cloth trade and powerful craft gilds, remained a hotbed of social unrest for many centuries to come. The points in dispute were the method of electing the aldermen and the levying of taxes. The margraves Otto and Conrad were called in as arbiters and decided in favour of the aldermen, decreeing that they should remain in office for the rest of the year and then elect their successors without interference from outside; that they should decide upon the *modus* of taxation, and that rich and poor were to pay equally; that the gilds should not impede the decisions of the council and should inform it of the results of their own meetings. Whoever defied this arbitrament would be guilty of a felony and would forfeit his life and goods to the margraves.[25]

A new revolt of the gilds of Stendal broke out in 1345, and this time it was successful. Aldermen and gilds agreed upon a reformation of the constitution: from now on the council was to be composed of two representatives of the commons and ten of the gilds (two each of the clothiers, clothmakers, and merchants, and one each of the furriers, shoemakers and curriers, butchers, and bakers), and only four aldermen were to continue in office in the following year; decrees of the aldermen required the consent of the gilds' wardens who were first to refer the matter back to their members; if no agreement were reached the aldermen were to have the last word; all decrees were to be read in burghers' assemblies and in the churches.[26] A number of patricians had to quit the town,[27] and were only re-admitted in 1350, after having agreed that the aldermen should be elected from the gilds, and that the clothiers' gild should not hold a privileged position.[28]

The violent conflicts of these years in the whole of the Brandenburg Mark were connected with the appearance, in 1348, of the 'false' margrave Woldemar, who claimed to have returned from the Holy Land after twenty-nine years' absence, but in reality was a usurper used by a powerful coalition of princes against the house of Wittelsbach. For the most part the towns sided with Woldemar and his allies and were granted especially far-reaching privileges [29]; of the nobles many remained loyal to the Bavarian margraves. In the Ucker Mark the gilds and commons belonged to the party of the false Woldemar, while the aldermen were on the side of the Bavarians [30], in the New Mark the towns went so far as to destroy the castles and fortifications of the nobles.[31] Unfortunately, the documents do not give many details about this aspect of the struggle around the person of the false Woldemar. When the Bavarian margraves slowly reconquered the Mark from the hostile coalition they had to make important concessions to the towns: they handed over several castles to them,[32] and promised to abstain from building any new ones,[33] to destroy those erected during the war[34] and to leave their armed forces outside the towns.[35] The towns had now reached the height of their power.

In the Old Mark towns fresh strife broke out in the second half of the century. In Salzwedel the gilds and commons rose in 1361, but without success. Margrave Lewis the Roman intervened, punished the ringleaders himself while leaving the others to the aldermen's jurisdiction, and ordered the wardens of the gilds to swear obedience to the aldermen and the margrave every year and to report everything harmful they heard of.[36] In 1387 the lower gilds of Stendal (the curriers, shoemakers, bakers, linenweavers, furriers, and clothmakers) bound themselves not to swear any more oaths to the aldermen, nor to submit to decrees which were not accepted by the gilds, and to help everybody to whom violence was done with their lives and goods.[37] This indicates that since the revolution of 1345 a reaction had taken place, probably beginning soon after the reconciliation of the town with the clothiers in 1350. In 1365, 1368–9 and 1372 the majority of the aldermen again came from those clothiers' families which had dominated the council before 1345.[38] The so-called 'three gilds' of the clothiers, merchants, and butchers now administered the town and provided the aldermen.

Conflicts took place about the same time in Berlin. An alderman of the town, Tyle Wardenberg, fomented a rebellion[39] against the Emperor Charles IV (of Luxemburg), who had taken the Mark by force from the Wittelsbachs in 1373 and had become margrave in their stead. Because of this rebellion Wardenberg was not re-elected to the town council. He then agitated among the commons, declaring that he had been excluded from the council because he opposed its corruption and wasting of money; he succeeded in getting the commons to annul several decisions of the aldermen, prevented any help being sent to the margrave, promised to free the burghers from all taxes, and did not cease his agitation even when re-elected as an alderman. Finally he was obliged to quit the town,[40] after which the unrest seems to have died down. In 1412, however, there was a fresh conspiracy against the aldermen in Berlin, the participants assembling in a church and taking an oath to obey their leaders. But once more the undertaking had no success,[41] and the rule of the patricians continued.

In 1411 King Sigismund made Frederick of Hohenzollern, burgrave of Nuremberg, governor of the Brandenburg Mark; in 1415 he ceded the country to Frederick, who was solemnly invested with it two years later. Thus the Hohenzollerns replaced the Luxemburgers as margraves of Brandenburg.

During the following decade, there were revolutionary movement
in a number of Brandenburg towns. It may be that such rebellions seem
more frequent in the fifteenth century because the source material for
this period is much richer; but probably the number of conflicts grew as
the result of the increasing wealth and importance of the towns, the development of strong gilds, and the more oppressive rule of the aristocracy.[42]

In 1420 strife broke out between the aldermen and commons of
Frankfort. Margrave Frederick decided that the burghers should elect
twelve men from the gilds and six from the commons, and that the aldermen should then choose four of the former and two of the latter as
representatives who were to be present at the collection and auditing of
taxes and to have power to vote for the commons, if the aldermen wanted
their decision, or, if they chose, to refer the matter back to the burghers.[43]
Only three years later the margrave had to settle a fresh dispute in the
town, the commons attacking the nepotism of the aldermen.[44] In 1424
the parties agreed that from then on the aldermen should not elect their
sons, brothers, nephews, or sons-in-law to the council, nor should aldermen be eligible as jurymen, who were to be drawn from the gilds and
commons.[45] In the previous year the margrave had decided disputes in
Treuenbrietzen in favour of the aldermen; the burghers were not to make
any innovations, and no gild wardens were to sit in the council.[46]

In 1425 the burghers of Prenzlau rose against the aldermen and
drove the patricians out of the council. In the following year Margrave
Frederick's son John was sent to settle the dispute; he judged that the
commons had complained without reason and admonished them to obey
the aldermen. He himself appointed a council, which was to elect its own
successors, and forbade the burghers to plot against it in any way.[47] Several ringleaders were put to death.[48] In the following year the same
prince was called into the Neustadt of Brandenburg to arbitrate between
the aldermen and the gilds and commons. Again he decided that the
former were to retain their power, but should choose sixteen representatives of the burghers and render every year an account of revenue and expenditure to them; if there were any disagreement he would himself
settle it.[49] In the next year fresh unrest broke out in Brandenburg because
of the tax levied for the war against the Hussites.[50]

In 1429 the lower gilds of Stendal, the clothmakers, furriers, and
linenweavers, rose in open revolt against the patricians and had to be
put down by the armed force of Margrave John who was supported by
other Old Mark towns.[51] Two clothmakers were beheaded, others had to
leave the Mark. The clothmakers had to promise never to increase the
number of masters above one hundred and to admit only their children
to the gild; furriers and linenweavers could no longer become aldermen.
All gilds and the commons had to swear to obey the margrave and the

aldermen and never to form any union against them, but the clothiers and landowners received a document that they were not to blame for the revolt.[52] Another revolt against the clothiers took place in the Neustadt of Salzwedel, and here also the burghers were ordered by Margrave John to be obedient to the aldermen.[53] In both towns the clothmakers had probably tried to gain the right to cut cloth, which was reserved for the clothiers. The first Hohenzollerns thus protected the rule of the aristocracy, making it dependent on their help and thereby strengthening their own power.

In the Middle Mark, Margrave John in 1429 accused Frankfort of having usurped the highest jurisdiction, a prerogative which he claimed to be his father's,[54] though it had been granted to the town in 1388.[55] To these and other complaints made by the margrave against Frankfort, the four towns of Brandenburg, Frankfort, Berlin, and Cölln, which had also incurred the margrave's enmity,[56] replied by forming, in 1431, a new union for mutual aid if any of them were deprived of their privileges or liberty.[57] In the following year, the aldermen of Berlin and Cölln settled various quarrels and reunited the two towns under a joint council, court, and administration.[58] This unification consolidated the power and prestige of the aldermen, the gilds apparently having no share in the town government. About 1438 the Old and Middle Mark towns drafted the terms of a new union, by which they refused to vote taxes, to swear the oath of allegiance, to render military service outside the country, or to help in wars started by the margrave without their consent, unless it were by common agreement of all the towns, or to surrender their privileges, whether these were threatened by attack from without or within.[59]

All this indicates that tension between margrave and towns, and between aldermen and gilds, was high when margrave Frederick II succeeded his father in 1440. When Berlin and Cölln paid homage to him, he prudently did not vow to the saints, but promised 'simply with words' that he would keep their honour and rights, without having confirmed their privileges before the homage.[60] Two years later, the gilds and commons of the town appealed to Frederick to help them against the aldermen, to revoke the act of unification and to install separate councils again. On 26 February he appeared with armed forces in Berlin, had the keys of the gates delivered to him, and appointed two new separate councils which were to elect their successors after one year, their election being subject to his confirmation and right of substitution; all unions and alliances of Berlin with towns inside and outside the Mark were declared null and void.[61] On 29 August Berlin and Cölln had to cede to the margrave their common town hall, their right of staple, the higher and lower jurisdiction, and a site in Cölln for the construction of a castle.[62] Thus they lost their most important privileges, their independence, and their unions with the other towns and the Hansa. The remaining Brandenburg towns also were forbidden to send delegates to the Hanseatic diets.[63] In July 1443 the aldermen of Salzwedel wrote to Hamburg that they could not come to the assembly at Lüneburg 'because of the great invasion which has taken place'.[64] In the same month Margrave Frederick laid, at Cölln, the first stone of the new castle,[65] which was called *frenum antiquae libertatis* by later chroniclers.[66]

This castle, growing before their eyes, roused the anger of the humiliated burghers. In January 1448 they opened a sluice in the town moat so as to flood the building, and Frederick vainly ordered it to be closed again.[67] Soon afterwards the Berliners arrested the judge whom he had appointed, put him into prison, and expelled officials and partisans of the margrave from the town; his intervention on behalf of the arrested man had no success.[68] Finally, an enraged crowd stormed his residence, forced the doors of the archives, and destroyed or carried away letters and documents.[69]

A new conflict became inevitable. Both sides prepared and looked for allies. Berlin and Cölln asked the Brandenburg towns as well as Lübeck, Hamburg, Lüneburg, and Magdeburg for advice and help, tried to restore the old unions and everywhere denounced the margrave for his violation of their rights.[70] The response was poor: only some small Brandenburg towns, Neu-Ruppin, Mittenwalde, and Perleberg, declared their willingness to help [71]; the others either did not reply or declined to do anything; for Frederick had been travelling round the country, summoning the burghers and asking for their support. Spandau and Bernau, near Berlin, were the first to promise it, then other towns followed suit and sent men-at-arms to Frederick.[72] In May 1448, deserted by their allies and attacked by the margrave and his followers, Berlin and Cölln had to agree to submit the dispute to a court of the estates.[73] It met in Spandau, where Frederick had assembled his forces, and listened to his description of all the offences and outrages of the two towns.[74] On 25 May it announced its verdict which confirmed Frederick's orders of 1442 in every point: the castle, the court, the common town hall, the right of electing the aldermen, the staple, and the toll had to be yielded afresh to the magrave.[75] On 19 June the burghers of Berlin and Cölln had to vow never again to violate the agreement of 1442 and to be obedient and humble subjects in the future.[76] One after another, the rich burgesses had to appear before Frederick and to surrender their persons, goods, fiefs, and even their wives' jointures; they lost their landed properties, at least in part, and had to pay enormous fines.[77] Several had to quit the town.[78] So great was their fear of the margrave that neither Frankfort nor the towns of the Old Mark sent delegates to the Hansa diet of 1450.[79] Two years later, Berlin and Cölln formally renounced their membership of the League because it had not helped them against the margrave.[80] Their opposition was finally broken, and the loss of their privileges and trade rights reduced them to unimportant country towns.

During the later years of his reign Frederick had to quell fresh conflicts in various towns. In 1467 he decided a dispute at Potsdam in favour of the aldermen, abolishing the assessors elected by the commons, and threatened to punish anyone who attacked the aldermen in future.[81] In the following year he subdued the rebellious gilds of Gardelegen, in the Old Mark, by punishing the leaders and making the wardens of the gilds swear obedience to him and to the aldermen.[82] He thus continued the policy of his predecessors of protecting the aristocracy.[83]

Though Berlin and Cölln had been subjugated by the margrave, the Old Mark towns, especially Stendal and Salzwedel, still held their old powerful position. The quarrel between them and Frederick's brother and successor, Albrecht, began immediately on his accession in 1471, over the question whether he should confirm their privileges before or after they swore the oath of allegiance.[84] The following years were taken up by a dispute between margrave, nobles, and towns over the *modus* and re-partitioning of a tax to pay his debt of 100,000 guilders. The margrave proposed for the first time to raise the money by an excise on beer, but the towns, in which the brewing and export of beer were very important trades, refused to grant such a tax so that he had to revert to the customary land tax, the towns having to contribute 50,000, the nobles 30,000, and Albrecht himself 20,000 guilders.[85] Later on, he informed the estates that he intended to raise his share by a new toll on all merchandise, from which the goods of prelates and nobles were to be exempted.[86] When a court of the estates, each time composed of a large majority of nobles, approved of this [87] and decided against the towns of the Old Mark and Prignitz, which were now refusing to pay their part of the 50,000 guilders,[88] the towns rose in open revolt. In April 1473, Stendal, Salzwedel, and Gardelegen refused to allow collectors of the new toll to be installed; in Stendal the burghers threatened to cut off the heads of the margrave's councillors, who were believed to be responsible for the introduction of the toll. Everywhere in the Old Mark the burghers stood on guard, and all were summoned to arms.[89] The towns of the Prignitz also refused to pay the toll; at Havelberg the collectors were driven away. In the Middle Mark, Brandenburg, Frankfort, and Rathenow joined the opposition. The commons of Frankfort demanded that the toll should be repealed, and that this claim should be conveyed to Albrecht not by an alderman, but by a member of the commons. The town would refuse to send him any military help in the future if he insisted on the toll. In the Pomeranian towns there was a rumour that the Brandenburg towns had *all* joined in this refusal.[90] The margrave accordingly had to give way for the time being.[91]

When Albrecht asked the estates for fresh financial aid in 1480, the prelates and nobles came back to the proposal to raise the money by an excise on beer, but the towns resisted vigorously.[92] Those of the Old Mark declared that they were too poor to give anything at all, while the others agreed only to give the usual land tax.[93] Thereupon Margrave John, governor of the Mark in place of his father, submitted the case to a court of the Middle Mark estates, bringing up all his old and new complaints against the towns of the Old Mark, especially against Stendal, the centre of resistance, which he accused of usurping many rights, particularly of jurisdiction.[94] Again the court, with its large majority of prelates and nobles,[95] decided in favour of the margrave, giving him the right to confiscate all goods of the Old Mark towns, wherever he found them, until they had paid their taxes.[96] In the following year, the prelates and nobles of the Old Mark, who had hitherto supported their towns, declared that they would pay their share whether the towns did so or not.[97] The latter, now standing alone, were unable to continue their opposition and offered, in place of the 17,000 guilders demanded, 13,000 guilders, which were accepted by the margrave.[98]

In 1488 Margrave John, who had succeeded his father in 1486, at last found the desired opportunity to subjugate the powerful towns of the Old Mark and their gilds.[99] When he asked the estates for fresh financial aid in February, the prelates and nobles and the Middle Mark and Prignitz towns consented to raise the money by an excise on beer. The consent of the prelates and nobles was secured by a clause that the beer they brewed themselves in their castles and manors was to be free from the duty, while that of the towns may have been won by conceding them one-third of the yield of the tax.[100] Only in the Old Mark did the lower gilds rise against margrave, nobility, and aldermen, which seems to show that the aldermen there were also inclined to accept the excise.

In Stendal the lower gilds and commons compelled the aldermen and the ruling 'three gilds' [101] to give a written promise to resist the excise and to make other concessions.[102] Then the burghers marched out of the town, pillaged and burned the residences of the nobles, of whom they captured several and seized others when they rode into Stendal to redeem their goods. Three nobles were tried and executed, the rest were cast into a dungeon.[103] The burghers of Salzwedel also marched against the nobles, sacked their manors and put several of them to death.[104] Similar riots, directed against margrave and aldermen, took place in all the towns of the Old Mark. In Seehausen the shoemakers were the leaders; here too the aldermen were forced to sign a document granting concessions.[105] In Salzwedel the burghers grew frightened after their outbreak and sent a message to the margrave saying that they put their persons, goods, and

privileges into his hands. But when he was already on his way to Salzwedel, they changed their minds again and stormed and occupied the convent of the Holy Ghost outside the town.[106]

Supported by the nobility, Margrave John could now master the Old
Mark towns by force. On 25 March Tangermünde, on the Elbe, surrendered to him.[107] From there he marched on Stendal, begged to do so,
according to chroniclers' reports,[108] by the deposed aristocracy. On 22
April the burghers of the town, who seem to have offered no resistance,
surrendered all their old privileges, e.g. those of not rendering military
service outside their town walls and of choosing another sovereign if oppressed by the margrave, further the original letters of their unions and
alliances with other towns, the higher and lower jurisdiction, and the
right of electing their aldermen freely. They had to agree to pay the beer
duty, raised to double the amount, not for seven but for fourteen years,
as well as damages to the nobles. The five seditious gilds, the clothmakers, shoemakers, furriers, bakers, and linenweavers, lost their gild status.
All the burghers had to do homage on their knees and vow never again to
plot against the margrave or the aldermen who represented him.[109] Three
ringleaders were beheaded,[110] and many others had to quit the town.[111]
A few months later, John confirmed the gild rights of the merchants,
butchers, and clothiers because of their obedient and pious behaviour
during the riots.[112]

From Stendal the margrave went to Osterburg, and from there to
Salzwedel, which surrendered on 28 April. It too had to yield up all its
privileges, which included exemption from military service and the right
to destroy the castles in the Old Mark, its jurisdiction, its rights of alliance, gild and free election of aldermen, the keys to the town gates, and
the weapons of the burghers. Like Stendal, it had to pay damages to the
nobles and to agree to raise the beer duty for a longer period and a
higher amount. The houses near the margrave's castle were to be demol-
ished and he was to be allowed to build a sortie from it, while the gates
between the Altstadt and the Neustadt, which had been taken down during the rising, were to be restored and closed again.[113] Two burghers were
executed.[114] During the first days of May, Seehausen, Werben, and Gardelegen also handed over their privileges, conceded the excise either for
seven or for fourteen years and signed similar documents of submission;
this Tangermünde and Osterburg had already done.[115] The power of the
Old Mark towns was broken, and it never revived.

A few years later, Margrave John followed up his victory of 1488 by
harsh treatment of the two towns of the Middle Mark standing next to
Berlin in importance. In 1490 he forbade the gilds of the Neustadt of
Brandenburg to summon the burghers to the town hall or to make any
agreement with the gilds of the Altstadt; for he refused to let the gilds
dominate the aldermen in the towns.[116] In 1496 Frankfort had to sur-

render the higher jurisdiction and the right of electing its aldermen freely, as well as to concede an increase of taxes.[117] The connections between the Brandenburg towns and the Hansa were now finally severed. In 1517 Stendal, Salzwedel, and Berlin left the League; they were declared non-members in the following years,[118] and Frankfort was pronounced one in 1525.[119]

At the close of the middle ages, the political and economic power of the Brandenburg towns was completely broken; the craft gilds and commons were subservient to the patricians, and the latter depended on the margrave. Throughout the period, the policy of practically all the margraves, to whichever house they belonged, had always been one of supporting the rule of the patricians and lending them their help to hold down the lower orders. As the latter were the mainstay of the opposition to any attempts at subjugation of the towns as a whole, effective resistance was made impossible by the aristocracy's policy of calling in the margraves.

Trade rather than manufacture had always been the main activity of these towns of the colonisation area, and this had two consequences: first, that the craft gilds and commons were not strong enough to gain power; and, secondly, that the loss of trade rights and privileges was fatal to the development of the towns. Where, formerly, strong communities had governed themselves, undisturbed by outside interference and protected by alliances with each other, and, as members of the Hanseatic League, had carried on trade with Scandinavia and Flanders, town life now decayed. Self-government, so far as it survived, developed into a dull routine and the magistrates became obedient state officials. Even in the years of the Reformation, when all over north-eastern Germany, from Lübeck, via Stralsund and Stettin, to Danzig and Königsberg, the commons rose in a last desperate revolt, there was hardly a stir in the Brandenburg towns.[120]

In the fight against the towns the margraves had to rely more and more upon the support of the nobles who were greatly strengthened by their common victory. The balance of power in society henceforth was in favour of the nobility. When, in the sixteenth century, the Junkers rose to be the ruling class in society, there no longer existed any force strong enough to contest the issue. Medieval democracy had lost its battle, and the burghers of the towns did not raise their heads again until the nineteenth century, when once more they were defeated by the forces which had vanquished them four hundred years earlier. Both the historical weakness of democracy in Germany and the formation of the Prussian State are intimately connected with the subjugation of the towns at the end of the middle ages.

Appendix

Margrave	House	Ruled in Brandenburg
Woldemar	Ascanian	1309–1319
Lewis the Elder ⎫ sons of King	Wittelsbach	1324–1351
Lewis the Roman ⎬ Lewis the	"	1351–1365
and Otto ⎪ Bavarian		
Otto ⎭	"	1365–1373
Emperor Charles IV . . .	Luxemburg	1373–1378
Sigismund, son of Charles IV .	"	1378–1397, 1411–1415
Jobst of Moravia . . .	"	1397–1411
Frederick I	Hohenzollern	1415–1440 (governor from 1411)
John ⎫	"	governor till 1438
Frederick II ⎬ sons of	"	1440–1470 (governor from 1438)
⎪ Frederick I		
Albrecht (Achilles) ⎭	"	1470–1486
John (Cicero), son of Albrecht .	"	1486–1499 (governor from 1470)
Joachim I, son of John . .	"	1499–1535

NOTES

* For list of margraves see Appendix.

1 Of more than sixty towns of the Brandenburg Mark over fifty per cent. have Slavonic names, and over twenty-five per cent. were major settlements before the German immigration started, but they were merely fortified places, and not *civitates* in the German sense, with self-government, special laws and privileges, aldermen and gilds of artisans.

2 Privileges as follows: Stendal, 1215; Prenzlau, 1305; Neu-Ruppin, 1315; Berlin and Cölln, Spandau, Frankfort, Landsberg, 1317; Brietzen, 1319; Wriezen, 1337; all towns of the New Mark, 1340 and 1344; Eberswalde and Bärwalde, 1350; Sandau, 1351; Straussberg, 1354; Alt-Landsberg, 1355; and many other towns: *Codex diplomaticus Brandenburgensis*, ed. A. F. Riedel (quoted as Riedel), xv, no. 5, p. 7; xxi, no. 22, pp. 104–5; iv, no. 4, p. 284; xii, no. 1, p. 350; xi, no. 32, p. 23; xviii, no. 9, p. 376; xxiii, no. 17, p. 14; ix, no. 11, p. 357; xii, no. 7, p. 417; xxiv, no. 55, p. 30, no. 62, p. 34; xii, no. 23, p. 296; xix, no. 34, p. 20; B ii no. 951, p. 329; xii, no. 42, p. 74, no. 22, p. 498.

3 Privileges of Berlin and Cölln, 1317; Salzwedel, 1343: Riedel, xii, no. 1, p. 350; xiv, nos. 115–16, pp. 82–3.

4 In 1375 the *iudicium supremum* was either sold or pawned in at least sixteen towns, including all the larger ones: *Kaiser Karl's IV. Landbuch der Mark Brandenburg*, ed. E. Fidicin, pp. 28–32. Cp. Riedel, i, no. 59, p. 155; ix, no. 33, p. 377; xviii, no. 56, p. 36, no. 39, p. 85, no. 22, p. 228, no. 51, p. 308; xix, no. 121, p. 249; xxi, no. 142, p. 197.

5 Privileges of Rathenow, 1295; Brietzen, 1319; Bärwalde, 1350: *ibid.*, vii, no. 4, p. 410; ix, no. 11, p. 357; xix, no. 34, p. 20.

6 Privileges of Stendal, 1324; the district of Lebus, 1327; Berlin and Cölln, 1328: *ibid.*, xv, nos. 104–5, pp. 77–8 (renewed in 1344: no. 157, p. 118), xx, no. 34, p. 203; *Historisch-diplomatische Beiträge zur Geschichte der Stadt Berlin*, ed. E. Fidicin (quoted as Fidicin), ii, no. 22, p. 28.

7 Riedel, xxi, no. 61, p. 134 (1324).

8 The principles of this law were communicated by Berlin to Frankfort in 1253: 'Consules autem qui nunc sunt sequentis anni consules eligere habent et statuere. . . . Omnes vero exercentes officia, videlicet pistores, sutores, carnifices, seu cuiuscunque operis fuerint, non liceat eis habere quod dicitur Innicghe in civitate, nisi de voluntate et permissione consulum. . . . Magistri etiam pistorum a consulibus statuantur. . . .': *ibid.*, xxiii, no. 3, p. 4.

9 Count Günther von Arnstein granted the law of Stendal to the town of Neu-Ruppin in 1256: 'Consules consulibus suo tempore substituendis consulant assumtis quibusdam discretioribus civitatis. . . .': *ibid.*, iv, no. 2, p. 283.

10 See *ibid.*, iv, p. 224.

11 *Ibid.*, iv, p. 208. Cp. below, p. 78.

12 Privilege of Margrave Lewis the Elder for the town of Pritzwalk of 1335: 'Unde cum concors electio consulum, per universitatem vestram pro nunc facta, ipsi nostrae civitati et nobis . . . utiliter conveniat, ut denuo consules . . . secundum civitatis nostrae Sehusen aliarumque nostrarum civitatum ritum et modum communem eligere habeatis, vobis . . . conferimus . . . facultatem. . . .': *ibid.*, iii, no. 48, p. 367.

13 Since 1258 the Brandenburg Mark had been divided between two branches of the Ascanian house, the Johannine and the Ottonine line.

14 'Nos una cum consilio omnium civitatum domini Johannis, marchionis Brandenburgensis, firma fide inter nos quandam fecimus unionem in hunc modum quod si aliqua violentia seu iniustitia alicui praedictarum civitatum insurgeret, tunc nos eidem civitati pro nostra possibilitate astare volumus consiliis pariter et expensis. . . .': Riedel, xiv, no. 63, p. 50. The documents *ibid.*, ix, no. 10, p. 7, and in *Urkundenbuch zur Berlinischen Chronik*, ed. F. Voigt (quoted as Voigt), no. 38, p. 25, are slightly different in wording.

15 'Si aliqui cives traherentur ad placita terrae, quae in vulgo dicuntur Lantdinc, extunc, sicut exnunc, expensae communes esse debent. Item si aliqua enormitas sive violentia per potentes aliquos fieret in nostra civitate, dummodo consules talem sibi assumerent violentiam, tunc iterum expensae communes esse debent. . . .': Riedel, ix, no. 14, p. 10; xiv, nos. 64, 66, p. 51.

16 Between Königsberg, Schönfliess, Härwalde and Mohrin, in the New Mark, in 1320; between the towns of the Middle and Old Mark and those of Lower Lusatia in 1323; between the Old Mark towns before 1323, in 1334, 1344, 1353, 1369, 1393, 1436 and 1478; between Prenzlau, Pasewalk, Angermünde and Templin, in the Ucker Mark, in 1348; between the Middle Mark towns in 1393 and 1399; between Berlin and Cölln, Brandenburg, and Frankfort in 1431: *ibid.*, xix, no. 21, p. 184; iii, no. 38, p. 361; xv, no. 103, p. 76; xvi, no. 10, p. 8; xiv, no. 124, p. 88; vi, no. 138, p. 100, no. 17, p. 409; xxv, no. 146, p. 278; vi, no. 168, p. 120; xxv, no. 295, p. 399; xxi, no. 96, p. 161; xi, no. 95, p. 66; xxiv, no. 96, p. 393; Fidicin, iv, no. 123, p. 95; ii, no. 97, p. 123, no. 104, p. 152. Probably many more such unions were formed.

17 Riedel, xv, nos. 104–5, pp. 77–8; xiv, no. 87, p. 65 (1324); xx, no. 34, p. 203 (1327); Fidicin, ii, no. 22, p. 28 (1328); Riedel, iii, no. 71, p. 378; ix, no. 68, p. 43; xi, no. 54, p. 37; xvi, no. 17, p. 13, no. 27, p. 328; xxi, no. 100, p. 164; Supplementband, no. 19, p. 233 (all issued by the 'false' margrave Woldemar in 1348).

18 See Riedel, B i, no. 106, p. 80; xiv, no. 13, p. 9; xv, no. 35, p. 24; *Hansisches Urkundenbuch*, i, nos. 593, 850, 865, pp. 208, 292, 299.

19 In the Old Mark Stendal, Salzwedel, Gardelegen, Seehausen, Tangermünde, Osterburg, and Werben; in the Prignitz Perleberg, Havelberg, Pritzwalk, and Kyritz; in the Middle Mark Berlin and Cölln, Brandenburg, and Frankfort: W. Stein, 'Die Hansestädte; (c) Die Städte der Mark Brandenburg', *Hansische Geschichtsblätter*, 1915, pp. 119–24, 135–7.

20 Thus 1459, 1476, 1482, 1485–6: Riedel, xv, nos. 348, 407, 409, 431, 443, 446, pp. 289–402; xvi, no. 621, p. 176.

21 'Af ichteswelke lude unrechte sameninge, twidracht, uplop und vorsturinge der stede in desen steden meynen to makene . . . to ereme live und gude scal men richten sunder gnade. Worden se ok vorvluchtich, der er scal men in den anderen steden nicht liden. . . .': *ibid.*, vi, no. 168, p. 120.

22 *Ibid.*, xxii, no. 3, p. 488 (1438?).

23 *Hanserecesse von 1256–1430*, vi, no. 557, p. 555. Renewed in 1447, 1470 and 1487: *Hanserecesse von 1431–1476*, iii, no. 288, pp. 177, 186–7; vi, no. 356, p. 332; *Hanserecesse von 1477–1530*, ii, no. 160, pp. 142–3.

24 'Cum in civitate nostra Stendal aliqualis mota fuisset discordia super iure civitatis, dissentientibus divitibus ac pauperibus. . . .': Riedel, xv, no. 42, p. 34.

25 Riedel, xv, 34. For a conflict between the aldermen and gilds of Neu-Ruppin in 1315, see *ibid.*, iv, no. 4, p. 285; and for one between the aldermen and commons of Pritzwalk in 1335, see *ibid.*, iii, no. 48, p. 367; ii, p. 14.

26 *Ibid.*, xv, nos. 167–8, pp. 123–5.

27 In 1346 Margrave Lewis the Elder promised to protect the burghers who were 'outside the town' and to help them in again: *ibid.*, xv, no. 175, p. 132.

28 The reconciliation was effected by Archbishop Otto of Magdeburg, the aldermen of the other Old Mark towns, and those of Brandenburg: *ibid.*, xv, nos. 179–80, pp. 135–6.

29 See the privileges given to Berlin and Cölln, Brandenburg, Spandau, Tangermünde, Osterburg, Pritzwalk, and Prenzlau: *ibid.*, Supplementband, no. 19, p. 233; ix, no. 68, p. 43; xi, no. 54, p. 37; xvi, no. 17, p. 13, no. 27, p. 328; iii, no. 71, p. 378; xxi, no. 100, p. 164.

30 In Prenzlau, Pasewalk, Angermünde, and Templin: *ibid.*, Supplementband, no. 28, p. 26.

31 The towns of Soldin and Königsberg: *ibid.*, xviii, no. 25, p. 458; xix, no. 71, p. 215.

32 Berlin, Frankfort, Spandau, and Köpenick each were to occupy one of the margrave's castles: *ibid.*, B ii, no. 891, p. 259 (1349).

33 Reconciliation with Königsberg and Soldin of 1349; with Stendal of 1351: *ibid.*, xix, no. 71, p. 215; xviii, no. 25, p. 458; xv, no. 185, p. 140.

34 At least in the Old Mark: reconciliation with Stendal of 1351, repeated in 1360; with Sandau of 1351: *ibid.*, xv, no. 185, p. 140, no. 201, p. 152; B ii, no. 951, p. 329.

35 Reconciliation with Spandau of 1349; with Rathenow and Sandau of 1351; with the Altstadt of Brandenburg of 1355; with the Neustadt of Brandenburg of 1365: *ibid.*, xi, no. 55, p. 38; vii, no. 16, p. 416; B ii, no. 951, p. 329; ix, no. 77, p. 49, no. 87, p. 55.

36 *Ibid.*, xiv, nos. 175–7, pp. 124–5.

37 *Ibid.*, xv, no. 235, p. 182.

38 Forty-three of the seventy-two aldermen known for the period 1365–1400 came from the families which had predominated in the council before 1345; among the twenty-nine others there were certainly members of the clothiers' gild who had joined it after that year: L. Götze, *Urkundliche Geschichte der Stadt Stendal*, pp. 174–5. The cloth trade of Stendal was very important: Riedel, xv, no. 360, p. 299.

39 This must have taken place between 1373 and 1378. The only source for these events exists in the form of notes in the oldest town records of Berlin of 1397 (?): Fidicin, i, pp. 176–80. Cp. Fidicin, *Berlinische Chronik*, p. 117.

40 In 1382 margrave Sigismund, the son of Charles IV, wrote in favour of the expelled Wardenberg to the aldermen, gilds and commons of Berlin: Fidicin, iv, no. 48, p. 51 = Voigt, no. 24, p. 204.

41 Apparently it was discovered at an early stage. Some details in Riedel, Supplementband, no. 63, p. 269. Cp. Fidicin, i, p. 223.

42 Cp. above, p. 77.

43 Riedel, xx, no. 96, pp. 256–7.

44 *Ibid.*, xxiii, no. 226, pp. 164–5.

45 *Ibid.*, xxiii, no. 229, p. 177.

46 *Ibid.*, ix, no. 86, p. 408.

47 *Ibid.*, xxi, nos. 219–20, pp. 260–2; *Die Magdeburger Schöppenchronik*, ed. K. Janicke (*Die Chroniken der deutschen Städte vom 14. bis in's 16. Jahrhundert*, vii), p. 374.

48 F. Priebatsch, *Die Hohenzollern und die Städte der Mark im 15. Jahrhundert*, p. 61.

49 Riedel, ix, no. 164, p. 129.

50 *Deutsche Reichstagsakten unter Kaiser Sigmund*, ix, ed. D. Kerler, pp. 238, 261.

51 The margrave expressed his thanks for help against Stendal to the towns of Seehausen and Tangermünde: Riedel, vi, no. 34, p. 365; xvi, no. 60, p. 52.

52 Riedel, xv, nos. 286–8, pp. 230–3; Götze, pp. 192–6.

53 Riedel, xiv, no. 114, p. 245.

54 *Ibid.*, xxiii, no. 240, p. 193 = Fidicin, iv, no. 158, p. 136.

55 Riedel, xxiii, no. 176, p. 125.

56 H. Prutz, *Preussische Geschichte*, i, p. 145.

57 Fidicin, ii, no. 104, p. 152. According to G. W. von Raumer, *Codex diplomaticus Brandenburgensis continuatus* (quoted as Raumer), i, p. 155, the Old Mark towns formed a union in the same year.

58 Riedel, xii, no. 38, pp. 510–11. Fidicin, iv, no. 162, pp. 143–4.

59 Riedel, xxii, no. 3, pp. 487–9.

60 Notes of Berlin's town-clerk: *ibid.*, D i, p. 304 = Fidicin, i, pp. 252–3.

61 Riedel, Supplementband, no. 88, pp. 287–90; Fidicin, ii, no. 126, pp. 180–6. Reports of chroniclers: *Das Stadtbuch des alten Köln an der Spree*, ed. P. Clauswitz, pp. 43–44; *Chronik des Franciscaner Lesemeisters Detmar*, ed. F. H. Grautoff, ii, p. 83; A. Krantz, *Wandalia*, liber xii, cap. x; A. Angelus, *Annales Marchiae Brandenburgicae*, ed. 1958, p. 214; P. Hafftitius, *Microcronicon Marchicum*, in Riedel, D i, p. 62; N. Leuthinger, *De Marchia et rebus Brandenburgicis* . . . , ed. J. G. Krause, p. 777. The modern literature on the subject is discussed by E. Kaeber, 'Die Beziehungen zwischen Berlin und Cölln im Mittelalter und der Konflikt der beiden Städte mit Kurfürst Friedrich II.', *Hansische Geschichtsblätter*, liv (1929), pp. 19ff.

62 Raumer, i, no. 67, pp. 207–8.

63 Voigt, note to no. 111, p. 387.

64 Fidicin, iv, no. 171, p. 176 = Voigt, no. 111, p. 387.

65 Voigt, no. 112, p. 388.

66 Krantz, *loc. cit.*; Angelus, *loc. cit.*; Z. Garcaeus, *Successiones familiarum et res gestae illustrissimorum praesidum Marchiae Brandenburgensis*, ed. J. G. Krause, p. 174.

67 Fidicin, ii, no. 136, p. 197; *Berlinische Chronik*, p. 172.

68 Riedel, Supplementband, no. 93, p. 294; Fidicin, iii, no. 401, p. 229; ii, no. 141, p. 211.

69 Fidicin, ii, no. 140, p. 208.

70 *Ibid.*, ii, nos. 140–1, pp. 206–12; *Hanserecesse von 1431–1476*, vii, no. 531, p. 842.

71 Riedel, iv, no. 103, p. 336; xi, no. 28, p. 245; Fidicin, iv, no. 173, p. 177; ii, no. 138, p. 199; iii, p. 330; cp. *ibid.*, iv, no. 174, p. 178.

72 Detailed letter of the aldermen of Neustadt-Eberswalde to those of Berlin and Cölln, dated April 10th: Riedel, xii, no. 67, p. 328.

73 The first proposal to submit the dispute to the decision of such a court had been declined by the two towns: Fidicin, ii, no. 141, p. 211.

74 See *ibid.*, ii, nos. 140–1, pp. 200–12.

75 Raumer, i, no. 68, pp. 209–10, also giving the names of the judges, their large majority being nobles.

76 *Ibid.*, i, no. 69, pp. 211–12.

77 According to the, perhaps incomplete, lists in Fidicin (ii, no. 142, pp. 214–15) four families had to pay 3,000 guilders each, two 2,000 each, five 1,000 each, seven 700 each, one 200, and seven 100 guilders each. Later on, some fines were reduced or remitted: *ibid.*, ii, no. 142, pp. 216–17, no. 144, pp. 219–20; Riedel, Supplementband, no. 97, p. 296. As late as 1458 his fiefs were given back to one burgher: Raumer, i, no. 114, p. 243.

78 Fidicin, ii, no. 142, p. 217.

79 *Hanserecesse von 1431–1476*, iii, no. 649, p. 485, no. 672, p. 512.

80 *Ibid.*, vii, no. 531, p. 842. Later on Berlin became again a member, but did not resume sending delegates to the diets: *Hansisches Urkundenbuch*, viii, p. 308 n. 4; *Hanserecesse von 1431–1476*, vi, no. 185, p. 164; Stein, pp. 133–4; Kaeber, pp. 87–8. Cp. below, p. 89.

81 Riedel, xi, no. 37, p. 182.

82 Priebatsch, pp. 82, n. 1, 105. Cp. the later addition in the town's statutes: Riedel, xxv, no. 239, p. 362.

83 Beginning in 1438 in Salzwedel: Riedel, xiv, no. 333, p. 262.

Ibid., xiv, no. 420, p. 349. Cp. above, p. 83.

85 For details see Riedel, xiv, no. 420, pp. 350–1; C ii, no. 63, pp. 62–3.

86 8 August 1472: *ibid.*, xiv, no. 426, p. 357.

87 23 February 1473: *ibid.*, C ii, no. 72, pp. 72–5.

88 8 March 1473: *ibid.*, C ii, no. 75, p. 89. In both instances several judges belonging to the towns withdrew before judgment was given, obviously because they disagreed.

89 Reports of the knight Busso von Alvensleben and Bishop Frederick of Lebus, of 3 and 9 April respectively: *ibid.*, C ii, no. 87, p. 101, no. 91, p. 113. Cp. *ibid.*, xiv, nos. 427–8, pp. 358–9.

90 *Ibid.*, B v, nos. 1939–40, 1945–7, 1950, 1952, pp. 205–33; C ii, no. 87, p. 101.

91 In 1476 the Prignitz towns bought their freedom from the new toll for 1,500 guilders, and the Old Mark towns for 6,000: *ibid.*, i, no. 114, p. 194; Priebatsch, p. 144.

92 Raumer, ii, no. 50, pp. 47–8 = Riedel, C ii, no. 196, pp. 245–8.

93 Letter of Margrave John to his father, of 10 August 1480: Riedel, C ii, no. 205, p. 257. Cp. his correspondence with the Old Mark towns: Raumer, ii, nos. 57, 60, pp. 55, 57.

94 In detail, Raumer, ii, nos, 59, 63, pp. 56–9.

95 See *ibid.*, ii, nos. 58, 63, pp. 56, 59.

96 *Ibid.*, ii, no. 63, p. 60.

97 *Ibid.*, ii, no. 65, p. 62.

98 Letter of Margrave Albrecht to his son, of 10 October 1481: Riedel, C ii, no. 217, pp. 267–8; Priebatsch, pp. 254–63.

99 For his sharp action against the gilds of Perleberg and Wittstock, in the Prignitz, in 1482 see Riedel, i, no. 118, p. 198, p. 291; iii, no. 232, pp. 486–7.

100 *Ibid.*, C ii, no. 265, pp. 333–6.

101 See above, pp. 79–80.

102 Riedel, xv, no. 452, p. 408.

103 Riedel, xv, no. 451, pp. 407–8, nos. 477–9, pp. 429–30.

104 *Ibid.*, xiv, no. 496, p. 422.

105 *Ibid.*, vi, nos. 69–70, pp. 384–5.

106 *Ibid.*, xiv, no. 496, p. 422.

107 Priebatsch, p. 171.

108 A. Krantz, *Saxonia*, liber xiii, cap. xiv; Garcaeus, p. 240.

109 Riedel, xv, no. 452, pp. 408–10.

110 Krantz, *loc. cit.*, and Angelus, p. 255, simply say that a number were executed. Götze, p. 237, and Priebatsch, p. 171, give the above number, while C. F. Pauli, *Allgemeine preussische Staats-Geschichte*, ii, p. 388, puts it as high as eight to twelve.

111 Riedel, xv, no. 459, p. 416.

112 *Ibid.*, xv, nos. 456–7, pp. 413–14; xxv, no. 333, p. 430.

113 *Ibid.*, xiv, no. 496, pp. 419–23.

114 Document built into the steeple of St. Mary's at Salzwedel in 1496: Götze, p. 243.

115 Riedel, vi, no. 212, p. 149, no. 69, p. 384, no. 52, pp. 431–2; xvi, p. 118.

116 Raumer, ii, no. 87, p. 83 = Riedel, ix, no. 314, p. 241.

117 Riedel, xxiii, no. 366, pp. 305–6; Priebatsch, pp. 173–4.

118 *Hanserecesse von 1477–1530*, vii, no. 39, p. 61, no. 108, p. 176.

119 *Ibid.*, ix, no. 132, p. 260.

120 Only in Stendal and Tangermünde, in the Old Mark, did a minor rebellion break out in 1530 which was easily suppressed by Margrave Joachim; in Stendal six ringleaders were beheaded: for details see Riedel, xv, nos. 613–15, pp. 526–9; xvi, no. 178, pp. 143–5; Supplementband, nos. 47–8, pp. 417–18; Pauli, ii, pp. 562–5. In 1525, the year of the Peasants' War, everything remained quiet in the Brandenburg Mark: see the letters of Margrave Joachim and the knight Christoph von Taubenheim in *Akten zur Geschichte des Bauernkriegs in Mitteldeutschland*, i, 2, ed. O. Merx and G. Franz, no. 922, p. 573, no. 963, p. 600.

19

The Late Medieval Poor
in Town and Countryside

F. GRAUS

IN TRYING TO OUTLINE a history of "the poor" in the late Middle Ages I am very conscious of the difficulties in my way and of the provisional character of my attempt. However, I have decided to go ahead, for at least two reasons. In the first place, while historians investigate the economic history of the late Middle Ages [1] in great detail and take a lively interest in its political events and political theory, and in changes in the structure of the state, there is no major work on social evolution in this period, and the lower social groups have been especially neglected. It is important to fill this gap.[2] In the second place, in revolutionary movements we see the upsurge of a group which the sources ordinarily call "the populace" or "the scum of the people". Although such texts are not very explicit, they reveal the existence of a group that was capable of taking the lead in mass uprisings, even if only briefly. At such moments the action of this group was decisive.

Certainly the existence in medieval society of people who had very little social importance is no secret to historians. Scholars have long since ceased to view medieval society as a model of harmony and equilibrium with no very rich (except for feudal lords), nor any extreme poverty except for a few beggars. A clear distinction is now seen between two groups to be found in every urban and rural population, those of the rich and the poor (*divites et pauperes*). Medieval sources reiterate this distinction, but no one has fully explored its significance.

The antithesis between rich and poor, taken from the Bible, runs through all medieval literature. Medieval sources apply these broad terms to all sharp social oppositions, so that the words *pauper, pauvre, arm, chudý* (in Czech) actually have a variety of meanings. Often one has to do considerable research to discover whether the word refers simply to an unimportant person or to a serf.[3] The meanings can vary at the same period.[4] I refer to the social import of the words, not to their juridical meaning. In dealing with the serfs, who in the Middle Ages were often described as "the poor," I shall not be concerned with their juridical status.

The notion of "the poor" rests on a long tradition of Latin literature. The Church Fathers faced the problem of differences of wealth, which were very marked in the society of the late Empire.[5] They had to take a position, especially from the 4th century on, in regard to flagrant social inequalities. At the same time they had to appease the poor and the slaves, who, according to the Christian faith, had been created by God in the same way as the rich and the powerful. The Church Fathers were far from agreement in defense of wealth. Some insisted that the rich man be generous, give large alms, help the Church, and lead an evangelic life. Very soon some voices were even raised in condemnation of property in general. Saint Jerome himself cited the old proverb, "Every rich man is either evil or the heir of evil." [6] On the whole, Christian literature glorifies poverty. The story of Lazarus (Luke, 16:19), stretched out sick and starving before the rich man's door and receiving his reward in the future life, enjoyed a great vogue; preachers and moralists tell it again and again.

From the theological point of view poverty was safer than wealth; [7] to be saved the rich man had to give alms generously, for, "It is easier for a camel to pass through the eye of a needle than for a rich man to enter into the kingdom of Heaven" (Matthew, 19:24). Ecclesiastical literature further early created the ideal of "the holy poor"—*sanctus pauper,* later also *sanctus rusticus*—that is, of the poor man who bore his poverty patiently without complaining to God and who would receive his reward in "the other world." As to the rich, they could redeem their sins by abundant alms-giving.[8] All was therefore for the best. Poverty was in theory an ideal state, the poor man having the immense advantage over the rich of greater certainty of salvation.

The ruling classes were in no way threatened by this exaltation of poverty. They assured the poor of their reward in the world beyond and by the same token denied their right to any active resistance. All the members of society were traditionally compared to the parts of the body, necessarily bound to help each other. Along with the glorification of poverty went a denunciation of the cruelty of rich men who oppressed the poor, whom "one saw murdered every day." [9] These denunciations were sometimes extraordinarily fierce. But if the moralists addressed themselves to the rich and the powerful of this world, exhorting them to pity the poor and the oppressed, poverty in itself is not, in ecclesiastical writing, held to be an evil in the proper sense of the term; on the contrary, it is that state which best allows man to lead an evangelic life.

Social conditions were very different in the late Middle Ages from what they had been in the last days of the ancient world. But the condition of the poor remained the same, as though to justify the saying of Scripture (Deuteronomy, 15:11, Matthew, 26:11), that there will always be poor in this world. It is true that a new doctrine appears, that of a threefold division of the people.[10] The old antithesis between rich and poor nonetheless remains the cornerstone of learned speculation while the poor continue to vegetate in the shadow of cathedrals and of wealthy monasteries. However, something is changing in the later centuries of the Middle Ages.

In the 13th century there are protests arising, in ecclesiastical circles, against the traditional idealization of poverty. Furthermore, authorized members of the Church (not only, as formerly, heretics) demand that she herself observe "apostolic" poverty. The Dominicans replied, not only by representing Jesus Christ with a purse in his hand, but by recalling the point of view sustained by Saint Thomas Aquinas, namely, that poverty is not indispensable to the state of perfection.[11] Theologians continued their praise of poverty—a "lay" poverty—in trying to persuade the poor (using old literary forms as a model) that they were in reality "happier" than the rich. Various collections of sermons [12] delight in the tale of the pauper who lives in contentment so long as he is poor but whose happiness fades away as soon as he gets hold of a too well-filled purse.

As early as the 11th century, some voices had been denouncing poverty as the cause of evils and of abuses.[13] These voices multiplied in succeeding centuries, especially in the 15th century, until we reach the famous verse of Villon: "Necessity makes men hate, And hunger makes the wolf leap from the woods." [14] This is the culmination of a bourgeois literary current which, far from seeing poverty as an ideal, sees in it nothing but evil and misery.

With the 13th century the behavior of "the poor" themselves also changes. Suddenly this period of "feudal crisis" [15] is shot with storm and social agitation. "The poor" begin to act as an *independent element*. They are found acting in opposition to the middle classes (especially, in the towns, to the gild masters) and formulating demands of their own. In the 14th century the movement extends from the towns of Flanders to Italy, from England to faraway Moravia. For the first time the laborers raise organized revolt in the countryside; [16] they reinforce the revolutionary violence of the Hussite movement in Bohemia (1419–1437). Was not the initial phase of that revolution dominated by "the poor"? [17] Yes, without doubt. But these "poor" are already different from "the poor" of earlier periods.[18]

We shall be convinced of this if we look at the urban poor as they appear in the documents recording the insurrections which break out

...hroughout Europe in the 14th and 15th centuries. In every instance it is clear that we have to do with very heterogeneous groups. The urban poor included people who were "outside society"—thieves, cripples, prostitutes, and vagrants—in a word, all those who were reduced to a parasitic life; but it also included all kinds of wage workers, from the servants of rich bourgeois to day laborers,[19] and journeymen whom gild rules had kept from becoming masters. Indeed the stratum of "the poor" came to include an important group of gild masters who had fallen into economic dependence on well-to-do artisans or merchants: this phenomenon occurred, for example, in the cloth industry, as the result of extensive specialization and of the limitation, in some towns, of the right of sale.[20] Finally we must add students and wandering clerks, those truculent and disorderly men whose precarious and poverty-stricken way of life was early revealed in the poetry of the Goliards.

The number of these "poor" varied with the importance and with the social structure of a town. The development of production clearly accentuated the differences between the different elements in the group. There was actually no common denominator between a beggar and a journeyman, a wandering clerk and a small master fallen into economic dependence. Further, these different elements were more or less stable; while some—the poor artisans—were city dwellers, others came and went (journeymen and especially wandering clerks). Each group had a special juridical status; [21] students and journeymen could hope to attain in time a better social position. The only bond between these disparate groups was poverty: in the language of contemporary documents they were "the poor."

In the towns antagonisms varied in intensity under differing social conditions. Thus beggars were in effect incapable of fomenting any action. Nor could the vagabond clerks make their protests heard at all widely; besides, they tended to think themselves superior to the rest of "the poor." As to struggles between journeymen and masters, these for the most part took the form of wage demands. To repeat: the sole link between these different types of men was poverty. They were capable of joining together in a revolt, but the union would not last long. They were drawn together by the common hate and envy that they bore the rich, but lasting unity was not possible. It was only in exceptional conditions—at the start of a rising—that "the poor" acted together; their resistance quickly crumbled, breaking up into individualistic actions that were frequently at cross purposes.

Apart from exceptional cases, the number of "poor" in the towns was very limited. Regulations kept down the number of journeymen and the demand for wage workers was relatively slight; besides, the epidemics of plague decimated their ranks.[22] It is well-known that medieval population clearly failed to grow in the 14th century. In view of the circumstance that the town "poor" could always try their luck by moving else where, we need not be surprised to find movements of revolt spasmodic and short.[23]

We cannot therefore speak of any true self-consciousness on the part of "the poor." They were united only by wretchedness.[24] The bitter antagonisms that developed broke out also between the different kinds of "poor." The only ideological unity they possessed came from above, through the medieval doctrine of poverty.

The rural "poor" were more homogeneous. Although here too there were fugitive outlaws and people too infirm to work, the majority of the "poor" was made up of wage workers, including farm girls, and of peasants with insufficient land for subsistence.

Differentiation among the rural population was accentuated in the late Middle Ages by the increased importance of monetary exchange, notably in regions where mixed farming was little by little being abandoned for concentration on a single main product. The massive pentration of money into the countryside allowed of the formation of a new rich group which increasingly asserted itself.[25] How many writers of the period deplore the luxury affected by peasants aspiring to become the equals of petty feudal lords! On the other hand, the infiltration of money brought new problems for the small peasants who were struggling to produce for the market. In my view it is impossible to give any more detailed general chaacterization of this trend that would be valid for all of Europe, for it took different forms in different places.[26] However, we can note the rise everywhere of a minority of rich peasants while the number of poor peasants increased.

True, in several countries workers' wages rose during the second half of the 14th century. This must have been due to local diminutions of the population coinciding with a greater demand for wage workers.[27] Often the lords set juridical restrictions on the fragmentation of holdings. Fragmentation might diminish their revenues, for the agricultural techniques of the age did not allow of much production on small servile holdings. Thus peasants often had to work more land than they wanted.[28]

The fundamental social opposition in the villages of Europe, with the possible exception of Italy, was that between lord and villein, although the condition of the villein in the 14th century differed from one village to another. This class opposition between lord and subject was, however, often reduced by the social antithesis between rich and poor within the peasant population itself. Already in the 10th and 11th centuries, the author of the well-known poem *Unibos* (*One-ox*), shows sympathy towards a poor but sly peasant.[29] In the late Middle Ages social oppositions had developed to such a state that Andrew of Ratisbon,[30] in his anti-Hussite treatise of the early 15th century, sought to frighten peasants by the prospect of their servants demanding a share of their property.

Juridically speaking, all villeins belonged to "the poor"; yet the poor villein looked on the well-to-do peasant as a rich fellow, and the hostility that he felt for him was sometimes deeper than that which he felt for his lord who was more distant from him.

Daily life distracted the peasantry from social struggle in numerous ways, for example, by the dispersion of the population among so many villages and by inter-village strife, notably over pasture rights or enclosures. Often it was not the lords who drew the hate of their subjects, especially on the great estates, but their agents who, being in direct contact with the peasants, were accused of many abuses.[31] This phenomenon was widespread in all of Central Europe as late as the 18th century. If we add the existence of loyalty toward the king, which was so marked during the French Jacquerie and in the English uprising of Wat Tyler, we shall be the less surprised in noting that—despite the evidence of deepened class lines within the village population—serious insurrection broke out only when special circumstances drove the villagers desperate: the movement of the Jacquerie in France is the classic example.

What were the relations between the two groups, the rural "poor" and the urban "poor"? Did a common misery unite them or was the traditional opposition between town and country too strong? There is no easy answer to these questions. If we look at the troubles of the 14th and 15th centuries, from Flanders to Bohemia, we see resistance on the part of the rural "poor" converging at certain times with that of the urban "poor."[32] Cooperation between them never lasted long. Cooperation, however, did appear in a number of different places, so that it was clearly not a matter of chance; it has to be explained.

Economic opposition between town and country was aggravated in the 14th century by the growing gap between the prices of agricultural products and those of artisan products. The town "poor" were driven to oppose any influx, however slight, of country workers,[33] for the arrival of such workers could not fail to make their own position worse. The villeins were not only juridically inferior to the "poor" of the great cities, who were personally free, but were looked down on by the citizen population. Bourgeois literature is stamped, even more so than the poetry of vagabond clerks, by anti-peasant bias. Chivalric literature, on the other hand, did occasionally, if rarely, idealize country life.[34] The peasant who came to town always felt that people were not only cheating him but trying to make a fool of him. This certainly did not make for harmony between town and country. They could cooperate only exceptionally, under the pressure of crisis.

If I were to draw any conclusions from this little sketch, I would say that in the towns "the poor" formed a fairly compact social group, united in a common poverty. It was this that fundamentally distinguished them from the proletarians of the future. The country "poor," less dissimilar in their origins, were too dispersed in their numerous villages and, if we may use a modern term, had no class consciousness.

In the late Middle Ages, and until the late 18th century, unrest in Central and Eastern Europe typically takes the form of spasmodic revolt: it breaks out here and there in separate regions and quickly collapses without spreading on any large scale. Yet in the first half of the 15th century there is clearly a new type of rising, in the powerful Hussite movement in Bohemia. Here we have a true revolutionary movement, a spreading storm, in the course of which "the poor," and sometimes other elements of the population, were truly united, not only under the pressure of common distress, but also by a common ideology.

This phenomenon shows differing degrees of intensity in the late Middle Ages, for example, in the rising of the Ciompi at Florence or in the revolt of the Zealots at Salonica, or again in the movement of Wat Tyler in England. In all these cases, the rebels are fighting to put an end to particular abuses. It is true that they also in devious ways appeal to some "higher justice," usually giving religious reasons.[35] On these occasions portents of the future appear in various forms. In the Hussite revolution these features are particularly striking. But all of these movements were more than mere revolts against immediate oppression. Their causes lie deeper and show traces of a true ideology. To analyze them, we must return to the point of departure of this article, that is, to current opinions on the subject of poverty.

Late medieval literature and ideology had its "progressive" current in bourgeois writing, which exercised a marked influence both on poetry and on prose, especially in romance. As regards theories of the State and of society, bourgeois thinking favored royal power. Indeed, bourgeois society formed its ideology in the course of the struggle that the Kings waged against feudal society and against the Church; it provided the sovereigns with their most important theorists, who set themselves to formulate a secular theory of the State. The attack on ecclesiastical theory was naturally not an open attack, for the bourgeoisie could not risk this. All the same, it is obvious that conflicts with the Papacy came to a climax during this period and that the whole of life was slowly and surely, if we may use a somewhat deceptive term, becoming laicized.

"The poor" however could hardly share this way of thinking, for there was nothing in it to meet their aspirations. The bourgeoisie were necessarily obliged to defend inequalities of wealth. Besides, their alliance with Monarchy brought further obligations.[36] "The poor" could not take this road. How could a man living in chronic need understand the values of people who lived in wealth and ease? On the contrary, the luxury of the rich appeared to him to be the cause of his own want.[37] It was for this reason that in the course of uprisings the hatred of the poor often seemed concentrated on objects of luxury.[38] It was easy for them to conclude that wealth was the cause of poverty. The ideal state of things was to be sought in the remote past, in the ancient "age of gold" when all had shared equally in the goods of this world and had a sufficiency. This tradition, however, except insofar as it had penetrated popular culture in the form of fairy tales or fables, was hardly enough to satisfy a farm hand or a poor journeyman. These looked to a future where all would be equal, where there would be no more want, no difference between master and subject, where all would live in peace and none would have to work for his daily bread. The only doctrine which offered an answer to these longings lay in the Christian teaching of the Kingdom of God, where even the wolf would live in peace with the lamb, where there would be no difference between "thine" and "mine," where there would be neither want nor suffering.

Church doctrine recognized this happy state but placed it in the future,[39] teaching that it would come when God willed, and that it was not for man to try to hasten its arrival. On the other hand, the popular movements definitely seek to hasten it and to install the kingdom of God on earth. True, it is only in the chiliastic phase of the Hussite revolt [40] that the movement of "the poor" found theorists (certain priests) to formulate such a program for them. Here it was clearly affirmed that in the future kingdom of God on earth (according to their clerics, it had indeed already arrived) temporal power and, indeed, all constraints, would disappear.[41] In the absence of such theorists, aspiration took the form of dreams and vague half-conscious longing. One finds the aspiration all over Europe, sometimes vague, sometimes clearly written into the program of a movement.

Lacking structural unity, the group of "the poor" had not really, as a whole, become a force working for change. Only a part of it represented such a force, but this took form only little by little, and much time was to pass before it could formulate its own program. "The poor" of the late Middle Ages, except to some extent in the Italian towns, were merely a typical element of medieval society, without real unity as a group. Incapable of producing an ideology oriented toward the future, they clung to traditional ideas. Yet both in the towns and in the countryside the uprisings of the late Middle Ages have a new character: "the poor" are now a relatively important element of society, capable of vitalizing social movements in a way that had never been seen before.

NOTES

[1] See a very good survey, M. Mollat, P. Johansen, M. Postan, A. Sapori, Ch. Verlinden, *L'Economie européenne aux deux derniers siècles du Moyen Age,* Xe Congrès Inter-

national de Sciences Historiques, Rome, 1955, Relations VI, pp. 801–957. Its only fault is a certain neglect of Central Europe.

2 The most important material is to be sought in analytical work on medieval literature. This has often formed the subject of doctoral theses in German universities. There is also much material dealing for the most part with local revolt in the collection entitled *Staedtische Volksbewegungen im 14. Jahrhundert*, Berlin, Akademie-Verlag, 1960. In this article I am limiting myself to a very few bibliographical notes.

3 For the German word *arm* see, for example, *Deutsches Rechtswoerterbuch*, I, Weimar 1914–32, col. 821–824; for the Czech term *chudý*, V. Brandl, *Glossarium illustrans bohemico-moravicae historiae fontes*, Brno, 1876, p. 80. The term could be used very broadly. See, for example, the letter sent in 1390 by the town of Torun to the town of Wroclaw where even the merchants were called "arme lute" by the Grand Master of the Order (Hansisches UB, IV, no. 1001), p. 440.

4 L. Verriest, in *Institutions Médiévales* (Mons et Frameris, 1946), I, pp. 33ff. and K. Bosl, in *Franken um 800. Strukturanalyse einer Fraenkischen Koenigsprovinz* (Munich, 1959), p. 16, apply the 9th century term *pauperes* to vassals, without, however, giving their reasons.

5 On this subject see O. Schilling, *Reichtum und Eigentum in der altkirchlichen Literatur. Ein Beitrag zur sozialen Frage* (Freiburg-on-Bresgau, 1908); R. von Pöhlmann, *Geschichte der sozialen Frage und des Sozialismus in der antiken Welt* (3rd ed., Munich, 1925), II, pp. 475ff.; and especially R. W. and A. J. Carlyle, *A History of Medieval Political Theory in the West*, I, 2nd ed., 1927.

6 *Comm. in Jeremiam*, 5, 26ff. in Migne, *P.L.*, t. 24, col. 719 n. For other examples, see O. Schilling, *op. cit.*, p. 159.

7 Thus Tertullian (*De patientia*, c. 7) already states that God "semper pauperes justificat, divites praedamnat." For analogous opinions, see Pöhlmann, *op. cit.*, p. 475.

8 See, for example, a sermon from the *Vita Eligii ep. Noviomag.* II, 15 (*P.L.*, t. 87, col. 533): "Potuit nempe Deus omnes homines divites facere, sed pauperes ideo in hoc mundo voluit, ut divites haberent quomodo peccata sua redimerent". (God could have created all men rich, but he wanted paupers in this world, so that the rich might have some way to redeem their sins.) The *Vita* was written in the middle of the 8th century from an older model. The idea cited was quite common.

9 See as early as St. Ambrose, *De Nabuthe Jezraelita*, I, 1 (*P.L.*, t. 14, col. 731). Throughout medieval literature, from collections of sermons to romances, there are stories of the oppression of the poor who have everywhere and always asked in vain for their rights.

10 The origins of this doctrine have not yet been established. There is a very suggestive allusion in the *Vita Dagoberti regis Francorum*, c. 4 (MG, *Script. rer. Mer.*, II, p. 515).

11 *Summa* 11–2 qu. 188 a. 7. Aquinas carried authority on this point.

12 See, for example, Th. F. Crane, *The Exempla or Illustrative Stories from the Sermones Vulgares of Jacques de Vitry* (London, 1890), nos. 66, 78, 108 and the notes to these. Among older Christian sources, see St. Augustine, *De civ. Dei*, IV, 3.

13 *E.g.*, Ruodlieb, V, v. 427ff., ed. K. Langosch (Berlin, 1956), p. 138. Ruodlieb expresses the point of view of the small feudal lord. This idea persisted through the medieval centuries.

14 *Le Grand Testament*, XXI.

15 This is not the place to discuss the various points of view on this crisis. See my article, "Erste Krise des Feudalismus," *Zeitschrift fuer Geschichtswissenschaft*, 1955, pp. 552–592. See also B. Zientara, "Zagadnienie depresji rolnictwa w XIX–XV w. w swietle najnowszej literatury," *Przeglad historyczny*, 1960, pp. 262–274.

16 F. W. N. Hugenholtz, *Drie boerenopstanden uit de veertiende eeuw* (Haarlem, 1949), a comparative study of the three 14th century revolts (Flemish, French, English).

17 The fundamental work from this point of view is the recent book of J. Macek, *The Role of Tabor in the Hussite Revolutionary Movement* (Prague, 1956), 2 vols. (in Czech).

18 I have dealt with the problem of the poor, principally in Bohemia, in the 14th and

early 15th centuries in the following: *The Urban Poor in the Pre-Hussite Period* (Prague, 1949) and *History of the Peasantry in Bohemia in the Pre-Hussite Period* (Prague, 1957). In these books I develop in more detail the arguments of this article.

19 An account of a pastoral visit of the Archdeacon of Prague, dating from 1379, refers to a place in Prague where women servants were hired. (Archives of the Chapter of Prague, Cod. XIV, f. 53v.)

20 For example in Bohemia, which in the pre-Hussite period had little export trade in cloth.

21 Especially the wandering clerks, who were not subject to the municipal judges.

22 I shall not discuss here the much-debated role of the Black Death in ending population growth. I am skeptical on this point because its importance for Central Europe has certainly been exaggerated. It must be emphasized that crisis conditions had already appeared *before* the plague.

23 This applies equally to Flanders, although it was so advanced, the isolation of the different movements being due there in part to inter-urban competition among gild masters and merchants.

24 The poor suffered continuously from the depreciation of small coinage, the regressive nature of municipal taxation, and juridical discrimination.

25 It is very significant that the ecclesiastical authorities began to concern themselves at this period with country usurers. These were not only town usurers operating in the country, but also rich peasants.

26 Everywhere, but especially in England, the percentage of large holdings tends to increase.

27 Local conditions played a very important role and in my opinion we should not generalize about a fall in the number of workers.

28 In 14th-century Bohemia it was certainly more advantageous for the unfree to cultivate a holding of average size in a fertile region. But this is merely a typical feature of a region favorable to grain-growing, as Bohemia was at that time.

29 Recently edited by K. Langosch, *op. cit.*, pp. 251ff., also notes, pp. 379ff.

30 Andrew of Ratisbon, *Dyalogus de Hussitis*, in C. Höfler, ed., *Geschichtsschreiber der Hussitischen Bewegung in Boehmen* (Vienna, 1856), I, p. 567: "Fuit quidam rusticus, qui conferens cum quodam presbytero dixit: Bonum videtur, quod sic non gravaremur per dominos. Dixit presbyter: Et quomodo? Respondit rusticus: Certe quod omnia essent aequalia. Dixit presbyter: Si tibi istud sic placeret, numquid tibi etiam placeret, si ingrediens domum tuam, in qua tu es dominus, servus tuus vellet esse similis tibi? Respondit rusticus: Certe non. Dixit presbyter: Quare non? Respondit rusticus: Res ista stare non posset. (Dixit presbyter): Quare res ista, quemadmodum tu asseris, stare non potest; quid tunc debet fieri? Respondit rusticus: Melius est ut antiquo more, servato ordine, superioribus inferiores sint subjecti."

31 Late medieval French literature testifies to this, and in all of Europe similar tales circulated, recounting how the Devil had carried off a cruel bailiff or punished collectors of severe taxes. See A. Hilka, *Die Wundergeschichten des Caesarius von Heisterbach* (Bonn, 1937), III, pp. 106–107 and Joannes Pauli, *Schimpf und Ernst,* ed. J. Bolte (Berlin, 1924), II, pp. 277–278.

32 "The poor" were only one element in a larger movement. In general, the risings among peasants and among townspeople converged at a definite stage.

33 The lords were equally opposed for fear of seeing all their workers depart. The attitudes of patricians and of gild masters varied in different circumstances.

34 This literary idealization dates from classical antiquity and appears in very different ages.

35 Given the social evolution peculiar to Italy, this feature is naturally not strong in the uprising of the Ciompi. The latter were in any case better organized than other groups and clearly had some elements of *political* ideology.

36 From the ideological point of view, this cooperation is especially striking in France. There is an analogous development in England. E. H. Kantorowicz has depicted this well in *The King's two Bodies: A Study in Mediaeval Political Theology* (Princeton, 1957). His only fault is that he underestimated the very marked current of bourgeois opinion and that he separated too much the evolution of political ideas and

political events. The fact that this alliance was very weak in Germany is due to the backward ideological state of that country. On the other hand, it appears in a very significant manner in urban attitudes to Louis of Bavaria and to some extent in urban attitudes to Wenceslas IV.

37 It was not only the poor who thought this. Learned theorists also expressed the opinion, as for example in a letter of Alcuin written in 793 (MG, *Epistolae,* IV, p. 43–44, p. 16).

38 In Wat Tyler's rising as well as in the early Hussite movement, it is curious to note that objects of luxury were not stolen but burnt, as though they were responsible for the impoverishment of "the poor."

39 Ecclesiastical chiliasm was older and different, awaiting the end of the world. This is quite clear, for example, in Gregory the Great. Here this expectation is haunted by fear, by the idea of the horrors that will strike the world. Medieval literature is filled with this theme.

40 See J. Macek, *op. cit.* and also E. Werner, "Popular Ideologies in Late Mediaeval Europe: Taborite Chiliasm and its Antecedents," *Comparative Studies in Society and History,* II (1960), pp. 344–363.

41 The Chronicle of Laurence of Brezová in 1420 lists this opinion as point 22 of the heretical errors of the chiliasts.